A Concise Companion to Postwar American Literature and Culture

D0415845

Blackwell Concise Companions to Literature and Culture

General Editor: David Bradshaw, University of Oxford

This series offers accessible, innovative approaches to major areas of literary study. Each volume provides an indispensable companion for anyone wishing to gain an authoritative understanding of a given period or movement's intellectual character and contexts.

A Concise Companion to Postwar American Literature and Culture

Edited by Josephine G. Hendin

Blackwell
Publishing

350 Main Street, Malden, MA 02148-5020, USA
108 Cowley Road, Oxford OX4 1JF, UK
550 Swanston Street, Carlton, Victoria 3053, Australia

First published 2004 by Blackwell Publishing Ltd

Library of Congress Cataloging-in-Publication Data

A concise companion to postwar American literature and culture / edited
by Josephine G. Hendin.
    p. cm. – (Blackwell concise companions to literature and culture)
    Includes bibliographical references and index.
    ISBN 0-631-20709-0 (alk. paper) – ISBN 1-4051-2180-7 (pbk. : alk. paper)
       1. American literature – 20th century – History and criticism –
    Handbooks, manuals, etc.   2. World War, 1939–1945 – United States –
    Literature and the war – Handbooks, manuals, etc.   3. Vietnamese
    Conflict, 1961–1975 – Literature and the conflict – Handbooks, manuals,
    etc.   4. Literature and society – United States – History – 20th century –
    Handbooks, manuals, etc.   5. Politics and literature – United States –
    History – 20th century – Handbooks, manuals, etc.   6. World War,
    1939–1945 – United States – Influence – Handbooks, manuals, etc.
    7. United States – Civilization – 1945 – Handbooks, manuals, etc.
    I. Hendin, Josephine.   II. Series.

    PS225.C66 2004
    810.9′0054 – dc22

                                                        2003020731

A catalogue record for this title is available from the British Library.

Set in 10/12.5pt Meridien
by Graphicraft Typesetters Ltd, Hong Kong
Printed and bound in the United Kingdom
by MPG Books Ltd, Bodmin, Cornwall

For further information on
Blackwell Publishing, visit our website:
http://www.blackwellpublishing.com

Contents

Contents

Notes on Contributors

Albert Auster is associate professor (clinical) in the Department of Communication and Media Studies at Fordham University. He is co-author with Leonard Quart of *How the War was Remembered: Hollywood and Vietnam*, *The Films of Mike Leigh*, and *American Film and Society Since 1945* (now in its 3rd edition). Dr Auster has also written for the *Journal of Film and Television*, *Television Quarterly*, *Cineaste*, and the *Chronicle of Higher Education*.

John Bell is assistant professor of performing arts at Emerson College; a puppeteer; and a founding member of the Great Small Works theater company. He started his serious theater work with Bread and Puppet Theater, was a fulltime member of the company for over a decade, and continues to perform with them. His work with Bread and Puppet on four continents allowed him to understand the possibilities of theater. He expanded his studies of theater history at Columbia University under Martin Meisel, where he focused on modern theater, drama, and performance, and earned his doctorate with a dissertation on the rediscovery of masks, puppets, and performing objects on European stages from the 1890s to the 1930s. His recent books include *Strings, Hands, Shadows: A Modern Puppet History* and *Puppets, Masks and Performing Objects*. He wrote a regular column on off-off Broadway theater for *Theaterweek* magazine, and is now a contributing editor to *TDR* and book review editor of *Puppetry International*. With Great Small Works he wrote and directed *A Mammal's*

Notebook: The Erik Satie Cabaret, a collaboration with pianist Margaret Leng Tan which premiered at La MaMa Theater in New York in 2001.

Sterling Lecater Bland, Jr, is associate professor of English at Rutgers University in Newark, New Jersey, where he is also associate dean of the Graduate School–Newark. He received his MA in English from Rutgers University and his MPhil and PhD in English from New York University. He is the author of *Voices of the Fugitives: Runaway Slave Stories and their Fictions of Self-Creation* and the editor of an annotated three-volume collection entitled *African American Slave Narratives: An Anthology*. His scholarly articles have appeared most recently in *CLA Journal* and the *Journal of the Association for the Interdisciplinary Study of the Arts*. His research and teaching interests include nineteenth-century American literature, African American literature and culture, autobiography, narrative theory, and theory of the novel.

Mary Jo Bona is associate professor of Italian American studies and English at SUNY–Stony Brook. She is the author of *Claiming a Tradition: Italian American Women Writers*, the editor of *The Voices We Carry: Recent Italian American Women's Fiction*, and co-editor, with Anthony Tamburri, of *Through the Looking Glass: Italian and Italian American Images in the Media*. Her articles have appeared in *MELUS* (Multiethnic Literature of the United States), *LIT: Literature, Interpretation, Theory*, *VIA: Voices in Italian Americana*, and *Forum Italicum*. Bona wrote the introduction to *Fuori: Essays by Italian American Lesbians and Gays*. Her poetry has appeared in the *Paterson Literary Review*, *VIA*, and several edited collections. She is the guest editor of *Italian American Literature*, a 2003 issue of the journal *MELUS*, and is co-editing, with Irma Maini, a collection of essays on multiethnic literature and the canon called *It Ain't Over Yet: Multiethnic Literature and the Canon Debates*.

Daniel Fuchs is emeritus professor of English at the College of Staten Island, City University of New York. He has also taught at the University of Chicago and has been a Fulbright Lecturer in American literature at the University of Nantes, the University of Vienna, the Free University of Berlin (where he has also been a Bundesrepublik Gastprofessor), the Beijing Foreign Studies University, and the Jagellonian University in Krakow, as well as visiting research professor at Kansei University, Osaka. He is the author of *The Comic Spirit of Wallace Stevens* and *Saul Bellow: Vision and Revision*, which was selected by *Choice* as an Outstanding Academic Book in 1984. He has written numerous essays, one of which, "Ernest Hemingway, Literary Critic," won the Norman Foerster Prize for the best essay published in *American Literature*. Professor Fuchs has been a fellow at the Villa Serbelloni, Bellagio; at Yaddo, Saratoga Springs; and at the Wurlitzer Foundation, Taos.

Fred L. Gardaphé is professor of European languages and literature and directs the American and Italian/American studies programs at the State University of New York at Stony Brook. He is current president of the Multiethnic Literature Society of the United States, past president of the American Italian Historical Association, and a pioneer in the field of Italian American studies. His books include the landmark study *Italian Signs, American Streets: The Evolution of Italian American Narrative, Dagoes Read: Tradition and the Italian/American Writer, Moustache Pete is Dead!: Italian/American Oral Tradition Preserved in Print*, and *Leaving Little Italy: Essaying Italian American Culture*. He is editor of the series in Italian American culture at SUNY Press and co-founding editor of *VIA: Voices in Italian Americana*, a literary journal and cultural review. He is also an active journalist contributing columns on literary and cultural subjects to the Chicago journal *Fra Noi*.

Josephine G. Hendin is professor of English and Tiro A. Segno professor of Italian American studies at New York University. Her novel *The Right Thing to Do* won an American Book Award from the Before Columbus Foundation in 1988–9 and was reprinted by the Feminist Press in 1999. Her critical works include *The World of Flannery O'Connor*, which was selected one of the Outstanding Academic Books of 1970 by *Choice Magazine*, and *Vulnerable People: A View of American Fiction Since 1945*, which was selected by the American Library Association as one of the fifty Notable Books of 1978 for its "significant contribution to the expansion of knowledge." Her most recent work is *Heartbreakers: Women and Violence in Contemporary Culture and Literature*. She is a former chair of the Department of English and former director of the expository writing program at New York University. Her awards include a John Simon Guggenheim Fellowship in literary criticism and the Elena Lucrezia Cornaro Award for scholarship. Her literary essays have appeared in the *New Republic, Harper's Magazine, American Literary History, MELUS*, and other publications.

Pat C. Hoy II is director of the expository writing program and professor of English at New York University. He has held appointments at the US Military Academy and Harvard. He received his PhD from the University of Pennsylvania. Professor Hoy is the author of numerous textbooks and articles related to the study of composition, including *The Scribner Handbook for Writers* (4th edition, with Robert DiYanni). His essays have appeared in *Sewanee Review, Virginia Quarterly Review, Agni, Twentieth Century Literature, South Atlantic Review,* and the *Wall Street Journal.* Eight of his essays have been selected as "Notables" in *Best American Essays. Instinct for Survival: Essays by Pat C. Hoy II* was selected as a "Notable" collection in *Best American Essays of the Century* (eds Joyce Carol Oates and Robert Atwan). Professor Hoy won the 2003 Cecil Woods Jr. Prize for Nonfiction from the Fellowship of Southern Writers. He regularly teaches freshman composition. He is a retired US army colonel.

Frederick R. Karl received his BA from Columbia College and his PhD from Columbia University. A distinguished literary and cultural historian, critic, and biographer, he is a prolific contributor to scholarship. He is the author of the following biographies: *Joseph Conrad: The Three Lives, William Faulkner: American Writer, Franz Kafka: Representative Man,* and *George Eliot: Voice of a Century.* He is editor of a series of volumes on biographical writing, *Biography and Source Studies.* His volumes of literary criticism include: *American Biography and Source Studies, Fictions: 1940–1980,* its successor volume, *American Fictions: 1900–2000, Modern and Modernism,* and more recently *Quest for Biography* and *A Chronicle of Wasted Time.* He is also general editor and volume co-editor of *The Collected Letters of Joseph Conrad* (six of the eight projected volumes have appeared thus far). Married, father of three daughters and grandfather of five, he has taught at the City College of New York, Columbia, and New York University. He is currently writing a book on the interaction between baseball and America from the 1920s to the present.

Perry Meisel is professor of English at New York University and a noted cultural, jazz, and literary critic. He has covered jazz and rock for the *Village Voice,* the *Boston Phoenix,* and *Crawdaddy.* His books include *The Myth of the Modern, The Cowboy and the Dandy,* and *The Absent Father: Virginia Woolf and Walter Pater.* He is also editor of *Freud: A Collection of Critical Essays,* and co-editor of *Bloomsbury/Freud: The Letters of James and Alix Strachey, 1924–25.* His literary essays and reviews have appeared in *Partisan Review, Salmagundi,* the *Nation,* and the *New York Times Book Review.*

David Mikics is an associate professor of English at the University of Houston. He is author of *The Limits of Moralizing: Pathos and Subjectivity in Spenser and Milton* and *The Romance of Individualism in Emerson and Nietzsche*, as well as articles on Shakespeare, Milton, contemporary literature, and literary theory.

Patricia Monaghan is associate professor of interdisciplinary creative writing at DePaul University in Chicago. Her most recent book is *The Red-Haired Girl from the Bog: The Landscape of Celtic Myth and Spirit*. She is the author of *The Encyclopedia of Celtic Mythology and Folklore*.

Cyrus R. K. Patell is associate professor of English at New York University, where he teaches courses in nineteenth- and twentieth-century US literature and on the literature and culture of New York City. He is the author of *Negative Liberties: Morrison, Pynchon, and the Problem of Liberal Ideology* and of the "Emergent Literatures" section of the seventh volume of the *Cambridge History of American Literature: Prose Writings, 1940–1990* (ed. Sacvan Bercovitch). A new study, *Beyond Hybridity: The Futures of US Emergent Literatures*, will be published by Palgrave.

Leonard Quart is professor emeritus of cinema studies at the College of Staten Island and the Graduate Center of the City University of New York. He is a contributing editor of *Cineaste* and has written essays and reviews for *Dissent, Film Quarterly,* the *Forward, London Magazine,* and *New York Newsday*. His major publications, co-authored with Albert Auster, include *American Film and Society, How the War was Remembered: Hollywood and Vietnam,* and *The Films of Mike Leigh*.

Robert E. Rhodes is professor emeritus of Anglo-Irish literature at the State University of New York College at Cortland, where he taught in the English Department for 30 years, specializing in Irish and Irish American literature. He is the co-editor (with Daniel J. Casey) of *Views of the Irish Peasantry, 1800–1916, Irish American Fiction: Essays in Criticism,* and *Modern Irish-American Fiction: A Reader*. Author of numerous articles and book reviews in the field of Irish-American literature, his essays include a study of William Trevor. He is a past president (1985–7) of the American Conference for Irish Studies, has served on the executive committee for 20 years and has been a member of the conference for 40 years. He has delivered scores of papers, slide lectures, and other presentations on Irish and Irish American subjects. He received the SUNY Chancellor's Award for Excellence in Teaching in 1976, and in 1987 was named a SUNY Faculty exchange scholar. He teaches an occasional course and continues to publish and to present programs on Irish topics.

Marvin J. Taylor is the director of the Fales Library and Special Collections at New York University. He holds a BA in comparative literature and an MLS from Indiana University, where he also studied music at the IU School of Music, and holds an MA in English from NYU, where he specialized in late-Victorian and Transition period fiction, queer theory, and postmodern literature. His thesis won the Gordon Ray Victorian Studies Award in 1997. He joined the Fales Library in 1993 after service at the IU School of Music Library, the Lilly Library at IU, and the Rare Book and Manuscript Library and the Health Sciences Library at Columbia University. Taylor founded the Downtown Collection at the Fales Library in 1994. It contains over 10,000 printed books and 4,000 linear feet of manuscripts and archives, and documents the post-1975 outsider art scene that developed in Soho and the Lower East Side. It is the only collection of its kind in a major research university and contains works by such artists and writers as Kathy Acker, Lynne Tillman, David Wojnarowicz, Dennis Cooper, Keith Haring, and many others. Taylor currently writes on Victorian sexuality, the post-Vietnam downtown New York arts scene, and the epistemology of libraries and archives.

Regina Weinreich has edited and introduced Jack Kerouac's *Book of Haikus*. The author of *The Spontaneous Poetics of Jack Kerouac*, she was co-producer/director of the documentary *Paul Bowles: The Complete Outsider* and writer on *The Beat Generation: An American Dream*. Her essays on the Beat Generation have appeared in the *New York Times*, *Washington Post*, the *Boston Globe*, the *Review of Contemporary Fiction*, *Twentieth Century Literature*, *American Book Review*, the *Village Voice*, *Entertainment Weekly*, *Hamptons*, and the literary journals the *Paris Review*, *Five Points*, and *Chelsea Hotel*, among other publications. She teaches at the School of Visual Arts and Columbia University in New York.

Chapter 1

Introducing American Literature and Culture in the Postwar Years

Josephine G. Hendin

The brilliance and diversity of American writing since World War II are at once testimony to the ideals of inclusiveness that inform our civil culture and an intense exposure of our limitations. At once celebratory and feisty, argumentative and lyrical, our writers identify and express the living contradictions of our culture. Through all the chapters that follow there emerges a collective portrait of a period and place marked by every conceivable fault and virtue, split by differences of wealth and position, by habits of outrage or praise, by ethnicity and race, by agendas of the left and right, by narrative realism and innovation, but nevertheless united, if by nothing else, by a sheer intensity of creative drive. The purpose of this companion is to provide a guide through that creative ferment, describe its shaping ideas and the writers who represent the variety of its energies and achievements.

Emily Dickinson's praise of that certain "Slant of light" that sharply exposes "internal difference, / Where the Meanings, are" underscores the power of "difference" to inspire. Out of the argument between the artist and business culture, between those on the margin and those in the mainstream, postwar United States culture has forged dynamic new fusions and combinations. The United States that emerges through our fiction, drama, music, and film is a rhetorical figure for modernity in all its disruption and progress. A nation whose cohesiveness relies on consent to and interpretation of the ideals of its founding documents has nourished an art animated by the power of those ideals to accommodate change and dissent, to provide strategies for the recognition and reconciliation of differences.

The growth of American writing in the postwar period has been affected not only by sharply depicted polarizations, but also by the ability to sustain variety and dialogue in the constructions of art. That power animated Walt Whitman's quest for "the fusing explanation and tie – what the relation between the (radical, democratic) Me ... and the (conservative) Not Me ..." might be. Taken together, those competing urges are reflected in the power of American cultural ideals to legitimize dissent, to recognize and embrace both the innovative artist and the traditions art disrupts. Postwar art illustrates the prominence of an ever-greater diversity of voices and perspectives. The construction of this book pays homage to that diversity in formulating the categories and dialogues shaping the consideration of postwar writing.

An ever-increasing incorporation of diverse voices, an ability to absorb, sustain, and respond to the inevitable argument between art and experience, imaginative writing and commercial concerns, and a frequent reconciliation of the claims of each, easily defy notions of a static opposition between insurgent art and stable, pragmatic traditions. The innovative music, drama, film, and literature of the time all negotiate with the very times and habits they seek to change. However strenuous the interplay of argument, backlash and comeback, of embrace or rejection of experiments in form, the result is neither silence, nor the long-predicted "death" of the novel, nor chaotic instability, but only a greater acceptance and refinement of that negotiation. Yesterday's avant-garde poet can be tomorrow's éminence grise. All this suggests that the enduring American gift may be precisely that constant process of exchange and incorporation that brings about a repositioning of the center.

The culture, literature, film, and drama of the United States in the postwar period are subjects each of the contributors to this volume has approached from his or her own perspective. Yet all constitute a revelation of art forms that defy simple characterization as either purely traditional or experimental and reflect a feisty engagement with American life. The ensuing new fusions have produced cross-disciplinary critical approaches to art, recast even the conception of archiving books and manuscripts, and enriched discussions across the borders of forms and genres. The result is an opening up of how literature, film, drama, music, and culture interact. As Perry Meisel makes clear, jazz does not simply constitute a negotiation with the very jazz history it transforms; it engages in close interaction in its origins, influence on American pop music, and cultural interaction with fiction. As Meisel writes: "hard bop is a superb metaphor for the many tensions that American music and culture hold in suspension in the years that follow World War II. . . . The reception of jazz and its musical heirs, rhythm and blues and rock and roll, has always been the product of a deep ambivalence in the American grain."

The argument of art with mainstream culture, the pull of creativity and the claims of commercial success, have produced writing, film, and music rich in ambivalence, celebrations, and attacks, but even richer in the subtlety with which such poles are negotiated. Much of our art calls into question American myths of innocence, conquest, tolerance, and optimism while sometimes invoking or holding onto them as ideals not yet realized, and always laying claim to openness and the right to be heard. In doing so, art carves a two-way street between newness and traditional American culture.

Frederick R. Karl explores both the unifying myths of the 1950s and the hidden currents that surged at home beneath the growing tolerance and prosperity of the United States in the immediate post-war years. His magisterial command of the sweep of postwar culture includes the cultural waves that crested after the fifties and rocked the turbulent decades to come. Regina Weinreich's essay, "The Beat Generation is Now About Everything," explores the innovative forms and shock art of the Beats and shows how they turned lifestyles that were wildly outrageous, exhilarating, or even dangerous into a force in mainstream art. Even in the suburban pastoral of mainstream writing, ideals of stability and security were pressured by the pull of rebellion and despair.

Writers committed even to traditions of American realism revealed problems that transcended ideologies of conformity or revolt. The suburban realism of John Cheever and John Updike with its mixtures of plenty and malaise was to register a dialectic between American optimism and uneasiness. The painterly short fiction of Flannery O'Connor, with its blend of violence, mystery, and moral obsession; the sharply imagined realities of the Detroit riot of 1967, etched by Joyce Carol Oates in *them*; the expansive psychological realism of William Styron, exposing the burdens of history in *The Confessions of Nat Turner* and *Sophie's Choice*; and the complex creations of E. L. Doctorow, who, in *The Book of Daniel* and *Ragtime*, mixed narrative forms in his innovative confrontations with the political past as personal as well as public legacy – all extended traditions of the realistic

3

novel in depicting vital social issues as well as manners and morals. They envisioned the past through the lens of a turbulent present.

The culture and canon wars of the 1980s polarized radicalisms on the right and left. A polemical intensity distorted discussions in American universities over the very definition of what should be taught. Discussions of the role of emerging voices in the study of contemporary writing twisted the legitimate claims of serious current literature into a false either/or. It was never necessary to argue that reading a contemporary African American or Hispanic writer meant the elimination of every preceding author. Reading Dante has not replaced studying Virgil any more than reading Shakespeare has required burning the works of Sophocles. The controversy over "multiculturalism" and the western canon had literature as its primary focus, but was about far more. The sheer intensity of its polarizations registered the pent-up anxiety caused by many social disruptions. Arguments over multiculturalism and "identity politics" expressed the ethnic pressures caused by the growing participation in the American mainstream of those who came after the Immigration and Nationality Act of 1965 had abolished quotas that favored immigrants from northern European countries. But the culture and canon wars also circulated around the Vietnam War, the youth revolution, the explosion of feminist outrage, the gay liberation movement, the sudden visibility of art based on long-taboo subjects, and an increasing attention to nontraditional literary forms.

Writing from today's perspective on precisely the mixture that so aroused controversy, Marvin J. Taylor describes the collision between art and society as it comes alive when the "Downtown" art movement in New York collides with the library, that "establishment" organ for defining value and categorizing forms. Curator of a unique collection of Downtown works, Taylor explains how "Downtown works . . . question the structures of society – the available discourses by which we describe things – question the library as a similar available discourse, one that does violence through categorization of materials that are not beholden to the same philosophical, political, cultural outlook as those discourses that inform the libraries' structures." He describes an art whose impulses were shared by a large number of writers:

> musicians, filmmakers, and video artists who . . . began to push the limits of traditional categories of art. Artists were also writers, writers were developing performance pieces, performers were incorporating videos into their work, and everyone was in a band. Along with the

profound disruption of artistic specialization, Downtown works themselves undermined the traditions of art, music, performance, and writing at the most basic structural levels. Rather than overthrow traditional forms and establish a new movement, Downtown work sought to undermine from within the traditional structures of artistic media and the culture that had grown up around them.

Writing on the Hollywood film, Leonard Quart and Albert Auster take on the reverse effect. Even as insurgent artists sought to transform establishment expectations, the establishment itself was incorporating insurgency as essential to reaching its audience. From within the commercial calculations of the filmmaking industry, and in the familiar genres of the western, the thriller, or the gangster film, Hollywood carried on its own interrogation of value by making the "murder mystery" and "moral mystery" mirror each other. Across genres there emerged, along with technical mastery and visual quotation, a questioning and darkening of populist optimism. Political and crime films interrogated American dreams and optimism, and exposed the faultlines in precisely the mainstream culture they could both fascinate and provoke. From the *Godfather* trilogy, through the twisty manipulations of fact in *JFK* or *Nixon*, to *Wag the Dog*, Quart and Auster make clear that Hollywood watched us, even as we watched its films.

American theater provided a more intimate site for the dramatic interplay between postwar life and dynamic art. John Bell explores a layering of attitudes toward theater as high art and commercial entertainment that guided the evolution of drama, shaping its forms and sharpening the conflicts between the claims of imagination and commerce, of idealism and necessity, tragedy and escapism, that were incorporated in the variety of dramatic forms. From dramas of intimacy to musicals, from Broadway to off-Broadway, Bell explores how theater captured America's self-consciousness about its place in the world and its changing views.

Nowhere are myths of an easy American triumphalism challenged more explicitly than in the literature of the Vietnam War, with its stark and powerful renderings of the soldier's effort to persevere with courage and even to maintain a measure of past hope and idealism when confronted with the actualities of an ill-conceived war. Belief confounded by disillusion emerges as a core experience in fiction that rendered the struggle for survival in a universe of doubt and death. Pat C. Hoy II enables an understanding of that literature as the crucible in which established certainties were challenged and often transformed.

Hoy brings an encompassing perspective to a rich and haunting literature shaped by the collision between "our destructiveness [and] our political failures . . . and signs of grandeur: willing sacrifice for the welfare of others, deep love for comrades, redemptive acts of mourning, the revelation of character, the knowledge of what it means to be responsible, the acknowledged ache of loneliness."

Vietnam writing continues the democratic tradition of American war writing – in play since Walt Whitman's poetry of the Civil War or John Dos Passos's *Three Soldiers* in World War I – of focusing on the common soldier. It exploits the use of the platoon of men from different races or ethnic backgrounds – reinforced in such World War II novels as Norman Mailer's *The Naked and the Dead* – as a microcosm for American differences reconciled in the interdependent wholeness of the platoon or squadron. But it would go further, subjecting each soldier to self-shattering, traumatic encounters, mixtures of violence and futility, of captured ground immediately evacuated, of bodycounts as success measurements, of the jungle itself as enemy, of the names of the soldiers often replaced by nicknames stripped of all associations with their past lives. This literature moved deeper into realms of consciousness where the soldier's American life disappeared and his heroic, pop icons, his John Waynes, became ironic figures as the challenge to certitudes of any kind grew deeper.

The Vietnam War made the world safe for postmodernism. The split between establishment hopes and actual experience, underscored by the harsh criticism of the war and its conduct by many who had committed themselves to a military career and whose patriotism and valor could not be faulted, itself demonstrated the pressure on once stable traditions. Cynicism over the possibility of unqualified belief in anything provoked fractures of faith in government that reverberated throughout the culture. Culture itself registered the blows to the system at large by accepting innovative forms that seemed perfectly suited to a time bent on interrogating its own myths and tearing up conventional wisdom. That very process provoked an extraordinarily rich literary response, one that constituted an assertion of the primacy of imaginative forms. David Mikics sees postmodernism itself as a reaffirmation of the importance of fiction – in its encyclopedic breadth, its search for the meanings hidden in the detritus of broken myths, and its "overcoming of, rather than a surrender to, skepticism about the powers of literature." Mikics finds in postmodern fiction new constellations and interactions between the private and public, the real and the fake, assent and repudiation.

Just as postmodern art reflects new aesthetic arrangements of social attitudes, so new social arrangements provoked a new aesthetic openness. Since the early 1980s, the crises once encoded in the "culture wars" has led to mainstream recognition of writing by groups once relegated to literature's undergrounds. Mary Jo Bona explores the evolution of gay and lesbian writing from social protest to personal report, from experiments on the margin to mainstream acceptance and, in some cases, commercial success, from a focus on the AIDS crisis to a larger sense of human fragility in the face of incurable disease. Encompassing fiction, drama, and poetry, gay and lesbian literature also includes a variety of ethnic, political, and racial concerns. Bona's meticulous treatment of its development enables an understanding of its depth and diversity. Spanning many genres and political goals, this literature underscores the extent to which postwar literature is an adventure in inclusiveness.

The interaction and even symbiosis between margin and mainstream nourished acceptance of new voices. That is nowhere better illustrated than in the postwar growth of African American and ethnic literatures as immense sources of creative energy. In Ralph Ellison's prescient novel *Invisible Man*, winner of the 1952 National Book Award and now canonical, the unnamed African American protagonist tells of his odyssey from South to North, rural to urban life, through experiences of dehumanization by ideologies of the right and left. He reaches a newfound faith in his own, individual voice as speaker of hidden truths: "Who knows but that, on the lower frequencies, I speak for you?," he asks.

Yet not everyone could accept minority, marginalized man as the voice for modern experience. Writing in 1966 in *Time to Murder and Create*, John W. Aldrich expressed a view, not unique to him, that too great an emphasis on the margins of society was causing the novel to lose its "educative" function, as the focus on "middle-class culture" was giving way to "the experience of the Jew and the Negro . . . not simply as social fact but as an experience symbolic of the universal modern sense of isolation and estrangement" (14). This could not resurrect the novel's universal appeal because, "regardless of how skillful these writers may be in dramatizing the full symbolic implications of that experience, there is always a point beyond which the most sympathetic non-Jewish and non-Negro reader cannot go, where the necessary suspension of disbelief can no longer be willed, and he is forced to say, 'That is not and cannot be myself'" (15).

However, in the insurgent 1960s and 1970s and even in eruptions from the 1980s underground, middle-class "insiders" didn't have to stretch their talent for a suspension of disbelief too far to feel like outsiders themselves, estranged from a once-familiar country whose stabilities of belief and mores once seemed secure. Middle-class certitudes were challenged by the series of assassinations – of President John F. Kennedy, Attorney General Robert F. Kennedy, and Martin Luther King – and widespread unrest from a growing anti-Vietnam-War movement, an expressive youth culture, often violent racial protest, cynicism after Watergate, and the feminist revolution.

Spurred by Betty Friedan's groundbreaking *The Feminine Mystique*, feminist perspectives would be captured in inventive satires of old ideals of American womanhood: in the landmark novel, *Memoirs of an Ex-Prom Queen* by Alix Kates Shulman; in Cynthia Buchanan's modernist satire on the Miss America contest, *Maiden*; and in that lively, picaresque sexual adventure, Erica Jong's *Fear of Flying*. Revolution was in the air, the office, and the pharmacy that filled prescriptions for the birth control pills that "always" worked. It was in the suburbs and coming ever closer in personal encounters from the boardroom to the bedroom. John Updike's *Couples* would document suburbia in "the post-pill paradise." All this eroded the confident sense of family and social stability and moderation at the core of traditional "middle-class culture." And Jewish and African American writers were to become important voices for many aspects of cultural dislocation that extended far beyond the bedroom.

Daniel Fuchs explores the collision between traditional values stressing moderation and responsibility and the appeal of an ever more unruly mainstream culture. Writing about Jewish American fiction, he provides an absorbing meditation that links the effects of the postwar temper on personal identity and on the narrative voice. His concerns include the intellectual and family crises caused by the challenge to American expressions of traditional liberalism – with its emphasis on stability, tolerance, and rationalism – and the argument launched against it by extremisms on all sides. Fuchs explores the variety of resources and responses Jewish American writers brought to the issue. Writing as both Jews and Americans, they redefined what each of those terms meant over time as they addressed issues of self-definition in relation to the larger culture. Fuchs's essay persuasively demonstrates that Jewish American literature constitutes a powerful meditation on both assimilation and difference that extends from the philosophic and political to the intimate and tragicomic, as it explores the pull of a culture of hedonism and gratification against the life of responsibility.

Openness to new and different voices after World War II intensified earlier interest in African American literature. Sterling Lecater Bland, Jr, enables an understanding of the evolution of that literature through the profound changes occurring between the Depression era and today. He notes:

> For African American literature, examinations of this change have tradi-tionally been reflected in discussions about the relationship between black writing and politics, culture, and the unyielding influence of memory and the past. Those alterations, however, have been informed by a series of adjustments that acknowledged traditional influences and relationships while simultaneously calling into question the assump-tions situated at the very basis of change. Basic perceptions of African American subjectivity shifted, the composition and boundaries of the African American literary canon were renegotiated, and the influences of gender, class, and sexual orientation acknowledged. The symbiotic relationship between the world's changes and black literature is felt nowhere more profoundly than in the constantly increasing audience for black writing in the decades following World War II.

Bland's essay demonstrates the power of African American literature to engage a tormenting heritage of slavery as well as changing cultural concerns and, through that active exchange, to establish its relevance to every aspect of our culture. African American writing has emerged as a diverse art, fluent over a variety of literary forms. Updating lyric, realist, and modernist practice, its writers have claimed through mastery of narrative forms a place and voice in world literature, a role under-scored by the awarding of the 1993 Nobel Prize in Literature to Toni Morrison. The dimensions of its success as a field of academic inquiry, and the high quality of the work of its scholars, have made African American studies a model that has inspired the growth of ethnic studies in general.

The growth and prominence of ethnic literatures are one of the remarkable features of postwar American writing. The many literat-ures that comprise ethnic studies incorporate, but redefine, traditions of American realism, aligning over time diverse narratives of diaspora, collisions with mainstream expectations, and even postmodern ren-derings of the current urban scene. These literatures unite the histor-ical and the mythic. They explore the disruption and reconstitution of ethnic and American identity, and approach the problem of modernity

9

through the experience of cultural collision and change. Ethnic writing sometimes defies formal categories, as writers employing ethnic heritage contribute to a variety of literary genres and forms.

The centrality of immigration to American experience defines it as a major transformative event for both the individual and the culture, encoding the pain of marginality and alienation in a larger American episteme – unity emerging from difference. The centrality of that episteme to postwar American experience has contributed to the incorporation of ethnic studies into university curricula. As a personal and national experience, immigration can generate a physics of high-speed collisions between cultures, an abrasive calculus of interactions with an often resistant mainstream, or even an ecstatic sense of liberation from old constraints in new American lives. Its literatures may incorporate a sociology of ethnic identity as fixed, but also include its potential as a source of adaptability and responsiveness to new challenges, as ethnic practices are not abandoned so much as reconfigured to meet the demands of a new environment. Although critical responses to ethnic literatures are varied, a central question concerns how the relationship between ethnic group and mainstream should be conceptualized or formulated. Formulations stressing opposition contend with an emerging body of criticism stressing mediations between ethnic margins and the American mainstream.

Approaches to ethnic literature have typically displayed road signs written in lexicons of opposition. Conflicts between marginal and mainstream culture, tradition-bound parents and their more assimilated children, and among ethnic groups have made tropes of distance and competitive rage commonplace in ethnic art. Jürgen Habermas has lamented that the claims of each group have seemed "all the more painful the more the tendencies to self-assertion take on a fundamentalist and separatist character" (118). Writing in *Our America*, Walter Benn Michaels explained why this seemed impossible to bypass: "There are no anti-essentialist accounts of identity. The reason for this is that the essentialism inheres not in the description of the identity, but in the attempt to derive the practices from the identity – we do this because we are this" (181).

Essentialist views of ethnic identity have nevertheless been questioned from a variety of directions. Ishmael Reed in *MultiAmerica* pinpointed the need to find ways of mediating between the divisive separatism that has shadowed the large achievements of ethnic studies and a universalism based on the erasure of differences. How best to negotiate that distance? Road maps have been hard to find. K. Anthony

Appiah has noted "that one reasonable ground for suspicion of much contemporary multicultural talk is that it presupposes conceptions of collective identity that are remarkably unsubtle in their under- standings of the processes by which identities, both individual and collective, develop" (156). Ross Posnock, writing in *Color and Culture: Black Writers and the Making of the Modern Intellectual,* has discussed the limitations of what he calls the "identity/difference model" (25). David Hollinger has explored the plethora of terms that have emerged to accompany the demand for change: "postethnicity," "affiliate" and "disaffiliate" relations, and "cosmopolitanism" and a "rooted cosmopolitanism" (6). Such questions reflect the growth of the vision of ethnic writing as a new intellectual movement among scholars, poets, and writers committed to a more inclusive and flexible ethnic discourse.

Conflicts between universalism and ethnic difference, traditionalism and innovation in the interpretation of ethnicity, have themselves been a source of creative energy, contributing to the growth and develop- ment of Asian American, Hispanic American, and Native American literatures. Cyrus R. K. Patell's essay on emergent literatures con- fronts that discussion. All these literatures reflect a concern with the preservation of cultural identity in opposition to mainstream uni- formity, but also a sense of the violence attached to hybridity as an ideal resolution. From that perspective they question American notions of individualism as something apart from community or even as won only by the destruction of community. As Patell writes: "*onto- logical individualism,* the belief that the individual has an *a priori* and primary reality and that society is a derived, second-order construct," is a persistent American attitude that, he notes, reverses the intention of the motto *e pluribus unum,* out of the many, one. Patell sees key intellectual architects of American individualism as stressing the reverse, that is, the "paring away [of] differences in order to reach a common denominator that will allow them to make claims about all individuals," rendering "cultural hybridity . . . a contingent, incidental, and ultimately irrelevant aspect of individual identity."

What complicates a simple either/or between ethnic heritage and an embrace of American mores is the ongoing conflict among writers of the same ethnic group over rewriting ethnic practices, tropes, myths, and signs. Patell opens up the contrast between traditionalist views of ethnic myths as fixed and immutable and the opposing view that the very value of the myths and practices lies in their applicability to the present and future, a relevance maintained by their ongoing adaptation. That discussion goes forward in virtually all ethnic literatures, but lends emergent literatures particular critical and cultural interest, even as its artists produce extraordinary writing that has already claimed mainstream recognition.

Ishmael Reed, writing in *MultiAmerica*, identified a "European American ethnic renaissance" (xx). Attention since the early 1980s has been paid to the experiences over time of European ethnic groups whose history in America includes terrible hardships, but who are now considered largely assimilated. Italian American studies is a prime example. Fred L. Gardaphé brings the approach of a sophisticated literary ethnographer and Americanist to his essay on Italian American film and literature. In doing so, he focuses on the work of a group that, between the 1880s and 1920s, constituted the largest proletarian migration in American history, and has produced a powerful body of fiction, poetry, and films.

Gardaphé's essay spans a vivid history in America that includes lynchings in the South, curfews, relocations, and internment, and suppression of the Italian language at the same time as Italian Americans were the single largest ethnic minority in the American army during World War II. The ironies and pitfalls of Italian American assimilation into the American mainstream, the role played by ethnic practices and traits within the group, and the interrogation or exploitation of those traits by its own writers and filmmakers all create a lively and changing negotiation within its own community and with the culture at large. Out of that ferment, Gardaphé shows, Italian American writers, artists, filmmakers, and critics have created varied art rich in perspectives on assimilation.

By exploring the interactions between American and ethnic art, by choreographing the relationship between margin and mainstream and among ethnic groups as a changing dance of mutual influences, and by exploiting the fluidity of ethnic tropes and signs, Gardaphé opens up new evolutionary approaches to ethnic studies. He enables us to see that from the kitchen of heritage, recipes for a flavorful new future can be developed. Italian American studies includes art and theoretic models in which ethnic "identity" is not fixed and immutable, but an open, unfolding social process of exploration and self-fashioning. In being so it provides models for public discourse that correlate with what Jürgen Habermas implies may be the paradox of identity formation itself: "Persons become individualized only through a process of socialization" (113). As part of that process of socialization, ethnic heritage and the American present create new forms of dialogue, interpretations of ethnic identity, and even conceptions of power within the urban scene.

A focus on urban politics is a particular concern of Irish American studies. "I have always taken comfort from the old Irish proverb, 'Contention is better than loneliness,'" wrote William V. Shannon, in one of the early landmarks in Irish American studies, *The American Irish* (1963). The Irish found plenty to be contentious about in American cities and, as Charles Fanning's *The Irish Voice in America* would underscore, discovered a unique political and literary voice. The largest wave of Irish immigration to the United States began as a result of the devastating famine that drove mostly rural, Catholic poor men and women to the United States, beginning in 1845 and extending beyond the famine's end in 1847. Irish Catholicism would shape and dominate the American Roman Catholic church. But secular power would be sought and eventually found by Irish men who had brought with them both a command of English most other immigrant groups lacked and an awareness of political dynamics honed in their long argument with Britain. Shadowed by mainstream contempt and derision, often conflicted in their relationships with other ethnic and racial groups, Irish Americans, as Noel Ignatiev details in his controversial cultural history *How the Irish Became White*, labored and fought to establish themselves in urban centers.

The election of President John F. Kennedy in 1960 seemed full vindication of the toughness of early immigrant struggle. It redeemed the hard journey to eminence even the successful described in terms of its attendant insecurities: the shame at crudeness that F. Scott Fitzgerald had encoded in 1925 in *The Great Gatsby* in Gatsby's determination to remake himself, and that made John O'Hara's beautifully dressed surrogate in *Butterfield 8* in 1935 bitterly declare: "I want to tell you something about myself that will help to explain a lot of things about me. You might as well hear it now. I'm a Mick." Kennedy seemed about to bring the era of too much insecurity to a close.

A man who had performed heroically in World War II, Harvard educated, magnetic, and superbly articulate, Kennedy was an American prince whose grandfathers had excelled in decidedly earthy, ward-boss politics. Although Kennedy's father had amassed a great fortune and served as American ambassador to the Court of St. James, even that could seem the perfect Irish American comeuppance to the memory of British contempt. Beginning his campaign for the Senate in 1946 by seeking and finding strong support in the Irish neighborhoods of Boston where his grandfathers had prevailed,

Kennedy's political path let outward toward American promise. His inauguration as president on January 20, 1961, underscored how far he and his family had traveled. Robert Frost read a commemorative poem heralding a new "Augustan age:" "A golden age of poetry and power / Of which this noonday's the beginning hour."

John F. Kennedy remains an embodiment of that blend of poetry and power in the fiction of ethnic groups other than the Irish. For Philip Roth in *American Pastoral* the highest term of praise for a handsome, larger-than-life Jewish success, nicknamed "Swede," is "He was our Kennedy." President Kennedy's assassination was presented in some fiction as an attack on American idealism. Kennedy emerged as the embodiment not only of the perfected hopes of generations of immigrant strivers, but of an American meritocracy of vigorous, benign, and rational authority. Roth imagines his assassination as enabling or ushering in the chaotic rebelliousness Roth calls the "American berserk." In the fiction of many ethnic groups, Kennedy occupies the haunting role of something more: a dream of ethnic merit achieved, embraced, and lost; of power perfected through its rational and benevolent exercise.

Robert E. Rhodes's essay, " 'Polytics Ain't Bean Bag': The Twentieth-Century Irish American Political Novel," explores the advent of the Irish into the American political mainstream, their ability to record that journey in fiction and drama, with all the internal differences and tensions that, as Rhodes indicates, led even Senator Daniel Patrick Moynihan, a former Harvard professor and the Senator most respected for his deep command of social issues, to assert his marginality and his roots by claiming: "I'm semi-assimilated." Rhodes addresses a spectrum of political meanings in fiction dealing with the rise of the ward bosses, from Wilfrid Sheed's portrait in *People Will Always Be Kind* of a "professional idealist," who brings to his idealism a hardcore cynicism, to novelist William Kennedy's assessment of all Irish experience as political. Rhodes's essay indicates how the political novel defines an assertive Irish American masculinity through a search for power in the world.

In "Grandmothers and Rebel Lovers: Archetypes in Irish American Women's Poetry," Patricia Monaghan focuses on the recourses of women encoded in poetry. Her essay on female archetypes in Irish American women's writing explores forms of empowerment outside the male world of politics. Invoking both mythic and ancestral female strength, women in contemporary writing supplement the traditional stereotype of the sorrowful, prayerful Irish mother with complex renderings of women's self-possession and skepticism. As Monaghan notes, in Tess Gallagher's poem, "Instructions to the Double," a woman finds her double is the androgyne within her, the "little mother of silences, little father of half-belief." Monaghan opens up that female curiosity that stokes subtle rebellions against the female role and the double subordinations experienced as women and poor ethnics.

Much ethnic fiction interacts in imaginative ways with American traditions of realism, using differences in social and economic status as crucial elements in narratives and characterizations. For example, Irish American realism, from novels by Edwin O'Connor and Frank O'Hara to Mary Gordon and Alice McDermott, depicts not only negative stereotyping, class and economic injuries, but also a variety of responses for coping with prejudice. O'Hara achieves control of the WASP world by dint of his knowing command of its manners in *Ten North Frederick* (1955) and his manipulation of his WASP characters. The comic ironies embedded in the title of his collection of stories *Sermons and Soda Water* (1960) suggest a mixture of success in life's serious moments and cocktail hours along with what William V. Shannon described as O'Hara's "rage and resentment of every Irish man and Irish woman who was ever turned down for a job in an old-line Protestant law firm, ever snubbed for the 'sin' of having gone to the wrong college, ever left out of a fashionable party, ever patronized for wearing slightly wrong clothes" (247).

Alice McDermott in *Charming Billy*, winner of the 1998 National Book Award, offered a scrupulous realism about the drabness of working-class life and the pitfalls of alcoholism, but introduced a woman's dream of romance as a possible cure for this grimness. In *Child of My Heart* (2002) art joins romance as antidote. McDermott writes of the virtual abandonment of their children by an alcoholic artist father and a sexually active mother, and the children's struggle for love and meaning, further clouded by intimations that one of the children will die. Yet the hard realities of children who are thrown back on each other, and grim prospects of death, are resolved through the resurrecting power of the artistic imagination. One child imagines her father has shown his love by an attentiveness to her that involves abandoning his devotion to Abstract Expressionist art to paint her in a "realistic" portrait that hangs pristine and lovely in the hallowed halls of the Metropolitan Museum of Art. Intimations of perfectibility and immortality through art echo William Butler Yeats's "Sailing to Byzantium" and invoke an Irish aesthetic heritage as if it were an ideal parent who could father an Irish American child. In the

15

perfected, eternal forms of art, that ideal parent cherishes and enshrines his daughter in an American sanctuary of beauty. Heritages of high or spiritual culture in countries of ancestry or origin haunt the corridors of realism in much ethnic fiction. Ethnic fiction supplies the memory or current experience of economic and social suffering, but also provides sustaining, often romantic, myths.

Postwar ethnic literatures illuminate the crossroads of historical continuity and historical displacement. From the vantage point of different cultures, one sees a persistence of themes: a focus on heritage and origins that includes, negotiates, or mediates difference; and an aesthetics that reconciles traditional or modernist visions of universalism as derived from the common well of repetitive archetypes with a new sense of a universalism based on shared experiences of urban dislocation and modernity. What is particularly fascinating is the growing emphasis on negotiating continuities rather than identifying oppositions. Instead of depicting the collision of cultures or of archetypal opposites such as insider/outsider as an inevitable train wreck, images of interpenetration and exchange increasingly hold sway. Here the artist's negotiation with the culture he or she struggles to transform positions heritage and newness as interactions, not fixed positions.

Cultural interpenetration has enabled a sense of modernity as the experience of multiversity: a polyglot urban linguistics, a close interaction between premodern cultures of heritage or immigration and the ultra-modern city, and even an imaginative incorporation of mystical, magical mythologies and the commercial, technological culture of the United States. Postmodern writers draw on ethnic materials to underscore such mixtures. For example, Don DeLillo's *Underworld* draws heavily on Italian American experience. An impoverished Bronx neighborhood serves as a site for immigrant waves – poor Italians and then poor Hispanics, to name only two. Yet all who come bring their mythologies of redemption and self-transcendence to those ghetto streets. In one scene a crowd waits expectantly for a miraculous vision to break through an ordinary advertisement. An orange-juice ad on a billboard reveals the hidden hand of God when "that certain Slant of light" cast by a careening elevated train illuminates a miraculous vision to the crowd. Marginality and solitude are defied in this community of rapture as the face of a local, dead Hispanic child emerges in the light as a divine apparition. The crowd's shared epiphany casts its own light, linking categories of meaning, connecting the resurrection of hope and innocence to commercial, secular culture, and reconciling ethnic differences.

16

The essays in this volume speak to and for the creative ferment in the United States that surged in new directions after World War II. They reflect an engagement with the play of tradition and innovation that transcends the narrowly political. Each essay should be read in the light of the others. Together they reflect our ongoing dialogue across genres and perspectives, a discourse filled with oppositions and inventive mediations between art and the times. Each essay reinforces the relevance of the tensions and excitement revealed in the others. Through the analysis of varieties of literature, of film and music, it is possible to see the vitality of the art produced in a society in transformation, maintaining its stability through its capacity to orchestrate over time the claims of individualism, community, and citizenship in and for the multiethnic, multiracial society America has become.

The terrorist attacks in the United States on September 11, 2001, were in part an attack on any effort to come to grips with accommodating difference as either an ideal prospect or an inevitable global task. In his meditation on the attack in *Harper's Magazine* in December 2001, called "In The Ruins of the Future," Don DeLillo described the attack partly as an attempt "to turn History on its end," by replacing the future with the past. He adopted a vision of those who died at the World Trade Center on September 11, who came from more than 120 nations and represented a plenitude of ethnic, racial, and religious ties, as "their own nation," stripped of all differences by death. But what was honored in their deaths was not their sameness, but their individuality. In the hundreds of pictures and loving descriptions of the missing that seemed posted everywhere in the city and in mourning them, they were missed for who and what they were. In the *New York Times*'s superb project in capsule biographies for each of those who died, what was recorded was what had made each of them loved, admired, and cherished by those who knew them. Asked what it was like to write their stories, one of the reporters on the project said, "I learned that there are no ordinary lives."

The sheer variety of writing in the postwar United States pays tribute to the endless strength of human creativity. It expresses in its multiplicity of forms and voices a full spectrum of experiences. DeLillo recalls walking weeks before the attack near the World Trade Center: "among crowds of people, the panethnic swarm of shoppers, merchants, residents and passersby, with a few tourists as well." Seeing a young woman praying on a mat facing east into a wall, he adds: "and it was clearer to me than ever the daily sweeping taken-for-granted

17

greatness of New York that will accommodate every language, ritual, belief and opinion" (*Harper's Magazine*: 40). "Accommodating difference," or Whitman's need "to find a fusing explanation and a tie," or Dickinson's "internal difference, / Where the Meanings, are": these are the crossroads where imaginative writing and American cultural ideals meet.

By exploring the reflexive relationship between the forms of art and the concerns of culture, by reconfiguring the relationship between margin and mainstream and among disparate groups as a two-way street, and by exploring the fluidity of experience and persistence of meaning, postwar writing bears witness to the genius and imaginative richness of these troubled times. In the chorale of narratives, no one voice or style holds absolute sway. But together they generate ever more creative ferment. Out of many differences, from the borders to the center of experience, in traditional or insurgent forms, postwar culture is enriched by ideals of openness and the affirmative value of the individual voice. With roots of heritage extending around the world, postwar writing in the United States flourishes as a bountiful art nourished by diversity. It joins in serving and contributing to a global ideal: the power of art to inspire recognitions and dialogues across cultures.

References and further reading

Aldrich, John W. *Time to Murder and Create: The Contemporary Novel in Crisis*. New York: David McKay, 1966.

Appiah, K. Anthony. "Identity, Authenticity, Survival: Multicultural Societies and Social Reproduction." In *Multiculturalism: Examining the Politics of Recognition*. Ed. Charles Taylor. Princeton: Princeton University Press, 1994. 149–67.

Fanning, Charles. *The Irish Voice in America: 250 Years of Irish-American Fiction*. 2nd edn. Lexington: University Press of Kentucky, 2000.

Gardaphé, Fred L. *Italian Signs, American Streets: The Evolution of Italian American Narrative*. Durham, NC, and London: Duke University Press, 1996.

Habermas, Jürgen. "Struggles for Recognition in the Democratic Constitutional State." Trans. Sherry Weber Nicholson. In *Multiculturalism: Examining the Politics of Recognition*. Ed. Charles Taylor. Princeton: Princeton University Press, 1994. 107–48.

Hollinger, David A. *Postethnic America: Beyond Multiculturalism*. New York: Basic Books, 1995.

Ignatiev, Noel. *How the Irish Became White*. New York: Routledge, 1996.

Michaels, Walter Benn. *Our America: Nativism, Modernism, and Pluralism.* Durham, NC: Duke University Press, 1995.

Posnock, Ross. *Color and Culture: Black Writers and the Making of the Modern Intellectual.* Cambridge, MA: Harvard University Press, 1998.

Reed, Ishmael, ed. *MultiAmerica: Essays on Cultural Wars and Cultural Peace.* New York: Viking, 1997.

Shannon, William V. *The American Irish.* New York: Macmillan, 1963.

Chapter 2

The Fifties and After: An Ambiguous Culture

Frederick R. Karl

As reflected in the culture of the decade, the 1950s more than most periods had several split personalities. By culture, we mean serious and pop, the arts and business, lifestyles and political ideologies, the totality of what makes a country into a nation and, by extension, a decade into a decade. As a silhouette of history the fifties have a definite contour: demarcated on one side by the end of the war and on the other by the uproar of the sixties. Unfairly, the fifties have often been narrowly perceived in mainly political and social terms, as the triumph of American prosperity; as the epitome of surging consumerism; as the victory of American culture and values over those of its closest rival, the Soviet Union; as a nation which has proven its uniqueness, in most ways God's chosen; and inevitably, as the time of reward for a generation of strivers who experienced and came through the Great Depression and a world war.

The split personalities of fifties culture are dazzling: Joseph McCarthy and the Beats; Richard Nixon and Elvis Presley; Eisenhower and Allen Ginsberg; warm, fuzzy family sitcoms and fixed, crooked quiz shows; the man in the gray flannel suit and the women of *Peyton Place*; the savagery of the Korean War and the peaceful, forgetful home front; John F. Kennedy and Martin Luther King; Joseph Papp and Roy Cohn; William Gaddis and Herman Wouk; Arthur Miller and Tennessee Williams; Robert Lowell and Wallace Stevens; Willie Mays and Maria Callas; John Cheever, the country club bard, and the Levittown people; the racism of the movie *The Searchers* and the civil rights movement; and so on through one cultural incompatible after another. Yet what runs through all such schisms, divisions, and splits – however bizarre – is a sense of the counterfeit, the deceptive, the fraudulent, the artificial, and the imitational; the forger's delight. In several ways, the decade was itself a forgery. It reveled in denial.

The 1950s in America, as a consequence, have a distorted reputation: more part of the myth of recovery than the reality of experience. As part illusionary, the decade has been dreamed up; what doesn't fit has been bundled into a formula. The period has been characterized recently (in lofty books by television anchors Tom Brokaw, Peter Jennings, and Dan Rather) as a time of growth, development, progress, enlightenment, and achievement of goals; as a renaissance of sorts and essential to what helped turn the country into a superpower under a benign, grinning, ex-hero of a president. The general argument is that the men and women who experienced the Depression returned from World War II to rebuild the country. This generation, accordingly, is a treasure, for not only did it revitalize the country domestically, it helped make the United States the beacon of the world, offering financial aid (Marshall Plan), food, and military muscle wherever required.

Yet when we look deeper, we see the jagged edges: tremendous valleys amidst some heights, great disparities between our vision or ideals and what we actually were. It was a decade of much deceit, pervasive counterfeit, not a little paranoia. A difficult, unbending visionary artist, Mark Rothko, was a cultural avatar of subtle and hidden dangers. His representative paintings were his huge rectangles, shaded so that the viewer is drawn in until all reality is submerged in color itself, not reflective of anything, but color shifting by degrees of intensity. Rothko hoped to capture a spiritual moment, and he may have succeeded. More likely, however, he grasped something as evanescent as the very impossibility of seeing because what was to be seen was hidden beneath layers and layers of artifice. Those rectangles are, in reality, disguises, distorted mirrors, dangerous exits and entrances.

Such perilous entrances and exits were everywhere: in the Korean War – all but forgotten, except by the families of the more than 50,000 Americans killed; the disasters of racial relationships – a national problem presented mainly as Southern intransigence; the growing schism between haves and have-nots, Michael Harrington's "other America" – the latter invisible since they had little representation or buying power; the sellout of intellectuals, who were coming aboard with chauvinistic acceptance of American dominion, with all the yawning chasms ignored. Two symposiums ("Religion and the Intellectuals" and "Our Country and Our Culture") held by *Partisan Review*, a once Trotskyite publication and a fervent believer in the intellectual life, reconsidered America in postwar garb. The participants were the stars who passed for the intellectual elite, although several had faltered badly: Lionel Trilling, Leslie A. Fiedler, David Riesman, Mark Schorer, Norman Mailer, Hannah Arendt, W. H. Auden, Reinhold Niebuhr, James Burnham, Louise Bogan, Max Lerner, Delmore Schwartz, Sidney Hook, Irving Howe, and Arthur Schlesinger, Jr, among others. Nearly all assumed America was becoming more conservative, more reliant on traditional beliefs, even religious; and more narrowly American, nationalistic, even chauvinistic. And with few exceptions – Norman Mailer derided them – they applauded the Americanization of the country. Perhaps because so few women and no minorities appeared on the panels, there were so few warning signals. For the panelists, then, since the fifties were so "sane," the sixties would seem to materialize from nowhere, and they were, equally, unprepared for the Vietnam War.

We might call into question not only the benign nature of the responses, but the short-sighted assumptions behind the symposiums and what they meant for the culture of the fifties. For their grounding was not too different from assumptions behind what *Partisan* considered its enemies, the editorial positions of *Time, Life,* and *Fortune,* or much of television, which is that Americans were coming together to reflect a common heritage, the opposite of Soviet villainy. The symposiums implied that Americans were homogeneous, coherent in their aims, bathed in values worth defending and saving (virtue, truth, integrity), and that traditional beliefs – church, community, family – once so maligned by intellectuals, may be sources of considerable strength. Much of this sounds like an echo of the 1930s "I'll Take My Stand," the manifesto of twelve Southern Agrarians who, excluding minorities and dismissing women, spoke of a coherent, homogeneous South; and by implication a template for American culture as a whole.

Yet the country was hardly coherent, much less cohesive. Forget for the moment Michael Harrington's somewhat later formulation of up to one-quarter of the population as "the other America" that was being by-passed and buried. If the Korean War with its more than 50,000 American deaths and hundreds of thousands of Korean casualties did not exactly tear us apart; if McCarthy and McCarthyism (the latter an even more dangerous residue than the original) did not rip us up; if the Cold War did not bring us to the brink of a deadly nuclear game with the Soviets, with the talk of a nuclear winter; then civil rights, poisonous racial and minority issues, and runaway corporate power would expose all the fault-lines in the country.

Those were the surfaces. Divisions ran far deeper: in matters of segregation and integration, in terms of political and private, states defied the law; government lagged in enforcement, or avoided it, or moved only under severe pressure. Millions were shorn of their right to vote, to obtain decent schooling, and to become equal citizens with whites. The Cold War was itself an enormous engine that drove nearly all considerations of security, national focus, the size of the military, and the reporting of news; corporate America through advertising seized the moment, with television rapidly developing and providing the latest push (Marshall McLuhan's "global village") – so that it was fair to say that programs were developed to provide filler for the commercials. The entertainment industry, most visibly the movies, was purged – far beyond the "Hollywood Ten" – in order to uncover a few subversives. Our Southeast Asia policies turned on who "lost" China; so that experts in the region were discredited or dismissed, and those who knew least – neither the history, languages, nor cultures – dictated policy. Planners considered how we could undermine the Geneva accords intended to settle an emerging, divided Vietnam. Still others, while helping the creation of South Vietnam, divided that country against itself, setting up the inevitable conflict.

Vice President Nixon suggested we help the debilitated French in Indochina with small nuclear weapons. Talk of nuclear winter resulted in a spate of films that featured alien invaders, gigantic bugs that overran the earth, and atomic or nuclear experiments which threatened human existence. The most noticeable were *The Day the Earth Stood Still*, in 1951, and *The Invasion of the Body Snatchers*, in 1956. The latter was considered so frightening that when it was shown on television, it was altered to include an explanatory prologue and epilogue.

Except for the Marshall Plan, which invigorated the defeated as well as the victorious countries, nearly every phase of foreign policy in the fifties proved short-sighted, a holding action without regard for the future. Repeatedly, we were told the future is now. The Marshall Plan itself was conceived as a means of providing markets for American products in the rest of the world, on the assumption that if we supply the means, other countries would come to market. The ideal of the loans – and there was an idealism and a vision – was rooted, nevertheless, in American expansionism. Those *Partisan Review* participants caught little of this overall incoherence in social and political policy, although, as we shall note, the arts did.

Everywhere we turn in the decade – and reflected compellingly in the so-called "high arts" – we find paradox and irony. Such were the fault-lines of the fifties that only the sardonic nature of irony or the negative aura of paradox could serve as adequate tools of criticism. What should have led us to greater feelings of confidence, or the ability to confront dominant issues including Soviet expansionism and our own racial conflicts, led instead to uncertainty, to perceived threats, and to disharmony in nearly every segment of American life. Change was becoming so much more rapid that it could no longer be readily assimilated. The sheer pace of change was so disruptive it was soon conflated with loss of values, or associated with conspiracy and subversion.

Reductive solutions gained credence. We observed some that were as simplistic as Frederic Wertham's citation, in his 1954 *Seduction of the Innocent*, of comic-book violence as the source of youth violence in America. Wertham assured Congress and the American public that the direct linkage existed between comic books and juvenile delinquency. Crime comics, he insisted, tear at community values and lead to antisocial behavior. His evidence is anecdotal, but as a psychiatrist he seemed so convincing he was believed; and although there may be some connection, as he pointed out, there are so many other factors in the creation of delinquency that any single one is inadequate. The public, however, was seeking an easy fix, rejecting larger cultural issues as too problematic: poor family life and status, low levels of education, the attractions of runaway consumerism, the easy access to alcohol and guns (later drugs), the possibilities of bad genes (heredity).

More complicated responses were put on hold, while simplistic ones were geared toward reasserting traditional values and national chauvinism. In a more complex equation, our political emphasis on national survival and American exclusionism became transformed into literary terms of counterfeiting and invisibility, the twinning of William Gaddis and Ralph Ellison, with a bow to Saul Bellow, Bernard Malamud, Flannery O'Connor, John Hawkes, and Philip Roth, among others. In the visual arts, abstract expressionism, as developed in Jackson Pollock's paintings, made large cultural statements. The Abstract Expressionists introduced a perfect, revelatory form for an ironic comment on a consumer-obsessed society. Into a culture obsessed with things it hurled an art of objectlessness, color as a mirror for receding form, the canvas emptied out of figures, the hallucinatory quality of non-figuration and geometric forms, and, in some cases, large areas of unfilled canvas. Abstraction forced meaning from the object to the eyes of the beholder; the individual is prioritized.

Not surprisingly, in popular culture, in the now rapidly developing area of television, the paradoxes characteristic of the decade prevailed, especially the capacity for the imitational, the forged, and the artificial. Surface triumphed over substance. Two programs, in particular, reveal how counterfeit and deceit pass as the real, one program a quiz show, the other a quasi-religious one, called *Life Is Worth Living*. That clichéd sentiment was repeated every week, a religious reductionism in the face of intractable political and social tensions. While quiz shows in the fifties were not entirely dominant – Milton Berle and Jackie Gleason among other comics drew in those who owned television sets – they did capture attention because of their giveaways. The money culture of the decade was perfectly mirrored in such shows: *The $64,000 Question* began in the summer of 1955 and was based on an earlier program made when money was less abundant, *The $64 Question*. This later program was also cloned into *The $64,000 Challenge* and into *Twenty-One*, all of which made television into such a misleading purveyor of information.

What came to count on *Twenty-One* as these programs developed were good looks, class standing, family background, and the aroma of elitism. *Twenty-One* would eventually live up to every aspect of the counterfeit by pitting a spotless Charles Van Doren, a Columbia University assistant professor and the scion of a distinguished family, against a grungy type, not a Columbia but a City College of New York man, a working student at a tuition-free school. It further pitted a model Christian young man against a stereotypical Jew: the Christian, son of poet and professor Mark and critic Dorothy Van Doren, was laid back and charming; the Jew, Herbert Stempel, was all push and shove and class resentment.

As it turned out, the large viewing audience had to be protected against the program's deceptions. *Twenty-One* had the brilliant idea of pitting contestants against each other, instead of against themselves and the questions. A winning contestant remained week after week, until the inevitable loss. Contestants, therefore, had to be interesting, or else possess a story that could become part of the show's larger narrative. They, in effect, became performers; and once that became clear, role-playing, not substance, counted. In this way alone, the quiz show became part of the selling of America in the fifties, part of the commodification of information and the reliance on appearances;

it fostered role-playing and rewarded it. In such a situation, counterfeit thrives, and public and private are indistinguishable.

The first big winner was the edgy Herbert Stempel, a man with an omnivorous memory for bits and pieces of information – what passed for "knowledge." He had his own aura, the working-class stiff hitting the jackpot; but after he had run up almost $100,000 in winnings, the producers felt he was wearing thin and that ratings needed boosting. (We see this played out in Robert Redford's 1994 movie *Quiz Show* and in the Kent Anderson book *Television Fraud*.) The plan was to introduce a competitor and run them head to head.

Enter Charles Van Doren, whose name alone elicited style over someone named Stempel (German for "rubber stamp" or "postmark"). Looks and tone mattered, and Van Doren was tall, slender, and handsome, with the special grace of the well born, a stylish American matinee idol as well as a would-be intellectual. In contrast, Stempel gave off immigrant sweat. Class lines, caste lines, and social lines were drawn; inevitably, just below the surface, a political point was established: that somehow Van Doren represented the best of America, whereas Stempel, although bright, was a second-class citizen. It was the Cold War in miniature.

At first, the two came out evenly, but in the second week, Van Doren scored and Stempel failed to answer a question on the writer and editor William Allen White. Van Doren was now the supreme being, and Stempel seethed. Without too much delay, he informed several New York newspapers that the show was rigged: that both he and Van Doren had been fed the answers. Incidentally, when Van Doren glittered on the program – he sweated, he pondered, he sank into deep thought – he received a five-year contract from NBC, including appearances on the *Today* show, not known then or now for its erudition. In many respects a forerunner of the telegenic John F. Kennedy, Van Doren had the ability to fake sincerity, an essential for those selling themselves as an up-scale product. Poor Stempel became, in turn, a forerunner of the bluebeard Nixon, dark, scowling, caught up by internal demons, no class, only ambition.

Van Doren, finally, began to wear a little thin and was eased out in favor of a woman; a lawyer, Vivienne Nearing. By then – just before the rigging revelations – *Twenty-One* and four other quiz shows dominated the top ten ratings. The following year before disaster struck, another six quiz shows were added to the list for eleven in all. This array of spin-offs and clones was itself a cultural phenomenon; for while demonstrating the voraciousness of television, it also showed its reliance on superficial knowledge and its need to recreate reality, to rely on performance over even superficial information.

In one respect at least, this development in pop culture paralleled what was happening in music, as Elvis Presley, when he shaped hillbilly and blues into rock and roll, turned audiences into screaming maniacs. Through all the reshapings Presley underwent on stage – he performed different bodily movements according to the nature of his audience – he still hoped to become a serious actor, a James Dean or Marlon Brando or Rod Steiger. Yet even as he aspired to climb from pop to serious stuff, his movies capitalized on his pop status. As numerous commentators observed, on stage he commodified his talents, using voice and bodily movements to communicate an intense sexuality, leaving little to the imagination. What passed for authentic, as with Van Doren, was the faking of sincerity for the sake of performance, very much a microcosm of what part of the decade stood for and vaunted.

What astounded the quiz show audience was that despite his all-American looks Van Doren was a "crook." He was quickly removed from NBC activities, although rigging quizzes was not itself an illegal act. Van Doren continued to deny his role until, called to testify before a House Committee in 1959, he recognized he could be indicted for perjury and confessed. His argument even then was pure show business, for he claimed that he, a university professor, did not see how the quiz program differed from entertainment and, therefore, the truth could be stretched. He had merely given the program a fictional narrative. But after these revelations quiz shows failed, and television for a time tried to separate news or information from entertainment: an effort that failed.

Television culture came in many shapes, not least in a program that blurred the line between religion and entertainment: *Life Is Worth Living*, with Bishop Fulton Sheen. Here God becomes a player – perhaps the unknown in another kind of quiz show. The bishop's message and appearance (penetrating eyes accompanying comforting talk) were elements of television's folding of all information and news into entertainment, including General MacArthur's triumphant return from Korea after having been dismissed by President Truman, or Richard Nixon's "Checkers" speech, which saved his vice presidency, or the Army McCarthy hearings, which were, ostensibly, over the soul of America, or the Senator Kefauver hearings, which looked like a sitcom, smelled like a gangster film, and played like a comedy, but almost vaulted the Tennessee, coonskin-cap-wearing senator into the presidency.

Bishop Sheen's television sermons had a simple function: to boost America and Americanism and, somehow, to link both to matters of faith. Like the somewhat later televangelists with their brew of God and patriotism, he offered solace, charity, and salvation for those capable of being redeemed. It was therapy with a difference; while Freud may have been acceptable for the Northeast, Sheen was for the rest of the country. Yet his initial function as a television spokesman was simply to make a dent in Milton Berle's runaway popularity on NBC. As much cultural as religious, the bishop's offering fitted well into the chauvinistic groundswell, a nationalism that pitted our values against a morally bankrupt enemy abroad.

Bishop Sheen had an impressive appearance: dark clothes (like Darth Vader), a gold cross hanging on his chest large enough to discourage Dracula himself, plus a cape and skull cap, all arranged to make him seem not quite of this world. But his message was. He was relentlessly upbeat, at a time when terrible things were occurring in the Korean War, in racial relationships, in the trampling of civil rights under McCarthyism. He cleared his own space and took his audience into it, a place close to the Earthly Garden, achievable through one's seeking of God's grace. If sin did exist, it could be expiated; if one were positive, one could be redeemed. Much less expensive than the burgeoning field of Freudian psychoanalysis, Sheen offered public therapy to millions, or at least those who could afford to own television sets. He closed his program with "God love you," the strange grammar turning the sentence into an imperative – part of the bishop's mystique.

Yet he was approachable, a regular fellow, someone you could confess to and come away cleansed, more accessible than many of those heavily accented analysts with the dictatorial manner. The bishop seemed as all right as Ike himself. Like the president's language, the rhetoric was simplistic, the message sentimentally upbeat, the faith thin gruel indeed, the philosophizing sophomoric, the tones those of a medicine man, a shaman. Everything fitted into a small box. One of the more famous episodes involved the bishop's reading of the burial scene from *Julius Caesar*, in which he replaced the names of the Shakespearean characters with the villains of the Soviet Union: Stalin, Malinkov, Vishinsky, and Beria. He intoned that one day they would all be judged, and lo and behold! Stalin suffered a stroke that killed him a few days later. Television's bishop was a prophet.

How much of this was actual belief on Sheen's part and how much was shaped for a not-too-well-educated television audience we cannot know. What we do recognize is that two such widely different offerings as a quiz show and a religious program were driven by many of the same forces. Popular culture, television, elsewhere most movies, magazines, and newspapers – all these were connected to more serious cultural phenomena by common themes of the counterfeit, the dissimulated, the deceitful. With his genial chants claiming that universities were agents of Satan and that social reform was creeping socialism, Sheen was little different from quiz masters who turned so-called information into counterfeit knowledge.

Yet clearly not all was pop. At a far deeper level of cultural achievement, in William Gaddis's mid-decade novel, *The Recognitions*, we discover counterfeiting as the meta-narrative for the country – clearly a response to postwar America losing its mind and soul in misinformation.

Halfway through this immense novel – half a million words – a character named Otto acts out what serves as a motif for the novel and for the period after the war. It serves, also, as a theme for Gaddis's later novel, *JR*. Otto is a failed playwright, a young man striving for the truth within a context of plagiarism and counterfeiting. He is unable to achieve recognition or insight and searches reflections of himself to find the "real person," and by doing so, could perform a true act of recognition. If he could attain that reality, then he would be able to write a valid play, instead of one full of borrowed feelings and imitated language. His glimpse of his plight comes when he tells the story about a forged painting; a forged Titian that had been painted over another old painting. When the Titian was scraped away to get at the old painting, the latter was found to be worthless. But under that worthless painting was something else, and when that was scraped off they found a real Titian which had been there all the time. Otto draws the point that under the surface of the counterfeit may be the original, if one keeps scraping away.

How traditionally American – Emersonian or Melvillean – a vision of hidden, but discoverable authenticity and, most of all, how applicable to the decade in which it appeared. Layers of untruth piled on; beneath it, somewhere, the real, while all the while we accept the forgery. We recall how in the 1950s tags were used ostensibly as instruments of information and forms of discourse – Cold War, pinkos, left-wingers, liberal intellectuals or eggheads, Red China, godless communism, McCarthyism, the red menace, traitors such as Alger Hiss, the Rosenbergs, Robert Oppenheimer – as though labels were a kind of totem. A reductive vocabulary transmitted only the artificial and factitious.

The Recognitions becomes our archetypal experience for the fifties, a paradigm for the way in which we saw and will continue to see ourselves. Rhetoric acts like a palimpsest, layer after layer disguising the real or actual. Exaggeration, hyperbole, rhetorical trivia all disguise the old master's painting underneath the forgery and fake. Gaddis's method, of seemingly disconnected segments coalescing at the level of the protagonist's metaphysical quest, questions the slice-of-life fiction and poetry characteristic of much of the fifties: William Styron's *Lie Down in Darkness*, Saul Bellow's *The Adventures of Augie March*, Bernard Malamud's *The Assistant* and *A New Life*, Allen Ginsberg's "Howl," or, at the end of the decade, Philip Roth's lead story in *Goodbye, Columbus*.

In *The Recognitions*, the epigraph to section VII (part one) compares Jesus Christ, who took upon himself human nature in order to redeem mankind, to the artist who must redeem us from those who defile creation; that is, those who support imitation. Yet Gaddis is careful not to make some hackneyed plea for the superiority of the artist over life; instead, he invokes the fixity of vision that rejects complicity in the marketplace notion of the real and the actual that fails to unearth the authentic. At stake, finally, is not solely art, but the quality of life. As in the religious parables, when the sinner achieves salvation, the less real is more real, especially when those who market both do not care which is which. In recapitulating the paradoxes of the fifties, *The Recognitions* reveals its several split personalities.

In the real world of art in the decade, among the so-called Abstract Expressionists or action painters – Jackson Pollock, William de Kooning, Franz Kline, Barnett Newman, Lee Krasner, Grace Hartigan, Clyfford Still, Robert Motherwell – the purity of the individual work was the subject of fierce debate, and never more so than in the career of Mark Rothko. As we observed, Rothko saw his large abstractions as spiritualized and as creating an aura, he felt, which was lost once the paintings were given a museum or gallery setting. This purity was traduced not only by formal settings, but also by anything considered decorative. He withdrew his large paintings for the Four Seasons restaurant, a lavish spot in Manhattan, because he felt his work would be considered not art but decoration, with people sitting around, eating, cavorting, getting drunk. One of the themes running down the middle of the decade is folded over into Rothko's obsessive need to control what happened to his paintings after they left his studio, an obsession that led to holding back as many as 800 from the marketplace as part of the Rothko Foundation. Gaddis's Wyatt Gwyon, the principal forger and counterfeiter – of paintings the old masters *might* have painted – would rather destroy all his work and even his studio than supply the marketplace. The theme runs thick, and deep, in the decade and is clearly a response to consumerism and affluence.

And just what was the marketplace? The marketplace was, in large part, a suburban vision; a vision based on an amorphously expanding population, which, without any roots in a given place, was filling up the edge communities outside city limits. These were shapeless masses, motivated not by any commonality but by a shared desire to escape the city and to set up as an isolated unit.

While full of American enterprise and energy, such new establishments created radically new cultural patterns with often undesirable consequences. Most obviously, it initiated that "other America," that America which became mired in an urban culture of poverty; a cycle accelerated by the white rush to the suburbs. The decision in *Brown v. Topeka Board of Education*, in 1954, to desegregate the school system nationwide energized the white move to the suburbs to escape integrated schools, and also saw the establishment of private academies, which were not government financed or controlled. The civil rights movement as a whole, although a necessary moral and legal corrective, proved divisive, highlighting racial tension and unresolvable elements as much as it created a greater sense of justice and equity. The flight to the suburbs revealed Americans once again as a palimpsest, in which layers of poverty lay beneath the prosperity; and those layers – with almost one-third of the population – contained differing identifications which remained virtually invisible.

The statistics demonstrate the movement: in the fifties the blue-collar workforce was down to 47 percent, and the service workforce was up to 53 percent. While this meant that work was available, it also meant that livable jobs declined, and would continue to decline. It showed that industrial jobs, the backbone of a lower middle and middle class, were weakening, even as the general prosperity increased, thus widening the gap between the white-collar suburbs and the blue-collar city, where once livable jobs were vanishing. Yet even poverty-level jobs were disappearing, for unemployment in this affluent society went from 3.1 percent to almost 7 percent by the turn of the decade. What was occurring in this cycle played out nationally. As jobs vanished, unemployment in certain defined sectors increased, service jobs provided poverty-level wages, and urban areas began to dry up, becoming lifeless, with little tax base, few services, and lowered expectations. Alienation became part of the cultural currency, as we see in several important studies of fifties youth by Paul Goodman (*Growing Up Absurd*) and Kenneth Keniston (*The Uncommitted: Alienated Youth in American Society*), among others. Alienation as a central theme carries over into innumerable fictive works, even into Philip Roth's *Goodbye, Columbus* stories at the end of the decade. The most facile explanation of alienation came in the hugely popular film *Rebel Without a Cause*, where James Dean established himself as the poster boy for alienation, attitude, and rebellion (along with Marlon Brando, another alienation icon). Yet Dean's alienation depends on a distant father, and once that is resolved, he is ready to "come home." Real alienation went much deeper, and is socially the other side of counterfeiting. For the alienated youth was attempting to validate himself (or herself) in a society which, in his or her perception, emphasized the counterfeit.

The difficulty of self-identification in a counterfeit or imitational context becomes apparent in several of the novels in the earlier part of the decade – Ralph Ellison's *Invisible Man*, Saul Bellow's *The Adventures of Augie March*, James Baldwin's *Go Tell It On The Mountain* – and in the stories of Flannery O'Connor. In these, the very quality of what it means to be an American has become confusing and ambiguous. Each protagonist is on a quest or search, in which in the face of rapid change he or she has to grasp some form of self or autonomy. Each must resist being blown away by a tornado or swept away by a monstrous tidal wave – the very energies and indifference of postwar American life.

In *Augie March*, Saul Bellow, in a realistic fiction, explores the divided selves of the fifties. In one of the compelling scenes early in the novel, Einhorn, the spunky, proud cripple, castigates Augie for having become involved in a cheap robbery of handbags. "All of a sudden I catch on to something about you. You've got opposition in you. You don't slide through everything. You just make it look so." The "opposition" Einhorn observes is Augie's dualism, that alternation of will and ennui, even anomie, which impels the novel and reflects so much culturally of the decade. It moves along on two tracks: the driving energy of the "I" narrator, Augie, and the enervation of the senses and emotions which acts as a countering force. On the one hand, Augie has the energy of Ulysses and something of his wily ability to survive; but on the other, he acts like Orpheus, although lacking specific artistic talent. Here in contemporary terms – of someone whom we expect to explode – is a meeting of the forties and fifties: energy confronting enervation and ennui.

Bellow, throughout, is delicately trying to get the feel of a period difficult to capture in literary terms, since one could not escape the contradictions of political and social life. Idealism is foolish, as Augie's brother Simon recognizes; he instructs him to seize the moment. Augie is not so sure. He resists adoption, he cannot be bought, he rejects the hard, practical advice of Simon even when action seems most appropriate, and this makes him seem directionless. He is, like a contemporary version of Henry James's Marcher in "The Beast in the Jungle," waiting for exactly the right moment, which may never arrive.

In his concern with the self, with multiple personalities, and with divided, enervated beings, Bellow was distressed that the American overevaluation of self – and its lack of discipline – derived from Rousseau, not from Nietzsche. The latter saw the self as associated with Apollo, god of light, god of harmony, music, reason, whereas the group or tribe was associated with Dionysus. In Nietzsche's formulation, Bellow stresses, the self served a real function, as part of the mediating process between the "individual and the generic." It was not an all-consuming commodity which demanded to be fed, as it was in Rousseau and as Bellow perceived it in postwar America. In these excesses of self, the American moves to antipodes of experience, from nihilistic denial of an individual's own mysteries to the feeding of the self and the exclusion of the world.

The whole modern trend – in opposition Bellow became increasingly shrill in his sixties and seventies fiction – means that public and private have become unbalanced. In the onslaught of the public against the individual in twentieth-century technology, the individual has fought back by assuming superiority through sickness, retreat, enervation, exhaustion, divided and warring personalities, and displays of self without engagement of self. By implication, Bellow saw a postwar America not as a mosaic but as full of warring and divided elements, nourished by directionless selves.

One of the most disaffected, alienated, rebellious, divided documents of the decade came not in fiction but in the screed by Whitaker Chambers, in *Witness*. Chambers, a principal in the conviction of Alger Hiss (for perjury), wrote a novelistic treatment of his life, which is one long alienated plaint. Chambers created roles for himself, many of them counterfeit, some of them verifiable. As he developed he blended the counterfeit in himself and the counterfeit he perceived in the godlessness and materialism of the pre-war years, which became intensified in the years after. He saw redemption only through pain and suffering, in being nailed to the cross and crying out to God for succor. In his exposure of Hiss as a spy for the Soviets – Hiss was his urbane opposite in many ways – Chambers satisfied his need for self-sacrifice; pain became his meal ticket.

Chambers's confession of alienation and maladjustment was part of a large cultural shift which included Norman Mailer's *Barbary Shore*, as well as his essay on existential daring, "The White Negro," followed in the mid-sixties by *An American Dream*. We see it, of course, in the entire Kerouac–Ginsberg–Burroughs–Gary Snyder – Beat movement: taking to the road, liberation through drugs and varietal sex, creating a counterculture as more valid than Ike's America. Whatever the differences, a common denominator emerged: to substitute the individual self for the counterfeit "out thereness," whether social, political, or broadly cultural. The breakout in the sixties is already implicit here.

Some of the intellectual energy for alienation and self-identification came from unlikely sources, such as Wilhelm Reich, best known for his invention of the orgone box. Reich's orgonomics was intended to cut to the core of human feelings, and to accomplish this by slashing through all the intermediate layers which stalled the normal. Whereas Freud – rapidly becoming America's "doctor," along with Benjamin Spock – had stressed the mind as the way of alleviating physical ailments, Reich had reversed the process, treating the body so as to alleviate mental fatigue. Reich wanted to remove tightness, and one way was through the orgasm, another through the experience of the orgone box. Improved emotional balance, better physical condition, and enhanced sex were part of Reich's prescription; and in an America both satisfied and dissatisfied with its position of power and affluence, Reich, at least in theory, seemed prophetic.

By the time of World War II, Reich was placing patients in his specially constructed boxes made of interwoven wood and metal to accumulate energy. By implication, such an accumulator was the way to self-definition; it allowed for the release of the orgasm, it helped cure cancer, it opened up body and mind to new sensations and experiences. Something of the same sort was implied in Alfred Kinsey's late forties "scientific" report on the sexual habits of the American male and, in 1953, on the female – alternate modes as ways of release. Reich himself began to go off the deep end by the fifties, although the box had become to many what mood-altering drugs would become later on. Reich saw the box as the miraculous cure-all; and in one stretch of the imagination, it was thought to affect even the weather. Conformity in psychoanalytic circles was represented by Freudians: heresy by Reichians and Jungians. The impact of Reich was that ability to pare away all the inessentials and to force the individual to confront a self "unlayered," as we see in Saul Bellow's *Henderson the Rain King* and in later works. Norman Mailer and William Burroughs bought the entire yard of Reichian discoveries in *Naked Lunch, Junky*, and *Queer*. Reich himself died in federal prison, in 1957.

The Reichian experience, however one defines it, finds its analogy in the larger culture. What happens when the country's myths and ideologies no longer coincide with reality? What occurs when the historical present nullifies both our expectations and our assumptions? What happens when the language itself loses its qualities, loses its very meaning, and is replaced by slogans and catchalls which address our emptiness with good cheer? What takes place when we realize we are individually powerless, and that effective power lies somewhere in the interstices of corporate America, the military, and leadership incapable of leading? Finally, how can we avoid what Erik Erikson called "identity diffusion" – feelings of a disunited or unresolved self – when the answers to the above questions come wrapped in counterfeit and deceptive ideas?

The Erikson term suggests a new kind of alienation. It implies, in one respect, what R. D. Laing, the Scottish psychiatrist, called social schizophrenia, something societally induced rather than an individual affliction. The new alienation, which is broadly cultural, results from a population's inability to adjust to constant change. Childhood and adulthood are discontinuous; social fragments cannot become whole; the very political climate subverts intellectual values. Passage from one phase of life to another is problematic and difficult, and the triumphs of technology so characteristic of the fifties cannot compensate. Innovation does not make up loss. The consequence is malaise and fatigue amidst affluence and prosperity, most of all drift and discontinuity, loss of commitment, a disbelief in social and political power – in all, the new alienation.

Someone like Senator Joseph McCarthy fed off such distrust, pessimism, resentment, and anxiety. Until alcohol befuddled him, he pushed just the right buttons as chair of a powerful Senate subcommittee he manipulated to subvert reason and to reinforce fear, while he established his own agenda of the counterfeit. By publicly making deceit and conspiracy the very stuff of the governmental process, he found the means to tip the country toward his own form of paranoia. In searching for subversives, he reinforced alienation. And yet while

McCarthyism did little for the mental health of the country, it did enter broadly into the arts in the fifties and thereafter. We see it in Arthur Miller's *The Crucible*, Mailer's *Barbary Shore*, Lionel Trilling's *The Middle of the Journey*, John Williams's *The Man Who Cried I Am*, Philip Roth's *Our Gang*, Mary McCarthy's *The Groves of Academe* and *Cannibals and Missionaries*, E. L. Doctorow's *The Book of Daniel*, and Robert Coover's *The Public Burning*, among several others. The final legacy of McCarthyism was that government had proved itself the enemy of government, an idea which escalated in the sixties into the counterculture.

Much of fifties rebellion was predicated not on establishing altern- ate visions or ideologies, but on penetrating the counterfeit. The pattern was a "return" to origins. What McCarthy and his cohorts had done was to reinforce the idea of the world as unstructured and uncentered; what rebellion or opposition hoped to do was to regain stability, and, in some instances, to regain innocence. It was a fantasy chasing a chimera, but quite the vogue. Bellow, among others in the fifties and early sixties, cannot be understood without sensing his desire for regaining lost innocence, his recognition it is an impossible quest, and yet his drive and energy to fight the battle for re-entry into the Garden. Roth's *Goodbye, Columbus* is all about fallen man, the expulsion from Eden, the avid desire to re-enter the earthly paradise, the cultural blockage of that effort. *Rebel Without A Cause*, the most obvious of the fifties films in this vein, is an effort to regain the paradise of fatherly strength and commitment; to put balance back into a relationship, and not to struggle toward any innovative social or political rebelliousness.

As the fifties progressed in this area, with the Beat generation an essential part of that hunger for regaining something now seemingly lost, such discontent began to merge with a more widespread rebel- lion in the early sixties. Civil rights, women's rights, gay and lesbian rights, and environmental rights, for instance, were all movements striking a more equitable balance for various identity groups. Even the most marginal of the rebellions were less for ideological restruc- turing than for achieving justice, cutting through artificial barriers – Marxism, for example, never caught on, nor did even a sustained third party movement.

It was becoming clear by the fifties that the culture was stacked against the so-called "people." Increasingly, now that mass media had with television a new way of penetrating into the American home, large segments of the population were being shaped by external forces.

Politicians might continue to speak of the right to know, but that was really quite different. One found it in Ginsberg's plaint, "Howl," where he "saw the best mind of my generation destroyed by madness, starving. . . ." Popular culture reflected homogenization, or the danger of it: films like *The Man in the Gray Flannel Suit* and *No Down Payment*, or novels such as *Peyton Place*, and, of course, television sitcoms (*Leave It to Beaver* and its numerous clones). In such works and in government manipulation of the press, the people were being transformed into a mass, for which, as sociologist C. Wright Mills pointed out, media markets were the form of communication. Small was replaced by large – America was more immense than even Whitman imagined – either the corner grocery store by giant chains, or the local politician by a nationally oriented figure behind a mike. Marketing became the new form of counterfeit. The public was not people but commercial outlets.

Everything depended on keeping a public united in the Cold War; and even movements such as civil rights found resistance not only on racial or ethnic grounds but on those of fear of the "other" and what that might signify. The tepid Kennedy response in the early sixties to the civil rights movement was grounded in the fear of disunity. The paradox was there: we argued American sameness as part of our democratic fight against Soviet imperial homogenization.

More paradoxes: the secular priests – Reich, Freud, Erikson, Laing, among others – preached an individual experience which was not borne out at the national level. The needs of the military alone – to secure against Soviet transgression, to preserve the *Pax Americana*, to reinforce American leadership and superiority – created an inevitable divide: the individual carving out his or her own identification in the context of an armed mass which existed for one's very protection; and further for the protection of one's so-called "rights." To defend themselves against nuclear winter was, for many, a real and present necessity; those underground bunkers, often guarded by guns, peppering the countryside were real holes built for real people.

Consequently, while the media organized us around stereotypes, while the military insisted on a united front for our own good, while national politics demanded that we pull together in the face of extreme danger, countering elements were equally strong: that we could only survive as individuals by catering to our selves; that we had to experience the anxiety implicit in individual exploration; and that while stereotyping and the mass provided mental security, they were, all in all, counterfeit, divisive sensations. Not unexpectedly, the

FBI chief J. Edgar Hoover asserted that "Beatniks" – who were testing alternate experiences – were among America's major threats to our existence.

A performer such as Elvis Presley could emerge to ecstatic success not solely because of his blending of musical forms – that is, his appeal, as a white performer, fusing blues and rhythm with rock and roll – but because he combined the perfect mix for the times: audacious on stage, sexually aggressive and provocative, yet courteous and polite off-stage. He played his role perfectly, and that ability to carve out a role in the fifties was as important as the talent itself. While other singers had talent, Elvis had sufficient rebellion in his stage performance to call up the "other side" of America: not only the poor and stranded, but a segment that considered itself deeply wounded and marginal. Elvis brought them in. As much as his voice, his bodily movements signaled the very qualities which made a novel like *Peyton Place* so popular for its sensual appeal, its physicality, its sense of the forbidden, and, not least, its vulgarity. All of these qualities only intensified the split personality of the decade, the insistence on political conformity confronting cultural aspirations that reached toward sixties rejection.

The mass media, in these recovery years after the war, helped fuel a vision of Americans as mellow, "good-feeling" consumers, big mouths ready to be fed. The vision was, however, a form of colonization. That neocolonialism based on merchandizing American-produced goods swept not only the USA but the world – American cars, refrigerators, washers, dryers, and planes – catering to needs at all levels of technology. Somehow questions of good and evil became matters of have and have-not. The refreshing quality of Bellow's *Henderson the Rain King* (in 1959) was based on "being," the metaphysical quest of one man for selfhood and autonomy, an antidote to consumerism. It should be read alongside Sloan Wilson's *The Man in the Gray Flannel Suit,* two very different books except that they converge in fifties yearning. As much as Sloan's novel is an account of one type of counterfeit conformity, the Bellow novel is a plea to break out into me-ness, with a strong grounding in subversive Reichian energy.

The Wild One, a 1953 film directed by Stanley Kramer, and featuring a very hostile Marlon Brando, is as much about consumerism as about so-called wildness. The opening shot is of a long stretch of empty highway that is slowly filled by roaring motorcycles bearing down on the viewer, until the entire screen is covered by bikers, like so many large bugs crawling over the landscape. They have come to have fun, but in actuality they make a fashion statement – Brando's black leather jacket and his jeans, his cocky hat, perched at a cute, aggressive angle; the bikes themselves, marvels of a technological culture, full of gimmicks and accessories; and even the spoken language: a fashionable jive transformed into a national language, a rock and roll lingo intended to exclude the older generation. The Brando character is questioned about what he is rebelling against, and he asks, in return, "What've you got?" But he is rebelling against what he considers to be American counterfeit conformity, and in reality he is embracing another kind of counterfeit, a consumer-driven cult grouping. Paradoxically, in this split personality film, as he seeks escape from a narrow, imitational life, he finds small-town narrowness and provincialism as somehow wholesome. He is nowhere, simply looking for thrills, a rather decent kid dummied up to seem dangerous, all attitude and no substance, a fashion statement.

In fashion itself, the fifties revealed a clash of styles and a clutch of personalities. Gray flannel suit for men at work, but jeans and leather jacket for boys at play; haute couture now being revived with American funding alongside leisure clothes, silks and velvets paralleled by denim, jersey, and cotton. The point about fashion was that there was no fashion, only social statements: gray flannel suggesting a suburban culture, haute couture an urban setting, denim and jersey marking a frantic leisure. The latter was middle-class, with new cars, larger houses (Levittowns were levitating as developments of neat, affordable, one-family houses spread everywhere), fulfilling dreams of amenities in suburbia. Leisure wear became a suburban fashion statement. The aim was comfort, settling in, a form of lifestyle, and part of the common man theme generated by Harry Truman early in the decade and by Ike later. Such middle-class fashion announced one's arrival, a spot among the haves, removal from the have-nots, distinctions overlapping with race, class, and caste.

Fashion in the fifties became so significant because it validated an affluent society, and in this, fashion played its role with colorful shirts such as the Hawaiian print and others. *From Here To Eternity*, the popular film made from the James Jones novel, featured one particular civilian dress, the Hawaiian shirt; President Truman flaunted it. It conveyed not only leisure but an attitude of coolness under fire, of togetherness, of the individual making a democratic statement within a stereotypical style. Alongside leisurewear was the sense that styles were becoming nearly anything, that there was neither continuity nor a pattern. Social styles were emblematic of a decade which futilely tried to contain unresolvable elements. In a fiction far removed from style or fashion, Ellison's *Invisible Man* revealed even deeper unresolvables in the country, not only racial, class, and caste divisions, but perceptions, angles of vision; the way we see. The very term "invisible" suggests that not even what is seeable is indeed visible; that the invisible remains the stronger element; the more powerful and insistent presence.

Style or fashion in the fifties was particularly meaningful in demarking roles for women. One aspect of the decade's fashions was to make women seem slim and desirable – as housewives they were expected to maintain the physical qualities which first drew husbands to them. A woman's figure, despite children and an affluent kitchen full of enticing foods, had to be whatever it had been. In just the period before Betty Friedan's *The Feminine Mystique*, fashion was sculpted to emphasize physical over any other achievements. Fashion makes the woman, as the cliché has it, and even underwear was aimed at preserving a slim sexuality, an uplift bra here, stiletto-like heels there, the perky look that made her a sexual object. The sole exception to this came with women who rejected it for the other extreme of the decade, the Beat, frazzled look; clothes that created their own style, a political and social statement.

In more serious divisions, questions of race were played out in the civil rights marches and demonstrations, as well as sit-ins and other forms of so-called civil disobedience. But what is often forgotten is how little of that penetrated to most sections of the country. True, the South was under siege and the college campuses were beginning to rise up, but most of the population was insulated against what was occurring, except what they read or saw in the media. Yet the exclusionary language surrounding race did begin to change, and that perhaps more than demonstrable changes impacted the nation as a whole. A film like *The Defiant Ones* in 1958 – although created in the generic stereotypical terms in which most people perceived race – helped in that change of language. Some of the fear of "the other" was dissipated.

Everything about the film is a cliché, and yet it is effective in its thrust because of the context: two escaped convicts in the South must flee the police while shackled together. While the film settles for stereotypes, the situation makes the viewer realize that the black man and his white companion are eventually linked by brotherly love, the very element most whites found so hard to accept. It is ironical that the language of "brotherly love" is offered in a culture which demonized homoeroticism and homosexuality; paradoxical that it is effective when most Americans had already rejected the exercise. Furthermore, the men's names suggest that irreconcilables will not meet realistically: the white character played by Tony Curtis is Joker; the black played by Sidney Poitier is Noah. Nevertheless, in its imitation of a resolution or at least a guiding light, the film makes the viewer feel warm and comfortable, that two men joined together and hateful of each other can eventually break the visible bonds and link themselves with invisible ones of loyalty and even affection.

The real fault-lines, however, lay in far deeper territory. At the time of World War II, blacks fought in segregated units; there were no blacks in major league baseball – they played in their own leagues; Southern blacks were blocked from registering to vote, and even if they gained that, they were often stopped before reaching the polls. The public schools in the South were segregated, separate, and unequal, and blacks who did not migrate found it difficult to move beyond menial work. Blacks in the North faced de facto segregation, especially in the larger cities with their specified minority districts and neighborhoods.

A decade of civil rights sit-ins, marches, and demonstrations under Martin Luther King and his colleagues made a dent in the laws, but James Baldwin's *The Fire Next Time*, a long essay on injustice, summed up racial matters in the fifties and early sixties. In the first part, "My Dungeon Shook I," comprising a letter to his nephew on the hundredth anniversary of the Emancipation, Baldwin laid out a deterministic role for his relative. "The limits of your ambition were . . . expected to be set forever. You were born into a society which spelled out with brutal clarity . . . that you were a worthless human being." He is expected to "make peace with mediocrity." From this, Baldwin turns to the main part, "Down at the Cross," which frames the civil rights movement thus far, and indicates how far it still has to go.

Baldwin is concerned with how the perception of black life on the part of whites leads not only to white brutality but also to black self-hatred. He visits the headquarters of the Black Muslims and is the guest of its head, Elijah Muhammad. He listens to the latter's point that all whites are devils – what Malcolm X at first preached – that blacks can flourish only as a separate race, and that if it perseveres, the black nation owns the future. Baldwin recognizes how tempting that is, but he also rejects it as too ideologically narrow, as impractical, and as filled with the very hate he condemns in whites. But nothing is easy, for Baldwin, raised in a strict Christian household, realizes how Christians have themselves subverted their own beliefs with behavior decidedly un-Christian. Moreover, Baldwin finds himself floating free of all association: turning to friends, black and white, and away from all institutions. He sees himself as an existentialist entity disconnected from whatever might give him support, except those friends who have accepted and embraced him.

Baldwin locates himself in the alien land of the fifties American, black or white, deracinated, without conviction, full of conflicting ideologies, none of which is coherent. He seems an isolated, anguished individual caught by fear and trembling not only for himself but also for the state of the world. The rhetoric of *The Fire Next Time* is Baldwin's, but the sentiment is the decade's plaint: a society superficially working together which papers over hostilities in ideology, in racial and ethnic matters, in conflicts between urban and rural, between urban and suburban. Great generalized areas of disconnect were submerged under a veneer of good cheer, a president who smiled away his inattention to detail, a Congress that was unresponsive to large segments of the population, states which openly defied the federal government with impunity, and, overall, leaders who seemed to function in different worlds from the people they represented.

Unlike Ralph Ellison, Baldwin in his essays and novels saw black life in America as full of horrors; Ellison, even in *Invisible Man*, had insisted that whatever social conditions the Negro (his designation) had to submit to, he or she still had a mind no one could take away. Baldwin, however, sees a wasteland where black life is concerned: "For the horrors of the American Negro's life there has been almost no language." Whites have the power, and, thus, they have the ability to define the world in which blacks live. Baldwin is not sanguine about change, indicating it must be forthcoming from vast shifts in the political and social structure, going much further than King's non-violent insistence on voting rights and on non-preferential seating in buses and restaurants, and pleas for respect and dignity. Baldwin warns that if blacks are not given their share of power, they can "precipitate chaos and ring down the curtain on the American dream. Next time there will be fire."

King preached a different message, an emanation from a parallel universe: non-violent resistance and constant pressure on the white establishment. Not all gains derived from King, but inevitably he gave them body and substance with his oratory, culminating, perhaps, in the best American speech since Lincoln's Gettysburg Address, in his "I Have a Dream," made at Washington's Lincoln Memorial on August 28, 1963.

Baldwin and King both constructed narratives that led into cultural shifts from the fifties to the sixties. And while our novelists – William Gaddis, Norman Mailer, Joseph Heller, John Barth, Saul Bellow, and Philip Roth, among others – did not take up civil rights issues as such, their criticisms of the country were continuous with what Baldwin and King would express. Missing, however, in the novelists was King's fervent belief in a better future, but this novelistic lack was due to a secularity which foreclosed on the preacher's leaps of faith. Instead, in Baldwin himself and in the major novelists, we find the end of euphoria, journeys into despair and despondency, a pervasive attitude that the country had passed up opportunities which would never again emerge.

The civil rights gains were not systemic. Schools remained segregated, with private academies becoming part of a parallel school system. Citizens' Councils in the South created economic and personal distress for blacks who were now protected by federal law. In the North, inner cities by and large remained unaffected by any of these events, but we could observe an ever-greater division between haves and have-nots, despite some growth in a black middle class.

A note of reality: segregationists in Little Rock, Arkansas, in 1957, led by their governor, Orvil Faubus, rebelled against the federal government. It was a matter of schooling, and it took the armed forces to protect the first black students who tried to enter their classes. This was three years after *Brown v. Board of Education*, which was now the law of the land, outlawing separate and unequal schooling for whites and blacks. It was also several years after segregation in the armed forces ended, by executive order of President Truman, so that an integrated 55,000 could die in Korea with equal opportunity. It was a full ten years after Jackie Robinson cracked the color barrier of major league baseball and joined the Brooklyn Dodgers, becoming a great star and crowd pleaser.

It was the decade when the states and federalism struggled more heatedly than at any time since the Civil War: when states' rights inspired visible, organized popular support and launched strong anti-government candidates. It was a time that Joseph McCarthy as well as many other Congressional politicians could exploit; a time when states' rights meant rolling back the gains for minorities, for civil liberties, for all matters pertaining to race. Under these conditions, with a country split, the civil rights movement went forward.

Another condition for splitting the country was still lying fallow, only to emerge by the end of the decade and in the earliest years of the sixties. The war's end in Korea in 1954 did not mean the end of the war in Southeast Asia; rather, it signaled the beginning. The very elements that said we had "lost" China were now in positions of authority, and they came to dictate Asian policy, leading us slowly but inexorably into the Vietnam swamp. As mentioned, Nixon wanted to help the French in Indochina with the use of nuclear weapons; and when that fell through – as did the French forces – America refused to sign the treaty officially dividing North and South Vietnam. We refused to see what ensued as a nationalistic civil war, and our attempts to prop up a corrupt and irresponsible oligarchy eventually led to another 55,000 of our own dead and well over a million Vietnamese casualties. That was, however, not Ike's war, but Kennedy's and Johnson's.

As elements in the fifties culture clashed – or as personalities split into ever smaller pieces – we note the need to identify with a label what was occurring. All the conflicting interpretations of 1950s man gained an advocate: Kenneth Keniston's "uncommitted," Robert Lifton's "protean man," Leslie Fiedler's "new mutant," C. Wright Mill's "white-collar worker" or "new power elite," Herbert Marcuse's "one-dimensional man," the familiar "organization and gray flannel" man. The most extreme statement of this aspect of cultural identity comes from Timothy Leary, the fallen Harvard professor, who in *The Politics of Ecstasy* says that passions are forms of stupor, and only sensations, opened up through psychedelic drugs, can make us creative. The emotional life misleads, whereas the "sensational" life is fruitful. We must get beyond emotion, not to reason but to sensations. Norman O. Brown's astonishing address to the Columbia University chapter of Phi Beta Kappa at the start of the decade moved him beyond reason, beyond passions, into sensations. Called "Apocalypse: The Place of Mystery in the Life of the Mind," his address, with its celebration of Dionysus, helped anchor the decade at one end, while it would be secured at the other by Leary and like-minded sensationalists.

Two unlikely fictions, each from a vastly different cultural context, exemplify how elements we associate with the sixties were already surging in the fifties: William Burroughs's *Naked Lunch* and Grace Metalious's *Peyton Place*. Each represents sensations, chaos, and anarchic impulses, which nestle under the surface of a compliant, colorless society. Burroughs conceived of fiction as a plastic art, perhaps our foremost example of the writer borrowing from other art forms, amalgamating the arts by way of their infusion into the word. Like the action painters of the fifties, Burroughs conceived of the field (canvas or page) as a series of clashes and conflicts. Like the parallel investigators in electronic music or John Cage's compositional experiments, he found sounds more significant than traditional communication. And like those shaping modern dance – Martha Graham, for instance – Burroughs saw that movement existed for its own sake as much as for its continuity with other movements.

Burroughs sought a "montage language" that could parallel a common filmic technique. He positioned himself as no less than an American prophet, a doom-filled Emerson, a no less lyrical but subversive Whitman. What was at the time considered scabrous and dangerous in his work proved to be all American; like all explorers of new territory he was testing out the limits of freedom, which in his case were the limits of anarchy.

The singular work that recalls Burroughs's contribution is *Naked Lunch*, reviled and banned in its day. Published in Paris in 1959 (and in the United States in 1966), it heralded a postwar, even postmodern, avant-garde. Yet its food imagery – less gourmet than cannibalistic – recalls more conventional works, Dante's *Convivio* (or Banquet), Carlyle's *Sartor Resartus*, and Swift's "A Modest Proposal," where nourishment could derive from eating Irish babies. Burroughs said the title was suggested by Jack Kerouac, and that it was unclear to him until his recent recovery from addiction. "It means NAKED Lunch – a frozen moment when everyone sees what is on the end of every fork." That is, when the counterfeit, the forged, the imitational, and the deceptive are revealed for what they are. Then, one comes to know what one is eating!

Burroughs had his theme: to expose the fake, fakers, and fakery, to force the reader to confront degradation, and to insist that degradation is never distant from revelation. More generally, he emphasized that the self must martyr itself in order to approach a form of joy otherwise unattainable. One senses that Raskolnikov is ready to explode in each of Burroughs's fictions. Everything, to be valid, must be experienced on the edge – what Mailer attempted also in much of his fifties fiction and in his self-aggrandizing essays. For Burroughs, to gain the junkie's paradise, one must sink to the junkie's hell. His positioning of himself is always adversarial, and not unexpectedly he was banned, making him a cult figure in the literary and junkie underground. The form of discovery – as characteristic of fifties fiction – was the journey: the journey out, on the road, the journey inward, the journey to the interior of knowledge, into places no one dared venture. R. D. Laing in his examination of mental health and mental sickness was exploring somewhat similar territory, an anti-psychiatrist psychiatrist; and of course Wilhelm Reich was attempting to find a cure for such ills with his orgone box.

What makes Burroughs so compelling, besides the daring of his exploration, was his reliance on self, an emphasis which showed a side to the fifties that connected well with sixties culture. The self was the junkie's self-indulgent paradise; drugs as the ultimate trip and the elimination of boredom; Burroughs spoke of staring at his shoe for eight hours at a time. Self was a form of liberation – and here we see the perilousness of Burroughs's imagination, the Raskolnikov syndrome of doing whatever satisfies one's ego, wherever it might lead. In his novels after *Naked Lunch* – *The Soft Machine*, *The Ticket that Exploded*, *The Wild Boys*, *The Exterminator* – Burroughs probed for the "ultimate moment." He moved almost entirely in danger zones, going well beyond the subversive into testing the limits of human behavior. All comfortable elements became targets; every exploration a journey for the "real" Burroughs or his pseudonym, William Lee, all in a condensed, foreshortened prose. The prose, which Norman Mailer began to imitate in his later work, but especially in *The Executioner's Song*, is a kind of shorthand, lacking both definite and indefinite articles, omitting the "s" of the third person singular verb, a notational effect of illiteracy within something very literate and "created." The language cannot be dissociated from the vision. The literary advantage of Burroughs's surreal world of hanging boys, endless sex (mainly anal), crumbling cities, continuous and obsessive movement is that it highlights an America that lacks coherence, a real place which in its confusions and ambiguities equals a fantasy land. Borders are erased: territories that are fought over are missing definition. Mind and body are not distinct; coherence is not a resolvable issue. Burroughs's characters are part of his dystopic vision, populating a pastoral gone sour and transformed into hell: the Vigilante, the Rube, Lee (Burroughs), The Agent, A. J. Clem and Jody, the Ergot Twins, Hassan O'Leary the After Birth Tycoon, the Sailor, the Exterminator, Andrew Keif, "Fats" Terminal, Doc Benway, "Fingers" Schafer. These are the types of character we associate not with literary or novelistic creation (and no women here), but with some middle region of the imagination, some area of possibility, a puppet or circus show. We will encounter a similar cast in Pynchon's "Whole Sick Crew" in *V*.

What can account for the themes of desolation and despair which frame so much fiction of the decade? Although Christopher Lasch, the historian and social commentator, spoke in *The Culture of Narcissism* of a crippling narcissism – an intense fascination with self which leads to the loss of self – we cannot use such a social definition for individual cases. As we examine the fiction, we observe that each case of despair differs from any other, each depression is unique – mirroring the variety of American life. For a parallel universe to Burroughs's, we can cite a mid-level novel like *Peyton Place*, by Grace Metalious, a cultural phenomenon after its publication in 1956. It then morphed into a movie and a long-running television program. As a cultural, not aesthetic, manifestation, the novel presents a compelling narrative. Although most of its situations and episodes are stereotypical, they cumulatively represent a vivid slice of America, and since naturalism and pragmatism remained the twin nodes of popular American fiction well through the fifties, the stereotypes of *Peyton Place* are really literary conventions. The novel reveals both class and sexual mores in the wake of the Kinsey reports on the sexuality of American men and women. Further, it reveals that even in a work which makes only small pretensions to literature there is the avid desire to penetrate the counterfeit in American life and to uncover the authentic if it can be found.

More particularly, *Peyton Place* upends sexual mores. The fifties, we recognize, were an especially puritanical time, since homosexuality and infidelity were often equated with untrustworthiness, possible betrayal of the country, and providing fodder for Soviet spies infiltrating American policy decisions. Sexuality was political. Any hint of sexual display – homosexual or otherwise – confronted the FBI's (Hoover's) war on "Sex Criminals" and then Joseph McCarthy's assault on "sex perverts" who were open game for the communists. And yet this demonization, the Kinsey reports, the reissue of William Faulkner's novels with their sexual ambiguities and intimations of incest, the increasing use of once forbidden epithets in print, and the gradual breaking away from earlier codes in the movie industry; – all of these helped create a new pattern of sexual behavior in fiction.

In *Peyton Place*, these new patterns concerned, chiefly, three women – in this way, also, Grace Metalious foreshadowed another kind of "revolution," the women's movement that began in the early sixties to shape itself around Betty Friedan's *The Feminine Mystique*. Metalious's women are not heroic, but they are representative. The three: Constance MacKenzie, a woman heading toward middle age, unfulfilled, with an illegitimate daughter whose illegitimacy she has hidden from everyone; her daughter, Allison, who is trying to find her way through adolescence and her teenage years, a young woman fatherless and unsure of everything except her dreams of becoming a writer – a portrait of the young Grace Metalious perhaps, as an aspiring but confused feminist; and Selena Cross. Selena comes from a dysfunctional family: her mother is mentally and physically ill, given to ramblings and bouts of insanity, her father is a drunk and a brute who commits incest with his young daughter. Selena is the most developed of the three, since her passage to maturity is filled with hardship and obstacles that in fact call into question her ability to end up a rational, useful human being. Selena kills her father when he returns to their house and seems ready once more to abuse her physically, but the jury in the subsequent trial acquits her when the town doctor testifies that he aborted Selena's baby by her father and has the latter's confession to prove it. Added to incest, to the sexual innuendo and ambiguity is abortion, performed with impunity by the town's most respected man.

All the submerged horrors of small-town American life become exposed – and it is here that Metalious makes her largest contribution. She has taken up rural innocence, spun it around and revealed it for what it is: a pattern that does not fit Norman Rockwell, the *Saturday Evening Post*, television sitcoms, or the claims of politicians. Rural life was pleasant, as long as one doesn't forget it is also a viper's nest. A political statement lies behind these revelations: that whenever political capital is made out of rural life, as part of a bias against urban corruption or as a statement of true American values, *Peyton Place* puts the lie to it all. It wasn't just sex that Metalious exposed. She showed that it was the entire value system at stake: the undemocratic class and caste distinctions in a supposedly classless and casteless society. In the film (1957) and the television series (in 1964, called a television novel), the class basis for the fiction of small-town life was, not unexpectedly, diluted. Behavior that was hot-house in the book became weightless in the film in the performances of Mia Farrow, who played Allison MacKenzie, and Ryan O'Neill, who played the town tycoon, Rodney Harrington. The television series aimed only for the trashy effects of Jacqueline Susann's *Valley of the Dolls*.

If we contrast *Peyton Place* with another extremely popular novel in the fifties, *The Man in the Gray Flannel Suit*, and its sequel in 1963, we observe how the latter obliterated all the important themes. In following the fortunes of Tom Rath, the man who pursues a personal and career rat race, Sloan Wilson gives us almost no social context. Rath's suburban Connecticut town seems to exist only for the sake of the characters Wilson creates; there is no sense of diversity, no level of classes, castes, races, religions, no real semblance of bias or prejudice, only power politics in the characters' careers and in married relationships. Wilson concentrates most heavily on the war between the sexes – what John Cheever, John Updike, and Philip Roth were already beginning to explore in the fifties – but, unlike them, without the broader meanings conferred by social contextualization.

An even deeper cultural split appeared in literary culture: there was an academic concentration on close readings of the text, the so-called new criticism, while writers were moving in and out of something as amorphous as existentialism, which belied the formalism of the new critical method. Although the full range of existentialism does not play well in American culture, several novelists flirted with it. By the early 1950s, it had become a hip philosophy, an import from Europe and France in particular, with its Sartrean emphasis on the individual reinventing himself or herself, the stress less on being than on becoming, the sense that the individual is alone in a contingent or random world. There was immediate appeal, especially in the conceptions of restructuring the self, as we see in novelists as diverse as John Barth, Walker Percy, Saul Bellow, and Philip Roth, picking up the trail of Norman Mailer and his "existential errands."

Yet clearly the American sense of existentialism became part of our own culture; little of what the French had in mind was transferable. For nearly all of our writers, the aim was to avoid being or becoming consumers, to rebel not so much against death as against the culture of advertising and consumption that threatened to destroy the feeling self. For the Europeans existentialism was a way of defying death. Broadly, American estrangement and alienation overlapped with existential ideas. For those wandering Americans – whether Jack Kerouac's Sal Paradise and Dean Moriarty, Saul Bellow's Augie March, Philip Roth's Neil Klugman, or poet John Berryman's narrator of his dream songs – it was heartening that since the universe was a random place, the individual's choice controlled his or her fate.

The American emphasis on space and spatiality precludes the claustrophobia implicit in Europe's time-oriented societies. Existentialism is meaningful literarily only where death (time, mortality, inescapability) is an ever-present reality, not in a society where it can be disguised with all the resources of wealth, ingenuity, and mobility. Joan Didion's somewhat later, spare antiheroines take existential poses, consider themselves victims, and conspire in creating parapet-like lives for themselves. But at their most anxious – and here we link them to the antiheroes of Bellow, Roth, and Percy – they play with despair, in

Didion's case in snappy Corvettes and luxurious homes. American existentialism is as much American as it is existentialist.

Because other societies faced annihilation and had been forced to contemplate significance, their philosophy subsumes inescapability. Having confronted death in ways unimaginable to the American, the European constructed a philosophy of life that includes dying and death and that shapes itself on the edge of an abyss. This is a norm, not an anomaly, not a protest or a rejection of consumerism and affluence, but a desperate fallback position, the bottom rung before the fall. Philip Roth, we know, increasingly modulated aspects of Franz Kafka, perceived as a kind of existential antihero, in "I Always Wanted You to Admire My Fasting" or "Looking at Kafka." But these titles indicate he must showboat with Kafka, role-play or Americanize him. How can he – or those others in the decade who emulated Kafka – recover a witty Kafkan sense of frustration akin to annihilation, which is so basic to existentialism, in his own American experience? Here, frustration is connected to one's loss of momentum in self-love, to a blockage of happiness, or to a shutdown of erotic impulses or social success. No Kafka there, and only marginal existentialism can emerge.

The American man idealized in the fifties, despite calls for desperation from Mailer, Burroughs, and others, believes he can conquer death, just as in coming to the new world as settler, pioneer, or immigrant he placated the devil. The Puritanical quest for religious freedom was always caught in terrible paradoxes, and the reverberations journey right into the postwar decade. For even while the Puritans theorized about damnation and lived in the shadow of Satan, they sought out areas of life that bespoke renewal and resurrection of self. The very sermons of the clergy were couched in spatial, or escapist, terms, in the phraseology of cosmology, which provided either salvation or damnation. The unresolved elements of this dual or split ideology feed well into fifties counterfeit.

In working terms, the Puritan ministers of course viewed the individual as emblematic of a universal design, not simply as a performing secular self. In this respect, our fifties writers have gutted the Puritan sense of the individual in order to extract his, or her, importance and to deny any divine connection. Working along the margins of Puritan rhetoric, our writers stress the secularization of the individual in space, his potential for perfection or completeness, democratic progress interconnected with technological progress, all shorn of divine intervention and principle. Our fifties writers and artists, accordingly, in more general terms press forward with ideologies about progress and development, which, if not self-defeating, are themselves slippery, deceptive, counterfeit.

Bernard Malamud's *A New Life*, set in 1950 – and an early example of the Jewish fictional renaissance – is compelling as an intimation of what will come. It combines the utopianism of the Puritans with the grounded secularization of the postwar writer, so that only irony can offer a resolution (which, incidentally, never arrives). Malamud's S. Levin (a foreign name for an American seeker) heads for Cascadia College; he assumes he can achieve Thoreau's intensity and wholeness in the Edenic West, where he can efface the alcoholism of his past. Drunk on spatial hopes, with intimations of some kind of divine intervention from nature, with the European East Coast having proved a false friend, he opts for Western freshness and novelty. He seeks nothing less than salvation from a "creative" experience which somehow will act like God, but without God. When he arrives in this virgin paradise, prepared to exchange S. Levin for Adam, however, the chairman of Levin's department tells him his function is to satisfy the needs of the professional school. While Levin casts about for renewal in God's country, he is informed that the area's needs are based on a land economy; it needs "foresters, farmers, engineers, agronomists, fish-and-game people, and every kind of extension agent." There is no poetry in the forest, no lyricism to the empty space, no song in the hearts of would-be pioneers. Levin's job will be to turn timber into poetry.

Malamud set *A New Life* right on the edge of the Cold War era: the Korean War, beginnings of McCarthyism, and Nixon's red-baiting and polarization between the Ivy League East and the rest of the country, disenchantment with communists and former allies in the Soviet Union, now an expansionist empire, loss of wartime mutuality, and the start of the alliances that would forge the politics of the next three decades. How does Malamud translate these forms of cultural data into novelistic terms? S. Levin has hardly arrived in the West when he recognizes that he – a Jew, a reformed drunkard, a representative of European history and memory – is sadly misplaced; for his choices, which once seemed boundless, have narrowed to Cold War positions.

Give up notions of literature and accept grammatical drill, or else move on. But where to? He is already at the edge, and America has told him to choose. To survive, Levin must become a counterfeiter of feelings and ideals, a trickster. Even sex (with a waitress), which starts out as great and turns sour when a jealous Syrian student

– international complications, the Jewish enemy – interrupts. Levin and the young woman make their way (from a tumble in the hay) back to town without their clothes. Paradise has been reversed, with anguish, not pleasure, the consequence. Levin had dreamed of being Adam in Eden, and now he is merely a cog in something well beyond him, a spatial experience without divinity, inner purpose, or achievement.

How similar this is to J. D. Salinger's more popular and enduring *The Catcher in the Rye* (1951). Once again, the dream, here of Salinger's troubled Holden Caulfield, is of an Edenic, oceanic experience. This will, Holden hopes, counter all the counterfeit, squirmy, oily creatures whom he encounters at school and elsewhere. He will be authentic, a young man of good faith, even if it means going over the edge into mental instability. Holden is the embodiment of an ego that wants to grow into a self without passing through the counterfeit; and he is, as well, a struggling remnant of American innocence in the late 1940s and early 1950s. In a political or ideological reading of the novel, Holden is our archetypal decent American, the young man who lives, like Thoreau, without a sense of personal sin. The result is that he must retreat, play Huck Finn in a world of deception and imitation. Unlike Huck, however, he has no spacious Northwest territory to escape to, so he escapes to an institution, our more up-to-date version of isolation. He must, at all costs, remain beyond contamination, both social and political, where everything is tainted and corrupted, the world after the fall.

Although Salinger has defined Holden as the sole honest man in a dishonest world, in the institution the latter receives psychoanalytic help. If "cured," Holden will re-enter the system "next September"; but recovery means not unto himself but into life, into the world of the gray flannel suit. His ideal – which is to catch children playing in the rye before they fall over a cliff – will give way to some kind of conformity. The novel is a cautionary tale for the fifties, full of its divisions and ambiguities: that every quest for Eden is a form of utopianism bound to fail, and to fail is the peculiar American way of affluence, conformity, and embrace of the bourgeois.

From utopian visions to the living hell of nihilism, fifties fiction revealed all the fissures in America's posture as a sitcom. Utopianism was not only in the eyes of Levin and Holden, but in the idealism that drove the civil rights movement and Martin Luther King in the face of presidential slow-down; in the drive to bring justice, voting rights, and equal schools for Southern blacks; in the fight to preserve civil liberties in the face of McCarthyism and Congressional committees from both Houses; in the struggle of those who, while anti-communist, resisted basing all policies on the Cold War; in those who opposed American aid to every right-wing, military government which opposed communism, whether in Iran, Guatemala, or elsewhere. But despite the idealism which ran through the decade, nihilism would not be denied its day. Much of the drama of the period was dark, nihilistic, full of pitfalls – the revivals of Eugene O'Neill (especially *The Iceman Cometh* and *A Long Day's Journey into Night*), the minimalism of Edward Albee, the performances of Samuel Beckett's short, but devastating plays, the lyrical defeatism of Tennessee Williams (perhaps reaching its epitome in the fifties with *Camino Real*) and the moral outrage of Arthur Miller in *The Crucible*, following *All My Sons* and *Death of a Salesman*.

John Barth's 1953 novel *The End of the Road* is a tragedy of nihilism, unlike his first novel, *The Floating Opera*, which was a comedy of nihilism. The "I" narrator, one Jacob Horner (who sat in a corner), appears as one side of the Eisenhower decade, politically enervated and inactive, passive, virtually comatose, but also someone linked to the dark, to demonic impulses. Barth depicted a struggle against the Laocoön pressures of the 1950s, a decade, he felt, that strangulated in slow measure. In multiple demonic ways, he asks what occurs when the enervated individual seeking to avoid choice is slowly squeezed, like the figures in the *Laocoön*. A very American question, it echoes the queries of Herman Melville and Nathaniel Hawthorne more than a hundred years before. Expectedly, Barth uses the *Laocoön* sculpture directly as a key trope. Horner has a version of it on his mantel, a statuette of Laocoön's head alone, sculpted by an uncle now dead. Its "blank-eyed grimace" and ugliness confront his every choice, so that Jacob is aware of his limbs being bound, of his very spirit pressed inward by the twin serpents. Inescapable pressure derives from the serpents of "Imagination" and "Knowledge" and from the gaze of the awful head – now Medusa-like – fixed like fate on Horner. Everything presses in; nothing oozes out. At the novel's end, Jacob leaves behind the *Laocoön*, along with his life at the college and his former friends the Morgans, but he cannot rid himself of his fate, expressed in the final word to the cabby, "Terminal."

Jacob's main fault is his insistence on the truth, a trait he shares with so many antiheroes of fifties fiction, culminating in that representative figure of the decade, Yossarian, in Joseph Heller's *Catch-22*, a novel written over the entire length of the fifties. Barth's character strives hard to capture the early years of the decade: he insists that conscious motives (intentions) are insufficient to explain people's actions, that nonchalance is as important as energy, that what cannot be accounted for can be as significant as what can, and that drifting energy – directionlessness – can create confrontation as much as more purposeful displays of testosterone. Finally, all efforts to penetrate the counterfeit end up in misunderstanding – because the "truth," such as it is, only compounds the deception. Barth forecloses on idealism.

That familiar silhouette of the counterfeit which lies so close to Barth's fiction of the fifties, and to Heller's linguistic and formalistic patterns in *Catch-22*, is now organic: that is, the unraveling of counterfeit within counterfeit, of hypocrisy and deception within further deception, is profoundly linked to method. The method itself is predicated on ways of revealing by denying, on ways of unraveling by undercutting and dispersing. The wit of such novels moves well beyond the set joke into aspects of comedy delineated by Bergson and others, wherein the closer the individual comes to the mechanistic and inorganic, the more he becomes a comic figure. Thus, Heller can turn the military and those behind it, the whole decade's worth of deception, into figures of fun; as, later, Stanley Kubrick would do in the film *Dr. Strangelove* in 1964.

In this configuration, the novel is a kind of extended litotes, that form of understatement and irony in which something is expressed by way of the negative of its opposite. One says "not a few" instead of "not many," because the first confuses us as to whether there are a few or there are many. *Catch-22* is itself a form of litotes, because it expresses an underlying negative aspect: if you are crazy, you need not fly; but if you do not want to fly, that proves you're not crazy. It is a form of verbal irony, whereby what is stated differs from what is expected. When logic is overturned, we find a nearly perfect means of revealing counterfeit ideas, feelings, and acts.

The year 1961 saw the National Book Award go not to *Catch-22*, but to Walker Percy's *The Moviegoer*, itself concerned with much of the same material, only here shaped in a more conventional way. In that novel, Binx Bolling depends on film for certification of reality. He comes out of the rebellious side of the fifties, apparently, and with a somewhat different focus could have been a key figure of the Beat movement. While he is linked to money, manners, tone, attitude, he is, also, a mental dropout who senses the malaise, personal, social, and political, which lies at the heart of an affluent, energetic, frantic society. He is an Americanized Oblomov, the Russian bed-warmer in Goncharov's novel *Oblomov*. The malaise Binx Bolling feels, which comes over him like fog rolling over the countryside, is the adversary experience of a rational society, a New Orleans that appears to work but which is really illusory, a mirror image of the real.

Surrounding Binx are the inauthentic, those of false sensibilities, those who lack perception or who live in the past. Authenticity is difficult to quantify in the past, since people can fake sincerity so readily. As a result, Binx tries to find it in movies, where the search for the authentic is available, but where the movies sow further confusion because they resolve searches. Movies have to end, whereas searches extend. Nevertheless, the movies have a reality and authenticity life lacks. The mirror image has the force and penetration. Early in the novel, the actor William Holden strolls down the French Quarter and creates "an aura of heightened reality," as though in a movie. Yet even that peculiar reality – tied as it is to a form of art or craft – is a cheat; for it cannot displace the malaise. For his sickness unto death, Binx identifies with Charles Doughty's classic *Arabia Deserta*; that desert becomes his, that emptiness his, that "thereness" his failure to achieve a "thereness" of his own. Even money-making, the totem of the decade, fails to satisfy. Percy had his trope for the fifties.

Not unrelated in this search for something authentic, but from different perspectives, are John Hawkes and Flannery O'Connor. The work of William Styron, Norman Mailer, John Updike (later fifties, early sixties), and Bernard Malamud has received the most publicity, whereas the more trenchant work of the decade came from elsewhere, from Hawkes and O'Connor, among others. O'Connor was unique in that while she discovered a voice that was an emanation from the Catholic church, the emanation differed from that of any other Catholic writer. In her way, she was responding to the moral malaise of the period. Rejecting self-serving achievement and, especially, specious ambition, she responded with a value system that relied more on Jesus than on the church. O'Connor stands for endurance, integrity in the face of temptation, redemption even when one is criminal, charity even for the ignorant, and forgiveness even for those whom society has outlawed. She came to identify with Teilhard de Chardin, a priest and writer, whose "passive diminishment" suggested acceptance of an affliction. O'Connor, who suffered from lupus, a degenerative disease that was incurable, saw unavoidable affliction as accompanied by a strengthening of the will to confront it. Transmuted into fictional agons, O'Connor's work became a battleground of diminishment and response, of degeneration and redemption.

In longer fictions such as *Wise Blood* and *The Violent Bear It Away* and in short stories like "A Good Man Is Hard to Find," "The Artificial Nigger," "Everything That Rises Must Converge," "The Displaced Person," and "The Lame Shall Enter First," she is "Christ-haunted," but not conventionally so. For she sees the way taken by Christ as a weapon which cuts very deeply into the imitational aspects of the decade. She has fiercely rejected the period's easy acceptance of creature comforts, its drive toward secularity, despite lip service to its churches, its divisiveness instead of older, community values, its failure to provide any solid foundation except for expressions of self and me-ism. O'Connor struggled against her generation of writers, not to negate them, but to negate the world they represented; and she became, in her way, a cultural force, even for those who did not or could not believe in her Jesus.

John Hawkes thought that he, too, was concerned with epiphenomenal forces, but his gods, devils and temptations derived from a secular not religious origin. Hawkes further attacked the very traditional structures of fiction. Using montage, he was able to slip away from plot, character, narrative (linear or sequential development), and even conventional time and space. His work, starting in the later 1940s, ran parallel to the efforts of the Abstract Expressionists. Objects themselves became the enemy. Hawkes was toying with an American version of *l'ecriture blanche*, Sartre's characterization of Camus' prose in *The Strangers*, and what Roland Barthes would later label as "writing degree zero": neutral, colorless writing. The Hemingway–Fitzgerald–Dos-Passos axis in fiction, still a powerful force in the 1940s, was fading as European Modernism flooded in. By his twenties, Hawkes was an altogether different writer from his more popular but serious contemporaries. Unlike Bellow, Mailer, Styron, and Salinger, for example, he had a view of language that would permanently remove him from the popular arena. His method of discourse made him more a writer's writer than a reader's writer.

The Beetle Leg, in 1951, after the tour de force of *The Cannibal*, written while Hawkes was barely past his undergraduate years at Harvard, is an amalgam of what at his best he would do: the setting in the West, spacious and spatial; the language Faulknerian in its irregularity and historical reach; the terms and textures Kafkaesque. Hawkes wrote a western in the Kafka manner, his first line was a pastiche of the first lines of *The Metamorphosis*. A man is embedded just below the water level of a dam – a trope for the decade, or else something even larger, a trope for postwar America. The grave site recalls Eden, with earth, mountain, and water marking his burial place, but he is also buried with the detritus of modern civilizations: hoses, pumps, Big Cat.

An act of chance took the anonymous man, and yet because of that happenstance he becomes the center of the novel. Yet human values hardly count – pace O'Connor. Land and landscape rule both life and deaths – a silent, moving earth that is, like the Great Slide itself, burying life in its very movement. The Great Slide is an apt metaphor, for it is a natural occurrence, but also man-made, piles of earth and hard matter that exist from his doing. Yet even while man-made, such immensities of weight and pressure refuse man's dictates. They slide, and by sliding they bury and kill. Hawkes here had his theme, although in later years he lightened up and, in somewhat less effective works, offered sensuality instead of his earlier grimness.

By *Second Skin*, in 1964, Hawkes had reached the zenith of his earlier development as a spokesperson for the decade's confrontational and, ultimately, divisive forces. Here are the themes he would pass on to Thomas Pynchon. The ideological grounding, as always with Hawkes, is the valid, the valorized, as against the counterfeit. In *Second Skin*, we note his typically American reliance on space: a bus trip, an island off the Atlantic coast, a spice island, "a wandering island . . . located in space and quite out of time." Nevertheless, despite spatiality and obsessive movement, the novel is defined by an innerness that is peristaltic, virtually paralytic. Space is denied, even as it is proffered – the twin peaks and valleys, or bipolar sensibility, of the fifties now entering the early sixties.

The protagonist, Skipper, carries death in his wake: his father, wife, and daughter are suicides; his son-in-law has been murdered; his mother, having vanished, is now dead. And yet Skipper tries for renewal and plans new generations. The island is his medium for resurrection; he is an island god and the skipper of his own realm. Hawkes's narrative works as a double agent: the author peering down the ruins of his material and doing it through Skipper's memory, and Skipper himself peering down the ruins of his life and attempting to discover areas of meaning. Meaning itself lies in validation of self in the face of almost innumerable disasters, some circumstantial, some Skipper-driven.

Hawkes eerily reflects aspects of the decade by way of his probe of mainstream materials (journeys, disasters, mortality) alongside his delving into margins, seams, and "static silences." The reader, meanwhile, struggles for connective tissue – some overall meaning or grounding – even as he or she is being borne along on the crest of violence and death. This method, which also appears intrinsic to *The Cannibal* and *The Lime Twig*, catches the undertow of American attitudes, that other side of the "city of words": an inability to verbalize, a need, concurrently, to express in violence what words fail to express.

Although *Second Skin* seems remote from the details of American life in the 1950s, its contrariness expresses rather precisely how we were and what we felt, even those who thought little and felt less. The idea of a "second skin" is compelling as a signifier of our desire for renewal even as we assess the disasters of the past. But more than that, a second skin suggests that we can return to an earthly paradise if only we come into contact with our deepest feelings; then we might overcome not only adversity and circumstance but memory itself. Molting, seizing control of his destiny with a pen – Skipper writes a memoir of past disaster – writing his way out of his death-dragging memories, Skipper finds on his island a way of transforming entrapment into a new life by turning it into a narcissistic circuitry of memory. As Hawkes might have said in retrospect, welcome to the sixties.

Yet equally strong cultural forces in the fifties drew on middle-class, "middle-brow" values, on what critic Dwight MacDonald called "midcult." His specific target for midcult was Clifton Fadiman, admired by many as a man of letters, but for MacDonald the high priest of a polluted culture. Fadiman was perhaps the best-known judge of the Book-of-the-Month Club. The BOMC, the Literary Guild, and other clubs had become popular as purveyors of mainstream fiction, some mainstream nonfiction, a few books of great complexity, but on the whole a *Reader's Digest* alternative to high culture. The idea was to draw in an audience which ordinarily might not read at all, and Fadiman was most successful in presenting fiction to such readers and making them believe they were reading "literature." Meanwhile, in reviews and commentary, he was attacking the one great literary figure of the forties and early fifties, William Faulkner, and praising more accessible writers such as Sinclair Lewis and other Naturalists.

Fadiman made it seem as if culture was not demanding, that it could be absorbed by anyone who could turn pages; and his role as moderator of a popular quiz show, *Information Please*, cemented his role as a messenger of culture. Yet the quiz program was not culture; it was discrete information. It was not thought; it was data. And its success relied not on the experts' "knowledge," but on their ability to recall detail. The experts were witty, of course, and very informative: Oscar Levant, who could recognize any piece of music after a few bars; John Kieran, who covered all fields, but especially sports; Franklin

P. Adams, a columnist who tried hard to keep up; and Fadiman, the all-knowing master of ceremonies. The program lasted from 1938 to 1948, and then it became the basis for the avalanche of quiz programs and their monetary rewards in the fifties. Fadiman's role was to validate such a program as culture.

The play between high and low culture, or midcult, was, in several respects, the pull and tear of the decade's dichotomies that at most levels resisted all efforts at resolution. The Cold War and McCarthyism, a tandem cultural force, tainted nearly every aspect of society, even though it did not directly pervade the lives of most people. The Hollywood Ten who went to prison; those hundreds more who were blacklisted; the tenured faculty members dismissed from their university posts; the loyalty oaths required for nearly all state employees; the labeling of all who opposed the Chinese Nationalists under Chiang as pro-Maoist; the question of who "lost China" – all of this, while remote to the larger population, developed a narrative of authoritarian fear and trembling. The Cold War was kept alive through still other forms of intimidation stemming from the recognition of potential nuclear devastation. The bomb (the BOMB); the aftermath of attack as a nuclear winter; brinkmanship, the threat of nuclear confrontation from Eisenhower's Secretary of State, John Foster Dulles; the extensive building of underground bomb shelters – some to be guarded by firearms; the threat of communist subversion, not only from McCarthy, but from Congress and the administration down to the governors and mayors – all inflamed insecurity. Amidst all, some viewed the civil rights movement as un-American for weakening us in the face of an external enemy. Even more "un-American" were the first stirrings of the gay movement to offset homophobic state laws, all considered a bulwark against a weakening of American youth. We cannot ignore, also, the censorious acts which did reach deeper into the population, by allowing authorities to control library books, television images and language, film ideology, sexual situations, and, once again, permissible language.

Against such pressures was a counter-movement which represented a more open, democratic force that blasted through in the mid-to-late sixties. Even as issues of social justice, fairness, civility, and equity were endangered as the country girded for Cold War, there were oppositional elements. That outpouring which was labeled the "Jewish novel" was part of the decade's drive toward social justice. Saul Bellow, Bernard Malamud, and Philip Roth, for example, were all concerned with the role of the Jew in an overwhelmingly hostile (in their eyes) Christian community. The redefining of the Jewish role would be followed by a comparable effort by the African American writers, the latter energized by *The Invisible Man* and the novels and essays of James Baldwin, followed by the Harlem Renaissance in theatre arts, the novels of John Williams, the first stirrings of Toni Morrison, and the intellectual commentary of Harold Cruse.

While the main ethnic thrust came in fiction, novels and short stories also carried a heavy societal and even political weight. The fifties saw a shift from a purely Anglo-Saxon culture (Hemingway, Faulkner, Wharton) toward one of infinitely greater variety; and this move toward multiplicity immediately conjured up questions of what constituted a society and a nation that now seemed to be splitting into subcultures. Multiculturalism was an invention of a later decade, but we observe intimations of it in the fifties, as ethnic, religious, and racial subcultures began to redefine a different kind of America.

Censors and censoring were called into question. In a decade that ushered in developments in communication and media technology, censorship played no small part in splitting America and rerouting internal boundaries. In a monumental decision that was part of the opening up of the country to alternative experiences, the censor who banned Vladimir Nabokov's *Lolita* was overturned. Certainly, *Lolita*, with its nympholepsy, was an "alternative" experience. As a test of the First Amendment it sanctioned free speech and writing. Three years after its Olympia Press publication in Paris, *Lolita* appeared in America as part of an "on the road" genre with a European sensibility. Everything about *Lolita* is parodic and drenched in modernist irony: a celebration of the counterfeit, its methods based on mirrors and reflections. By joining Humbert, a polyglot European (Swiss, Austrian, French, a "dash of Danube," and English from his mother) and Lolita, a prototypical junk-food pre-teen American, Nabokov had a ready-made mirror that would reflect the imitational. Each participant attempts to adapt to the other: Humbert to Lolita's indulgence in fast food, guidebook scenery and "sights," movement and spatiality; Lolita to Humbert's indulgence of his child-passion, of constant touch and sexual play, most of which she can hardly tolerate.

The career of Nabokov in the fifties and early sixties, in fact, plays in and out of nearly every aspect of American culture. Through parody, satire, and burlesque, he bridged American yearning for new experiences and the European sense of failure. He became our model Modernist. *Pale Fire*, in 1962, is the other side of *Lolita*, more technically adventurous than the earlier book, but nevertheless full of the self-love at the heart of the Nabokov conception of art. In an age of narcissism and solipsism, he outdistanced his closest competitors, Mailer, Roth, and Bellow; while his ironic thrust, although self-serving, also allowed him to penetrate counterfeit ideas. *Pale Fire* seems like an artifact based on the imitational, but in fact it reveals how deception becomes part of memory and history, and enters the culture.

While the structure of the book may seem arbitrary, it is actually unified. The parodic nature of the material, including the arrangement, works as a probe to uncover the authentic. The 999-line poem by Shade, the commentary by Kinbote (which occupies three quarters of the book's length), and the index, apparently by the author, are interconnected. All are associated with Nabokov's insistence on being all characters and places in the novel. *Pale Fire* is in the long line of self-reflexive novels from *Tristram Shandy* to Marcel Proust's long invasion of self and memory; and in all instances, the self-reflexiveness creates a parodic view of the material, an intense examination of one's self which also serves as an antidote to corruption, deception, and hypocrisy.

In this view, *Pale Fire*, the poem, becomes armor-plating for the self. As the personification of the exile, Nabokov caught the marginalization of the "normal," and identified the residue of counterculture in a society which insisted on virtue and values. In his subversion of those qualities, and in his refusal to enter into the American community (literarily and otherwise), he links up with the larger forces which proved adversarial. Kinbote at one time thought Slade would call his poem "Solus Rex," the solitary king, a chess term, but also a trope for the marginal artist. This then links with Wyatt Gwyon in Gaddis's *The Recognitions*, as well as other portraits of the artist figure in Salinger, Bellow, and Roth. That image of the artist as solitary and exiled is not, simply, a romantic notion: it is part of the countering element in the decade that refuses the artificiality of official pronouncements.

The artist is a bulwark against false hope in a decade in which hope was offered freely and superficially, from the White House to television sitcoms and soaps. In its countercultural pose, the poem shows the American indifference to memory, to time past, to history itself. Kinbote's commentary must struggle against the poem's subversiveness. Shade has shown how America swallows memory, and Kinbote must demonstrate that some values still remain. The dialectic is very much part of the ideological struggle of the fifties, in that those who wanted to move forward (progressives, liberals, federalists) had to confront those who held the power and stood for states rights, passivity, nostalgia, and a superficial reading of history. It does not matter that Shade's poem is often a mockery of poetry – so parodic it descends into burlesque and incoherence – for what does matter is its representation of the chaos Kinbote must reshape to form a coherent world. In this mix of elements, the poet-artist must have visionary powers, and he might be the subject for assassination; kill the poet and one kills the vision. It was a prophetic note for the sixties.

Carved into segments (the poet, the commentator, the assassin), Nabokov's career is curiously like those of the American action painters who after years of one type of art (as realists or naturalists or color stylists) moved to another stage, as though in a different language. That sense of the protean, of constant change, of movable careers, which we find in Nabokov, is prototypical postwar American. Thus despite his discomfort as an American, despite his urge to parody New World styles and ways, despite his mockery of Cold War obsessions, Nabokov proved, in some ways, typical. Dislocation for the European fitted well into America's repeated reshaping of itself, as it moved back and forth from inauthentic to valid, from mainstream to counterculture.

While Nabokov yearned to be modern, so did postwar America. The rise of power for the country was accompanied by a desire for renewal. Ideas that had been well developed in Europe – as part of Bauhaus, functionalism, and other design groups – were now becoming part of America's perception of itself. Design in all its varieties, as furniture, architecture, kitchen utensils, and even television and radio which were virtual revolutions in themselves, underwent transformation. It was no longer sufficient for something to work, it had to "fit." In one respect, the emphasis on the modern was still another step toward secularity, and it also energized the argument that our living culture was setting us even further from tradition and traditional values. These are cultural wars that have continued into the twenty-first century.

How did the fifties define "modern"? In some respects, "modern" was expected to be the demarking image of the times: America as progressive, forward looking, the future as it was unfolding. "Modern," as design and in practice, would draw on the arts – especially the wave of abstraction that overtook the art market – and the sciences: constant discoveries of the new, the curative, especially in medicine, the exploration of frontiers. But "modern" would, also, explore new materials, synthetics, fabrics, tensile strengths, and related matters; and the new materials, made possible by developments in plastics and other synthetics, demanded new shapes. These materials, in calling for designs that allowed them to expand, influenced ceramics, fabric making, and body parts for cars, as well as architecture, engineering, and industrial development.

To be "modern" was, primarily, to be functional: the design should never go beyond what the material permits. Function, form, and substance cohere in an insistence on the meeting of art and design. Simplicity was required; lines for a public that wanted its transportation to look lavish. But "modern" meant even more; it was to indicate that fifties man and woman had mastered the machine and technology itself: that just as America had harnessed so much energy to win the war, so the peacetime society could muster comparable energy in harnessing science and linking it to art. But this linkage was not to be special; it was to be available to all, as the surge in television advertising would have it. The secularity of affluence met the democracy of practice. No matter how strict the purse, something modern should be available. That was the key to advertising: not only publicizing certain products – from soap to cars – but selling American democracy by selling products. In several areas, the intense drive to be modern was part of American pride as it assumed leadership of the free world: first in democratic procedures, it was thought, and first in its product availability. It was part of civic virtue to buy.

The housing that was to provide shelter for returning veterans – and subsidized by government loans – was, of course, in the modern mode, stripped-down, functional houses, with clean, sharp edges, and few or no ornaments or surprises. For some these houses were to be starter-uppers, but for most, they became home, often with additions as the family increased. A certain homogenization was unavoidable, as housing became mass assembled, on large tracts, where there was little if any distinction between one structure and another. Levittown, in suburban Long Island, was exemplary in this respect: long rows of similar houses stretching to the horizon, and no distinctive features unless the owner in time added them. All the houses had an unfinished space for additional room, an attic that might be developed, or a basement; but the basic structure oozed modernity, which came to mean straight, clean lines, as on an assembly line. There was something distinctly American about it: you got what you (or the federal government) paid for. No European entanglements here! Levittown was a Cold War triumph.

Yet behind every effort at perfection lies the counterfeit. The perfect – whether in design, practice, or theory – invites a utopianism, and utopianism, as some fifties intellectuals would discover, ended up on the dust heap of hopes frustrated or destroyed. We must remind ourselves that American pride, chauvinism, and Cold War bravura in the face of Soviet nuclear weapons made us feel superior and invincible. Having made our world so much better, we were ready – as Kennedy would spell it out in his Inaugural Address in 1961 – to bring the fruits of our adventures to others. The result of our utopian belief in American perfectionism was the passage from the clean lines of design to entanglements in areas of policy we had only partially grasped.

Little could be more utopian than the rapid growth of the suburbs in the fifties, the slow and then radical desertion of the city on the part of those who could. Levittowns proliferated, with a house in the suburbs defined as a kingdom or a princely residence, however tight the quarters. With GI loans and easy terms, the government offered an earthly paradise. The home was "picture perfect," as the expression has it, and the couple in it was also considered to be picture perfect. Television acted it out: in the music of the *Lawrence Welk Show*, the alternative to Elvis, and in the numerous family portraits (*The Adventures of Ozzie and Harriet, Leave It To Beaver, I Love Lucy*, among others) presented by the so-called "WASP-coms" which allowed for only minor imperfections; and these were easily papered over. These perfect households in the perfect suburbs appeared all white; blacks were not permitted into Levittowns and only in minuscule numbers in comparable developments.

For those lucky whites – and the whole country in the pre-civil rights era could seem hegemonically white, Christian, and male-driven – there were the perfect appliances; kitchens were part of every domestic woman's dream world. A version of medieval order prevailed: God in heaven (at least on Sunday), father at work, supporting it all gracefully, mother in the kitchen with all the time-saving appliances which kept her happy (or miserable), and the happy children playing or studying. No sex, no drugs, no alcohol, no transgressions, Junior was not a cross-dresser – just a little hurt here or there, a crush, a broken teenybopper romance, all troubles ready to be folded over into the family. With the draft still on, Johnny willingly went into the military, glad to do his service for a country that offered him so much.

But we know another fifties existed alongside this one, or at another level, as a kind of palimpsest. The foothills of what would later prove to be mountains were already forming. We have already cited the "rebel," whether with or without a cause, the beginning of what would be on a larger scale with "on the road" anarchy and sixties openness. In serious social and political terms, civil rights were beginning to become an issue that would roil historical conventions, a kind of second battle of the Civil War; and, as noted, gays were beginning the slow organization that would give them a strong group voice. Even the women's movement, more clearly associated with the later sixties, was stirring, intensified by women who had returned from war plants and the military, certain they could do the job as well as men. While the larger society – and certainly the federal government under a passive president – did not as yet respond, the lower slopes of change were being breached and a multicultural society would not be far behind.

The "other" America began to export its cultural products abroad, and nowhere more than in its music did America use popular culture as a form of power. Here the rebellious side of the decade dominated and revealed the paradoxical split between a seemingly ultra-bourgeois, acquisitive nation and what the arts, popular more than serious, were producing. The sound of the period was, substantially, rock and roll, although other musical styles also commanded audiences and recordings. Rock and roll, introduced by the disc jockey Alan Freed, dominated especially when Elvis Presley appeared in the mid-fifties; and then rock defined the sixties, *the* sound of almost every form of that decade's protest. A beginning was made with Bill Haley's "Rock around the Clock," a single with its rhythms picked up from guitar and drum. The record moved slowly until it became background music in the film *The Blackboard Jungle*, which delineated a troublesome school of delinquent students. Rock was, in this later respect, associated with rebellion, uncivil acts, even violence. With this, the record climbed to number one, and its association with an outlaw culture was fixed.

Rock was made for Elvis. However polite he was, his bodily gyrations and that smirking expression endeared him to a young audience. As Frank Sinatra in the previous decade had enthralled and excited young girl worshippers, so Presley transfixed youth, both male and female. As much as Chuck Berry, Buddy Holly, and Little Richard appealed, Presley came to embody rock and roll, until the late sixties, when his star began to fade and the Beatles were the new sensation, both soothing and rebellious.

A good part of Elvis's success was his immersion in different kinds of music: gospel, blues, and country, all of which he brought to this performance of rock. His Pentecostal background gave him the emotional basis which in his later development became full of sexual innuendo. As he developed a style, he hit upon a blending of a laid-back delivery and a high vocal line, really a whine and a cry for help. His manner communicated both defiance and vulnerability, and this became his attraction. Along other lines, part of Presley's appeal – and one must see this in terms of the racial culture of both his home-base of Memphis, Tennessee, and the country as a whole – was his presence as a young white man who sounded black. The appeal was immediate, since black performers were having difficulty finding acceptance at shows even while their sound was praised. A white face emitting a black musical voice was a racial dream, given the culture of the mid fifties. Early on, Presley's signature piece "That's All Right (Mama)" was, also, racially perfect: mothers were "in," whether black or white, and the words could be taken to prove that at heart he was a good boy. The hip swiveling and knee bends came later.

Popular musical culture was expansive, whether in movies, on the Broadway stage, or in individuals' appearances. In musical comedy, the Rodgers and Hammerstein successes continued from the forties, with musicals that swept through the fifties: *West Side Story, Kiss Me Kate, Brigadoon, Guys and Dolls, An American in Paris*, and *Annie Get Your Gun* helped solidify an American genre that became an export product. Individual performers, black and white, included Judy Garland, Frank Sinatra, Pearl Bailey, Harry Belafonte, Ray Charles, Nat King Cole, Bing Crosby, Gene Kelly, Fred Astaire, Liberace, Sammy Davis Jr, Duke Ellington, Lena Horne, Pete Seeger, Sarah Vaughan, and groups such as the Ink Spots, the Mills Brothers, and the Platters.

Yet Presley dominated. He also mirrored the undertones not only of rebellion but of despair in the country, especially in his groundbreaking "Heartbreak Hotel." He brought desolation to the airwaves, this in January 1956, a counterpoint to the good feeling the country was supposed to foster; in fact, something of a countercultural revolution in itself, an avatar of desolation that the Vietnam War and assassinations later would bring. The tone was of loneliness, precisely what the major plays of Tennessee Williams were also exploring; and, as cited above, not far behind were the revivals of Eugene O'Neill's plays, all "Heartbreak Hotels" of sorts, with the agonizing *Long Day's Journey into Night* and the sighs of loneliness, mortality, and isolation in *The Iceman Cometh*. America as lonely, nightmarish, desolate – quite a different cultural response from what television advertising was revealing. Then, during the popular surge of this record, Presley appeared on television, his gyrations somehow reinforcing the threat of "Heartbreak Hotel" to American complacency; until in subsequent appearances, he was photographed only from the waist up. The thought police were wary; the Catholic church and some Protestant groups, along with the United States attorney general, were eager to censor whatever offended church-going people. The media could only reveal so much, even as Presley began to stretch boundaries. It was becoming clear that popular culture did more to open up America than any other cultural form, despite all efforts to keep it closed.

Ambiguity, paradox, unresolvables, and disconnects remained bewildering elements. Three very different areas suggest how bizarrely America was facing postwar challenges. The universities, seemingly the last stand of sanity, capitulated to McCarthy and his Senate subcommittee, to Senator McCarran and his exclusion of the foreign-born, and to the House Un-American Activities Committee (HUAC). By the end of the 1940s, the universities had agreed that members of the communist party were not fit to teach, although membership in the party was not illegal and there was no indication that such professors were indoctrinating their students or bringing their party affiliation into the classroom. But a more expansive issue was that those who pleaded the Fifth Amendment – also a legal right – were now being driven from the academy, making it unclear what the Fifth Amendment protected the individual from. The Supreme Court – Frankfurter and Robert Jackson, among its members – followed a hands-off policy, allowing the legislative branch to decide what was allowable in the courts. In effect, the Court did not wish to impede the HUAC in its pursuit of anyone tainted with possible communist sympathies, and even of those who took the Fifth because they disapproved of the investigation of political beliefs, not because they were covering up any party affiliation or even sympathy.

As a consequence – in which many notables like playwrights Arthur Miller and Lillian Hellman were swept up – the universities accepted the fact they should not be allowed to regulate their own faculties. In nearly every instance, large urban universities ceded sovereignty to Congressional committees, several of them chaired by an alcoholic (Joseph McCarthy), a future jailbird (J. Parnell Thomas), or simply a know-nothing (like McCarran). In case after case, the Committees made judgments about the fitness of so-called subversive faculty. The aim was to discredit the faculty member as being disloyal or linked to a foreign power, and, therefore, incapable of being loyal to the university, the students, and the country itself.

The general public was in the main ignorant of any of these attacks on faculty members even in state universities. The public only came to hear of the incursion of Congress into intellectual life in the tangential case of Robert Oppenheimer, not in a university setting but in the nuclear program, where his high security clearance was removed because he was deemed if not disloyal then unreliable. No security breach was ever found in Oppenheimer's case, only left-wing connections; but his harassment by Congress and by the Atomic Energy Commission after he had supervised the Manhattan Atomic Bomb Project did bring home how reputations and lives could be invaded and even destroyed. In an equally damaging case, that of Owen Lattimore, the accusation that he was the leader of a Far Eastern clique of advisers that "lost China" – when the communists drove Chiang's forces to exile in Taiwan – was a loss of another kind. It meant that the State Department no longer had experts willing to speak their minds about a region which would draw us into the Vietnam War in ignorance of the land, its history and culture, its languages and nationalistic aspirations.

In another world, the world of baseball, the split personality of the country was palpable, and unbridgeable. For even as baseball began to integrate racially, following Jackie Robinson's joining the Brooklyn Dodgers in the National League in 1947 and Larry Doby's joining the Cleveland Indians in the American League shortly after, the country tore itself apart over civil rights for African Americans. Some baseball teams moved rapidly, with the Dodgers soon adding Don Newcombe, Roy Campanella, and Joe Black; others like the New York Yankees and Boston Red Sox remained white for several years more. Withal, the additions to both leagues created some of the biggest stars of the game: Hank Aaron, who would in time break Babe Ruth's lifetime home run record, and Willie Mays, considered by many to be the finest all-around ballplayer ever. The nature of the game was changing incrementally, for the entrance of black players meant that white athletes had to compete against a much broader spectrum of the population; and, shortly, black players – Aaron, Mays, Ernie Banks, Frank Robinson, Willie McCovey – came to dominate in batting averages, home runs, stolen bases, and other statistics. And yet the integration, finally, of America's sport was not reflected in other areas – neither in schools nor in housing. Resistance in the South to integration was violent, while in the North it was more subtle but almost as effective. Crowds applauded black (and Hispanic) achievements on the field as strenuously as they resisted racial integration elsewhere. America was truly divided, in ways that cut across social, political, class, and personal lines.

Finally, perhaps most revealing of all the split personalities in American fifties culture, are the words of our most sophisticated, high-toned poet, Wallace Stevens. Stevens stood for poetry as the supreme art, more significant than philosophy, asserting that we owe the idea of God himself to poetry and not to philosophy. Stevens believed in poetry as a "supreme fiction," a kind of secular Bible or set of Gospels for our time. Only in poetry can human beings find fulfillment, and only poetry provides the linkage between reality and the imagination. These are all ideas Stevens emphasized in his letters in the 1950s, as well as in his poetry and in his remarks on aesthetics. Yet Stevens, the aesthete, was also a chauvinist, an American in the gray flannel mold who believed that "there are infinitely more meanings for Americans in America" than in anything Europe could provide. Our curiosity about Europe, he wrote in 1950, could be easily satisfied, whereas much greater significance would attach itself "to some of our own things." Narrowness and provinciality ran alongside worldliness; Stevens in poetry and aesthetics is broad and inclusive, Stevens in social and political matters – the Hartford insurance vice president – is, as he says, part of the mass, self-satisfied, a nationalist, not an internationalist. This, too, was America in the postwar decade, split and divided, even as it grew rich.

References and further reading

Baldwin, James. *Go Tell It On The Mountain*. New York: Knopf, 1953.

Baldwin, James. *The Fire Next Time*. New York: Dial Press, 1963.

Barth, John. *The Floating Opera*. New York: Appleton-Century-Crofts, 1956.

Barth, John. *The End of the Road*. Garden City, NY: Doubleday, 1958.

Bellow, Saul. *The Adventures of Augie March*. New York: Viking Press, 1953.

Bellow, Saul. *Henderson the Rain King*. New York: Viking Press, 1959.

Brown, Norman O. *Love's Body*. New York: Random House, 1966.

Burroughs, William. *Naked Lunch*. New York: Grove Press, 1959.

Burroughs, William [under the pseudonym William Lee]. *Junkie*. New York: Ace Books, 1953.

Burroughs, William. *Junky*. New York: Penguin, 1977.

Burroughs, William. *Queer*. New York: Viking, 1985.

Chambers, Whitaker. *Witness*. New York: Random House, 1952.

Cheever, John. *The Enormous Radio and Other Stories*. New York: Funk and Wagnalls, 1953.

Cheever, John. *The Wapshot Chronicle*. New York: Harper, 1957.

Cheever, John. *The Housebreaker of Shady Hill and Other Stories*. New York: Harper, 1958.

Coover, Robert. *The Public Burning*. New York: Viking, 1977.

Doctorow, E. L. *The Book of Daniel*. New York: Random House, 1971.

Ellison, Ralph. *Invisible Man*. New York: Random House, 1952.

Erikson, Erik. *Childhood and Society*. New York: W. W. Norton, 1950.

Erikson, Erik. *Identity, Youth and Crisis*. New York: W. W. Norton, 1968.

Friedan, Betty. *The Feminine Mystique*. New York: W. W. Norton, 1963.

Gaddis, William. *The Recognitions*. New York: Harcourt, Brace, 1955.

Gaddis, William. *JR*. New York: Knopf, distributed by Random House, 1975.

Ginsburg, Allen. *HOWL and Other Poems*. San Francisco: City Lights Pocket Bookshop, 1956.

Goodman, Paul. *Growing Up Absurd: Problems of Youth in the Organized Society*. New York: Vintage Books, 1960.

Goodman, Paul. *Growing Up Absurd: Problems of Youth in the Organized System*. New York: Random House, 1960.

Hawkes, John. *The Beetle Leg*. New York: New Directions, 1951.

Hawkes, John. *The Lime Twig*. Norfolk, CT: New Directions, 1961.

Hawkes, John. *The Cannibal*. New York: New Directions, 1962.

Hawkes, John. *Second Skin*. New York: New Directions, 1964.

Heller, Joseph. *Catch-22*. New York: Simon and Schuster, 1961.

Keniston, Kenneth. *The Uncommitted: Alienated Youth in American Society*. New York: Harcourt, Brace and World, 1965.

Laing, R. D. *The Divided Self: A Study of Sanity and Madness*. London: Tavistock, 1960.

Laing, R. D. *The Politics of Experience*. New York: Pantheon Books, 1967.

Lasch, Christopher. *The Culture of Narcissism: American Life in an Age of Diminishing Expectations*. New York: W. W. Norton, 1978.

Leary, Timothy. *The Politics of Ecstasy*. New York: Putnam, 1968.

McCarthy, Mary. *The Groves of Academe*. New York: Harcourt, Brace, 1952.

McCarthy, Mary. *Cannibals and Missionaries*. New York: Harcourt, Brace, Jovanovich, 1979.

McLuhan, Marshall. *Understanding Media: The Extensions of Man*. New York: McGraw-Hill, 1964.

Mailer, Norman. *Barbary Shore*. New York: New American Library, 1951.

Mailer, Norman. *An American Dream*. New York: Dial Press, 1965.

Malamud, Bernard. *The Assistant*. New York: Farrar, Straus, Cudahy, 1957.

Malamud, Bernard. *A New Life*. New York: Farrar, Straus, Cudahy, 1961.

Marcuse, Herbert. *Eros and Civilization: A Philosophical Inquiry into Freud*. Boston: Beacon Press, 1955.

Metalious, Grace. *Peyton Place*. New York: Messner, 1956.

Mills, C. Wright. *White Collar: The American Middle Classes*. New York: Oxford University Press, 1951.

Mills, C. Wright. *The Power Elite*. New York: Oxford University Press, 1956.

Nabokov, Vladimir. *Lolita*. Paris: Olympia Press, and New York: Putnam, 1955.

Nabokov, Vladimir. *Pale Fire*. New York: Putnam, 1962.

O'Connor, Flannery. *Wise Blood*. New York: Harcourt, Brace, 1952.

O'Connor, Flannery. *The Violent Bear It Away*. New York: Farrar, Straus, Cudahy, 1960.

O'Connor, Flannery. *The Complete Short Stories*. New York: Farrar, Straus, 1971.

Percy, Walker. *The Moviegoer*. New York: Knopf, 1961.

Pynchon, Thomas. *V: A Novel*. Philadelphia: Lippincott, 1963.

Riesman, David. *The Lonely Crowd*. New Haven, CT: Yale University Press, 1950.

Roth, Philip. *Goodbye, Columbus and Five Short Stories*. Boston: Houghton Mifflin, 1959.

Roth, Philip. *Our Gang (Starring Tricky and his Friends)*. New York: Random House, 1971.

Salinger, J. D. *The Catcher in the Rye*. Boston: Little, Brown, 1951.

Stevens, Wallace. *Harmonium*. New York: Knopf, 1923.

Styron, William. *Lie Down in Darkness*. Indianapolis: Bobbs-Merrill, 1951.

Styron, William. *The Long March*. New York: Random House, 1952.

Styron, William. *Set This House on Fire*. New York: Random House, 1960.

Styron, William. *The Confessions of Nat Turner*. New York: Random House, 1967.

Susann, Jacqueline. *Valley of the Dolls*. New York: B. Geis Associates, distributed by Random House, 1966.

Trilling, Lionel. *The Middle of the Journey*. New York: Viking, 1947.

Updike, John. *Rabbit, Run*. New York: Knopf, 1960.

Wertham, Frederic. *Seduction of the Innocent*. New York: Rinehart, 1954.

Williams, John. *The Man Who Cried I Am*. Boston: Little, Brown, 1967.

Wilson, Sloan. *The Man in the Gray Flannel Suit*. New York: Simon and Schuster, 1955.

Wouk, Herman. *Aurora Dawn, or, The True History of Andrew Reale*. New York: Simon and Schuster, 1947.

Wouk, Herman. *The Caine Mutiny Court Martial*. New York: Doubleday, 1954.

Wouk, Herman. *Marjorie Morningstar*. Garden City, NY: Doubleday, 1955.

Chapter 3

The Beat Generation is Now About Everything

Regina Weinreich

"The Beat Generation is no longer about poetry. The Beat Generation is now about everything," wrote the poet Gregory Corso in a prescient 1959 essay "Variations on a Generation" (quoted in Charters: 183). By then, the important literary works by which the Beat Generation was defined as a countercultural movement had already made their mark: poet Allen Ginsberg had inaugurated his epic "Howl" at the pivotal Six Gallery reading in San Francisco, novelist Jack Kerouac had published his *On the Road* to a dazzling rave review in the *New York Times*, and satirist William S. Burroughs had unleashed his *Naked Lunch*, horrifying the conservative, repressive culture at large, which wished to stifle its "obscenities." Characterized by spontaneity, an unwillingness to revise, an anarchist spirit, and the influence of jazz music, these works were outrageous compared to the staid formalism of mainstream American literature.

Corso's claim that the Beats were "about everything" was perhaps supported by the extent to which literature and writers were equally famous for a "hip," disaffected lifestyle featuring unmannerly, "up-yours" behavior, irreverence, and sloppiness. The Beat avant-garde was so embedded in the zeitgeist its imagery had melded with the cultural images at large. In movies, disaffected Marlon Brando/*The Wild One* (1953) and James Dean/*Rebel Without a Cause* (1955) were hipster prototypes alongside Jack Kerouac's *On the Road* protagonists Sal Paradise and Dean Moriarty.

In other media, in the 1960s and 1970s, the Beat sensibility continued to cross over into popular culture: In rock and roll, the band
Steely Dan took its name from a dildo in *Naked Lunch*; David Bowie
wrote lyrics utilizing Burroughs's "cut-up" techniques; the very name
"Beatles" came from "beat."

Ever adaptable, the Beats embraced the culture and evolved with
its vagaries high and low: Burroughs, a star of sorts, did a turn on the
popular television satire *Saturday Night Live*, and played a junky priest
in Gus Van Sant's *Drugstore Cowboy* (1989). Embracing the Beats back,
Van Sant dedicated his award-winning *Good Will Hunting* (1997) to
the memory of Allen Ginsberg and William S. Burroughs. Clearly the
director felt an affinity with these writers – artistically and psychically.

Corso's complaint is resonant for yet another phenomenon: by the
1990s, Jack Kerouac and Allen Ginsberg were wearing khakis for
GAP advertisements, and William S. Burroughs was endorsing Nike.
It was a sign: the erstwhile beatnik societal misfits had become cultural icons. They had name recognition; they could sell products, and
it had little to do with what they wrote. ("The Beats were writers.
That is, they wrote," to paraphrase William S. Burroughs.) Literary
and cultural impact, however intertwined, remain separate issues.
And while the Beats are now given serious critical attention, a full
assessment has not yet taken place. Even fifty years past their main
literary achievements, much of the Beat image is still mired in cultural myth, a phenomenon they themselves cultivated.

By 1959 the Beats had already made their name on scandal and
exhibitionism: an acquaintance of Jack Kerouac, Lucien Carr, killed
his gay stalker, Dave Kammerer, when Kammerer dared Carr to do it,
and Carr accommodated him in this Gidean *acte gratuit*. Immediately
after, Carr showed up on Kerouac's doorstep, and the two were
arrested when they went to the police the following morning. Kerouac
eventually would recount this story in *Vanity of Duluoz* (1968), but its
spirit infused *The Town and the City* (1950). This first novel augured the
emergence of a new consciousness in America: "The New Vision,"
which explains the evolution of the kind of existentialism Kerouac
and the other Beat writers dramatized in their lives and work.

Anarchy in fact made art imperative. William Burroughs accidentally
shot his common-law wife, Joan Vollmer, in a William Tell routine in
Mexico City in 1951. Burroughs resolved to redeem himself, to exor-
cise the "Ugly Spirit" through writing, as he explained in the preface
to *Queer*, first published in 1985. Written in the fifties, the novel's linear
style is like that of *Junkie* (1953), the work which precedes it, even

though Burroughs was beginning to break up the narrative with his signature "routines," analogous to the tales told by drinkers at a bar.

From the early fifties, Beat writers abandoned traditional forms in favor of more experimental writing, producing the works on which their literary fame is based. Ginsberg's "Howl" (1955) utilized a long poetic line in the tradition of Walt Whitman, his cadences measured by breaths; Kerouac's *On the Road* (1957) was written on a continuous scroll in his spontaneous bop prosody; Burroughs's *Naked Lunch* (1959) was marked by a fragmented narrative form. To the Beats this stylistic experimentation was a necessary form of rebellion against what Seymour Krim has called "the critical policemen of post-Eliot U.S. letters" (Krim: 195), adhering to a strict formalism, which for the Beat writers was inadequate in reflecting the speeded-up and fragmented world they were observing. If there was in fact a "New Vision," then a new language would have to be created to represent it. Often misunderstood by their critics, who saw the work as sloppy, ragged, ungrammatical, ill-composed, or obscene, the writing of the Beats was just one more publicity stunt.

What is Beat?

The very term "beat" was essential to the early Beat writers' self-definition (Charters: xvii). A term used in jazz circles after World War II, beat meant "down and out," or "poor and exhausted." As legend has it, hustler Herbert Huncke coined the term in 1944, proclaiming, "Man, that's beat," introducing it to Burroughs when he went to Times Square looking for a fix.

Burroughs in turn introduced it to Allen Ginsberg, a Columbia College freshman who passed it along to fellow writer Jack Kerouac, who at the time had left Columbia for the merchant marine. Never losing its allusion to the musical beat, the term took on its own reverberations, and could mean the highest high spiritually, as in a shortened form of beatitude, or blessedness. Ginsberg also added "sleepless, wide-eyed, perceptive, rejected by society, on your own and streetwise" to the definition, while Kerouac insisted on a mysterious, spiritual inference in the manner of Bartleby, Melville's non-conformist who intoned, "I would prefer not to" (Charters: xviii).

"Beat" as in "Generation" could be problematic and imprecise as a critical category referring to the youth culture of postwar decades, or to a determined rebellion against a repressive sociological ethos.

Historically the term "Beat Generation" was officially launched in a *New York Times* magazine article on November 16, 1952, by John Clellon Holmes, the author of *Go* (1952) and *The Horn* (1958), early Beat novels. "This is the Beat Generation" characterized a revolution in progress, made by a post-World War II generation of disaffiliated young people coming of age in a Cold War world without spiritual values they could honor. Later in 1958, Holmes's "The Philosophy of the Beat Generation," published in *Esquire*, made it clear that the group that originated the idea of the Beat Generation was short-lived, and had consisted only of a group of friends: that original group, Ginsberg, Carr, Burroughs, Huncke, and Holmes, had scattered. But after the Korean War, the Beat Generation was resurrected. Postwar youth had picked up the gestures and soon the "beat" sensibility, as reflected in its political and social stance, was everywhere.

The literary hierarchy of the Beat Generation can nevertheless be categorized: the seminal beat figures are Jack Kerouac, Allen Ginsberg, and William S. Burroughs. A second tier included Gregory Corso and the West Coast poets Lawrence Ferlinghetti, Michael McClure, and Gary Snyder, who are equally renowned artists in their own right. Catalysts were Carl Solomon, Herbert Huncke, Neal Cassady; women Joyce Johnson, Hettie Jones, Diane di Prima; additional West Coast poets Philip Whalen, Kenneth Rexroth, Philip Lamantia, Lew Welch, Jack Micheline; the next generation Bob Kaufman, LeRoi Jones (now called Amiri Baraka), and those to follow: Anne Waldman, Jan Kerouac, William Burroughs, Jr, Ed Sanders, Kathy Acker. Not to mention any number of associates and affiliates and hangers-on, anyone who was there – and writing.

Seminal Beats

Jack Kerouac, from Lowell, Massachusetts, a New England mill town with a strong French Canadian community, found himself a national sensation when his second novel *On the Road* received, in 1957, rave recognition from a second string *New York Times* critic, Gilbert Millstein. Kerouac's first novel, *The Town and the City* (1950), was favorably reviewed but deemed derivative of the novels of Thomas Wolfe. Even as he was writing in the late forties, under "the anxiety of Wolfe's influence," he was dissatisfied with the pace of his prose. Inspired by the bebop music of the times, Charlie Parker and Thelonius Monk, and the manic verbal drive of a young hustler named Neal Cassady, the son of a Denver wino, who wrote an incredible non-stop letter dubbed "The Great Sex Letter," Kerouac developed his "spontaneous hop prosody," which he perfected through novel after novel, books of poetry, 19 in all. *The Dharma Bums* (1958), *The Subterraneans* (1958), *Visions of Cody* (published posthumously in 1973), *Desolation Angels* (1965) remain classics of his stylistic progression, his "road" books. A more nostalgic, rhapsodic style was developed in his "Lowell" books, concerning his hometown, memories of childhood and nightmare Catholicism, first love, and his saintly brother Gerard's death at age 9 when Jack was 4: *Dr Sax* (1959), *Maggie Cassidy* (1959), *Visions of Gerard* (1963). *Vanity of Duluoz* (1968) remains a masterpiece of his mature style. He considered these works his "true life" novels and wished they could all be seen as a Divine Comedy of the Buddha, as one vast book, his Legend of Duluoz.

On the Road's composition is legendary. Not only was the book a stylistic departure, written on a roll of teletype as one huge sentence, grammatically *exclamatio* (in the manner of Melville's *Moby-Dick*) as if every moment was a simultaneous highest high and lowest low, describing the antics of two travelers across the vast body and expanse of America in a fast car; it was a thematic departure as well, with its refrain of "Everything is collapsing." Following upon *The Town and the City*, which had anticipated this breakdown of the very foundation of American life, the family, government, institutions, in its articulation of "The New Vision," the characters were considered revolutionary, hipsters, satiric in their defiance of American hypocrisies; American picaros, they were Huck Finn and Jim, the raft on the Mississippi supplanted by the automobile.

"The New Vision," inspired by the Beat writers' reading of Oswald Spengler's *Decline and Fall of the West,* is obliquely defined in Norman Mailer's 1957 essay, "The White Negro." Published in *Dissent*, the work contextualized these characters' nature, positing a connection between the beat outsiders and the anomie and depersonalization of the post-World War II period, when individuals could be quantified by the number of teeth which could be extracted from their mouths, the number of lampshades made from their skin. Mailer took the imagery of the concentration camps, and the post-Hiroshima period, to describe the correlative emotional state of the hipster. If the individual could be so threatened as to be collectively murdered, rolled into mass graves or atomically annihilated, then the teleology of organized religions, with their concerns with God's organization in matters of life, death, and afterlife, had no bearing on contemporary civilization. American existentialists lived in a perpetual now, disconnected from the past and future, as if each moment were their last. To be beat was to "encourage the psychopath in oneself, to explore the domain of experience where security is boredom and therefore sickness, and exist . . . in that enormous present which is without past or future, memory or planned intention, the life where a man must go until he is beat" (Mailer quoted in Charters: 584).

Using the character of Dean to depict this American archetype, *On the Road* celebrates a new kind of hero, one who embodies IT, IT being a radiant moment when time stops and all is in the perpetual NOW. The hero who embodies IT lives in the present without thought to past or future. As Kerouac wrote in the voice of his onlooker Sal Paradise, in admiration of those who embody IT:

> the only people for me are the mad ones, the ones who are mad to live, mad to talk, mad to be saved, desirous of everything at the same time, the ones who never yawn or say a commonplace thing, but burn burn burn like fabulous yellow roman candles exploding like spiders across the stars and in the middle you see the blue centerlight pop and everybody goes "Awww!"

Kerouac in his time became confused with the amoral hipster he so poetically portrayed, but his truth was far from it. Seeking all along the "hearthside" ideal, the solidity of family and home, and the girl next door, Kerouac's writing became the romantic quest for the promise of America, for the comforts of Catholicism, the peace and serenity of his adopted Buddhism. Finding himself marginalized by the "beat" label foisted on him by Allen Ginsberg, repulsed by the cultish aspects of the Beat movement and thereafter the hippies who claimed his paternity, Kerouac wished only to be considered in the mainstream American tradition, a man of letters like Herman Melville, Walt Whitman, Ernest Hemingway, and Jack London.

Controversial too was his dictum, "First Thought, Best Thought;" Kerouac refused to revise. This outrageous stance was in appearance a rebellion itself, revision being the artist's chief control. As an artist, his quest was for language – pure, natural, unadulterated language or the open heart unobstructed by what Kerouac saw as the lying of revision. And yet as book followed upon book roughly recounting the same material, the writer's life, he was in fact revising with each new novel. The original scroll of *On the Road* makes it quite clear that, in the words of Malcolm Cowley, his editor at Viking Press, he revised, and did so quite well (Gifford and Lee: 206).

Though he was best known as a prose fiction stylist, Jack Kerouac wrote books of poetry as well. Among the Beats, he was known as a poet supreme, who worked in several poetry traditions including sonnets, odes, and blues (which he based on blues and jazz idioms). His *Mexico City Blues* was published in 1959. After meeting the poet Gary Snyder in 1955, he also mastered the haiku, the 3-line, 17-syllable Japanese genre going back to Basho. Ezra Pound had modeled his short poem "In a Station of the Metro" after the Japanese haiku. Kerouac went further to define the American haiku tradition, departing from the 17-syllable, 3-line form.

Like Pound, Kerouac consciously felt he was creating a new version of this highly compact poetic genre, at least in English, as he remained convinced of the supremacy of the Japanese masters, Shiki, Han Shan, and Basho. In his "Origins of Joy in Poetry," he extolled the values of haiku as "pointing out things directly, concretely, no abstractions or explanations, wham wham the true blue song of man." He defined his practice in *Scattered Poems*:

> I propose that the "Western Haiku" simply say a lot in three short lines in any Western language. Above all, a Haiku must be very simple and free of all poetic trickery and make a little picture and yet be as airy and graceful as a Vivaldi Pastorella. Here is a great Japanese Haiku that is simpler and prettier than any Haiku I could ever write in any language: –

> A day of quiet gladness, –
> Mount Fuji is veiled
> In misty rain.
>   (Basho) (1644–1694)

Thus in this tradition, Kerouac wrote:

> Birds singing
>   in the dark
>   – Rainy dawn

> Elephants munching
>   on grass – loving
> Heads side by side

> Perfect moonlit night
>   marred
> By family squabbles.

> Missing a kick
> At the icebox door
> It closed anyway.
> (*Scattered Poems*: 67–9)

In terms of Kerouac's oeuvre, the short, compact poetic form is a contrast to the long, looping, panoramic, spontaneous sentences or riffs of his highly poetic novels. They reveal his creative range to include the crafting of both a long, sweeping pan and an instantaneous snapshot that deepens as it is contemplated.

Kerouac was curiously absent or non-participatory in some of the Beat literati's peak moments. At the pivotal 1955 Six Gallery poetry reading in San Francisco, an event said to have triggered the San Francisco Renaissance, Kerouac passed jugs of wine while Ginsberg wowed the crowd with a premier reading of "Howl." Ginsberg organized the October 13 reading, inviting Michael McClure, Philip Lamantia, Kenneth Rexroth, Gary Snyder, and Philip Whalen. Kerouac had of course been invited to read but claimed shyness. "'Poet ain't court jester, I say. He, tho, gets up on stage and howls his poems,' said Jack declining to read" (Kerouac, *Selected Letters 1940–1956*: 519).

Allen Ginsberg was from Paterson, New Jersey, his father a poet and English teacher, Louis Ginsberg; his mother Naomi had been a member of the Communist Party, and had taken her young sons Eugene and Allen to the local meetings. Ginsberg's childhood was defined by the tragedy of his mother's mental illness. He was her chief caretaker, shepherding her through various mental institutions where he also met poet/essayist Carl Solomon.

On that day, October 13, 1955, Allen Ginsberg was about to make his mark. He experienced the fifties as a stultifying time, a repression of real feeling. The personal tragedy of his mother's madness and the lack of access to tender emotion led to his writing "Howl." He had written the poem earlier that year during a period when depression over Carl Solomon's psychiatric crisis coincided with his own guilt over having authorized a lobotomy for his mother. He wrote the poem's first and lengthiest section in one sitting, breaking from his usual habit of writing by hand, composing directly on the typewriter. Convinced that his work was merely experimental, and with no prospect of publication, he eschewed the short-line style he was working in, in favor of the poetic long line and incantatory repetition, a homage to Walt Whitman's "barbaric yawp." He used a triadic ladder structure drawn from William Carlos Williams and improvisatory expansiveness inspired by Kerouac's spontaneous bop prosody, a form that both poets adapted from the saxophone riffs they heard in jazz clubs. Other sections of "Howl" were written and revised in the days and months to follow (Schumacher: 200–7). The middle section was inspired by a paranoiac peyote trip. Ginsberg discerned a robotic death's head, wreathed in smoke and glowing red, when he looked up at the ritzy St Francis Hotel. He found it emblematic of the materialist evil of the capitalist metropolis. The clanging of the Powell Street cable car intoned for the poet the word "Moloch," the Old Testament God to whom children were sacrificed (Watson: 183).

The Six Gallery unveiling of "Howl" had a political bent as well, expressing not only a personal outrage but also an indictment of society's hypocrisies. "We hated the war and the inhumanity and the coldness," said longtime friend, playwright and poet Michael McClure. "The country had the feeling of martial law. An undeclared military state had leapt out of Daddy Warbucks's tanks and sprawled over the landscape. As artists we were oppressed . . . We knew we were poets and we had to speak out as poets" (Sterritt: 106). The audience was indeed moved by Ginsberg's rage. They knew that "a human voice and body had been hurled against the harsh wall of America and its supporting armies and navies and academies and institutions and ownership systems and power-support bases" (Charters: xxvii–xxviii). Allen Ginsberg was the most politically active of the seminal Beats, his work a lifelong commitment to social change.

The Beats Abroad

Just as New York and San Francisco were key cities for Beat creativity, so too were Tangier and Paris. In the late fifties, Beat talents were fermenting, coming to fruition in such important work as Allen Ginsberg's *Kaddish* and William Burroughs's *Naked Lunch*. Gregory Corso would write his poems "Bomb" and "Marriage," Brion Gysin's Dream Machine would emerge, and experiments like the cut-ups would pave the way to Burroughs's "cut-up" trilogy: *Soft Machine* (1961), *Ticket that Exploded* (1962), and *Nova Express* (1964).

Except for Kerouac, who merely came for a visit, helping to type up and name Burroughs's work, the Beats were exploring new terrain, geographic as well as stylistic. The locus of this creative activity was Europe and North Africa. William Burroughs, the scion of the Burroughs adding machine company from St Louis, Missouri, had been a mentor to the younger Beats in their late forties Columbia University days, encouraging their reading of Oswald Spengler's *Decline and Fall of the West* and other books instrumental in formulating their "New Vision." After the Mexico City shooting of his wife, he moved to Tangier. His resolve to write as redemption for this act resulted in a work in progress, from "The Yage Letters," his correspondence with Allen Ginsberg, to "Interzone," writings of the International Zone that Tangier was before its revolution in 1956, to what became *Naked Lunch*. According to the writer Paul Bowles, Burroughs's pages were piled up on his hotel floor with bits of food and rat turds (Weinreich, "Interview with Paul Bowles").

Often acting as literary agent for his friends, Ginsberg showed an early manuscript, entitled *Interzone*, to Maurice Girodias of Olympia Press, a house that was making a name for itself publishing quality writing that was not likely to get past the censors in Britain or America – like Nabokov's *Lolita*, Beckett's *Watt* and *Molloy*, Miller's *Sexus*, *Plexus*, *Tropic of Cancer*, and *Tropic of Capricorn*. "Such a mess, that manuscript!," stated Girodias of Burroughs's work. "You couldn't physically read the stuff. The ends of the pages were all eaten away by rats or something, but whatever caught the eye was extraordinary and dazzling" (Miles: 32).

Then the *Chicago Review* published nine pages from *Naked Lunch*, which had garnered such a negative write-up in the *Chicago Daily News* that the issue was suppressed. Irving Rosenthal, its editor, then started up *Big Table*, featuring the work of Kerouac, Burroughs, Edward Dahlberg, and Gregory Corso. Hitting the stands in March 1959, *Big Table* was seized by postal authorities as obscene. While Burroughs despaired that the work would never be published, the scandal brought *Naked Lunch* to the attention of Maurice Girodias, who was ever eager to champion a suppressed work, even though he had already rejected it when Ginsberg first brought it around. Girodias contacted Burroughs through his assistant, Sinclair Beiles, suggesting he would like another look at the book. In a few weeks Burroughs received a contract, an advance of $800, and a deadline of 10 days to prepare the manuscript for the printer.

Ginsberg, Kerouac, the poet and classical scholar Alan Ansen, who had been secretary to W. H. Auden, all came to help Burroughs assemble the work once it was clear it would be published. Various titles had been suggested, including "Sargasso Sea." Kerouac, who did much of the manuscript's typing, suggested the winning *Naked Lunch*, a title that illustrated the novel's principal metaphor: addictions, quite literally what is at the end of one's fork.

Brion Gysin also devoted himself to *Naked Lunch*'s publication. An American painter, born in England of a Swiss father and a Canadian mother, Gysin had been a restauranteur, raconteur, writer, as well as an artist in Tangier, where Burroughs initially met – and rejected – him. Gysin stated that the raw material of *Naked Lunch* overwhelmed them: "Showers of fading snapshots fell through the air: Old Bull's Texas farm, the Upper Reaches of the Amazon . . . Tangier and the Mayan Codices . . . shots of boys from every time and place . . ." (Burroughs and Gysin, *The Third Mind*: 43). They wondered, "What to do with this? Stick it on the wall along with the photographs and see what it looks like . . . Stick it all together, end to end" (Burroughs and Gysin, *The Third Mind*: 43). Despite the difficulty, they completed the novel on time.

Though *Naked Lunch* was composed from the routines Burroughs included in his correspondence to Ginsberg from Tangier in the period 1954–7, the version that was finally published in Paris was quite different from what Kerouac, Ansen, and Ginsberg typed up in Tangier. The problem of how to edit finally resolved itself with the understanding that a linear narrative would never come of these pages. And yet, as Allen Ginsberg has noted, the novel has a "psychic structure" (Sawyer-Laucanno: 278.)

From Tangier and other points of travel, the Beats one by one had moved on to a hotel in Paris, where Burroughs and Gysin – as well as Allen Ginsberg, Peter Orlovsky, Gregory Corso, and Harold Norse, among others – took up residence. Located on a little medieval lane running down to the Seine from rue St André des Arts on the Left Bank, around the corner from the Place St Michel, at 9 rue Git le Coeur, the hotel was found by Allen Ginsberg when he was looking for a cheap place to stay. This hovel of a hotel had no name until Gregory Corso dubbed it the Beat Hotel.

It was a class-13 hotel, which meant that it met the absolute minimum level of accommodation: tenants shared a Turkish-style hole-in-the-floor toilet on each floor's landing, there was hot water available only three days a week, and anyone wishing for a bath had to commission the hot water and pay extra. Electricity outages left tenants in frequent darkness; nevertheless, the 42 rooms were in great demand, with a long waiting list. The proprietor, a blue-haired Madame Rachou, was very mysterious and arbitrary about whom she let in. Rooms were 5 francs a night or 120 francs a month (about $30); Madame sometimes permitted residents to pay their rent with paintings or manuscripts, which she did not keep because she never believed they would be valuable. Best of all, she ignored the improprieties of the clientele – whores and petty criminals as well as artists, poets, and jazz musicians – and even protected them from the prying gendarmes whose police station was just across the street. Madame maintained a good relationship with the police by feeding them lunches, thereby sparing her tenants searches and harassment. The hotel had a natural odor of hashish, and Burroughs was said to have hidden his stash underneath the floorboards.

Ginsberg and his lover Peter Orlovsky were the first to settle in; then Ginsberg invited Burroughs to join them, which he finally did in January 1958. Orlovsky was leaving the next day and Ginsberg feared that Burroughs would want to pick up where they had left off in an unresolved intimacy in 1953. But Burroughs had changed, and stopped putting pressure on Ginsberg for sex. Burroughs moved into room 15 on the fifth floor, equipped with a two-burner gas stove on the table in one corner, a washstand on the other, a wardrobe, two chairs, a bed, and a table on which stood his old Spanish portable.

Four wire baskets hung on the wall over the table, lit by a single naked light. The window looked out onto a blank wall. Prior to that, in 1953, when Brion Gysin was living in Tangier, the initial meeting of these figures who would become a couple was far from friendly. The expatriate American composer and writer Paul Bowles, the author of *The Sheltering Sky* (1949), had suggested that Gysin might want to meet a literary friend who had recently come there to live, William S. Burroughs. Known to the native boys as "El hombre invisible," Burroughs had a cadaverous demeanor and was so heavily into drugs that Gysin, who was obviously no stranger to these substances, noted him with some disgust: "Caught a glimpse . . . glimmering rapidly along through the shadows from one farmacia to the next, hugging a bottle of paregoric . . . Willie the Rat scuttles over the purple sheen of wet pavements, sniffing," Gysin later recollected (Burroughs and Gysin, *The Third Mind*: 49). Immediately turned off, he decided to have nothing to do with Burroughs.

In Paris, Gysin renewed links with Burroughs and started one of the closest collaborations between two artists. Brion Gysin had had a past in Paris. In 1935 he was to have been included in the Surrealist Show, but, as one version of the story goes, his work was removed at the last minute on André Breton's orders because Breton hated homosexuals. Gysin had another distinction: it was he who provided the recipe for hashish brownies for inclusion in Alice B. Toklas's famous cookbook, much to her horror. Now Gysin too had moved on to Paris after the demise of his Tangier restaurant, The Thousand and One Arabian Nights, and was staying with the Princess Ruspoli (he was always fancying himself on the Princess circuit), but he needed to find another place when he moved into the Beat Hotel.

In the process of preparing the *Naked Lunch* manuscript, the Burroughs–Gysin friendship was becoming so intense that they became inseparable. Burroughs said that Gysin was "the only man I ever respected. I have admired many others, esteemed and valued others, but respected only him. His presence was regal without a trace of pretension." Ginsberg and Corso often found their relationship incomprehensible, finding that Gysin "exaggerated some of Bill's worst tendencies – his suspiciousness, his anti-female stand, his penchant for seeing people as agents." Added Corso: with Gysin, "Burroughs got into some very heavy psychic things" (Sawyer-Laucanno: 281).

But that is precisely what interested Burroughs most. With Gysin he could explore power and psychic control, magic, and superstition. They began to experiment with altered states of consciousness. They practiced the medieval technique of scrying, staring at a stainless steel dowsing ball in which scenes of a paranormal nature could be perceived. They also stared into a mirror until the image began to distort, enabling them to see different incarnations of themselves. Once, in a trance, Brion saw something and wrote it down on a piece of paper: "The Ugly Spirit shot Joan." From then on Burroughs understood that event, which had taken place in Mexico City in 1951: the accidental shooting of his wife, which he then claimed caused him to become a writer. Their mutual interest also allowed them to explore alternative ways of writing: they developed the "cut-up technique." One day in late September 1959, Brion was in his hotel room mounting some drawings, slicing through the boards with his Stanley blade and at the same time slicing through some newspapers, *New York Herald Tribune*s, he was using to protect his table. He noticed that where a strip of page was cut away, the newsprint on the next page could be read across, combining stories with hilarious results. He was laughing so hard others in the hotel thought he was having a hysterics attack. And of course he was.

Burroughs had been out to lunch with some reporters from *Life Magazine*. He immediately saw the importance of the cut-up discovery and they began experimenting with the *Saturday Evening Post*, *Time Magazine*, texts by Rimbaud and Shakespeare, likening the method to that of "The Wasteland," the work of Tristan Tzara, and Dos Passos in the "Camera Eye" sequences in *USA*.

Claiming that writing was 50 years behind painting in its ability to depict reality, they found the cut-ups to be a solution to the problem of bringing writing closer to its origins in calligraphy and hieroglyphics – picture language. The first cut-ups applied the painters' techniques to writing: "Cut right through the pages of any book or newsprint . . . lengthwise, for example, and shuffle the columns of text. Put them together at hazard and read the newly constituted message. Do it for yourself. Use any system which suggests itself to you . . . Words have a vitality of their own . . . and you or anybody can make them gush into action" (Burroughs and Gysin, *The Third Mind*: 34).

Burroughs and Gysin introduced the technique to Corso and Sinclair Beiles, and they had heated arguments about the merits of the collage writing. Still they produced enough of it to compile into the collaborative book *Minutes to Go* (1960); that same year *Exterminator*, another cut-up book by Burroughs, appeared. Interestingly enough, the cut-ups seem to explain the fragmentary style of *Naked Lunch*, which of course came before. *The Soft Machine*, *The Ticket that Exploded*, and *Nova Express* all make use of the cut-up as well as a variation, the fold-in.

In the late summer of 1959, Harold Norse, a poet and fellow resident at the Beat Hotel, the author of the cut-up text *Beat Hotel* and *Memoirs of a Bastard Angel*, introduced Burroughs to a young mathematics student at Cambridge, telling him that the young, fair, nervous, birdlike man liked older men. Ian Sommerville was spending his vacation in Paris working at the Librairie Mistral in exchange for a free bed. He soon became Burroughs's lover. He shared with Burroughs and Gysin an interest in experimenting with language and soon expanded from the cut-and-paste method to tape recording. Later the experimentation would extend to computer permutations of a given text.

In December of 1958, Brion had accidentally discovered the effect of shimmering light on the brain: a "transcendental storm of color visions today in the bus going to Marseilles. We ran through a long avenue of trees and I closed my eyes against the setting sun. An overwhelming flood of intensely bright patterns in supernatural colors exploded against my eyelids: a multidimensional kaleidoscope whirling out through space" (quoted in Sawyer-Laucanno: 285). When Gysin, who was not sure what happened to him, tried to explain it all to Burroughs, he suggested a book called *The Living Brain* by William Grey Walter, which described such phenomena.

Sommerville also knew of the book and became intrigued by the idea of creating a mechanism whereby Gysin's experience could be replicated. In February he wrote to Burroughs and Gysin that he had made a "simple flicker machine: a slotted cylinder which turns on a gramophone at 78 rpm with a light bulb inside. You look at it with your eyes shut and the flicker plays over your eyelids. Visions start with a kaleidoscope or colors on a plane in front of the eyes and gradually become more complex and beautiful, breaking like surf on a shore until whole patterns of color are pounding to get in" (quoted in Sawyer-Laucanno: 285). Soon Gysin made his own Dream Machine at the Beat Hotel, and he and Burroughs became avid devotees.

While Burroughs was completing *Naked Lunch*, Gregory Corso was also enjoying a fertile artistic period. He wrote his poems "Bomb" and "Marriage" in the same week. To get its "bomb" shape, he had to type it out, cut out each line and paste it onto construction paper, in the mushroom-cloud form of a nuclear explosion. Lawrence Ferlinghetti, poet and publisher of City Lights Books, based in San Francisco, came out with a broadside of "Bomb," which immediately sold out its 2,000 run. Ferlinghetti had not anticipated how much readers had become preoccupied with the bomb, and, finding Corso's poem fascistic, he decided not to put out a City Lights edition of Corso's poems. Somehow Ferlinghetti was not convinced that the poem's embracing of nuclear explosions was satiric. But that was Corso's voice; by mocking the institution of marriage in the poem of that title, Corso scrutinized so-called "civilized" behavior much as Twain did in the character of Huck Finn a century earlier. These, perhaps Corso's most famous poems, were included in his *Happy Birthday of Death*, complete with "Bomb" fold-out, finally published by New Directions in 1960. Corso also produced some cut-up poems in *Minutes to Go* (1960) with fellow Beat Hotel residents – begrudgingly. He was not satisfied with the cut-up as a literary strategy.

If Burroughs's cut-ups and Gysin's Dream Machine can be considered the cold aesthetic of the Beat Movement – art by scissors, by flickering light – Allen Ginsberg's aesthetic is its warm, tender heart. Unlike Burroughs, who did not care where he was, Ginsberg explored Paris with vigor. He wrote to his father on September 30, 1957, "Paris is the only city I've seen so far that would tempt me to expatriate and settle down" (Schumacher: 269).

A year and a half after his mother's death, Ginsberg was determined to write an elegy to her, especially as only seven people showed up at her burial, not enough for a minyan, the ten Jewish men required to be present for proper prayer. On November 13, 1957, he was alone at the Café Select, a legendary bar from the 1920s, and he began, weeping as he wrote:

Farewell
with long black shoe
smoking corsets & ribs of steel Farewell
communist party & broken stocking
Farewell
O mother Farewell

He did not complete the entire work, but he regarded the poem as an opening up, bringing him access to his grief in Paris. He also went to the Père Lachaise cemetery and sat at the grave of Apollinaire, sketching the tombstone and writing about the visit:

Sat here with bearded Beson on a tomb & stared at your
    rough menhir
– a tall grey ragged stone 8 feet tall – and a flat square piece with
    grooves for little flowers
Someone placed a jam-bottle
full of water filled with daisies,
Someone else a red cheap funeral 5&10c surrealist typist
ceramic rose with artificial flowers
a cross fading into the rock, – under a fine mossy tree
neath which I sat – with snaky trunk.

Ginsberg later claimed to have written the Apollinaire poem to identify him with his literary antecedent, much as he claimed kinship with Whitman in "A Supermarket in California." He hoped that others would read these antecedent poets as his literary fathers and see him as following their traditional, well-blazed poetic path.

Meanwhile, back in the United States, the Beats were becoming known as much for their flamboyance as for an artistic vision at odds with the conformist fifties. However, the times were changing rapidly, owing in part to them. In 1957, Lawrence Ferlinghetti went on trial for obscenity in San Francisco, for publishing the epic "Howl" in his City Lights Pocket Poets series. In 1959, Robed Frank was photographing the non-Ozzie-and-Harriet America (Ozzie and Harriet were a popular television family which came to epitomize the American ideal) for his collection *The Americans*, with an introduction by Jack Kerouac. Frank, who came from Switzerland, was interested in Americans who were not imaged in the popular culture. *On the Road* got such a rave review in the *New York Times* it became an instant bestseller, its author a superstar of that time, and synonymous with the word "Beat."

By the sixties Kerouac had finished most of his significant writing, accomplished in the long period between the writing of *On the Road* in 1952 and its actual publication in 1957. An alcoholic, he eventually drank himself to death in 1969. Living in St Petersburg, Florida, with his third wife, Stella Sampas, as well as his mother, and given to inciting brawls outside bars, he died a week after he had been beaten up, of internal hemorrhaging, while watching *The Galloping Gourmet* on television.

Several critics, the poet Richard Howard among them, are of the opinion that Ginsberg's work after this early period declined. Yet Ginsberg's *White Shroud* (1985) remains one of his most moving collections, especially in the title poem, where the poet enters the Land of the Dead and encounters his mother. In his later years and until his death at age 70 in 1997 Ginsberg held a professorship at Brooklyn College, where he continued to promote the literature of the Beats.

William S. Burroughs died later that year at 83, of heart failure, in Lawrence, Kansas, where he was living in a little red house with dozens of cats, a fishpond out back, and a shooting range for his shotgun paintings. In the 1980s he wrote his final trilogy, *Cities of the Red Night* (1981), *Place of Dead Roads* (1984), and *The Western Lands* (1987), filled with the usual Burroughsian tropes of sex, drugs, violence, and preoccupations with political conspiracies, Mayan gods, and viruses. The critic Ann Douglas finds this trilogy "taken as a whole his greatest work" (Douglas: xxi); certainly it is his most traditional narrative.

An ingenious adventure, *The Western Lands* features dramatis personae re-enlisted from other books: Joe the Dead, Kim Carsons, Dr Benway, and Hassan i Sabbah all make cameo appearances. The central framing intelligence is William S. Hall, a Burroughs surrogate afflicted with writer's block and living in a boxcar on an abandoned dump. Mired in the junk heap of his own clichés, he wants to write his way out of death, to ensure his own immortality. Unlike Burroughs's other work, *The Western Lands* has closure: Burroughs's Hall has a happy ending, redeeming himself as a writer writing.

Guilt by Association

A famous 1961 photograph taken in the garden of Burroughs's Tangier outpost, the Hotel Muneria, features Alan Ansen, Gregory Corso, Ian Sommerville, Allen Ginsberg, and longtime American expatriate

Paul Bowles. A family portrait of sorts, the photo links the Beats to others of like mind. Ginsberg has said that Paul Bowles shared with Burroughs "a bleak implacability of metaphysics" (Weinreich, "Interview with Allen Ginsberg 1990"), but when asked whether the author of *The Sheltering Sky* (1949) was Beat, Ginsberg said, "No, but there's guilt by association."

"Guilt by association" works for many who hung out with this crowd but best sums up the situation of women vis-à-vis the Beats. Among women Diane di Prima, Joyce Johnson, and Hettie Jones stand out as literary figures as well as girlfriends, wives, women cohorts. They have written substantial books of poetry and novels. Carolyn Cassady, wife of Neal, and Bonnie Bremser, wife of poet Ray Bremser, have made their names as memoirists, with *Bean Beat* (1976) by Cassady and *Love of Ray* by Bremser (1971). Of the second-generation Beats, Anne Waldman stands out as having inherited the literary legacy of both the women and the men.

Joyce Johnson's *Minor Characters* (1983) is a landmark memoir recalling her relationship with Jack Kerouac and the others, but is most significantly the tale of a young girl's coming of age during this time of social change. Hettie Jones's *How I Became Hettie Jones* (1990) is not only a window into her life with poet LeRoi Jones, a.k.a. Amiri Baraka, but an account of interracial marriage of the time.

The women writers, however, are not known for the stylistic innovations that marked the writing of the seminal Beats. Their innovations lay in the life they portrayed, untraditional and courageous at a time when alternative lives, often defined by unmarried sex and illegal abortions, could be life-threatening, decades before *Roe v. Wade*. In Joyce Johnson's memoir of her two-year relationship with Jack Kerouac, during the crucial time of his overnight fame in 1957, a most poignant portrait is that of her best friend from Barnard College, a young poet named Elise Cowen. Cowen embodied the emotional turmoil of the time, particularly for women; having had a crush on Allen Ginsberg – she had typed up his *Kaddish* – she hurled herself through a glass window to her death in 1962 at age 28.

While the men are the most recognized figures of the Beat Generation, the women were "often present as the most observant and sober witnesses" (Waldman: xi). Bonnie Bremser is a glaring example of a stand-by-your-man sensibility. Her husband Ray had been arrested for armed robbery and wrote much of his first volume of poetry in jail. In Veracruz, Mexico, Bonnie Bremser helped him elude the courts by supporting him and her infant daughter as a prostitute. She later gave her child away, all of which is recounted in her gutsy, graphic memoir *For Love of Ray*, retitled *Troia*.

Poet Diane di Prima, an Italian American, wrote of the newly published "Howl" that what Ginsberg was describing in his opening, "I saw the best minds of my generation," would change poetry forever; that by simply getting it published Ginsberg "had broken ground for all of us," referring to "The New Bohemians" with whom she was associated. She, like Kerouac, sought a vernacular in her poetry. She is best known for her *Revolutionary Letters* (1971), poetry inciting liberation as in letter 35:

> rise up, my
> brothers, do not
> bow your heads any longer, or pray
> except to the spirit you waken.
>
> (47)

Before that, Maurice Girodias had published her *Memoirs of a Beatnik* (1969), inviting her to write her life story as erotica for Olympia Press. Eager for cash, she described what it was like to participate in a Beat orgy, how being in bed with Ginsberg, Kerouac, Orlovsky, and Corso was "warm and friendly and very unsexy – like being in a bathtub with four other people" (quoted in Watson: 273). "Di Prima's memoir not only provided a vivid picture of bohemian New York in the mid-1950's, but restored to erotica real bodies, lived-in humor, and a canny comfort about sex surpassing that of the Beat males" (Watson: 273).

Poet Anne Waldman co-founded (with Allen Ginsberg) the Jack Kerouac School for Disembodied Poetics at Naropa institute in Boulder, Colorado. In the 1970s she ran the St Mark's Poetry Project, an important venue for Beat poetry readings, as famous for the significant new verse being read as for the antics in its courtyard. Waldman had the organizational skills to make a success of this school, with its goals of bridging Eastern and Western values in the arts. As a poet, Waldman complained that the men were simply not passing on the wisdom to the women. If they were recommending books to one another, they were not nurturing the women's reading. Nevertheless, utilizing the long line Ginsberg took from Whitman, the incantatory catalogues of verse, Waldman published her "Fast Speaking Woman," and following Ginsberg's penchant for performance, she vocalized her poetry, influenced by the "male elders" in the Beat movement, as well as rock performers. Calling her epic sequence, *Iovis,* an "all encompassing exploratory collage/argument with male energy," and seeking a "poetics of transformation beyond gender" (Waldman, *Women of the Beat Generation*: 290), Anne Waldman has taken the aesthetics of the Beat Generation into a feminist stance.

The Beat Generation is Now about Everything

As the Beat movement calcifies into mainstream memory-cum-history, distortions are discernible. In 1995 the Whitney Museum of American Art mounted an exhibition called "Beat Culture and the New America 1950–1965," with the Beats' East and West Coast divisions. The show felt alien to Allen Ginsberg and painter Robert LaVigne's memory of their own beat experiences, as they walked around somewhat surprised at the array of works yoked together under the Beat banner. In the same year, perhaps hoping to capitalize on the Whitney's success, Barney's department store had display windows featuring a beat pad complete with clutter and a pile of poetry books: Corso, Lamantia, Whalen – a cliché of "beat." Someone clearly did his or her homework and then blew it – there was a book by Allen Ginsberg, spelled "Alan" on the spine. Granted a commercial display is not a reference source, and is as permanent as yesterday's weather, still it is a small reminder of the subtle ways that time distorts. If an uptown luxury department store can misspell the poet's good name, imagine further distortions as we go farther from fact, and the need for the factual.

On a more significant scale Joyce Johnson has watched with dismay the emergence of no fewer than a dozen Kerouac biographies since his death in 1969, noting errors in their texts and their pretense at history. Particularly vexing to her are several references to his insensitivity to her writing by agenda-driven biographers wishing to establish Kerouac's negativity toward women, or more to make claims for his homosexuality. This assertion is repeatedly illustrated by his taking pages from her first novel manuscript to write letters to his pals. It is of some importance whether Kerouac acknowledged the writing of a fellow novelist, as significant as is his attitude toward women. For some, the only real woman in Kerouac's life was his mother. Nevertheless, as Johnson made clear, Kerouac was extremely encouraging of her work, cautioning her against revision; she in turn chided him for his thriftiness as he removed the telltale manuscript pages she had tossed from the trash (Johnson, *Door Wide Open*: xi–xxvi).

The Beat sale at Sotheby's auction house on October 7, 1999, offered a further glimpse of the Beat Generation through its artifacts: photos by Ginsberg with his poetic scrawl at bottom. A copy of *Howl* inscribed to Gregory Corso, handmade by Lawrence Ferlinghetti for its first City Lights edition, had the white flap affixed to the black background with such good glue it still held up after 40 years. Later editions were not so artsy. Also on the auction block was Jack Kerouac's varsity letter H from when he played football at the Horace Mann School, from Edie Kerouac Parker's estate. She was his first wife, and as legend has it he fell in love with her after she ate six sauerkraut hotdogs at a New York deli in 1941. Ginsberg's statue of Buddha, and Lawrence Ferlinghetti's manual typewriter, on which he wrote his famous *Coney Island of the Mind*, went on sale along with Kerouac's own copy of *Lolita* personalized with Nabokov's picture and an inscription, "What Decency is, Can Never be Outraged." Quite a statement given the history of censorship and derision which has followed the Beats!

As Beat is a posturing, or a stance, no one exudes "beat" as Gregory Corso did, nobody ostensibly at the extreme, nobody ostensibly down and out. Beat is bad, "up-yours" behavior as well as go-for-broke performances. Beats today are so by kinship, by affinities, intellectual, emotional, or by design. Rock star Patti Smith has affected the poetry and the pose. The author of the books *Babel* (1978) and *Complete* (1998), she illustrates "beat" in performance, for example in her playing at the Cathedral of St John the Divine in May, 1998, for over 2,000 at Allen Ginsberg's memorial. She played as if her life depended on it. So Beat was her playing, she broke her tooth. "The only thing I was ever vain about was my teeth," said the least vain woman around; "I was playing so hard, I chipped this one in front," she said, grinning wide to show it (conversation with author). "Guilt by association" works well for the beat legacy. A famous photo of painter Jean Michel Basquiat shows him clutching a copy of *The Subterraneans*. The actor Johnny Depp purchased Jack Kerouac's raincoat and plaid shirt from Kerouac's estate.

What does it mean? Is there something of a passing on to the next generation of rebels? Among the memorabilia in Marilyn Monroe's collection auctioned at Christie's in October, 1999, was a first edition of *On the Road*. Where did she get it? Was she a fan? Did she, as did so many of her time, feel an affinity with the poet cut loose in a rigid society? She too died before her time, of a drug overdose. The question remains, was it suicide or murder? Was it the price of fame? The link to Kerouac doesn't seem so odd at all, especially in view of the ambiguities surrounding their deaths, as if these enduring mysteries could unite them in a most American fate. Literary icon meets pop icon in heaven. Why, one is even tempted to say, man, she was Beat.

References and further reading

Bremser, Bonnie. *For Love of Ray*. London: Compton Press, 1971.

Burroughs, William S., and Brion Gysin. *The Third Mind*. New York: Viking, 1978.

Burroughs, William S., and Brion Gysin. "Introduction." In *Queer*. New York: Viking, 1985. v–xxiii.

Charters, Ann, ed. *The Portable Beat Reader*. New York: Viking, 1992.

di Prima, Diane. *Revolutionary Letters*. San Francisco: City Lights, 1971.

di Prima, Diane. *Recollections of my Life as a Woman: The New York Years*. New York: Viking, 2001.

Douglas, Ann. "'Punching a Hole in the Big Lie:' The Achievement of William S. Burroughs." In *Word Virus: The William S. Burroughs Reader*. Eds James Grauerholz and Ira Silverman. New York: Grove, 1998. xv–xxviii.

Gifford, Barry, and Lawrence Lee. *Jack's Book: An Oral Biography of Jack Kerouac*. New York: St Martin's Press, 1978.

Ginsberg, Allen. *Collected Poems 1947–1980*. New York: Harper and Row, 1984.

Ginsberg, Allen. *White Shroud Poems 1980–1985*. New York: Harper and Row, 1986.

Ginsberg, Allen, and Louis Ginsberg. *Family Business: Selected Letters between a Father and Son*. Ed. Michael Schumacher. New York: Bloomsbury, 2001.

Holmes, John Clellon. *Nothing More to Declare: Of the Men and Ideas That Made This Literary Generation*. New York: Dutton, 1967.

Johnson, Joyce. *Minor Characters: A Beat Memoir*. Boston: Houghton-Mifflin, 1983.

Johnson, Joyce. *Door Wide Open: A Beat Love Affair in Letters 1957–1958*. New York: Viking, 2000.

Jones, Hettie. *How I Became Hettie Jones*. New York: Dutton, 1990.

Kerouac, Jack. *Scattered Poems*. San Francisco: City Lights, 1971.

Kerouac, Jack. *Selected Letters 1940–1956*. Ed. Ann Charters. New York: Viking, 1995.

Kerouac, Jack. *Selected Letters 1957–1969*. Ed. Ann Charters. New York: Viking, 1999.

Kerouac, Jack. *Book of Haikus*. Ed. Regina Weinreich. New York: Viking Penguin, 2003.

Krim, Seymour. *Shake It for the World, Smartass*. New York: Dial, 1970.

Lardas, John. *The Bop Apocalypse: The Religious Visions of Kerouac, Ginsberg and Burroughs*. Urbana and Chicago: University of Illinois Press, 2001.

Miles, Barry. *Beat Hotel: Ginsberg, Burroughs and Corso in Paris, 1957–1963*. New York: Grove, 2000.

Norse, Harold. *Memoirs of a Bastard Angel: A Fifty-Year Literary and Erotic Odyssey*. New York: Morrow, 1989.

Sawyer-Laucanno, Christopher. *The Continual Pilgrimage: American Writers in Paris, 1944–1960*. New York: Grove, 1992.

Schumacher, Michael. *Dharma Lion: A Biography of Allen Ginsberg*. New York: St Martin's Press, 1992.

Smith, Patti. *Babel*. New York: Putman's, 1974.

Smith, Patti. *Complete*. New York: Doubleday, 1998.

Sterritt, David. *Mad to Be Saved: The Beats, the '50's, and Film*. Carbondale: Southern Illinois University Press, 1998.

Tytell, John. *Naked Angels: The Lives and Literature of the Beat Generation*. New York: McGraw-Hill, 1976.

Tytell, John. *Literary Outlaws: Remembering the Beats*. New York: Morrow, 1999.

Waldman, Anne. *Fast Speaking Woman*. San Francisco: City Lights, 1975.

Waldman, Anne. *Iovis. Books I and II*. Minneapolis: Coffee House Press, 1993.

Waldman, Anne. "Foreword." In *Women of the Beat Generation: The Writers, Artists and Muses at the Heart of a Revolution*. Ed. Brenda Knight. Berkeley: Conan, 1996. ix–xii.

Watson, Steven. *The Birth of the Beat Generation: Visionaries, Rebels, and Hipsters, 1944–1960*. New York: Pantheon, 1995.

Weinreich, Regina. *The Spontaneous Poetics of Jack Kerouac: A Study of the Fiction*. Carbondale: Southern Illinois University Press, 1987.

Weinreich, Regina. "Interview with Allen Ginsberg, 1990." In *Paul Bowles: The Complete Outsider*. Documentary film, 1993.

Weinreich, Regina. "Interview with Paul Bowles, November, 1988." In *Paul Bowles: The Complete Outsider*. Documentary film, 1993.

Weinreich, Regina. "Interview with Allen Ginsberg." *Five Points: A Journal of Literature and Art* II.1 (1997): 30–46.

Chapter 4

From Bebop to Hip Hop: American Music After 1950

Perry Meisel

Jazz Myth, Jazz Reality

The reception of jazz and its musical heirs, rhythm and blues and rock and roll, has always been the product of a deep ambivalence in the American grain. In the 1930s, the first professional jazz critics celebrated jazz for its redemptive primitivism. In the process, they had to slander the very achievement that they praised. For Carl Van Vechten, the more brutal the poverty of black life, the more authentic was the music to which it gave birth. The Yale-educated John Hammond, who drove his car throughout the South and Midwest on the trail of legendary performers, valued musicians who could not read music more than those who did. Their illiteracy testified to the natural urgency of their expression. In the 1950s, Jack Kerouac and Norman Mailer honored jazz for similar reasons. For Kerouac, the spontaneity of jazz improvisation was proof of its mindless honesty. For Mailer, the power of black music lay in the presumably savage power of the black people who had invented it.

What is troubling about the modern reception of jazz is what is historically familiar about it. Behind it looms an earlier mode of reception that it recapitulates even as it overturns: the history of American minstrelsy, the practice by which "blackface" white performers, beginning in the North in the 1830s, parodied black American music even as they deigned to exalt it. The minstrel tradition persists well beyond the 1950s. Recall, alas, the vexing performance of John Belushi and Dan Ackroyd in the 1980 film *The Blues Brothers*. Unlike their blackface inspiration, they cannot even sing or dance. Because of studio money, however, they have been able to enlist as companion performers some of the greats of blues and rhythm and blues, from Ray Charles to James Brown. This is mockery, like it or not, sub-tended by a domination based not only on the almighty buck, but on a racism rooted in the minstrelsy that continues to accompany the mainstream appreciation of American music.

Is there another way of assessing the history of jazz and its progeny that is free of racist presupposition? Ralph Ellison is the best guide:

> Although since the twenties, many jazzmen have had conservatory training and were well grounded in formal theory and instrumental technique, when we approach jazz we are entering quite a different sphere of training. Here it is more meaningful to speak, not of courses of study, of grades and degrees, but of apprenticeship, ordeals, initiation ceremonies, of rebirth. For after the jazzman has learned the funda-mentals of his instrument and the traditional techniques of jazz – the intonations, the mute work, manipulation of timbre, the body of tradi-tional style – he must then "find himself," must be reborn, must find, as it were, his soul. (208–9)

Jazz has a structure and a history, rooted not in the soil or in blind instinct, but in the self-conscious artistry of the musicians who play it. Jazz is a learned tradition. Like the history of any aesthetic form, it is defined by a complex interplay of convention and revolt. After 1950, the complexity deepens. Reactions to it produce a whole new epoch whose apotheosis is rock and roll.

Jazz and Rhythm and Blues

The history of American music after 1950 falls into a three-part sequence: the emergence of bebop as a response to swing, and bop's eventual decline after Charlie Parker's death in 1955; the emergence of rhythm and blues after 1955 as a response to bop, and r & b's reinvention of swing's easy danceability in a newer key; and the emergence of rock and roll as both a resolution of this prior history and the suppression of some of its key elements, particularly its African American foundations. To tell the story by focusing on rep-resentative or "canonical" figures will also provide a lesson about how so-called "popular culture" works by tale's end.

Swing music dominated New Deal America and kept spirits high in the canteens of World War II. But it had a history and its future had a horizon. If combo Dixieland had given way to the small-orchestra "jazz" of the 1920s and the Jazz Age ideology that appropriated it, then "jazz" had given way to the expansive vision of swing in the big-band sounds of Duke Ellington and Count Basie. By the end of World War II, however, swing's infrastructure began to crack economically. The mood of American culture had likewise become brooding and alienated in the shadow of the Bomb. Bebop was the music of the Beats, and Beat emphasized the solitary and the existential. The reflective bop soloist was its ideal emblem.

Parker's battle with the influence of Lester Young is the key site of musical struggle in the shift from swing to bebop, despite the attempt by some historians to blame it all on Dizzy Gillespie and his milder revision of swing trumpet. Muting the horn and graveling its tone (Gillespie also bent the bell of his instrument by accident one afternoon, leaving it that way because it looked cool), Gillespie was good for publicity. By contrast, Parker drastically alters the tone, attack, and harmonic choices of saxophone forever. He expunges the most saccharine of swing horn mannerisms, vibrato, and introduces a tonal amplitude to saxophone that never capitulates to Young's breathiness. Parker also combines a technical appetite unmatched in jazz before or since with a depth of blues feeling second to none except for that of Louis Armstrong.

Although Parker's influence within jazz proper remains decisive well beyond his death in 1955 – not until John Coltrane does a musician of peer power emerge to change the nature of saxophone again – by the late 1940s a new player appears on the jazz stage to challenge bebop's dominance and take its place in popularity with the black listening public: rhythm and blues. Louis Jordan and his Tympani Five are the founding group, appearing at Minton's in Harlem for the first time in 1938. Jordan himself sang in a swing style over the horn section's jump riffs and played an early version of what is really rock and roll saxophone. The latter's real father, however, is saxist Earl Bostic. If Parker invented bop out of swing, then Bostic, with his raucous transformation of swing vibrato into rock and roll flatulence, invented r & b out of swing.

Rhythm and blues eventually crossed with bop to produce "hard bop": a fusion of bop phrasing and harmonics with r & b rhythms, particularly the funky beat that becomes the *via media* for a music enduringly beset by the burdens of Parker's precedent. Bop had often used Afro-Cuban instrumentation; the presence of conga and timbales added an extra layer of density to its experimentation with rhythms and time. But the reasons for hard bop's emergence are more than circumstantial. LeRoi Jones and Arnold Shaw both regard hard bop as an umbrella of protection from Parker musically and from bop ideologically. Shaw even suggests that hard bop was a way lesser musicians, especially sax players, had of swerving from the demands of bop technique. The same could be said of a black public that, as Nelson George has documented, had grown exhausted listening to Parker and Gillespie, and that wanted easier, groovier music that it could simply relax to.

The absence of a canonical center for hard bop – one could choose among any number of group leaders, chief among them Horace Silver and Art Blakey – is a perfect example of its sensibility. Hard bop seeks the erasure of personality in the very act of securing it through deliberately generic, even formulaic means. Whether it is Cannonball Adderley, who played with Miles Davis, or King Curtis, who played with both Lionel Hampton and the Coasters, all of jazz goes on to feed on the synthesis of hard bop. As a common point of origin, hard bop joins the sound of the roadhouses of the 1950s with the revolutionary music of Ornette Colman, Eric Dolphy, Archie Shepp, and John Coltrane in the 1960s. Miles Davis's inspired (and still criticized) brand of "fusion" jazz beginning in the early 1970s – a mix of jazz and rock – is hard bop's greatest legacy, and the basis of virtually all later developments in jazz and rock alike. So significant is Davis's jazz-rock fusion that his earlier role in the history of bop proper is often over-shadowed by it. If Parker changes saxophone, it is Davis, not Gillespie, who changes trumpet. Not only does he take on the influence of the single most powerful influence in all of jazz, that of Armstrong, and modulate its enthusiasm into wariness. He also takes on the influence of Parker, for whom he served as trumpet sideman in the late 1940s and early 1950s. Davis's invention of "cool" jazz after 1955 – a calm, selective mode of solo improvisation – is his resolved response to Armstrong and Parker alike.

Hard bop is a superb metaphor for the many tensions that American music and culture hold in suspension in the years that follow World War II. The consummate jazz trope for any resolving or miscegenating style, hard bop is the stance of any number of familiar American mythologies: the fusion of cowboy and dandy in the roughneck spirit of gangster heroes from Jay Gatsby to Michael Corleone; the fusion of country and city in the churchy urbanity of African American writers from W. E. B. Du Bois to Alice Walker; the fusion of low-life slang and the learned vocabulary of English Romanticism in the fiction of Raymond Chandler. Philip Marlowe is not only a hard-boiled detective; with his combination of suavity, grit, and mischief, he is a hard bop detective, too.

John Coltrane, who served as Davis's tenor sideman in the late 1950s, is the last of jazz's major figures. Dead in 1967, Coltrane's influence had replaced Parker's, and remains the dominant style in jazz soloing even today. Like his contemporaries, Coltrane grew up in a climate that featured the consensus of hard bop; it also offered up hard bop's resources for sale if you wanted to be original. Coltrane was always a dialectical musician. The biting cascades of sound represent both his debt to Parker and his flight from him; the replacement of finger-snapping by the graver blues tone-poem is his surest difference from the bop approach to phrasing, even as it is scarred by the desire to escape it. How does Coltrane win his originality and overcome Parker's influence? By returning, not to Young, but to Bostic. Here he finds a means of inspiration in Bostic's earliest of models for r & b phrasing, when it is still attached to the rigors of swing. As a youngster, Coltrane had actually recorded with Bostic at a date in Cincinnati in 1952, when he was also touring with the altoist Eddie "Cleanhead" Vinson and hard bop organist Jimmy Smith.

Coltrane's revisionist propensities run so deep that they also required him to follow one album with a response in the next, especially in his last phase. *Meditations*, for example, a fearsomely shy and hesitant work, is greeted, with almost preternatural haste, by the squealing, growling adventures of *Ascension*, which became a kind of holy text for the "out" jazz movement of the late 1960s. The epochal *A Love Supreme* is the most fiercely self-conscious effort in the history of jazz recording: each of the album's movements comments upon and alters the phrasing of the movement before. Here, Coltrane breaks free of jazz history as no saxist before or since, although he does so, inevitably, by negotiating with the very history he transforms.

Soul

If jazz made some measure of peace with itself with hard bop, a wider form brought together rhythm and blues with the "gospel" tradition of Thomas A. Dorsey Jr to produce an entirely different kind of synthesis. The result is what is often known as "soul." Soul is rhythm and blues in a post-Jordan mode. Jordan's singing, including the ensemble chorus behind it on hit tunes such as "Choo Choo Ch'Boogie," was still in the tradition of swinging jazz vocalists, chief among them Cab Calloway. Post-Jordan r & b is distinct from it thanks to Dorsey. It crosses the swing manner with another and presumably opposed sensibility, the sound of the hymn. Soul is, like hard bop, also the result of the synthesis of two apparent antinomies, in this case the secular and "dirty" stance of the blues and the stance of black religiosity derived from spirituals.

While always a religious man, Dorsey did not place the hymn on a pedestal, as did the earliest concert performers of the African American spiritual, the female Jubilee Singers of Fisk University in Nashville, who toured Europe in 1871. Dorsey the musician came belatedly to the invention of a religious or gospel music, having first been a blues musician who arranged for such luminaries as Bessie Smith and Ma Rainey. When Dorsey first heard the music of Charles A. Tindley at the annual meeting of the National Baptist Convention in Philadelphia in 1929, his own compositional instincts found both kinship and a foil. Tindley, too, was blues-based, but not confined to the strict, 12-bar world of its musical grammar. Using the song models of Anglo-Irish spirituals, with 16-bar structures often supplemented by a bridge, Tindley's lyrics and moods were transcendent rather than circular and despondent. Dorsey joined the resources of this new discovery with the musical modalities of the blues itself. After 1929, he never looked back.

Thus, gospel was from the start a synthetic sound, a transformation of the traditional Anglo-Southern hymnal by means of the "classic blues" of the 1920s that had also informed the prehistories of swing, bop, and r & b all alike. The discovery of a fresher realm from the belated vantage point of classic blues is not a surprising one in the history of blues tradition. Just as Dorsey discovers the sacred on the starboard hand of the secular, so Rainey had discovered the sound of the country blues that preceded classic blues only after she had thrived as a city musician. Nor does Dorsey himself cross only sacred and secular; he also crosses country and city. Like the storefront churches that sprang up in the poor neighborhoods of Northern cities that counted more and more Southern emigrants among their populations after World War I, gospel is a theater of Southern inspiration within a Northern frame. By the time soul reaches its apex in the big-city studio sounds behind the voices of Otis Redding, Wilson Pickett, and Aretha Franklin (all gospel musicians who had graduated to the mainstream), the pattern was polished, and accounted for much of the music's broad appeal.

Dorsey's gospel sound blends with the jump sound of early r & b, however, through a mediator: the magnificent sound of the 1950s and early 1960s that we associate with doowop. While doowop's roots extend to the Ink Spots, an elegant vocal recording group of the swing era that emphasized tight harmonies, falsetto, and "tuba" bass, the sound's imitators included kids without benefit of instruments, the necessity that became a virtue. It created doowop's a capella sound.

By the late 1940s, doowop had grown into a full-scale ghetto genre. By the middle-1950s, its recordings finally crossed over racial marketing lines with hits by the Cleftones, the Flamingoes, the Moonglows, and Frankie Lymon and the Teenagers. The next generation of doowoppers – the Platters, the Coasters, and the Drifters – paved the way for a number of solo artists whose names we know far better than those of their ancestors.

Now rhythm and blues hits its full stride. Sam Cooke's career is a case in point. He was the first gospel star to cross over into commercial success. In 1957, after six years as lead singer of the Soul Stirrers, the country's leading gospel group, he recorded "You Send Me," a number-one hit and the watershed that marks the transition from gospel proper to soul. The course of Marvin Gaye's career a few years later on is even more representative. Like Cooke, Gaye began by singing gospel music as a child, although his route to soul stardom included an explicit journey through doowop as a teenager. It also included marrying into the family of Motown founder Berry Gordy, Jr, who produced Gaye's first hits in the early 1960s.

With Motown, all the elements in the history of jazz, rhythm and blues, and gospel come together in the most fully realized sound ever achieved in American popular music. Memphis had the Stax house sound of Booker T. and the MGs; Atlantic Records had an outpost of progress at the Muscle Shoals studio in Alabama. But the crown jewel of soul production was Gordy's Motown label in Detroit. Motown was, as Smokey Robinson remarks in his autobiography, "a university." Unlike "high culture" versions of urban art such as T. S. Eliot's *The Waste Land*, the sound of Motown presents the components of tradition not as fragmented and broken off from a whole, but as related in a multitude of ways. Gordy is a gleeful archeologist of blues knowledge, using the shuffle beat of Chicago blues, the walking bass lines of hard bop jazz, and the harmonies of doowop-inspired vocal back-ups as backdrop and collateral for an astonishing array of solo singers that included Gaye, Robinson, and Stevie Wonder.

101

After Sam Cooke, the epicenter of soul is Jackie Wilson. With Wilson, rhythm and blues singing becomes a school or strict canon. Wilson plays Milton to Cooke's Shakespeare, structuring the diction of a newly unfolding tradition. Even more than Cooke, Wilson isolates a doowop device – the devastating falsetto, with roots in the ancient history of fieldhouse blues – and remakes it into a vocal strategy central to the subsequent history of r & b singing as a whole. Wilson's 1957 hit, "Reet Petite" (also Gordy's first published song), features a voice in self-conscious dialogue with itself, jump-cutting from the falsetto that is now its dominant timbre to forays into the depths of a more guttural naturalness of expression.

In Wilson's train follow, like the Romantic poets following Milton, Robinson and Al Green, to name only two of the principal proponents of soul as it moves into the 1960s and 1970s. Smokey resolves Wilson's influence by resolving Wilson's self-dialogue between tenor and mezzo soprano into a single falsetto pitch. Green resolves it again by returning to the self-dialogue. Green agonizes, in the Greek sense of the word, over his relation to Wilson. Green's preacher father actually dismissed him from the family's gospel choir as a boy when he caught him with a Wilson record. To contain the anxiety of Wilson's influence, Green, with some irony, continued to rely on religious tradition, taking much of his performance persona from the Passion of Christ. In 1980, Green the soul star also became a minister of God.

Urban Blues

If Dorsey married the hymnal and classic blues, what kind of blues did gospel and doowop marry to produce the synthesis of soul? They crossed with the sound of urban blues, particularly the sound of Chicago blues. Here, concrete history is symbolic. The emergence of Chicago blues can be dated with fair accuracy from the moment of Muddy Waters's arrival in Chicago from Mississippi in 1943. Waters had already garnered fame as a Delta bluesman, and, in 1944, traded in his acoustic guitar for an electric one. The terms of his achievement expanded radically. Not only is his journey up Highway 61 reminiscent of the movement from country to city that defines much of the mythology of black American experience in the twentieth century. Through the electrification of his guitar, Waters adds to the journey the modernist lament of a fall into the nightmare of technology, away from the grace of nature. But this is to read him too jejunely. The most perpetually surprising thing about urban blues is that you sometimes can't tell the difference between the singer's voice and his guitar. Waters, characteristically, muddies the waters separating the two. Here the difference between blues tradition and the white culture that surrounds it is especially clear. Waters in effect deconstructs the presuppositions behind the most presumably natural difference of all – the difference between nature and culture.

The Southern urban bluesmen who emerge out of T-Bone Walker in Texas are a more tailored bunch than their Northern colleagues (Walker actually precedes Waters, amplifying a swinging guitar with Charlie Christian's help in the late 1930s), but the same deconstruction of the difference between the savage and the civilized is at work. B. B. King of Memphis is exemplary. The dialogues between voice and guitar do not just cast the guitar (Lucille) as having a singing voice of her own; by implication, they also cast King's own sweet-as-can-be voice into an instrument *par excellence*. Coming as it does after Christian's invention of electric jazz guitar in the 1930s as a light and supple-toned instrument, Waters's brutal rhythm guitar of the 1940s is a self-conscious anachronism. It is deliberately atavistic. Its creation of a new, self-consciously primitive persona for the city blues carries the same irony as does any Romantic quest for beginnings. Its earlier African American counterparts include Du Bois's notion of the "folk" and Zora Neale Hurston's invention of a rich and fecund South designed to override historical trauma. In all three cases, a Northern perspective creates a rawer Southern appeal.

Now Chuck Berry's pivotal position in the early rock and roll canon comes into focus. Recording on Chess records in the mid-to-late 1950s, Berry worked for the same Chicago label most closely associated with urban blues. But there the similarity ends. The pure singing voice right out of a boys' choir, riding high over jump riffs of a kind unique for electric guitar, presents a *prima facie* case for a major new turn in the history of American music. A master at managing overdetermination, Berry is not just a combination of gospel and urban blues. A complex mediation hides the shift that they only enable. The guitar timbre may be that of Waters, who mentored his younger Chess colleague. Something else, however, is afoot. The jump riffs of "Johnny B. Goode" or "Maybelline" come from a plain source, even though the continuity involved is surprising. There is autobiographical testimony to confirm it, and the invocation of the "other" Dorsey's name as well. It was, says Berry, Tommy Dorsey, the white swing bandleader, who most influenced him as a teenager, and it was

Dorsey's hit, "Boogie Woogie," that haunted him most of all. In other words, Berry's signature guitar riffs are really the horn section of a swing orchestra translated into the language and technology of electric guitar. Berry's signature riffs retrieve the sound of the big bands suppressed by electric blues, but voice it in the latter's new electric guitar mode. Canceling each with the other, Berry acknowledges and deflects his two principal influences simultaneously. In the process, he also shifts the center of American music from jazz to rock and roll.

Rock and Roll

Gospel music not only created the tradition of soul. It also created the tradition of country music. While country began as an amalgamation of Dixieland, banjo, and picking blues guitar in the form of hillbilly bluegrass, it also began in Texas in the form of country swing. Country swing was an extraordinarily sophisticated music that joined the horn section with a fiddle to revise the sound of the black big bands of Kansas City. The Grand Ole Opry radio broadcasts from Nashville always counted black listeners among their audience; listeners and musicians both knew how thin a line separated, or failed to separate, white America from black, especially in the South.

No wonder Buddy Holly's role in rock and roll history is decisive. Born in the Texas panhandle (he died in a plane crash in 1959), Holly blended country with rhythm and blues to produce a foundation for rock and roll that enabled the Beatles, the Beach Boys, and even Bob Dylan. It is Hank Williams's voice together with the instrumentation of bluegrass that provides Holly and other white Southern musicians with the mode with which they can cross or miscegenate rhythm and blues. Both r & b and country were too close to home. The invention of rock and roll allowed Holly, Jerry Lee Lewis, and Elvis Presley to render the components of both traditions uncanny – something at once familiar and strange. Holly's "Reminiscing" exemplifies the crossing. King Curtis's highly manicured rhythm and blues horn dresses up Holly's wailing vocals over a tight, funky studio band that is missing the one instrument that serves as the model for both the singing and the saxophone: the sound of the banjo that is common to the origins of country and blues alike.

Much, then, as hard bop came to organize jazz by the mid-1950s, a synthesis of country and rhythm and blues came to organize rock and roll by the mid-1960s. The Beach Boys are its richest example. So strategic is their achievement, however, that the country dimension of their sound, unlike, say, that of the Everly Brothers, is neatly repressed. Southern white musicians cannot call in the definitive resource that the Beach Boys could: doowop. For the Beach Boys, it is the newer sound of the inner city that mediates between country and rhythm and blues. Surf music is a form of urban folk. If the Beach Boys' voices revise the wail of the Ozarks by virtue of doowop, surf guitar revises the sound of blues guitar by virtue of Chuck Berry.

The eventual model for folk rock, of course, is Bob Dylan. Dylan the singer joins the voices of Muddy Waters and Woody Guthrie; Dylan the songwriter joins Main Street and the Imagist lyric. Once Dylan went electric at the Newport Folk Festival in 1965, the die was cast. He also joined, as Waters had, voice and instrument in a byplay of sounds that deconstructed the differences among them. The crossing of lines informs Dylan's career as a whole. As a youngster playing New York's Folk City, he sounded like a gnomish old man; as an aging country enthusiast moving toward religion, he sounded like a boy. No rock and roll songwriter has had the degree of Dylan's influence as a composer, since no other rock and roll songwriter has controlled the overdeterminations of tradition so well.

But it is, with great irony, a non-American rock and roll – the music of the British Invasion of the early 1960s – that catapults rock and roll into the hysterical popularity that has defined it ever since. Jackie Wilson caused female fans to faint at his performances, but not until the Beatles did the phenomenon reach the world of white girls. Heirs to Buddy Holly, the Beatles were, even more than the Beach Boys, also heirs to Chuck Berry, who had transformed the sound of the big-band horn section into the sound of electric rhythm guitar. The rock and roll synthesis was nearing completion.

The Rolling Stones finished the job. Keith Richards's rhythm guitar, like John Lennon's, carried with it the whole history of the jazz horn section, although now it is reimagined in overdrive, with the help of the Chicago bluesmen. Not an ecumenical band like the Beatles, the Stones were less interested in doowop back-up effects than in taking on the entire history of jazz as amplification revised and refigured it. The distance from America made the British climate richer in invention. The most influential solo guitarists in rock history, Eric Clapton and expatriate American Jimi Hendrix, also found an imaginative home in England in these same years.

The school of Chuck Berry was by now paying staggering dividends. Hendrix was Berry's most original disciple, hiding his dependence on the master with the groaning, shuddering swerves that define the very sound of his guitar. "Purple Haze" is an overt revision of "Maybelline." Listen to the two songs back to back, or, better yet, "sample" them – play them at the same time and look out for the uncanny combination of repetition and difference that the relation between them produces. But the school had more than a valedictorian in Hendrix. It also featured guitarists such as the Yardbirds' Jimmy Page, who, with the formation of Led Zeppelin in 1968, completed Berry's transformation of swing horns into electric guitar by helping to invent the sound of heavy metal. The fashion of the ear-splitting trash guitar band is no fashion. It is the central fact in American musical history that joins the big-band sound of the last era of a popular jazz, swing, with the sound of rock.

The two major trends in rock and roll in the 1970s, disco and punk, have, at least on the surface, little in common. But the good-time party strut of disco and the engine-like thwack of punk rhythm guitar share one central thing: an overheated and overpressured beat, up-tempo and built deep into high-hat, bass, and bass drum. Their common legacy is likewise plain: it is hip hop. Whether it is the Ramones and Donna Summer, or the Sex Pistols and the Village People – sampling them together is a worthwhile exercise – the grinding overdrive of punk tempos and the syncopated oompah of disco cymbals are resolved by hip hop time and stance. Reggae – hip hop's nominal source – provides a strategy to cover the anxiety of influence felt from both.

Despite its seeming radicality, hip hop is a profoundly conservative form musically. Its radicality lies not in the diction of its lyrics, but in its fusion, or re-fusion, of rhythm and blues and rock and roll. It is a synthesis of the two. From Run-D. M. C. to 2 Live Crew, hip hop emphasizes a back beat as a heavy metal rock group would, but also resists it by its conversational vocal stance, which is temporally skewed in relation to it.

Where does the back beat, the most recognizable of rock and roll tropes, come from? The marching band. Much as Armstrong bends the oppressor's bugle and invents jazz, so rock and roll, following the black tradition of syncopated marching bands in New Orleans and throughout the South, discovers the back beat as an answer to the sharp cadence of rule. The back beat turns rule back on itself. In the process, it gains a rule of its own.

The Myth of Popular Culture

No discussion of postwar American music can avoid an eventual confrontation with Theodor Adorno's infamous estimate of jazz in particular and "popular music" in general. Despite his allegiance to the left, Adorno appears to think very little of the ability of African Americans to think very much at all. Nor is his paradoxical Marxist contention that all "popular music" is lifeless and commodified sufficient intellectual cover for a palpable quality of hatred whose origins only an encounter with the street, or with a psychoanalyst, could explain. In his brackish essays on jazz, Adorno cannot keep bop separate from swing, or New Orleans separate from Chicago. Nor is he embarrassed by his Eurocentrism, which measures all things against classical time signatures and the authority of the maestro rather than the groove. But the crux of Adorno's dismissal of jazz and, by implication, of blues tradition as a whole comes in an astonishing passage on the difference between "higher music" and "popular" in the *Introduction to the Sociology of Music*:

> The higher music's relation to its historical form is dialectical. It catches
> fire on those forms, melts them down, makes them vanish and return
> in vanishing. Popular music, on the other hand, uses the types as
> empty cans into which the material is pressed without interacting with
> the forms. Unrelated to the forms, the substance withers and at the
> same time belies the forms, which no longer serve for compositional
> organization. (26)

What a dazzling display of allusion. Adorno, the closet Platonist, is actually an aesthete, although a poor one whose appeal to Marx ("withers") creates a smokescreen to keep the reader from reflecting on what he or she has just read. If the history of jazz and its legatees is anything, it is "dialectical." Far from using its "types as empty cans" – the metaphor is typically flattering – jazz and its musical heirs take the "forms" that enable them as their very subject. However, the distinction between "form" and "material" in any kind of music is misleading, since music has no semantic plane that it signifies, only an endless series of "formal" ones. The "vulgarity" that Adorno assigns to "popular music" is a projection. What is vulgar is the analysis and its presuppositions.

Properly speaking, there is no difference between the "popular" and the "higher," for a simple reason. All traditions are structured dialectically. Whether it is the relation between *Mary Tyler Moore* and *The Dick Van Dyke Show* or between *I Dream of Jeannie* and *Bewitched*, the revisionary ratios are manifest for any interested viewer. The ceaseless transfigurations in the history of "popular culture" reveal something else, too: the presence of the canonical master, who manages historical overdeterminations and anxieties of influence as the stock in trade of his or her business. Chuck Berry's ability to transform big-band boogie woogie into the jump sound of rock and roll guitar is what makes him canonical, not the imposition upon him of a "moral" or "thematic" role from outside the terms of his medium. He is canonical because he transforms material, to insist on Adorno's own vocabulary, dialectically. Like painting or literature – or, God forbid, like classical music – blues tradition is a self-conscious and learned tradition. To enjoy it requires education, too, although not, ideally speaking, at a German university.

References and further reading

Adorno, Theodor W. *Introduction to the Sociology of Music. 1962.* Trans. E. B. Ashton. New York: Continuum, 1976.

Berry, Chuck. *Chuck Berry: The Autobiography.* New York: Harmony Books, 1987.

Charters, Samuel B. *The Country Blues.* New York: Rinehart, 1959.

Christgau, Robert. *Any Old Way You Choose It: Rock and Other Pop Music, 1967–73.* Baltimore: Penguin, 1973.

Davis, Miles, with Quincey Troupe. *Miles: The Autobiography.* New York: Simon and Schuster, 1989.

Ellison, Ralph. *Shadow and Act.* New York: Random House, 1964.

George, Nelson. *The Death of Rhythm and Blues.* New York: Pantheon, 1988.

Giddins, Gary. *Riding on a Blue Note: Jazz and American Pop.* Boulder: Da Capo Press, 2000.

Gillett, Charlie. *The Sound of the City: The Rise of Rock and Roll.* New York: Pantheon, 1970.

Gilroy, Paul. *The Black Atlantic: Modernity and Double Consciousness.* Cambridge, MA: Harvard University Press, 1993.

Gitler, Ira. *Swing to Bop: An Oral History of the Transition in Jazz in the 1940s.* New York: Oxford University Press: 1985.

Gordy, Berry. *To Be Loved: The Music, the Magic, the Memories of Motown. An Autobiography.* New York: Warner Books, 1994.

Guralnick, Peter. *Sweet Soul Music: Rhythm and Blues and the Southern Dream of Freedom.* New York: Harper and Row, 1986.

Hebdige, Dick. *Subculture: The Meaning of Style.* London: Meuthuen, 1979.

Jones, LeRoi. *Blues People: Negro Music in White America*. New York: Morrow, 1963.

Keil, Charles. *Urban Blues*. Chicago: University of Chicago Press, 1966.

Lott, Eric. *Love and Theft: Blackface Minstrelsy and the American Working Class*. New York: Oxford University Press, 1993.

Malone, Bill C. *Country Music U.S.A.* Austin: University of Texas Press, 1985.

Marcus, Greil. *Mystery Train: Images of America in Rock "n" Roll Music*. New York: Dutton, 1975.

Palmer, Robert. *Deep Blues*. New York: Viking, 1981.

Robinson, Smokey, with David Ritz. *Smokey: Inside My Life*. New York: McGraw-Hill, 1989.

Russell, Ross. *Jazz Style in Kansas City and the Southwest*. Berkeley: University of California Press, 1991.

Schuller, Gunther. *The Swing Era: The Development of Jazz, 1930–45*. New York: Oxford University Press, 1989.

Shaw, Arnold. *Honkers and Shouters: The Golden Years of Rhythm and Blues*. New York: Macmillan, 1978.

Southern, Eileen. *The Music of Black Americans: A History*. New York: Norton, 1971.

Chapter 5

American Drama in the Postwar Period

John Bell

Introduction

The postwar era in American culture, from 1945 to the end of the twentieth century, was especially marked by a self-conscious sense of place in the world. Whether or not the twentieth century was the "American Century," the postwar period was certainly the time when citizens of the United States began to believe that it was, in fact, their century, and that theirs was "the greatest country in the world." Ascendant economic growth and an accelerated birth rate (the "baby boom"), as well as a feeling that the United States was specifically responsible for "winning" World War II, gave Americans self-confidence about leading the world, but, at the same time, an underlying, nagging doubt about their ability do so. The dynamics of these two opposite cultural sensibilities played themselves out during the postwar era, reaching a kind of climax during the 1960s and 1970s, when the civil rights movement and the Vietnam War set the American desire confidently to make things right against glaringly apparent failures of purpose.

Postwar drama reflected such duality as it developed from 1945 to the end of the century and was expressed in the dynamic between commercial and aesthetic visions of drama. Unlike European drama, which as a cultural artifact was apprized as an essential part of each European nation's patrimony, American drama had emerged in the beginning of the twentieth century as a strictly commercial venture, admired and considered useful largely to the extent that it could make money. The Little Theater Movement which began in Chicago in 1912 (initiated by Maurice Browne, an Englishman) changed this situation by asserting the need for something more, something beyond simple economic success, as a motive for making theater. Its most famous alumnus, Eugene O'Neill, changed the course of American drama by combining commercial success with a sense of drama as cultural treasure, and as a form constantly in need of reinvention.

But also, and perhaps more importantly for the postwar period, O'Neill's experience was an emblem of a cultural duality in American drama characterizing not only the New York theater scene, but United States theater as a whole. O'Neill's initial plays were presented at the Provincetown Playhouse, downtown in Greenwich Village, but beginning with *Beyond the Horizon* (1920) his dramas found commercial success on Broadway, thus embodying a basic dichotomy of American drama: the contrast between the uptown theaters of Broadway, with all their potential box-office success, and the downtown playhouses of Greenwich Village, where theater could be made for the sake of cultural, social, or political ideals. The distance from Greenwich Village to Broadway and 42nd Street was short geographically, but represented a potential chasm in the collective psyche of playwrights, actors, directors, designers, and audiences. Was downtown theater artistically "purer," or was Broadway drama, with its combination of artistry and commercial success, a truer representation of American culture? Did success on Broadway (like success in Hollywood) mean artistic compromise? Was the artistic "freedom" of off-Broadway theater worth the penury it often demanded of its practitioners? And ultimately, was there in fact really that much of a difference between uptown and downtown theater, or were they the co-dependent halves that made up the whole of American drama?

The successes of the Little Theater Movement, and later the controversies surrounding the Depression-era Federal Theater Project, brought out this cultural dualism in American drama. In the decades after World War II, the energies of "art" theater coalesced under the term "off-Broadway," which specifically noted the geographical realities of the commercial/non-commercial split, and by defining non-commercial drama as the "other" theater ceded priority of place, power, and influence to Broadway's continuing cultural and economic power. Off-Broadway (and later "off-off-Broadway") theater had always to concede its connections to and a certain dependence on its successful uptown sister, but in the 1960s it surpassed Broadway theater as the source of new American drama. A sense of the possibilities of drama outside the Broadway spectrum also emerged in the growth of regional theaters across the United States, which asserted themselves not only by their authority as community-based American cultural centers, but also as artistic rivals to a Broadway theater scene which they considered moribund.

While the uptown/downtown aspects of American drama characterized its twentieth-century development, the development of mechanical and electronically mediated alternatives to live theater – film and radio – meant that live drama was slowly but surely being pushed from the center of the cultural spotlight. Thornton Wilder wrote to Gertrude Stein that 1940 was "the year that the movies have finally risen and surpassed the stage," and in the postwar era television not only joined earlier forms of mass media, but soon superseded them (Stein: 254). Television delivered dramatic entertainment directly into American living rooms, eliminating the necessity of a trip to a theater, on Broadway or anywhere else. Live theater was no longer the medium through which most Americans experienced drama, but a more and more rarefied form of performance. This shift in the nature of postwar drama lead to a cultural and physical decline of Broadway theater, which would not be reversed until the late 1990s redevelopment of Broadway as the live unit of mass media, corporate conglomerate entertainment.

Classic Postwar Drama: American Realism

As World War II drew to a close in 1945, Broadway theater's persistent traditional strengths were refracted through the cultural lens of its five years of wartime service as the United States' live, patriotic representation of Anglo-American culture. *Oklahoma!*, which revolutionized the American musical by seamlessly combining song and story when it opened in 1943, was still running, and the Theater Guild, a downtown stalwart of the 1920s which had figured out in the 1930s how to succeed on Broadway, opened Rodgers and Hammerstein's *Carousel*. English expatriate actor Maurice Evans's *G. I. Hamlet* (an abridged version of Shakespeare's play) had arrived on Broadway after playing to soldiers in South Pacific war zones, and numerous plays featured actors in uniform. Over a dozen "Hollywood film stars" (Blum: 307) temporarily forsook Los Angeles movie studios for the New York stage – a marker of what was by now a well-established split between live theater and the world of film. African American actors appeared as ethnic exotics, in *Carib Song*, featuring dancer Katherine Dunham, and in Margaret Webster's production of *The Tempest*, which cast as Caliban Canada Lee, a black actor who had emerged in the Harlem Renaissance of the twenties. Despite these stereotyped roles, which carried on an American tradition going back to minstrel-show days, there were more sophisticated black characters in Broadway dramas: interracial couples were the subjects of both *Deep Are the Roots* and *Strange Fruit*. The persistence of older character conventions, the emergence of newer ones reflecting the changes brought about by the war (for example, the racial integration of the US Army); the esteem for English theater and especially Shakespeare, and the blossoming of the American musical were all reflections of tradition and change in postwar drama.

Perhaps the most important Broadway moment at the beginning of postwar American drama was the acclaim that greeted Tennessee Williams's first Broadway play, *The Glass Menagerie*. It won the 1945 Drama Critics Circle Award, and set the stage for a succession of Broadway successes over the next 15 years that established Williams as one of the central playwrights of the postwar era. Williams's partner, as it were, in defining the tone of this first phase of postwar drama was Arthur Miller, whose *All My Sons* won the Drama Critics Circle Award two years later, and who, like Williams, contributed a consistent record of Broadway successes until the 1960s, when his and Williams's popularity faded in the face of new subjects and playwriting styles.

Williams's *Glass Menagerie* set the tone for postwar America drama by combining an interest in realism – specifically the social realism most prevalent in the Group Theater's work of the thirties, especially its productions of the dramas of Clifford Odets – with an introspective, almost psychoanalytical focus on the depths of the individual consciousness tortured by the day-to-day struggles of American society. While the realistic domestic drama was the dominant form through which American playwrights contributed to twentieth-century literature, 1930s versions of the form, especially by Odets, often offered quite specific political critique of the rigors of American society on the make and its constant pressures to succeed in the free-for-all of the American economy. However, in the postwar years, such critiques tended to serve as a framework around dramas which focused more on individual characters. In Williams's *The Glass Menagerie* and *Streetcar Named Desire* (1947), as well as in Arthur Miller's *All My Sons* (1947) and *Death of a Salesman* (1949), the middle-class characters all face economic and social challenges. But these conditions are ultimately secondary to the person-to-person conflicts driving the plays – conflicts which, especially in Williams's work, are ultimately inner struggles.

Tennessee Williams's early domestic tragedies focus on the harsh exigencies of modern American life: the likelihood of personal despair for rootless individuals caught up in the desire – or the necessity – of success in any one-for-one's-self society which served as a microcosm of postwar towns and cities across the United States. Williams's innovation on the domestic tragedy was to open up the psyches of his protagonists as beautifully vast, deep, and hidden worlds whose richness is often wasted, undetected by the brutish instincts of more unfeeling characters who are nonetheless equally trapped in the same tough milieu. *The Glass Menagerie*, for example, is set in a St Louis apartment in the Depression era, where the mother and brother of crippled Laura Wingfield try to fix her up with an old high school friend. The attempt is typically ill fated, and a general level of despair affects all the characters of the play, chiefly because they are having such a hard time making ends meet. Laura's mother urges her to compensate for her emblematic physical condition with "charm and vivacity," but of course this does not work. The mystery and lush vividness with which Williams creates the three Wingfields is countered by larger-than-life forces which not only deny the family the "Happiness" and "Good Fortune" they wish for, but force Tom, the son, to leave town.

Williams, of course, was a homosexual playwright at a time when homosexuality was considered deviant, a subversive condition that must remain hidden. And so many of Williams's characters (like Tom Wingfield, who consistently disappears into the evenings to go to "the movies") have an added depth of mystery, a hidden life further enriching Williams's interior worlds. A few years later on the French stage Jean Genet would evoke more explicitly homosexual characters and worlds, with a lush richness of character similar to Williams's. But a difference between American stages of the forties and fifties and their European counterparts was that the Cold War moral climate of the United States meant that Williams's work had to remain "closeted." Part of what makes his work so strong, in fact, is the tension between the appearance of daily American life and the conflicted passions that struggle beneath its surface. While this sense of hidden conflict is clearly connected to Williams's homosexuality, it reverberated among American audiences of the forties and fifties on a bigger scale, as a general marker of the postwar anxiety.

The Aesthetics of Partial Realism

While the plays of Williams and Miller might appear to set a standard of realistic American drama, an important aspect of their aesthetics is that they persistently include significant, non-realistic elements that blatantly call attention to the artifice of the stage. This partial realism was not their innovation, since it appears, to an even greater extent, in the wildly experimental techniques of Eugene O'Neill's plays of the twenties and thirties. But this portrayal of a compromised realism, a realism that calls attention to itself, points to basic connections between the mainstream achievements of Miller and Williams and the later avant-garde experimentation of the sixties and seventies that is often considered its antithesis.

A significant element of *The Glass Menagerie* is its combination of realistic – even naturalistic – characters with certain elements of nonrealism, especially in the stage pictures the audience might see. In his "Production Notes" for the play, Williams called for "a new, plastic theater which must take the place of the exhausted theater of realistic conventions if the theater is to resume vitality as a part of our culture," and he initially wanted magic-lantern slides to project images and titles on an onstage screen (Worthen: 337). The projections did not make it to the Broadway production, but other aspects of new, nonrealistic conventions did. For example, Tom Wingfield not only participates in the stage action, but narrates the play, and when he first appears on stage addresses the audience directly, initiating the constant breach and re-establishment of the "fourth wall" which characterizes the drama. "Yes, I have tricks in my pocket," he begins:

> I have things up my sleeve. But I am the opposite of a stage magician. He gives you illusion that has the appearance of truth. I give you truth in the pleasant disguise of illusion. To begin with, I turn back time. I reverse it to that quaint period, the thirties, when the huge middle class of America was matriculating in a school for the blind. Their eyes had failed them, or they had failed their eyes, and so they were having their fingers pressed forcibly down on the fiery Braille alphabet of a dissolving economy. (Worthen: 338)

Williams's sense of the stage as a realm of both magic and realism, and his sense of the social economy of the United States as a harsh social framework in which individual stories unfold, is also present in Arthur Miller's equally influential work.

In Miller's *Death of a Salesman*, for example, the dominant stage image is the house of doomed salesman Willy Loman and his family. But, as Miller relates in the stage directions for the play (realized by Jo Mielziner in one of the most influential set designs of the postwar period), "[t]he entire setting is wholly, or in some places, partially transparent. The roof-line of the house is one-dimensional; under and over it we see the apartment buildings" (116). Miller's tragedy – in which an ordinary, middle-class American family man is crushed by the bitter-sweet vagaries endemic in the lower echelons of the business world – unfolds, like Williams's play, in a magic stage world where time slips backward and forward, and characters from Loman's past can suddenly appear in his present. This temporal fluidity contrasts with the bright, solid realism of the characters themselves, whose dialogue captures the day-to-day expansiveness of postwar American society. For example, consider the opening exchange between Willy and his wife Linda, after Loman has abruptly given up selling and suddenly returned home:

> LINDA (*Very carefully, delicately*): Where were you all day? You look terrible.
> WILLY: I got as far as a little above Yonkers. I stopped for a cup of coffee. Maybe it was the coffee.
> LINDA: What?
> WILLY (*After a pause*): I suddenly couldn't drive any more. The car kept going off onto the shoulder, y'know?
> LINDA (*Helpfully*): Oh. Maybe it was the steering again. I don't think Angelo knows the Studebaker. (117)

The dramatic tension here lies between the almost banal evocation of an unhappy car trip and its underlying meaning, which Linda is delicately trying to discern: Loman is simply no longer capable of selling. Miller evokes classic images of Americana the way Edward Hopper, or even the more kitschy Norman Rockwell, might paint them: the road to Yonkers; a place to stop for coffee; the Studebaker with a bad steering wheel. Miller's attention to character and its symbolic material connections evokes Ibsen's evocations of middle-class existence, or, even more so, Chekhov's meticulous attention to the details of such life.

Between Chekhov, Strindberg, and Ibsen's dramatic innovations in late-nineteenth-century European drama and Miller's postwar emergence as a playwright came the experiments of America's Little Theater

Movement, in the work of O'Neill and his Provincetown Playhouse colleague Susan Glaspell; in the abstract realism of Thornton Wilder's experimental evocations of Americana, and in the Depression-era social consciousness represented by Group Theater productions and their tributaries. The plays of Miller, Williams, and other postwar realists such as William Inge (whose *Picnic* appeared on Broadway in 1953) consequently combined particular focus on the rhythms, vocabulary ("y'know?"), and everyday subject matter of American speech with an opposing urge to define the stage as a place where grand illusions might be performed – and then analyzed. The vernacular realism of these playwrights' characters was perfectly matched by the Stanislavski-based acting styles of the most important American acting schools, such as the Actors Studio, founded by Group Theater veterans Cheryl Crawford and Lee Strasberg.

The maturation of an American twentieth-century drama in the postwar years was a culmination of dramatists' writing, the development of an American realistic acting style, and the consciousness of stage design as art. All of these developments had been inspired by European theater practices of the pre-war decades, but by the 1940s they had coalesced into a mature American drama. American playwrights were self-conscious about their role as creators of an artistic voice for the dominant postwar power which their country had become, yet still suffered from a sense of New-World inferiority which had traditionally branded American drama as a humble and suspiciously shallow newcomer to the world of theater. Arthur Miller was conscious of this when he wrote a 1958 introduction to *Death of a Salesman*. One of the fascinating aspects of the essay is his attention to Aristotle's *Poetics*, and his concern about Willy Loman's status as a lowly salesman instead of one of Aristotle's tragic kings: Miller feels the need to justify his play on Aristotle's terms, as if to meet the standards of classic European drama (Miller, "*Death of a Salesman*").

Miller's argument, that a salesman's death might be considered as tragic as a Greek hero's, reveals the consistent power of Aristotle's dramatic theory on the new continent well into the twentieth century, but also marks Miller's confident sense of time and place: that this particular moment in American drama was one in which comparisons to classic dramas of the past were not simply appropriate, but probably necessary, as if this postwar era was indeed the moment in which American drama came of age. Which was, in fact, the case.

John Bell

Piscator and the Birth of the Postwar Avant-Garde

When the American version of Stanislavski-influenced acting first appeared in the 1930s, it was inextricably connected to the social (or more aptly, *socialist*) idealism of the Theater Guild, a predecessor of the Group Theater. But by the time of the Cold War environment of the postwar years, the revolutionary techniques of American realist drama – especially the naturalistic "Method" acting style which characterized it – had disengaged from an outward embrace of political activism, and such concerns now appeared as background elements of Miller's and Williams's plays, in contrast to their function as content, for example in Clifford Odets's Group Theater dramas. While particular forms of dramatic realism – particularly in language and acting style – characterized the dominant revolutionary aesthetic of the immediate pre-war years, various forms of explicit non-realism came to characterize the avant-garde theater which slowly emerged after the war.

An interesting link among the different strands of American theater of these years is Erwin Piscator's Dramatic Workshop at New York City's New School for Social Research (1940–51). Piscator, the renowned German director who, together with Bertolt Brecht, invented what came to be known as "epic theater," joined the many émigré leftist intellectuals who had left Nazi Germany for the United States in the late 1930s. An extraordinary array of theater artists taught and studied at his Dramatic Workshop. Stella Adler, Sanford Meisner, Herbert Berghof, Mordecai Gorelick, Lee Strasberg, John Gassner, and Barrett Clark were among the teachers there. Marlon Brando, Tennessee Williams, Tony Curtis, Tony Randall, Rod Steiger, Judith Malina, Vinnette Carroll, and Miriam Colon (founder of the Puerto Rican Travelling Theater) were among the students. Piscator taught his students a holistic approach to theater which sought to consider all aspects of the stage (including machine technology and film) as colors in a director's palette – all this consistent with modern European theories of the director as artist which had marked the revolutionary ideas of Edward Gordon Craig, Constantin Stanislavski, Vsevolod Meyerhold, and Max Reinhardt in the pre-war decades. Piscator combined this concept of the dramatic production as a unified work of art with a sense of the purpose of drama, which ultimately hearkened back to Friedrich Schiller's Enlightenment belief in theater as a profoundly moral institution whose ultimate purpose was to help shape a nation.

Tennessee Williams had studied in Piscator's Dramatic Workshop during the war, and clearly his imagistic staging ideas (for example, the projections called for in *The Glass Menagerie*) were supported, if not entirely inspired by, his work with Piscator. The Broadway production of Williams's drama, however, downplayed his interest in particular epic elements to focus instead on the realistic intensity of the actors' presence. Williams acquiesced to the signal predominance of realistic acting methods, explaining that "the extraordinary power of [Laurette] Taylor's performance [as Amanda Wingfield] made it suitable to have the utmost simplicity in the physical production" (Williams: 337).

The Glass Menagerie as Broadway theater is fascinating because so many influences on postwar American drama are at play in it: the domestic drama, with its traditional social-realist intensity now serving in the background as a tonal marker, is now free to delve into rich evocations of tragic American characters, made vivid by the intense emotional connections enabled by American versions of Stanislavski-style acting techniques. The modern vision of dramatic production as a director's art, in which unity of theatrical vision is paramount, has by this mid-century moment aligned American drama with its European counterparts, but the somewhat more radical visual experiments of epic theater, and certainly the political sense of visionaries like Piscator, have been necessarily tempered by the continuing exigencies of Broadway as commercial venue, and by the persistent sense of American drama as primarily entertainment. The European sense of drama as a central cultural activity, as art which defines society, is a bit too high reaching, too "high falutin'," for the American stage. And, in the developing Cold War climate which dominated all forms of American culture from 1945 through the 1970s, a certain amount of repression was in order: homosexuality and leftist political sentiments were not just uncomfortable lifestyles or beliefs, but dangerous to the United States' sense of its very existence as the leader of the "Free World."

It is in the immediate flux of the postwar period that Bertolt Brecht's *Life of Galileo*, with Charles Laughton in the title role, appeared briefly onstage in Los Angeles and then on Broadway, in 1947. Critics recognized connections between Brecht's drama and the 1930s innovations of the Federal Theater Project's "Living Newspaper" productions, and Brecht sought to make a connection between the iconoclastic Renaissance scientist and the emerging postwar world by writing a prologue for the Broadway production which specifically compared Galileo's plight to the moral conflicts faced by contemporary scientists charged with developing atomic bombs (Bertolt Brecht: 226). But the moment was clearly not right for Brecht's epic theater to succeed on Broadway. Actors trained in Stanislavski methods were unprepared for Brecht's utter lack of interest in such techniques as "emotion memory." In rehearsal they wondered "What's our motivation?" The Brechtian response was to offer another question: "What's the motivation of a tightrope walker not to fall off the high wire?" (Lyons: 187). Brecht wanted actors to deliver lines with the high artistic intensity – and also the focused emotional detachment – of circus performers.

The consternation Brecht's epic methods aroused in some American theater artists was reflected on a larger scale by his run-in with the House Un-American Activities Committee in Washington, DC. As one of a group of Hollywood artists suspected of communist sympathies at the beginning of an era of blacklisting which would prevent or severely inhibit their work and that of many others, Brecht testified ambivalently to Congress in 1947, and then left the United States for Europe, a few days before *Galileo* opened in Broadway's Coronet Theater. It was a minor blip on the screen of the Broadway season that year, which was marked above all by the outstanding successes of Williams's *A Streetcar Named Desire* and Miller's *All My Sons*, dramas which came to define postwar United States drama by combining the modern sense of unified theatrical art with a particularly American fascination with the performance of character, especially when that was done with the virtuoso, Stanislavski-style intensity of actors such as Marlon Brando, whose career took off that year in Williams's play.

Arthur Miller and Tennessee Williams clearly set the pace and tone of Broadway theater of the late forties and fifties, but were accompanied by the similar focus of such playwrights as Robert Anderson (*Tea and Sympathy*, 1953), Carson McCullers (*Member of the Wedding*, 1950), and Herman Wouk (*The Caine Mutiny*, 1954). The postwar period greeted the appearance of Eugene O'Neill's later plays (*The Iceman Cometh*, 1946, and *Long Day's Journey Into Night*, 1956) with great respect; they were, significantly, in contrast to his 1920s experiments, O'Neill's most fully realistic works.

Alternatives: The Living Theater and Off-Broadway Drama

While mainstream postwar drama headed into the Cold War era with a firm sense of what it was doing and how to do it, the beginnings of postwar avant-garde drama were emerging from some of the same roots. Despite its humble origins, avant-garde American drama would have an impact around the world equal to or perhaps even greater than that of mainstream drama.

The Drama Workshop student who most fervently pursued Erwin Piscator's expectations for modern theater was Judith Malina, a rabbi's daughter from New York City who together with artist Julian Beck conceived the Living Theater in 1947. Malina emerged as the company's director, and Beck the theater's main designer. The initial struggle they faced was one which marked the development of American avant-garde theater for the entire century: the search for space in which to perform. For while Broadway theaters in the vicinity of 42nd Street and Times Square had evolved an effective, self-perpetuating system of presenting new theater to the public, what became known as off-Broadway theater, as well as its 1960s sibling, off-off-Broadway theater, had a much more difficult economic challenge in finding support for the pointedly non-commercial plays they wished to produce.

Malina fully embraced Piscator's sense of the unity of art and society, as her 1945 notes to one of his lectures attest:

> Can we build society like an eight-cylinder car [she wrote, paraphrasing Piscator] by understanding its elements? Can we do this without considering spiritual form, in the sense of human happiness? Spiritual, meaning growth and intelligence. We need art to complete the incompleteness of life. But first we need society and security in society. We perfect the world through the nation and through the self, and we must take a step toward this in our theater. Political theater is art theater . . . The art theater was always bound to thinking, and always seeking for truth. Thus the art theater was always political theater. The theater turns even unconsciously to politics. (Malina: 67)

Malina and Beck ended up presenting the first Living Theater productions in their Manhattan apartment, but by 1951 they managed to produce a season at the Cherry Lane Theater, downtown in Greenwich Village and not far from the Provincetown Playhouse which had launched American avant-garde theater over 30 years earlier. The productions of the Living Theater's 1951 season are an instructive blueprint for the development of American avant-garde drama in the years to come. The season featured Brecht learning plays (*He Who Says Yes and He Who Says No*), European avant-garde classics (Alfred Jarry's *Ubu Roi* and Pablo Picasso's *Desire Trapped by the Tail*), poetry transformed into drama (T. S. Eliot's *Sweeney Agonistes* and Federico Garcia Lorca's *Dialogue of the Manikin and the Young Man*), poetic plays (Gertrude Stein's *Doctor Faustus Lights the Lights* and Kenneth Rexroth's *Beyond the Mountains*), and new ventures into drama by the icono-clastic American social philosopher Paul Goodman (*Childish Voices*). The contrasts with postwar domestic realism could not be clearer.

While Williams and Miller focused their attention on the creation of compelling, realistic American voices in dialogue, the plays chosen by the Living Theater directly evoked the kind of inner voices at which the realistic plays hinted. Arthur Miller ended *Death of a Salesman* with Linda Loman's uncomprehending farewell to her suicide husband:

> I can't understand it, Willy. I made the last payment on the house today. Today, dear. And there'll be nobody home. (*A sob rises in her throat*) We're free and clear. (*Sobbing more fully, released*) We're free. (*[Her son] Biff comes slowly toward her*) We're free . . . We're free . . . (226)

But in contrast to Miller's clearly limned, emotional climax, the Living Theater's production of Stein's *Doctor Faustus Lights the Lights* presented a very different kind of passion, beginning with the title character saying:

> I am Doctor Faustus who knows everything can do everything and you say it was through you but not at all, if I had not been in a hurry and if I had taken my time I would have known how to make white electric light and day-light and night light and what did I do I saw you miser-able devil I saw you and I was deceived and I believed miserable devil I thought I needed you, and I thought I was tempted by the devil and I know no temptation is tempting unless the devil tells you so. (Stein, *Doctor Faustus Lights the Lights*: 203–4)

Context, in the Stein play, is left open; the play text is a provocation, begging for response from the actors, designer, and director who would stage the play. While the Miller play seeks illustration on stage, the Stein play wants to evince an unprogrammed, creative response in performance.

American realistic dramas, even with the fantastic, magical, nonreal appurtenances of their postwar innovations, draw on the shared conventions of a Euro-American tradition of stage language going back ultimately to the nineteenth century, while the emerging avant-garde, represented by the first efforts of the Living Theater, draws on the evolving conventions of avant-garde theater ultimately going back to the 1890s experiments of Jarry and other symbolist theater-makers in France. Most importantly, the avant-garde impulse sees the play-text as one element in the simultaneous presentation of actors, images, sounds, and words, while the tradition of realistic drama tends to honor the play-text as the primary element and marker of any live performance.

The Living Theater's off-Broadway experiments were soon augmented by Circle in the Square, which opened in Greenwich Village in 1950, the Phoenix Theater (1953), Joseph Papp's New York Shakespeare Festival (1954), and later, in 1967, the Negro Ensemble Company. Productions of Tennessee Williams, Samuel Beckett, T. S. Eliot, and Edward Albee plays began to establish off-Broadway theater of the 1950s as a venue for more adventurous experiments in theater form. Off-Broadway also functioned, as the Little Theater Movement had in the pre-war decades, as a complement to Broadway theater, a proving ground where plays could develop before entering the mainstream. Albee, for example, the foremost American playwright of the postwar European dramatic genre that Martin Esslin labeled "theater of the absurd," had difficulty finding a venue for his first play, *Zoo Story*, which he wrote in 1958. The two-person drama, set on a bench in New York's Central Park, is an encounter between a "normal" postwar American man, Peter, who has a job, wife, home, and pets, and Jerry, a nonconformist who seems to embody the existentialist lifestyle described in the then-popular writings of Jean-Paul Sartre and Albert Camus. Their chance meeting leads to discussions about the purpose of life, and then to a confrontation as Jerry provokes Peter to bellicose anger. At the play's climax, the "normal" Peter stabs Jerry to death, without really knowing why – a marker of the absurd contingencies of contemporary American life.

Zoo Story opened off-Broadway in 1960, on a double bill with Samuel Beckett's *Krapp's Last Tape*. It never moved to a Broadway theater, but nonetheless helped establish Albee's reputation as a serious dramatist. His critique of American life was more pronounced than Miller's or Williams's, and his connection to the "absurdist" strains of European dramatic experiments probably made his off-Broadway start inevitable.

However, it was not long before Albee's innovative playwriting style found a mainstream audience. By 1962 his savage classic *Who's Afraid of Virginia Woolf?*, which pitted a college professor in vicious battle with his bizarrely outrageous wife as they mutually destroy their marriage, opened on Broadway, winning great acclaim and the Drama Critics Circle Award. *Who's Afraid of Virginia Woolf?*, less "absurd" than *Zoo Story*, but far more brutal than most contemporary realistic dramas, is a family drama reminiscent of *Streetcar Named Desire* in that domestic relations are characterized by an intense personal conflict. Albee's play, unlike, say, *Death of a Salesman*, eschews Miller's sense of individuals caught up in an overwhelmingly powerful social and economic structure, to focus instead on byzantine depths of character, and on how civilized twentieth-century Americans might find within themselves surprising reservoirs of the most uncivilized thoughts and deeds. The modern capacity for ugliness, hate, and evil, Albee's early plays seem to say, lurks beneath the well-brushed veneer of postwar American society. That Albee's sensibility had to emerge off-Broadway bespeaks the extent to which Broadway theater had, by the 1960s, become rather conventional. But the fact that Albee's plays soon found their audience *on* Broadway points out another, more important, aspect of Broadway's durability: its ability to include any dramatic form that will draw an audience.

Not all off-Broadway playwrights of the 1950s did succeed on Broadway, of course. The Living Theater produced *The Connection*, a 1959 jazz-scored drama about heroin addicts by Jack Gelber, and Kenneth H. Brown's 1963 play *The Brig*, which was an intense indictment of American military punishment in Japan, influenced by Antonin Artaud's "Theater of Cruelty" and Vsevolod Meyerhold's Biomechanic acting techniques. These stunning innovations in American drama played only off-Broadway, and it's clear that the Living Theater was not interested in becoming more mainstream than that. Other off-Broadway playwrights, such as Arthur Kopit and Adrienne Kennedy, also pursued their other-than-mainstream writing styles that only later were recognized for their artistic merit.

Related to, but separate from, the world of off-Broadway drama was the new world of performance created not by playwrights and directors, but by composers, dancers, artists, and poets, which began at Black Mountain College in North Carolina. In the 1930s that institution had received émigré artists from Germany's Bauhaus, who introduced to the American students and faculty the ideas of experimental Bauhaus theater. By 1948 composer John Cage and choreographer

Merce Cunningham were teaching there, as well as painter Willem de Kooning and visionary designer Buckminster Fuller. They reconstructed seminal works of the European avant-garde, such as Erik Satie's *Ruse of the Medusa*, and invented their own performances combining image, music, and text (Goldberg: 125). By the mid-fifties, Cage and Cunningham had moved to New York, and Cage was teaching a course on the composition of experimental music at the New School. This soon became a colloquium for all sorts of theories and practices of experimental theater – an incubator for the burst of creativity that would redefine American theater in the mid-sixties.

Another Alternative: Regional Theater

Broadway theater has regularly seemed synonymous with American drama, but in fact the two retain quite separate identities. First of all, Broadway theater, to the extent that it focuses on the practical challenge of providing live entertainment to a wide audience, has always opened itself to whatever stage spectacles might fill its seats. So, even in the heyday of serious drama on Broadway – the decades from the twenties through the forties – the works of "serious" playwrights were vying (successfully) for attention with vaudeville shows, musicals, and youth-oriented concerts featuring Frank Sinatra in the thirties, and rock and roll in the fifties.

The spread of mass media, and especially television, in the postwar decades helped lead to the decline of Broadway as a center for serious drama, and, some would say, the decline of live drama in general across the United States. Broadway theater was no longer the central point in a nationwide network of theaters; that system, organized at the turn of the century by such producers as the Theatrical Syndicate, Oscar Hammerstein, and the Shubert Organization, had been declining since the advent of film and radio in the 1920s. In the postwar decades, proscenium arch theaters in cities and towns across the United States were turned into movie houses or abandoned.

However, beginning in 1947, a new effort to spur live theater in cities across the country began in Dallas. This was the regional theater movement, and, like avant-garde theater, it would change the way American drama was defined and produced, if not the way it was written. The regional theater movement, like the Little Theater Movement at the beginning of the century and the Federal Theater Project of the thirties, sought both to decentralize American theater culture and to draw attention to American drama as art rather than commerce. In the estimation of Joseph Zeigler:

> the first regional theaters became a way to say "no" to what their creators saw as the commercial values of Broadway – quick success, star power, the businessman's literature, and money as a god. The first regional theaters after World War II became a new world dedicated to the establishment of new theatrical values – permanence, the ensemble company of actors, classics on the stage, and art as a goal. This was to be the new alternative; and Broadway, the theatrical capital of the country, was to be stripped of its ideological power. (Zeigler: 16)

Beginning with Margo Jones's creation of Theatre '47 in Dallas, a string of regional theaters emerged across the United States in the following three decades, spurred in large part by the support of funding sources such as the Ford and Rockefeller Foundations. The regional theaters, including the Guthrie Theater in Minneapolis, the Actor's Workshop in San Francisco, Houston's Alley Theatre, the Long Wharf Theatre in New Haven, the Mark Taper Forum in Los Angeles, and, according to some definitions, Joseph Papp's Public Theater in New York (also considered an off-Broadway theater), created a new kind of nonprofit dramatic culture. The regional theaters' desire to makes themselves distinct from Broadway was sometimes physical; many of them adopted in-the-round stages instead of the traditional proscenium. They also attempted to maintain permanent companies of actors, unlike the Broadway system of casting each play separately and attracting audiences with a big star. The repertoire of the regional theaters, despite their radical intentions, was not as daring as the New York avant-garde experiments. Mindful of their middle-American audiences, the regional theaters stuck to classic European texts (Shakespeare and Molière, for example), as well as newer American plays by O'Neill, Williams, and Miller that were deemed to be new classic dramas, and, surprisingly enough, the political plays of Bertolt Brecht. In this way, the regional theaters were a powerful force in defining the postwar canon of serious American drama.

In some cases, regional theaters produced new works. Margo Jones, for example, nurtured William Inge's *Dark at the Top of the Stairs* in Dallas, as well as Tennessee Williams's *Summer and Smoke*, both of which later opened to great success on Broadway. What this indicates, of course, is that the regional theaters spelled not the end of Broadway so much as a new means of enriching Broadway's ability to present new American drama, an effect the off- and off-off-Broadway theaters would have as well. In spite of its protestations against Broadway's commercialism, then, the regional theater movement became an integral part of a new Broadway system of presenting new drama. By assiduously guarding and supporting the noncommercial aspects of postwar playwriting, the regional theater movement helped create dramas which *could* do very well on Broadway, while maintaining what were considered to be high artistic standards. Thus, for example, Howard Sackler's play about the black American boxer Jack Johnson was developed by Arena Stage director Zelda Fichandler from 1966 to 1968 into an attention-getting production which put Arena Stage on the national map as a producer of new works for theater. The ultimate destination for Sackler's *Great White Hope*, of course, was Broadway, where it became quite successful in 1968, and won Sackler the Pulitzer Prize. But Zeigler points out that to the extent that this drama became successful, it left behind its regional theater origins (195). The regional theater fostered the development of intriguing new drama, but could not change the central position of Broadway as the arbiter of American theater.

The early stage of regional theater development across the country during the 1950s was matched by something of a second wave of similar developments in the 1970s. For example, the Steppenwolf Theater in Chicago and the Magic Theater in San Francisco were part of a second wave of nonprofit regional theaters that, like their elder brethren, became sources of new drama.

Cold War Drama in the Fifties

During the 1950s, a perceptible shift took place in the creation of postwar drama. The Korean War and the division of the globe into capitalist and communist blocs competing with each other and vying for influence in the underdeveloped countries of Asia, Latin America, and Africa helped produce a domestic culture on guard and wary of destabilization. Although in some areas of American culture – the Beats, and off-Broadway theater, for example – destabilization seemed inevitable and in fact welcome, the safe road for mainstream film, television, and theater seemed to be the presentation of ultimately reassuring scenarios of American or American-style life.

In Europe the existing support structures for drama were making it possible for the "Angry Young Men" of Britain and the "absurdist" playwrights of France to reinvent drama for the postwar era. That kind of freedom to experiment, and to fail, was not really part of the Broadway environment, but it was a hallmark of off-Broadway theater. So, as off-Broadway theater took shape in New York City, and regional theaters sprang up around the United States, the shift in creativity in American drama was quite clear. "Serious" dramas continued to appear on Broadway, largely in keeping with the semi-realist form realized in the productions of plays by Miller and Williams. There were periodic appearances by Thornton Wilder's mature, more mainstream plays (*The Skin of Our Teeth* and *The Matchmaker*, both in 1955), and a late return to Broadway by Eugene O'Neill, with his autobiographical *Long Day's Journey into Night* (1956). The preponderance of the Miller/Williams standard did not at all mean a lack of innovation, for many new dramas, such as Carson McCullers's *Member of the Wedding*, or Lorraine Hansberry's *A Raisin in the Sun*, explored new subject matter outside the realm of plays by Miller, Williams, and Inge. Popular plays with great contemporary appeal followed the postwar realist style, perhaps without achieving the artistic heights that Miller and Williams clearly gained. Sidney Kingsley's version of Arthur Koestler's cautionary tale of Stalinist repression, *Darkness at Noon* (1951), was a success in this vein, as were popular stage plays such as *Dial "M" for Murder* (1952), *I Am A Camera* (1952, a heterosexualized version of Christopher Isherwood's novel of pre-war Berlin), and *The Caine Mutiny Court Martial* (1954). The vicissitudes of Broadway tastes were reflected by the fact that in this decade Tennessee Williams's Broadway career faltered with the failure of *Camino Real* in 1953, but rebounded with the success, two years later, of *Cat On a Hot Tin Roof*. Even an adventurous play such as Samuel Beckett's *Waiting for Godot* could appear on Broadway, although its rough, "absurdist" edges were rounded by vaudeville veteran Bert Lahr, who starred as Estragon in its 1956 production. The emendations and modifications apparently necessary for Broadway seem typical of the 1950s: Beckett's play made more satisfyingly and safely comic by Lahr; the suppression of homosexual overtones in Isherwood's bitter-sweet paean to Weimar Germany. All of these shifts probably made the works more successful on their uptown stages, but point to the clear artistic need for an alternative, which off-Broadway theater provided, not only for newer playwrights, such as Edward Albee, but also for established writers like Tennessee Williams, who could find support for his new writing at a time when his plays were no longer a sure-fire box-office success on Broadway. Even Bertolt Brecht finally found success on the New

York stage, in a long-running production of his collaboration with Kurt Weill, *The Threepenny Opera* (1954), although the production was attached to Weill's name rather than Brecht's.

American drama, especially on Broadway, has always judged its success in comparison to its musical theater, and the 1950s above all showed incredible achievements by the American musical. The decade was punctuated by the almost yearly appearance of works which have been recognized as the classics of postwar musical theater: *Guys and Dolls* (1950), *The King and I* (1951), *South Pacific* (1952), *The Pajama Game* (1954), *Damn Yankees* (1955), *My Fair Lady* (1956), *West Side Story* (1957), *The Music Man* (1957), *The Sound of Music* (1959), and *Bye Bye Birdie* (1960). The musicals which thrived in this period all celebrated and glamorized American culture and American society; attributes, of course, which were central to their success. The more difficult questions that drama, almost by definition, has perpetually raised were clearly not the kinds of issues mainstream American audiences of the 1950s sought to address, as they might have been more willing to do in, say the thirties, or, soon afterwards, in the sixties and seventies.

A real innovation in mainstream drama was Lorraine Hansberry's *A Raisin in the Sun*, which in 1959 became the first drama by an African American woman to be produced on Broadway. Significantly, *A Raisin in the Sun* was very much in the tradition of realistic, middle-class domestic drama developed by Arthur Miller, comparable in technique and story to his *Death of a Salesman*. This explains its acceptability to the mostly white audiences of Broadway, but also the criticism it received from some black critics who found Hansberry's middle-class, assimilationist stance too moderate. After all, this was the moment of the civil rights movement in the United States, and moderate appeals for racial integration were being countered by calls from more radical blacks for more access to political and economic power. Hansberry's play, in a way, takes up where Miller's *Death of a Salesman* leaves off, in that it opens with the Younger family of Chicago expecting the arrival of a $10,000 life insurance check for Mama Younger's deceased husband. The play follows the extended Younger family's tribulations as they decide, against various social and familial odds, to buy a house in a white neighborhood, and it ends, unlike Miller's tragedy, on a positive note: the black family makes progress in realizing the American dream of social and economic advancement. Hansberry was influenced by Ibsen and Strindberg, and her writing combines postwar realistic settings and plot structures with believable African American characters, not the stereotypes Hansberry saw populating existing American dramas. For example, here is Walter Lee Younger (played by Sidney Poitier in 1959) rejecting an offer by a white representative of the neighborhood to which the Youngers are moving to buy back their new house:

> WALTER *(starting to cry and facing the man eye to eye)*: What I am telling you is that we called you over here to tell you that we are very proud and that this is – this is my son, who makes the sixth generation of our family in this country, and that we have all thought about your offer and we have decided to move into our house because my father – my father – he earned it . . . We don't want to make no trouble for nobody or fight no causes – but we will try to be good neighbors. That's all we got to say. *(He looks the man absolutely in the eyes.)* We don't want your money. *(He turns and walks away from the man.)* (Hansberry: 145)

The voice Hansberry has created here for Walter is complex: articulate and strong, but also sensitive, yet not removed from vernacular speech. He starts to weep, yet still looks his white interlocutor in the eye. He says "we don't want to make no trouble for nobody," but also stands up to the threat of intimidation: "we have all thought about your offer and we have decided to move into our house." In short, the innovative element at work here is the articulation of a realistic black voice, a century after minstrelsy defined the African American on stage, and over three decades after "sympathetic" black characters had been written by Eugene O'Neill (*The Emperor Jones*, 1920) and Dubose and Dorothy Heyward (*Porgy*, 1927). Hansberry's decision to write her play in the realistic family drama mode is quite central to *Raisin in the Sun*'s success. The familiarity of the form eased the presentation of a topic which was difficult for white audiences to consider. In this way, American postwar theater on Broadway could reflect the kinds of conflicts that constantly roiled beneath the surface of Cold War culture, and yet, through the familiar form and content of the realistic family drama, achieve a satisfying and reassuring conclusion.

From Off-Off Broadway to Alternative Theater

To the extent that off-Broadway theater became established and respectable, it created the opportunity, beginning in 1960, for a more experimental off-off-Broadway community to emerge as a collection of nonprofit venues was established in basements, lofts, converted churches, and storefronts. Off-off Broadway theater, like its off-Broadway forebear, made substantial contributions to postwar American drama, but, unlike off-Broadway theater, some aspects of it also grew into self-sufficient entities focused not necessarily on uptown success, but instead on creating a viable substitute for it. In this sense, "off-off Broadway" might not be as apt a term for the movement as others: "experimental theater," "alternative theater," "radical theater," or the classic "avant-garde theater"; terms which, although none completely defines the movement, all straightforwardly avoid defining themselves solely in terms of a Broadway paradigm.

Perhaps part of the autonomous downtown focus of off-off-Broadway theater had to do with the extent to which the quasi-alternative nature of off-Broadway theater had, by the sixties, become inevitably enmeshed with the ways of commercial theater. Michael Smith, a *Village Voice* theater critic of those years, saw the mainstreaming of off-Broadway theater as the primary impetus for the formation of its more radical off-off-Broadway sibling. As the off-Broadway movement became more and more established, Smith wrote in 1966:

> rents went up, unions moved in, ticket prices climbed, audiences were reduced in number and ever more subject to "hit psychology." A play could be produced for a few hundred dollars in the middle fifties; in the sixties Off-Broadway productions have required initial investments ranging from a minimum of almost $10,000 to upwards of $40,000. To risk putting on an untried or unconventional play became foolhardy, at least without plenty of money and high-powered publicity. The pressure to play it commercially safe has steadily mounted and the opportunities for creative work have steadily diminished. The Living Theater, which for several years had been Off-Broadway's most adventurous theater, was closed for nonpayment of taxes in October 1963. Since that time, with a few exceptions, Off-Broadway has been in decline. (Smith: 5)

The distinctions between off-Broadway and off-off-Broadway theaters are, to a degree, murky and indistinct, because both emerged from the same urge to create modern American drama for artistic rather than commercial reasons. Of course, the history of American twentieth-century drama is the intense interplay of commercial theater and drama for drama's sake, and the 1950s urge to make drama primarily as art was the same impetus which compelled new dramatists to do so in the 1960s. The frustration Michael Smith defined in 1966 was, to a large extent, a response to the success of off-Broadway theater's ability to establish itself as a source of new drama. This conundrum – successful "alternative" drama becoming mainstream – was not to be avoided in the sixties, or for that matter in any of the decades preceding or following it. An awareness of this dynamic relationship, however, did result in the more independent viewpoint of off-off-Broadway theater in comparison to its predecessor. Success on the improvised stages of St Mark's Church, Judson Church, Caffé Cino, or La MaMa Experimental Theater Company was, for many of those involved in the productions, sufficient unto itself.

Those four venues, in fact, were the center of 1960s dramatic work downtown; work which further expanded the traditional parameters of American drama. If writers like Albee, Murray Schisgal, and Kennedy were influenced by the European "absurdists" (and, in Kennedy's case, West African culture), 1960s writers such as Sam Shepard, Maria Irene Fornes, Megan Terry, Lanford Wilson, and Jean-Claude van Itallie were influenced not only by postwar European drama, but by contemporary developments in dance, music, and the newly emerging genres of happenings and performance art.

Judson Church, for example, was an epicenter of 1960s theater-making, which benefited greatly from John Cage's music composition classes at the nearby New School during the previous decade. Judson Church presented not only playwrights and directors connected with the Judson Poets Theater (Al Carmines, Robert Nichols, Rosalyn Drexler, and Lawrence Kornfeld) but the creators of postmodern dance (including Yvonne Rainer, Trisha Brown, Steve Paxton, and Lucinda Childs), performance art (Robert Rauschenberg, Carolee Schneeman, Alan Kaprow), and even the puppeteer Peter Schumann, whose Bread and Puppet Theater helped articulate the emerging political urgency of the time with gigantic moving sculptures. It was a period, as Sally Banes describes it in *Greenwich Village 1963*, in which sculptors danced, poets acted, musicians made art, and dramatists took in and used all that surrounded them.

Sam Shepard emerged as the best known of the off-off-Broadway playwrights, and his work typifies the heterogeneous mix of influences on 1960s alternative drama. Shepard was famously involved with punk rock poet and diva Patti Smith, and at one point was the drummer for the alternative rock group The Holy Modal Rounders. His plays appeared frequently at Theater Genesis at St Mark's Church, and at Ellen Stewart's La MaMa. Shepard wrote into his plays the particular influences of postwar popular culture – rock and roll in particular – that were unknown or unfamiliar to the earlier generation of off-Broadway playwrights. His early work regularly ignored, or, perhaps more correctly, shattered the conventions of the realist or semi-realist stage of postwar drama, but, in fact, the voices he creates for his characters share the realistic edge which dominates the postwar genre. What was new about Shepard's voices, besides their often absurdist or shockingly abrasive contexts, was the way they articulated the ennui of postwar Americans living in suburban tract houses whose basements also served as bomb shelters from a potential nuclear war. In such a suburban American home, although one clearly infected with a domestic, malevolent menace, "Man" addresses "Boy" in Shepard's 1964 play, *The Rock Garden*:

> MAN: . . . Did you notice the rock garden? That's a new idea. It's by the driveway. You may have seen it when you pass by there in the mornings. It's not bad for my never having made one before. It's one of those new kind. You know? With rocks and stuff in it. It has a lot of rocks and stuff from the trip. We found afterwards that it was really worth carrying all those rocks around. You know? It's a nice rock garden. It gives me something to do. It keeps me pretty busy. You know? It feels good to get out in it and work and move the rocks around and stuff. You know? It's a good feeling. I change it every day. It keeps me busy.
> *A long pause. The Boy falls off his chair.* (Shepard: 29)

The Boy, Shepard's stage directions tell us, falls off his chair here, and at other moments in the scene, from the boredom the Man's speech induces. The absurdity of the situation is made troubling by the fact that both characters are dressed in their underwear, and that the short play ends with the Boy's quite explicit description of masturbation and sex. The scene is typical of Shepard's early experimental work, and of his later more mainstream plays, in that the authentic voices of richly drawn American characters are presented through situations in which absurdity and baleful violence seem to lurk just around the corner (themes which call to mind Edward Albee's plays). The fact that Shepard would emerge, by the end of the century, as one of the postwar era's greatest American playwrights speaks to the fact that his characters – whether set in the seventies experimental-theater context of a gladiatorial rock and roll fantasy world in *Tooth of Crime (1973)*, or in the American kitchens and living rooms of the more realistic family dramas *Buried Child* (1978) and *True West* (1980)

– consistently speak in an American voice that resonated almost automatically with American audiences. While Albee's plays of the same
era were easily included within Martin Esslin's 1961 articulation of a
"theater of the absurd," the incongruous situations created by Shepard
articulated a starker critique, not only of postwar American life, but
of postwar American theater structures. Unlike Albee's dramas, which,
ultimately, fit comfortably on a Broadway stage, Shepard's 1960s plays
attacked the whole nature of traditional drama, just as the works of
so many others in downtown New York stepped outside the bounds
of traditional drama to create conventions of a new genre called
performance.

While Shepard's characters spoke in a sure-handed American vernacular, the Cuban American playwright Maria Irene Fornes, although
similarly interested in the emerging postwar tradition of "absurd"
drama, made her conflicted characters betray an awkwardness with
language reflecting mistrust and apprehension. For example, in *The
Conduct of Life* (1985) here is how Leticia, the wife of a Latin American
military leader, explains to him her opposition to deer hunting:

> LETICIA: What! Me go hunting? Do you think I'm going to shoot a
> deer, the most beautiful animal in the world? Do you think I'm going to
> destroy a deer? On the contrary, I would run in the field and scream and
> wave my arms like a mad woman and try to scare them away so the
> hunters could not reach them. I'd run in front of the bullets and let the
> mad hunters kill me – stand in the way of the bullets – stop the bullets
> with my body. I don't see how anyone can shoot a deer. (Fornes: 914)

The sense of impending violence which appeared again and again in
1960s dramas – a reflection, of course, of the ongoing war in Vietnam
and the contentious, oppositional atmosphere it created in the United
States – is still rife here, just as it persists in many of Shepard's plays.
Fornes's Leticia, in fact, ends up killing her husband. But the voice,
however articulate, is somewhat formal ("I'd run in front of the
bullets and let the mad hunters kill me"), almost awkward, and points
out the extent to which many of Fornes's plays are themselves about
language as a barrier to, as much as a conduit of, information. It is
this difference in voice, in part, which allowed Shepard's comparat-
ively accessible plays, especially later works (*Buried Child* and *True
West*) to find larger audiences, eventually even on Broadway.

Other off-off-Broadway playwrights similarly created new characters
and their voices in dramas which confidently worked well outside

realistic norms of mainstream drama. Lanford Wilson wrote *The Madness of Lady Bright*, a one-act portrait of a drag queen, for performance in the intimate Caffé Cino in 1964. The brief play features Leslie Bright in his apartment, and a "Boy" and "Girl" who re-enact important moments of his unhappy life in a time-shifting mélange of moments. Here is Leslie's reverie, which shifts from self-praise to derision:

LESLIE: . . . I am Venus, rising from . . . and matching eye shadow. And nothing else. *(He looks in the mirror for the first time. Stops. Looks bitchily at his reflection.)* You. Are a faggot. There is no question about it any more – you are definitely a faggot. You're not funny but you're a faggot. *(Pause.)* You have *been* a faggot since you were four years old. Three years old. *(Checking the mirror again.)* You're not *built* like a faggot – necessarily. You're built like a disaster. But, whatever your dreams, there is just no possibility whatever of your ever becoming, say, a lumberjack. You know? (Wilson: 63)

The setting in which this character appears does not maintain a consistent level of realism, and the functions of the Boy and Girl are almost those of stagehands; in other words, the theatricality of Wilson's play is more similar to the happenings taking place nearby in Judson Church than to more realistic dramas in proscenium stages. But, again, Bright's voice rings true, in an almost naturalistic way, and this aspect of Wilson's playwriting is consistent with both other off-off-Broadway work and the mainstream traditions of postwar realistic drama. Like Shepard's, Wilson's later plays returned to more conventionally realistic worlds, while retaining the playwright's sense of potentially outrageous characters. Wilson and a number of other alumni from the Caffé Cino started the Circle Repertory Company as an off-Broadway theater in 1969, and it was there that Wilson's later plays, including *The Hot L Baltimore* (1973), *The 5th of July* (1978), and *Talley's Folly* (1980), reached larger audiences off-Broadway. Circle Rep's emergence from the off-off-Broadway scene into a position as a central source of contemporary American drama points to the extent to which off-Broadway theater had, by the seventies, become the true center of serious American drama, replacing the more hidebound, less flexible structures of Broadway, which was increasingly focused on musical theater instead of straight plays.

What seems to make the sixties and seventies version of alternative theater different from earlier postwar attempts to invent an alternative to Broadway is the sheer mass of the effort, as well as the tumultuous time in which it occurred. The desire to make alternative theater was connected not only to aesthetic issues, but to the turbulent political controversy over the Vietnam War, and to the other issues which emerged around it: women's rights, gay liberation, the Black Power movement, and countless other expressions of particular communities or identities which had seemed to acquire a kind of critical mass. The sense of "radical" which Arthur Sainer uses in his study of these theaters (*The New Radical Theater Notebook*, 1997) has two meanings: a radical break from the conventions of American drama so carefully constructed in the pre- and immediate postwar years; and a yearning for radical change in society, a desire which was everywhere in the air during those years, but which had vanished almost entirely by the twentieth century's end.

Stefan Brecht, in the three books of a series he calls "The Original Theater of the City of New York" from "the mid-60s to the mid-70s," calls such postwar American drama "abnormal theater." The radicalism of this theater, in Brecht's consideration, goes right to the root of drama as literature because he sees such off-off-Broadway work of the sixties and seventies as "a director's, not a writer's theater," which was "underground and radically non-literary" (Brecht, *Queer Theater*: back cover). The radically visionary theater of Robert Wilson clearly fits Brecht's sense of this postwar American drama-which-is-not-drama. Wilson's works of this period could eschew dialogue altogether, use "found" text in the surrealist tradition, or employ the work of an autistic writer such as Christopher Knowles; for example, this excerpt from a trial scene in Wilson's monumental *Einstein on the Beach* (1976):

> I feel the earth move . . . I feel the tumbling down tumbling down . . . There was a judge who like puts in a court. And the judge have like what able jail what it could be a spanking. Or a whack. Or a smack. Or a swat. Or a hit. This could be where of judges and courts and jails. And who was it. This will be doing the facts of David Cassidy of were in this case of feelings. (Knowles: 21)

Knowles's writing is reminiscent of Gertrude Stein's work, which had appeared on Broadway in the 1930s (*Four Saints in Three Acts*) and then again in the early 1950s productions of the Living Theater. Knowles's abstract evocations emerge from a different source than Stein's studied Modernist experimenting, but nonetheless function similarly onstage, as a kind of verbal setting, although Knowles's seventies sensibility is filled with references to contemporary pop music:

Carole King's seventies hit song "I Feel the Earth Move" and the teen idol David Cassidy.

Another anomalous but equally powerful element of seventies American drama was the "queer theater" movement. Connected in part to drag shows which had been a component of urban homosexual communities for the entire twentieth century, queer theater was an openly and proudly gay expression developing concurrently with the gay liberation movement. Beginning with the somewhat loopy loft performances of Jack Smith, and the cabaret spectacles of John Vaccaro and a group called Hot Peaches, queer theater reached its apogee with Charles Ludlam's Ridiculous Theater, which was strong enough to outlast Ludlam's death from AIDS in 1986. Ludlam, a playwright and director, together with his partner Everett Quinton and others, created outlandish spectacles whose extravagant humor and design was matched by Ludlam's classic sense of dramaturgy and his success at continually communicating on several levels of meaning – not unlike the dramatic work of Oscar Wilde.

Ludlam's sense of, and his delight in plumbing the depths of, the ridiculous lead to dramatic truths which all sorts of audiences could understand. Ludlam's hairy-chested impersonation of the ill-fated courtesan Marguerite Gautier, in his version of the classic melodrama *Camille* (1973), for example, was a wildly exuberant evocation of queer identity, but also a brilliantly successful achievement of melodrama as theater: the artifice of queer theatricality was a perfectly apt framework in which to truly understand nineteenth-century dramatic form. Unlike Lanford Wilson's unhappy drag queen in *The Madness of Lady Bright*, the gay characters of the Ridiculous Theater (and the artists creating and portraying them) did not consider themselves inevitably doomed to depression or insanity. Instead, they saw their performances as celebratory affirmations of gay life.

Queer theater was simply one aspect of the rich variety of dramatic forms being created by theaters in New York City and across the United States. In California the San Francisco Mime Troupe and the Chicano-based El Teatro Campesino were strong exponents of outdoor, street-based political theater, employing the traditions of commedia dell'arte, Mexican *carpa* (tent) theater, and the theories of Bertolt Brecht, to create dramas actively engaged in political issues and causes; for example, with those of the United Farmworkers Union, with which El Teatro Campesino was associated. In California, New York, and other states across the country, alternative theater was defined more by groups sharing a common technique than by individual playwrights working within a traditional theater-making structure. In New York City, for example, the Pageant Players, the Open Theater, the Performance Group, the Ridiculous Theater, the Bridge Collective, the Bread and Puppet Theater, and the Living Theater (which by now was the matriarch of American alternative theater) all created their own particular styles of dramatic creation, which then persisted in their various offshoots in the years to come.

The alternative theater movement of the 1970s produced its own complicated connections to existing American drama. The Living Theater's espousal of a politically committed American theater finally found good company in the general sense of activist art which characterized the moment, as if a younger generation had caught up to Malina's and Beck's Piscatorian idealism. A marker of the dynamics of the decade is that Herbert Blau – who as a founder of the Actor's Workshop in San Francisco and then the director of the Repertory Theater of Lincoln Center had already made a substantial contribution to America's regional and off-Broadway theater movements in the sixties – created his own radical theater group in the seventies, Kraken, to perform dramas which pushed theatrical boundaries even further than he had previously done.

The Black Theater Movement

Connected to both the regional and alternative American theater movements of the sixties and seventies was a nationwide black theater movement; a reflection of the civil rights movement's development from a focus on integration to the more radical desire for black political and economic power, and that desire's emergence as a cultural force in what has come to be known as the Black Arts Movement. In terms of drama and its functions, the black theater movement was a response to both the politics and dramatic form of Lorraine Hansberry's *Raisin in the Sun*. Some of the new generation of black dramatists questioned the whole goal of Broadway success, while others sought to build on Hansberry's achievement. The playwrights and theater groups of the movement burst forth in a variety of directions and forms, from the exhortations of Amiri Baraka's aggressively confrontational plays (*Dutchman*, 1964, and *Slaveship*, 1966), and Barbara Ann Teer's reinvented rituals for her National Black Theater, to the almost neoclassic, Chekhovian nuances and cadences of August Wilson's historical plays about African American life in Pittsburgh

(*Ma Rainey's Black Bottom*, 1984, and *Fences*, 1985, for example), which found regular success on the Broadway stage. In other words, like the experience of the regional and off-Broadway theater movements, the success of the black theater movement's desire to create new American dramas had a double effect: while it cultivated new dramatic themes and forms, and prized a decentralized cultural system outside of the Broadway mainstream, the success of some of its practitioners (August Wilson and Anna Deavere Smith, for example) lead right back to Broadway, where the new dramas enriched and enlivened (once more) that traditional theater scene.

Amiri Baraka, the best-known playwright of the early Black Arts Movement, became active in the 1960s as a Beat poet in the company of Allen Ginsberg, Jack Kerouac, and other writers and jazz musicians. Baraka (then known as LeRoi Jones) and Adrienne Kennedy took a playwriting workshop with Edward Albee in 1964, the same year Baraka's *Dutchman* opened off-Broadway at the Cherry Lane Theater. *Dutchman* was markedly different from *A Raisin in the Sun* (which had appeared only five years earlier on Broadway) because of its unapologetic denunciation of racism and its articulation of African American anger, in the subway confrontation between a seductive white woman, Lula, and her victim, a middle-class black man, Clay, whose normally repressed rage is ultimately pushed to the point of explosion by Lula's aggressive sexual and verbal attacks. Near the play's climax Clay finally bursts out:

CLAY: . . . You great liberated whore! You fuck some black man, and right away you're an expert on black people. What a lotta shit that is. The only thing you know is that you come if he bangs you hard enough. And that's all. The belly rub? You wanted to do the belly rub? Shit, you don't even know how. You don't know how. That ol' dipty-dip shit you do, rolling your ass like an elephant. That's not my kind of belly rub. Belly rub is not Queens. Belly rub is dark places, with big hats and overcoats held up with one arm. Belly rub hates you. Old bald-headed four-eyed ofays popping their fingers . . . and don't know yet what they're doing. They say, "I love Bessie Smith." And don't even understand that Bessie Smith is saying, "Kiss my ass, kiss my black unruly ass." (Baraka: 557–8)

Baraka's articulation of African American rage, here mixed together with the intense imagery of sexual desire and frustration, complicated by the culturally explosive pairing of a black man and a white woman, was a kind of cultural shock, even on the off-Broadway stage. Baraka's angry Clay (whom the evil Lula murders at the close of the play) was quite different from Hansberry's quietly dignified Walter Lee Younger, and represented a new kind of African American dramatic voice for the sixties. Despite (or because of) its evocation of a raw African American rage, and its button-pushing use of the charged theme of interracial sex, *Dutchman* struck a sympathetic chord with off-Broadway audiences, winning the off-Broadway "Obie" award in 1964 for best play. Two other Baraka plays opened in New York City that same year, establishing a new moment in African American postwar drama, with Baraka as its chief spokesman.

But Baraka quickly forsook the theaters of off-Broadway to create the Black Arts Repertory Theater and School in Harlem, and later the Spirit House collective in Newark, both conscious efforts to make theater quite outside traditional venues. This was the same impetus that impelled dancer and actress Barbara Ann Teer to create her National Black Theater in Harlem in 1968. Teer's "Sunday Afternoon Blackenings and Ritualistic Revivals," presented at theaters and universities in the United States, the Caribbean, and Nigeria, insofar as they attempted to create modern rites of functional value in societies bereft of ritual, were similar in form and intent to the ritual performance art and happenings of white artists in downtown New York, although Teer's consciously drew on specifically African roots.

Ed Bullins, like Amiri Baraka, wrote expressly political plays, and for a brief moment was connected with the radical Black Panther Party in Oakland, California. In 1967 Bullins worked with Robert Macbeth on the creation of the New Lafayette Theater in New York City, an ensemble in which, Bullins later wrote, "we committed ourselves to moving away from European references for our art and lives" (Bullins: 10). The plays Bullins wrote for the New Lafayette Theater included *Street Sounds* (performed at La MaMa in 1970), which, instead of a dialogic plot, presented a succession of monologues by 40 different characters on a Harlem street. Unlike, say, Lorraine Hansberry's intentional effort to present African American characters to a white audience, Bullins was not so interested in making things easy for an uninitiated public. "The reason that critics – Black/white/ American – cannot decipher many of the symbols of Black theater," Bullins wrote at the time, "is because the artists are consciously migrating to non-Western references," in order to revitalize "an innovative strain of Black Art" (Bullins: 8).

In the midst of these politically radical dramas by black male writers, Adrienne Kennedy was concurrently creating her own "innovative strain of Black Art" in off-Broadway plays such as *Funnyhouse of a Negro* (1964). But instead of straightforward explications of political or social situations, Kennedy wrote quite personal examinations of black identity in a race-conscious, white-dominated world. *Funnyhouse of a Negro* is a surreal, shifting drama about Sarah, a woman attempting to find her identity among an array of white and black characters, from Queen Victoria to Patrice Lumumba, which are all, ultimately, aspects or projections of Sarah's own psyche. Her Lumumba character, for example (called "Man"), speaks in the first person of a life quite similar to Kennedy's own experience:

> MAN: . . . My nigger father majored in social work, so did my mother. I am a student and have occasional work in libraries. But mostly I spend my vile days preoccupied with the placement and geometric position of words on paper. I write poetry filling white page after white page with imitations of Sitwell. It is my vile dream to live in rooms with European antiques and my statue of Queen Victoria, photographs of Roman ruins, wall of books, a piano and oriental carpets and to eat my meals on a white glass table. (Kennedy: 339)

It is easy to see how such drama would not be favorably received by critics interested in straightforward articulations of black political and social goals, and it wasn't. Kennedy's ambiguous attraction to the symbols of European culture, and the apparent confusion her character Sarah faced in her search for identity, were not at all the sureties of African American culture that the times appeared to favor, and consequently Kennedy's writing, in the sixties and seventies, was more respected as high modern culture than championed as popular political art.

While the black theater movement influenced playwrights such as August Wilson to create dramas in the realistic vein exemplified by Hansberry, it also inspired later playwrights to further develop new methods of writing African American theater works. Ntozake Shange, for example, wrote *For Colored Girls Who Have Considered Suicide/When the Rainbow Is Enuf* as a "choreopoem" combining dance, music, and a series of 20 poetic monologues (similar to Bullins's *Street Sounds*), in this case expressing the frustrations and small victories of seven young black women. Shange's play first appeared off-off-Broadway in 1975, moved to New York's Public Theater, and then finally played to great acclaim on Broadway the following year. A quite different alternative to traditional drama was developed by Anna Deavere Smith, who wrote and performed solo shows based on actual events, in which she would mimic all the characters involved, basing her words on interviews she had conducted with them. In *Fires in the Mirror* (1992), about riots in the mixed African American and Jewish neighborhood of Crown Heights in Brooklyn, and *Twilight: Los Angeles* (1993), a similar analysis of riots in Los Angeles, Smith created a kind of serial dialogue among the participants in these real events by juxtaposing her successive monologues. The technique, to be sure, had its precedents in earlier African American plays and in the ancient arts of storytelling, but was also a development of the growing tradition of performance art which had emerged from the sixties alternative theater to define a large percentage of off-off-Broadway performance of the eighties and nineties.

Postmodern Theater

By the mid-1970s, postwar American drama was being created in a wide array of forms in a wide array of fields. Off-Broadway theater, the regional theater movement, and alternative theater experiments had effectively widened the scope of American drama since the immediate postwar years when the Living Theater had stood out as a lone iconoclast. Broadway was still the glamorous center of American theater, but its most successful productions were musicals in the British operatic style of Andrew Lloyd Webber. The job of presenting "serious" drama was by and large left to off-Broadway theaters, many of them nonprofit organizations like Joseph Papp's Public Theater, which could develop new work in an environment temporarily separated from the immediate need for box-office success. Successful Papp productions, such as the musical *A Chorus Line*, which originated in the Public Theater in 1975 and became a long-running Broadway hit the same year, would then help maintain the reputation of their off-Broadway parent theater, as well as help pay for its new projects.

As the Vietnam War ended and the political intensity of American culture abated, theaters which in the sixties had channeled some of that energy into their work now searched for new inspirations and subject matter. The alternative theaters began to evolve. The Performance Group, for example, had been led by director Richard Schechner in productions such as *Dionysus in 69* (1968), a reworking of Euripides' tragedy into a Vietnam-era actors' spectacle. In a brilliant bit of foresight, the group purchased an automobile garage in New York's SoHo district and turned it into their own flexible theater space. But by 1975, members of the group decided to continue working without Schechner, and renamed themselves the Wooster Group. With Elizabeth LeCompte as director, and actors Spalding Gray, Willem Dafoe, Peyton Smith, Kate Valk, and Ron Vawter, as well as designer Jim Clayburgh, the Wooster Group went on to create the most celebrated dramas of what was then being termed a "postmodern" era. Beginning with the trilogy *Three Places in Rhode Island* (1975–8), the group turned away from the earnest exploration of sixties social and political issues in order to pursue a formally spectacular theater of image, sound, and body, in which "texts," not play-scripts, were one element in an array of theatrical sign systems. In a program note the group explained:

> The Wooster Group has developed an idiosyncratic work process. "Source" texts are quoted, reworked and juxtaposed with fragments of popular, cultural and social history as well as with events and situations which emerge from the personal or collective experience of Group members. These various elements are fused into a collage or score – the final text.
>
> The Group texts stand as an alternative theater language which redefines the traditional devices of story-line, character and theme. Each production reflects a continuing refinement of a nonlinear, abstract aesthetic which at once subverts and pays homage to modern theatrical "realism." (Wooster Group: n.p.)

In a fashion paralleling the concurrent developments in postmodern academic theory, as well as the collage and montage techniques of the classic European avant-garde, the Wooster Group created dramas in which stories, characters, and images overlapped and contradicted one another. *Route 1 & 9* (1981), for example, took parts of Thornton Wilder's 1938 classic *Our Town*; an educational movie about Wilder's play; a transcription of a routine by black comedian Pigmeat Markham; 1960s dance music; live phone calls to an actual fried chicken restaurant in Harlem; and the culturally charged American tradition of blackface performance to create a multi-leveled, often puzzling, but theatrically riveting spectacle about race and American culture. The Group's postmodern style rendered meaning ambiguous – quite a difference from the earnest sense-making of earlier alternative dramas in the sixties. This appealed especially to downtown audiences familiar with what was now the twentieth-century tradition of avant-garde drama, but was misunderstood by others, for example the New York State Council on the Arts, which cancelled some funding for the Wooster Group because it considered *Route 1 & 9* racist.

Playwright, director, and designer Richard Foreman also worked in an abstract, postmodern style, writing cryptic dialogic dramas for actors which took place in surrealistically odd environments: rooms filled with meticulous assemblages of odd everyday objects. Foreman's plays, in which words hardly ever made consistent logical sense, had above all much in common with Gertrude Stein's similarly abstract word play, and his reticence in expressing meaning straightforwardly through speech and story line matched the similar methods of the Wooster Group and Robert Wilson. For example, in a 1991 play, *Eddie Goes to Poetry City: II*, the perplexed title character hears an offstage voice (similar to those created by Adrienne Kennedy, in fact) comment on his quest for identity:

> SOFT VOICE: He looks into a mirror, tries to comb his hair, but it isn't there. So much for the surface of things, he says, but I don't cry, I just try to balance good on my own side of a spinning what-d-ya-call-it? And nobody could tell if I fell off the bed because it happened so fast I came in a seeming wink of the eye but who winked? Nobody I know. But then, I don't know everybody. I'm too much into milk, chocolate, and sometimes, maybe, a slice of apple pie. Who'll join me? (Foreman: 49)

Foreman's sometimes teasing dance of meaning wants to encourage audience speculation, or even philosophizing, while at the same time steadfastly avoiding the traditional power of drama to tell a story through the creation of consistent, understandable plot.

Spalding Gray, a veteran of Schechner's Performance Group and its successor Wooster Group, pioneered the late-century American genre of solo performance in a series of autobiographical "epic monologues," as James Leverett termed them, which explored Gray's psyche and his personal experiences. Gray's particularly engaging storytelling style made his introspective monologues a kind of therapy, not only for Gray, but also for his similarly introspective, post-sixties, middle-class audiences. Solo performance emerged at the end of the century as yet another new, nondramatic form of playwriting, which combined the old arts of rhetoric, public speaking, and stand-up comedy with the creative point of view associated with performance art. Eric Bogosian, Anna Deavere Smith, Holly Hughes, Karen Finley, Paul Zaloom, Roger

Guenver Smith, Danny Hoch, and many others developed the solo performance form into a persistent late-century dramatic genre, in new alternative venues such as P.S. (for "Performance Space") 122, The Kitchen, and Dixon Place. Bogosian, the two Smiths, Zaloom, and Hoch created fictitious characters they could perform onstage, while Hughes, Finley, and Gray used the form to present theatricalized versions of their own personae, often with explicit details of their sexual lives.

But traditional drama was not at all neglected by late-century writers. In addition to August Wilson's Pittsburgh cycle of black family dramas, playwright David Mamet wrote starkly realistic dramas about contemporary American life which willfully rejected most of the techniques developed by the alternative theaters from the sixties on. Mamet's plays, such as *Speed the Plow* (1988) and *Oleanna* (1992), are tightly written confrontations, of usually no more than a handful of characters, in which the apparent meaning of the characters' lines generally hides some complex scheming or trickery. Mamet, in a real sense, returns to the American family drama of Miller and Williams (like Sam Shepard), but without a sense of trust or confidence in even the ideal of American home life which propelled *Death of a Salesman* or *The Glass Menagerie*. In *Speed the Plow* a veteran movie-producer's apparently innocent secretary turns out to be more of a ruthless Hollywood deal-maker than he is, and in *Oleanna* an apparently innocent college girl turns into a remorseless, evil feminist who ruins a rumpled college professor's life by falsely charging him with sexual harassment. In spite of the persistent skepticism and recurrent misogyny in his work, one of Mamet's great gifts is his ear for American speech, and especially its disjointed rhythms, for example in this passage from *Speed the Plow*, in which Gould, the producer, is visited by his friend Fox:

> FOX: I have to talk to you.
> GOULD: Chuck, Chuck, Chuck, *Charles*: you get too old, too busy to have "fun" this business; to have "fun," then what are you . . . ?
> FOX: . . . Bob . . .
> GOULD: What are you?
> FOX: What am I . . . ?
> GOULD: Yes.
> FOX: What am I when?
> GOULD: What are you, I was saying, if you're just a slave to commerce?
> FOX: If I'm just a slave to commerce?
> GOULD: Yes.

FOX: I'm nothing.
GOULD: No.
FOX: You're absolutely right. (Mamet: 4)

Unlike the measured sentences of Miller, or Williams, which in contrast seem almost artificially eloquent, Mamet's percussive dialogue sets up a colorful field of sound, which we recognize as artifice in part because we suspect its speakers may not be at all sincere. And that, perhaps, is how Mamet's otherwise traditional playwriting can be understood in relation to other postmodern dramatic works: the love of language – particularly *American* language – is countered by a post-sixties mistrust of its meanings and its speakers.

Conclusion

By the end of the twentieth century, the relatively new traditions of American drama existed in a very different cultural world than that which existed at the close of World War II. Broadway was still the apparent center of American theater, but it was a Broadway redefined as a kind of theatrical theme park, revitalized with public and private redevelopment funds, but presenting mostly musical spectaculars, such as the Walt Disney Corporation's *The Lion King,* directed by puppeteer Julie Taymor. Taymor herself had, in the seventies, been a member of Herbert Blau's Kraken theater group and briefly worked with alternative puppeteer Peter Schumann, and clearly brought to her Broadway production the avant-garde's interest in applying all forms of old, new, Western, and Eastern theatrical forms to new dramatic work. There were serious dramas in Broadway theaters, but often tried-and-true plays, such as a revival of Sam Shepard's *True West.* The Broadway scene was able to accept the Wooster Group's version of Eugene O'Neill's expressionist play *The Emperor Jones* for a brief run in a production heavily influenced, in true postmodernist fashion, by Japanese kabuki theater. Meanwhile, scores of new dramas reflecting the multiple streams of the past fifty years' development of American theater opened and closed in off-Broadway and off-off-Broadway theaters, competing not only with film and television, but with home video rentals and the increasingly omnipresent internet which linked millions of home computers: all reasons for American audiences to stay home instead of journeying to a theater. Which is to say that, in spite of the increasing overload of spectacle sensations offering themselves to American audiences, live dramas still somehow seem to find an audience.

References and further reading

Banes, Sally. *Greenwich Village 1963: Avant-Garde Performance and the Effervescent Body*. Durham, NC: Duke University Press, 1993.

Baraka, Amiri. *Dutchman*. In *Modern Drama: Plays/Criticism/Theory*. Ed. William Worthen. Fort Worth: Harcourt Brace College, 1995. 551–8.

Blum, Daniel. *A Pictorial History of the American Theatre*. Philadelphia: Chilton, 1960.

Brecht, Bertolt. "Prologue to the American production [of *Life of Galileo*]." In *Collected Plays Volume 5*. Eds Ralph Manheim and John Willett. New York: Vintage, 1972. 226.

Brecht, Stefan. *Queer Theatre*. Frankfurt: Suhrkamp, 1978.

Brecht, Stefan. *The Theatre of Visions: Robert Wilson*. Frankfurt: Suhrkamp, 1978.

Brecht, Stefan. *Peter Schumann's Bread and Puppet Theatre*. 2 vols. London: Methuen, 1988.

Bullins, Ed. "Black Theater: The '70's – Evolutionary Changes." In *The Theme is Blackness: "The Corner" and Other Plays*. New York: William Morrow, 1973. 3–15.

Esslin, Martin. *The Theatre of the Absurd*. New York: Anchor Books, 1961.

Foreman, Richard. *Eddy Goes to Poetry City: II*. In *My Head was a Sledgehammer: Six Plays*. Woodstock: Overlook Press, 1995. 45–103.

Fornes, Maria Irene. *The Conduct of Life*. In *Modern Drama: Plays/Criticism/Theory*. Ed. William Worthen. Fort Worth: Harcourt Brace College, 1995. 914–22.

Goldberg, RoseLee. *Performance Art: From Futurism to the Present*. New York: Harry N. Abrams, 1988.

Hansberry, Lorraine. *A Raisin in the Sun*. In *Black Theatre U.S.A. Vol. 2*. Eds James V. Hatch and Ted Shine. New York: Free Press, 1996. 104–46.

Kennedy, Adrienne. *Funnyhouse of a Negro*. In *Black Theatre U.S.A. Vol. 2*. Eds James V. Hatch and Ted Shine. New York: Free Press, 1996. 333–43.

Knowles, Christopher. "Witness: I Feel the Earth Move." In *Einstein on the Beach: An Opera in Four Acts*. Philip Glass and Robert Wilson. New York: Dunvagen Music, 1992. 21–2.

Lyons, James K. *Bertolt Brecht in America*. Princeton, NJ: Princeton University Press, 1980.

Malina, Judith. "The Piscator Notebook." Unpublished ms, 1945.

Mamet, David. *Speed the Plow*. New York: Grove Press, 1987.

Miller, Arthur. *Death of a Salesman*. In *New Voices in the American Theater*. New York: Modern Library, 1955. 111–226.

Miller, Arthur. "*Death of a Salesman*." In *Playwrights on Playwriting*. Ed. Toby Cole. New York: Hill and Wang, 1960. 261–76.

Robinson, Marc. *The Other American Drama*. Cambridge: Cambridge University Press, 1994.

Sainer, Arthur. *The New Radical Theatre Notebook*. New York: Applause, 1997.

Shepard, Sam. *The Rock Garden*. Scripts 1.3 (January 1972): 24–30.

Smith, Michael. "Introduction." In *Eight Plays from Off-Off Broadway*. Eds Nick Orzel and Michael Smith. New York: Bobbs-Merrill, 1966. 1–16.

Stein, Gertrude. *Doctor Faustus Lights the Lights*. In *Selected Operas and Plays of Gertude Stein*. Ed. John Malcom Brinnen. Pittsburgh: University of Pittsburgh Press, 1970. 203–38.

Stein, Gertrude. *The Letters of Gertrude Stein and Thornton Wilder*. Eds Edward M. Burns and Ulla E. Dydo. New Haven, CT: Yale University Press, 1996.

Williams, Tennessee. "Production Notes." In *Modern Drama: Plays/Criticism/Theory*. Ed. William Worthen. Fort Worth: Harcourt Brace College, 1995. 37.

Wilson, Lanford. *The Madness of Lady Bright*. In *Eight Plays from Off-Off Broadway*. Eds Nick Orzel and Michael Smith. New York: Bobbs-Merrill, 1966. 57–92.

Wooster Group, The. Program for *The Road to Immortality, Part One (Route 1 & 9)*. New York: The Kitchen, 1986.

Worthen, William, ed. *Modern Drama: Plays/Criticism/Theory*. Fort Worth: Harcourt Brace College, 1995.

Zeigler, Joseph Wesley. *Regional Theatre: The Revolutionary Stage*. Minneapolis: University of Minnesota Press, 1973.

Chapter 6

Hollywood Dreaming: Postwar American Film

Leonard Quart and Albert Auster

In 1998, the American Film Institute issued its highly controversial list of the 100 greatest American films. These films were chosen not so much for the box-office receipts they garnered as for their aesthetic quality, intellectual content, and influence on audiences and film-makers. Of the top four films, three were produced before 1945. They included, as one might expect from its perennial inclusion on every-one's list of the greatest films of all time, Orson Welles's structurally complex and technically brilliant *Citizen Kane* (1941) at number one, Hollywood's romantic classic *Casablanca* (1942) at number two, and that grandiose epic of the Civil War and Reconstruction, *Gone With the Wind* (1939), at number four. What might have come as a bit of a surprise was that the third-ranked film, and the only one produced after 1945, was Francis Ford Coppola's *The Godfather* (1972) (American Film Institute).

What made *The Godfather*'s inclusion among the top four films sig-nificant was how different in tone and content it was from the films that preceded and succeeded it on the all-time greatest list. *Citizen Kane*, *Casablanca*, and *Gone With the Wind*, despite their differences in time period, characters, and themes, were all produced during the heyday of the old studio system (1920–60), and despite their dark moments, usually left one, at their conclusion, with some bit of hope in the human condition and the possibility of a happy life. Thus, as Rick says to the police chief Louis at the end of *Casablanca*, "This could be the start of a beautiful friendship," and even Kane's tragic ending seems to be mitigated by the knowledge that if he hadn't been separated from his mother and that sled his life might have turned out quite differently. In contrast, Coppola's brilliant final shot of the door closing on Michael Corleone (Al Pacino), as he accepts homage as the new Don Corleone, suggests that his ascent to power means that he is irrevocably separated from his wife, children, and personal dreams. It's a moment that combines a feeling of murderous triumph with a chilling sense of horror and loss.

It is this final moment in *The Godfather* that symbolically distinguishes some of the most important films made in the post-World War II era from the previous decades; and more frequently than not these later films were more likely to end in total despair, pessimism, and tragedy than their predecessors. Indeed, *The Godfather* and its sequel *The Godfather Part II* (1974) were nothing less than an epic of the disintegration of the American dream (American Film Institute). They were also films drenched in blood, and neither the depiction of strong family roots nor the old Don's (Marlon Brando) rough natural sense of justice could cancel out the image of a family whose business and success was totally involved in intimidation, violence, and murder.

Of course, *Godfather II* did not pretend to provide a sophisticated left critique of capitalism and its ethos. However, operating within the genre conventions, it was able to convey a great deal of the perniciousness of the American success ethic. The film is also an epic of dissolution, conveying how Americanization and mobility turned the murderous passion and tribal loyalty of the immigrant Mafia into an impersonal, rootless corporate nightmare. Implicit in the film was the feeling that the nightmare extended far beyond the parochial confines of the Mafia into the heart of American history and society itself.

This was not always the case in American film of the postwar era. Looking back, the period immediately after the war found an America at the height of its political, military, and economic power. With an army that had recently participated in the destruction of the Axis alliance of Germany, Italy, and Japan, the United States had emerged from the war physically and economically unscathed, and was in sole possession of the ultimate weapon, the atomic bomb. In addition, the United States produced one half of the world's manufactures, 57 percent of its steel, 43 percent of its electricity, and 62 percent of its oil. It owned three quarters of the world's automobiles, and as a portent of potential future ascendancy, a majority of the Nobel prize-winners in the natural sciences were American (Hodgson: 19).

It was this hegemony that has caused historians like James Patterson to call his volume of the Oxford History of the United States, which deals with the period from 1945 to 1974, *Grand Expectations*, or for Marxist historian Eric Hobsbawm to refer to the same period in his magisterial *The Age of Extremes* as a "Golden Age." It was coincidentally also the heyday of the Hollywood studio system, with eight major studios producing 99 percent of all films screened in North America and almost 60 percent of films shown in Europe. In addition, there were almost 90 million tickets sold each week in the US. Indeed the film industry was the sixth most important industry in the United States in 1945 (Littman: 13–19). Thus, with a certain degree of justice, one of the major film hits of the era could be titled *The Best Years of Our Lives* (1947).

Actually, William Wyler's *The Best Years of Our Lives* swept the Academy Awards, was the top box-office attraction of 1947, and garnered widespread critical praise. James Agee, for one, wrote that it was "one of the few American studio movies in years that seem to be profoundly pleasing, moving and encouraging" (Agee: 173). The Marxist writer-director Abraham Polonsky, soon to be blacklisted, wrote "the era of human character which *The Best Years* makes available to its audience is a landmark in the fog of escapism, meretricious violence, and the gimmick plot attitude of the usual movie" (Polonsky: 191–2).

Praise catapulted the film into the realm of the instant masterpiece, although that judgment was probably inflated, for the film tended to take few intellectual risks and could be at times sentimental. *The Best Years* still contained more truth and insight about the readjustment of veterans, including an amputee (played by a nonprofessional actor), to peacetime than any other forties film. At the same time, it was a stately, carefully balanced, and shrewdly manipulated tribute to the American way of life. It paid homage to American institutions like the small town/city and the family, and to Hollywood's belief in the redemptive power of love. However, the film tended to obfuscate social issues, dismissing class as a factor in American life by creating a world where the comradeship of veterans, who run the gamut from bank officials to soda jerks, could unselfconsciously carry over into civilian life without an awkward moment.

Despite its limitations, *The Best Years'* emotionally moving scenes, its formal luminosity (its eloquent use of deep focus, flowing camera movements, and stirring reaction shots), and its well-defined, nuanced characters did provide a genuine glimpse into the nature of postwar American life. Although it ultimately allowed each of its characters a graceful, albeit predictable, re-entry into postwar American society, it suggested there were genuinely real and traumatic problems inherent in returning from the war. There were also hints that underneath the film's essentially optimistic surface there existed some feelings of unease about America's future.

Those doubts were exacerbated and became explicit in subsequent years as Cold War tensions between the United States and the Soviet Union intensified, and as a domestic "red scare" took hold in US society. Though the country remained essentially prosperous, and, except for the brief period of the Korean War (1950–3), at peace, that undercurrent of anxiety that was briefly glimpsed in *The Best Years* became more and more manifest.

Although the studios churned out their usual quota of genre films, such as musicals, comedies, and thrillers, many of the best of them took on a somber, darker quality. For example, the western, which was a Hollywood staple and generally accounted for the lion's share of films produced each year from 1939 onward, tended toward a degree of pessimism that was generally at odds with its morally clear, heroic, generally optimistic tradition. Nowhere does one find this better represented than in the postwar work of John Ford, generally acknowledged in all quarters to be one of the film industry's unique geniuses. Ford's postwar work consisted of films that evoked a sense that the powerful myth of the West, with its combination of heroism and self-sacrifice (for example, *Fort Apache*, 1948), was losing its hold on the American imagination and character. In the fifties his work took on an even more pessimistic tone, culminating, as Stuart Byron noted, in what some considered Ford's most brilliant and influential film, *The Searchers* (1956) (Byron: 45–8).

The Searchers' narrative revolves around an embittered ex-Confederate soldier named Ethan Edwards (John Wayne), who searches for years to find his young niece, Debbie (Natalie Wood), who was kidnapped by the Comanches after her family was massacred. This simple plot became not only the basis for a story of heroic rescue, it also provided Ford the means of suggesting a hidden dimension of the Old West, of the Westerners', and by implication the American, obsession with race (though his Indian characters remained, for the most part, murderous savages or comic foils) (Byron: 45–8). Indeed as the years go by and Debbie's captivity lengthens, Ethan's goal becomes not so much to save her from her Indian captors as to kill her because she has become tainted in his eyes by having become one of them, including having had sexual relations with an Indian. Only Ethan's deepening, affectionate relationship with his surrogate son and Debbie's adopted brother, Martin Pauley (Jeffrey Hunter), who is one-quarter Indian, mitigates that rage, and ultimately results in Ethan returning Debbie to the safety of a white family and community, that garden in the wilderness for Ford.

Nonetheless, nothing is quite the same in this Ford western. Everything has become grimmer and darker. The landscape of Monument Valley, as always brilliantly framed, awe-inspiring, and transcendent in its desolate beauty, here seems threatening. The cavalry – in previous Ford films the embodiment of virtue, courage, and self-sacrifice – seem ineffectual and absurd. And finally, the hero, Ethan, is a sullen, violent man consumed by murderous rage, and doomed to wander. Ford's heroes usually reconcile their individuality with a sense of community, but not in *The Searchers*. There just is no community that an Ethan can ever be at home in, and his wandering is not an affirmation of freedom but the fate of a solitary man eternally condemned to live outside the domestic hearth.

To some degree Ford's gloomier view of the world was aroused by the fact that stable landmarks of the industry that had nurtured and supported his genius were fast receding. Buffeted by landmark Supreme Court cases that separated the studios from their theaters, and undermined by the new medium of television, which cut their audience in half and forced them to function in a climate of suspicion and paranoia fostered by an anti-communist blacklist, the old studio system passed away. It was to be succeeded by a new studio system shorn of all contract players, stars, directors, writers, etc., and solely focused on the financing and marketing of films. This latter narrowing of function undoubtedly arose from their losing their independence as corporations and becoming the moviemaking units of giant media conglomerates, some of which weren't even American owned (such as Columbia Pictures, which was taken over by the Japanese electronic giant Sony).

Though the end of the old studio system may have been a disaster for those like Ford, whose talent grew and was nurtured within its confines, to others its dissolution, along with the old censorship code (which had fostered all sorts of unrealistic ideas and euphemisms), was truly liberating. Now freed to explore sex and sexuality in all its manifold full-frontal nudity, and released from the necessities of "compensatory moral value," which required that no screen sin go unpunished, writers and directors could explore without hindrance the full range of the human condition.

Indeed this impulse, when added to the energy and radical spirit that emerged in the late sixties as a result of the counterculture and political movements such as the anti-war and civil rights movements, resulted in a renaissance in American filmmaking. So, Arthur Penn's *Bonnie and Clyde* (1967) harnessed the film techniques of the French "New Wave" to the older American genre of road films, such as Fritz Lang's *You Only Live Once* (1937) and Nicholas Ray's *They Drive By Night* (1949). This time-worn tale of two youthful outsiders who choose a life of crime held a powerful attraction for a 1960s audience who felt they were cut off from the channels of power and incapable of bringing about social and political change. In a similar fashion, *The Graduate* (1967), with its attack on the sterility of upper-middle-class American values, gave expression to the discontent and alienation of the young.

Unleashed from its traditional structure, the film industry began to take chances and reach out to relatively untried filmmakers such as Robert Altman, Martin Scorsese, Brian DePalma, Steven Spielberg, George Lucas, and Francis Ford Coppola. These "Easy Riders and Raging Bulls," as Peter Biskind referred to them, were distinguished by their awareness of film history, technical competence (sometimes gained from working on small-budget quickies or being trained in university film schools), and self-conscious and idiosyncratically personal visions. These directors also made films that veered from the formal stateliness and coherence – even, at moments, the sense of verisimilitude – of the classical narrative.

As evidenced by Coppola's *Godfather* saga, they were also unafraid to work at making ambitious, epic films that were critical of American culture and society. For example, Robert Altman's *Nashville* (1975) was an epic and ironic attempt to capture both middle American con-sciousness and the pernicious life energy of American popular culture. Indicative of its success in doing so is the comment of the *New York Times* columnist Tom Wicker, who called *Nashville* "a two and a half hour cascade of minutely detailed vulgarity, greed, deceit, cruelty, barely contained hysteria and the frantic lack of root and grace into which American life has been driven by its own heedless vitality" (quoted in Kass: 193).

In *Nashville* Altman interweaves 24 characters who are either particip-ants in or dream of entering the world of country and western music. Using an open-ended, improvisatory style, which centers on the actor, *Nashville* is built on seemingly disconnected moments, filled with dazzling aural effects and visual images, demanding close viewing from its audience to pick up the elusive detail in intricate frames packed with overlapping action. Altman evokes in the film a callous, grasping, violent world in which everyone either gropes for stardom or lives off the fantasies and myths popular culture creates. And his cool, ironic sensibility succeeds in transforming Nashville's country music industry into a metaphor for American life – a cacophonous din where everybody struggles for his or her own version of a gold record.

The new generation of directors reveling in their knowledge of film history also gave new spins to the old studio genres. Brian De Palma brought new energy to the Hitchcockian thriller in *Obsession* (1976) and Altman infused an alternative and socially critical vision into a number of genres, such as the western (for example, *McCabe and Mrs Miller*, 1971). But perhaps no older form from the halcyon studio days fit this mood of revisionism and angst better than Hollywood's film noir tradition. Already distinguished from the other genres of the previous era by its morally ambiguous heroes, seductively duplicitous heroines, and seedy and perverse minor characters, it offered a world enveloped in shadows that conveyed an eerie sense of menace or sometimes of entrapment in a corrupt prison. This type of filmmaking had been brought to America by refugees from World War II Europe like Fritz Lang, Billy Wilder, and Robert Siodmak, and seemed ready made for the new generation of directors.

Nowhere is this combination of the new mood of blackness and despair with the conventions of film noir better exhibited than in Roman Polanski's *Chinatown* (1974). Built on the hard-boiled detective narrative that was frequently used in film noir, *Chinatown* departs dramatically from both the themes and structures of the older genre and infuses it with an overt sense of tragedy and pessimism that could be hinted at but never fully realized in its older version. J. J. Gittes (Jack Nicholson), who is in the tradition of older detectives like Raymond Chandler's Marlowe and Dashiel Hammet's Sam Spade, but is distinguished from them by the fact that no form of sleazy case is beneath him (even divorce cases, which were anathema to the older detectives), becomes involved in a murder case that through labyrinthine twists and turns entangles him in a nightmare world of sexual and political corruption. Like his predecessors, Gittes finally unravels the truth. However, in their world, criminals were usually punished; here the most powerful villain, Noah Cross (John Huston), who had made a mistress of his daughter (Faye Dunaway) and intended to do the same with his granddaughter, and who through murder and corruption sought to control the whole Los Angeles water supply, is too powerful to be punished. Indeed all that Gittes is left with is the melancholy injunction and symbol of a world that cannot be altered or understood: "it's Chinatown." The depravity of thirties Los Angeles stands in for the moral confusion and bankruptcy of seventies America.

This anxious, pessimistic mood was heightened by the events of the mid-sixties and the early seventies, namely the Vietnam War and Watergate. The frustration that many Americans, particularly the young, felt about having any impact on American policies both at home and abroad was greatly exacerbated, as was their sense that the political system was tainted beyond all repair. Ironically, during the war, the film industry at least initially preferred to ignore it in favor of covert symbols such as the prevalence of screenplays involving deranged returned veterans, or if they dealt with it at all, it was in patriotic epics such as John Wayne's *Green Berets* (1968). However, once the war ended and some time passed, the film industry took on the war, and what emerged in grandly uneven films like *The Deerhunter* (1978) and *Apocalypse Now* (1979) was evidence of a mad, inchoate, futile war that was emotionally shattering and the cause of political rage and turmoil.

In no film was this mood better distilled than in Oliver Stone's Oscar-winning *Platoon* (1986). Stone was a Vietnam War veteran, whose film of remembrance and mourning had a cathartic effect for many Vietnam vets and non-vets alike. His Vietnam is a bleak, horrific world where the GIs face an almost-invisible, ubiquitous enemy. The film is most powerful when it uses minimal dialogue and telling close-ups to evoke with great immediacy the war's everydayness: the stifling discomfort of the jungle and bush, ants, heat, and mud; the fatigue of patrols; the murderous cacophony and chaos of night firefights; and the boredom and sense of release of base camp. Stone also understood, but never condoned, just how fear, exhaustion, and rage about the death of their fellow soldiers could undermine some of the GIs' sense of moral restraint and humanity and turn them into brutes who massacre civilians and torch villages. It's all seen through the eyes and voice-over narration of Chris Taylor (Charlie Sheen), an upper-middle-class Yale dropout and patriot who, like Stephen Crane's hero in *The Red Badge of Courage*, is initiated into manhood and personally transformed by the war. In the process Stone may not have captured the political and social meanings of the war, but the film echoed the dominant public feeling about Vietnam: that it was a self-destructive march into some kind of purgatory.

Platoon also marked, after years of avoidance, wavering, and regression, Hollywood's total acceptance of Vietnam as a serious subject for film. Stanley Kubrick's *Full Metal Jacket* (1987) had grander aspirations than *Platoon*, dealing less with the concrete reality of Vietnam than with the military as an institution that breeds killers, and projecting a vision of human nature as innately barbaric and corrupt. The vision of human beings as potential destroyers and lovers of death, coupled with an Olympian, coldly detached style, pervades almost all of Kubrick's work, notably *A Clockwork Orange* (1971), where a futuristic delinquent gang revels in orgies of destruction. The ultimate and most striking irony implicit in Kubrick's version of Vietnam is that the film's most vital figures are its most lethal and brutal. Although Kubrick may not endorse the world of his obscenity-spouting, bullying drill instructor, Sargeant Hartman (Lee Ermey), he clearly has sympathy for characters who are at home in a nihilistic world. For Kubrick it is the misanthropic soldiers, not the humane and sympathetic, who triumph amid war's barbarism.

Another irony, one that Kubrick couldn't have been even remotely aware of, was that just as he was presenting his Hobbesian view of the universe, the world was about to turn topsy-turvy. Indeed two years after the release of *Full Metal Jacket*, the Cold War, which had given rise to the tensions that resulted in a Vietnam, suddenly came to an end. On November 9, 1989, the Berlin Wall, which for decades had been the symbol of the murderous separation of East and West, democracy and communism, came tumbling down. Following the Wall's collapse, like a house of cards, Soviet hegemony over Eastern Europe ended, and within two years the world saw the splintering of the Soviet Union itself.

At the highest governmental levels, the end of communism was greeted with elation, albeit with a tinge of restraint; for the film industry the end of communism momentarily spelled uncertainty. Communism had provided decades' worth of villains to inspire dread, create conflict, and provide opportunities for heroic victories. The question loomed: what enemy was to replace them? Not missing a beat, however, Hollywood turned to a familiar fifties villainous holdover – aliens from outer space. In *Independence Day* (1996), gone were the messianic Giacometti-like aliens of Spielberg's *Close Encounters of a Third Kind* (1977) and his cuddly little *ET* (1982). Instead the earth was threatened by space meanies right out of *The War of the Worlds* (1953). These fiends from outer space had laid waste to most of New York City (including the Statue of Liberty and the Empire State Building), Washington DC, and LA. Everything looked bleak until a rainbow coalition that included an African American top-gun airforce pilot (Will Smith),

a Jewish computer nerd (Jeff Goldblum), and the Clintonian president of the United States (Bill Pullman) banded together to defeat their
monstrous intergalactic foe.

More significantly, an element of the triumphal tinged with nostalgia
began to turn up in American films. That triumphalism was best
expressed in Steven Spielberg's *Saving Private Ryan* (1998). Spielberg
was ideally suited for conveying the range and effects of heroic action.
By the time he began work on *Saving Private Ryan*, he had already
directed six of the top twenty box-office grossing films of all time.
Furthermore, ever since 1993 and his Academy Award-winning
Schindler's List, he had aspired to a seriousness of purpose and content
which was at the same time able to appeal to wide audiences. Spielberg
was also a master of film style (brilliant editing and control of pace)
and genre conventions (for example, adventure and science fiction),
who often brought fresh inventiveness and creativity to these techniques that left one with a feeling of exhilaration, as well as nostalgia
for those older forms of cinematic storytelling.

Spielberg's *Saving Private Ryan* strikes a patriotic note from the opening image of a giant American flag that fills the screen, with John
Williams's mournful musical score in the background. Then Spielberg's
camera follows an aged veteran and his family on his return to the
battlefields and cemeteries of Normandy, and through his memory
we experience the landing at Dog sector of frightened soldiers at
Omaha Beach on June 6, 1944. What follows is what military historian John Keegan in *The Face of Battle* has called "the most terrifying,
realistic thing ever done in the cinema" (quoted in Gussow: B9).

The first 25 minutes of the film evoke the Goyaesque horrors of
war, filling the screen with terrifying moments such as a wounded
soldier searching for his arm and a GI screaming for his mother as his
guts spill out onto the beach. In this sequence the soldiers are anonymous, and there are no false heroics as Spielberg indelibly captures the
image of war as abattoir.

Unfortunately the rest of the film hardly lives up to its virtuoso
opening, as it settles into a rather pedestrian war story, about a lone
patrol out on a dangerous mission. The patrol is an archetypal World
War II one that consists of, among others, a cynical wise guy from
Brooklyn, a Bible-quoting Southern sharpshooter, and a loyal, battle-
hardened sergeant. They are led by the vulnerable, wise Captain John
Miller (Tom Hanks), a small-town high school English teacher. He's
the kind of heroic everyman (out of Frank Capra) who just wants to

finish the job and go home to his wife. In this case the job is to find and bring to safety a Private Ryan (Matt Damon), whose four brothers had been killed during the invasion and elsewhere in the war.

In *Saving Private Ryan*, Spielberg, many of whose films in the nineties sought to bear witness to large themes such as American racism and the Holocaust (*Amistad, Schindler's List*), attempted to again bear witness, this time to the heroism of Americans who fought in World War II. *Saving Private Ryan* also allowed American audiences to revel in an historical moment when American military might and prowess was at its apogee. And it permitted Americans to savor a moment of triumph, something that eluded them as a result of the almost anti-climactic end of the Cold War. The generation that had weathered the Depression, fought against fascism in World War II, and endured the long "twilight struggle" (Reeves: 36) against communism now began to be referred to in nostalgic terms, as in TV anchorman Tom Brokaw's book *The Greatest Generation*. The suggestion was that our best days were behind us.

Others saw this period less in terms of nostalgia than as an era where America lost its innocence and the country fell from grace. Oliver Stone in his two presidential films, *JFK* (1991) and *Nixon* (1995), offered a serious inquiry into and even explanation for what had gone wrong with America since the beginnings of the Cold War. Stone's ambitious, brilliantly edited films (flashforwards, flashbacks, jump cuts, a mix of newsreels, still photos, etc.) touched a nerve, and even before their release journalists, politicians, and other assorted literati weighed in with denunciations and critiques of the films. Smug conservative critic George Will demonized *JFK* as an "act of execrable history and contemptible citizenship, by a man of technical skill, scant education, and negligible conscience" (quoted in Petras: 15). The Nixon family's comment on *Nixon* was the less eloquent but certainly more succinct "character assassination" (Weintraub: C18).

Stone was not without his defenders. In an article in the *Atlantic*, political and cultural polymath Garry Wills wrote that "great novels are being written with the camera – at least when Stone is behind the camera" (Wills: 96–101). Norman Mailer, no stranger to the pungent metaphor, said Stone "has the integrity of a brute" (quoted in Grimes: C15, 22), and in an especially insightful afterthought commented that *JFK* "should be seen not as history but myth, the story of a huge and hideous act in which the gods warred and a god fell" (Mailer: 124–9, 171).

What was missing in all the controversy over Stone's presidential films was any reference to connections between the two films beside the obvious historical links. Nevertheless, there were two essential links between the films. The first was that in an important sense both were mysteries, or more precisely one was a murder mystery (*JFK*) and the other was a moral mystery (*Nixon*). The second was that, taken together, they presented Oliver Stone's mythic interpretation of American history and politics since 1945.

JFK's status as a murder mystery is most clearly evoked by soft-spoken New Orleans DA Jim Garrison (Kevin Costner) in his summation to the jury (one that in actuality Garrison never delivered) in the Clay Shaw trial, in which he refers to the Kennedy assassination as "the murder at the heart of the American dream." The image, however, of DA Garrison heroically walking the mean streets of New Orleans in search of the Kennedy assassins is one that made critics of the film pause; especially when even die-hard conspiracy theorists considered Garrison's investigation and subsequent indictments "a grotesque misdirected shambles" (Summers: 11).

However, for Stone, Garrison's record as a thrice-elected New Orleans DA, his over 20 years' service in the military, and his later career as an appellate judge marked him as a patriot and an uncommon common man. Just as significant for Stone was the fact that Garrison was the only American law enforcement official ever to bring indictments in the Kennedy assassination. This allowed Stone to enter the surreal world of the Warren Commission report, giving him an opportunity to present a grand unified conspiracy theory of his own.

In Stone's version of the Garrison investigations, Garrison's persistence and unwavering courage and integrity bring him more and more into conflict with the dark side of American life, especially its incarnation in the military-industrial complex. At the very beginning, the film refers to this colossus in newsreel footage of President Eisenhower's 1961 farewell address warning of its power. Nonetheless, it isn't until Garrison's meeting with the shadowy former Black Ops agent, Colonel X (Donald Sutherland), that Garrison really begins to understand fully the forces he is confronting: a supposed cabal of high-ranking military men, Mafia Dons, oil millionaires, Cuban exile leaders, and CIA agents that Colonel X convinces him carried out a "coup d'état."

Using Colonel X as his Virgil, Dante's guide through hell in the Inferno, Stone also reveals the political subtext. According to Stone's dubious historical scenario, Kennedy was killed because he wanted to end the Cold War and begin withdrawing American troops from Vietnam – an assertion that obviously cannot be proven. So for Stone Kennedy's assassination not only resulted in the loss of a beloved prince, but embodied the end of American innocence and idealism.

The loss of idealism so central to *JFK* is also referred to time and again in *Nixon*. Idealism is of course the last thing one associates with Richard Nixon. Yet for Stone, Nixon is a complex figure, at once a gifted Machiavellian who had a great deal of political hubris, and a man who was equally paranoid, self-pitying, and guilt ridden. The mystery that Stone tried to solve in *Nixon* is the question of what the personal and moral sources of such a tragic and intricately self-destructive character were. In attempting to decipher that riddle Stone used visual references to *Citizen Kane* (for example, newsreels, oblique angles, vast dark rooms). His appropriation of this classic film as a central metaphor for understanding Nixon was logical given Welles's effort to penetrate the mysteries of Kane. Indeed this time instead of one "Rosebud" there is a host of possible rosebuds that offer clues to the enigma that was Richard Milhous Nixon.

The primary one is Nixon's mother Hannah (Mary Steenburgen), whom he described as a "saint" (Brodie: 76), but whose severity, self-righteous moralizing, and unintentional rejections would have eviscerated the soul of an even more self-confident child than little Richard Nixon. As a man, Nixon once referred to himself in a letter as "your good dog" (Brodie: 76). Stone also offers tantalizing clues such as the "four deaths" that Nixon refers to as stepping-stones to his presidency. These included most prominently the deaths of John and Robert Kennedy, and more personally the deaths of Nixon's two brothers (Arthur and Harold); the latter financially enabling him to attend law school and leaving him with a legacy of guilt.

Stone also allows us to ponder whether or not it could have been psychological and class resentment that motivated Nixon. As John Ehrlichman (J. T. Walsh) says to H. R. Haldeman (James Woods): "You've got people dying because he didn't make the varsity football team. You've got the constitution hanging by a thread because the old man went to Whittier and not Yale." Finally, there is double-dealing, hypocritical Henry Kissinger's (Paul Sorvino) portentous judgment: "Imagine, if this man had been loved."

Besides providing a somewhat facile psychological explanation for Nixon's political behavior, Stone also provides an intellectual-ideological rationale for some, albeit not all, of Nixon's political failings. By the time of *Nixon*, the cancer that Stone had diagnosed in *JFK* had evolved into an invincible, all-powerful government, an almost mythic creature that Stone refers to as the "beast" – a creature that no individual, no matter how powerful, can control.

The power of the beast, the hidden government that *Nixon* hints at, is the penultimate metaphor in Stone's conspiracy-driven vision of American politics in both *JFK* and *Nixon*. According to Stone, it is simply that had Kennedy lived he would have withdrawn from Vietnam and ended the Cold War. However, the threat of that caused such consternation in the lethal Leviathan/beast – the military-industrial–CIA–Mafia–Wall-Street complex – that they passed a death sentence on him. And in the wake of his death there occurred a period of political demoralization that culminated in the rise and tragic fall of Richard Nixon, with his combination of relentless political ambition, ruthless pragmatism, and self-destructive vindictiveness. Or as the anguished Nixon himself puts it one night as he passes before a portrait of Kennedy (whom he has been obsessed with) during the Watergate scandal: "When they see you, they see what they want to be. When they see me they see what they are."

This gap between the ideal and the real is nowhere better revealed than in the political films of the nineties. America in its fin de siècle is a long way from the simple optimism and idealism of Hollywood films like *Mr Smith Goes to Washington* (1939). The possibility that a Jefferson Smith (James Stewart) could take on political machines, lobbyists, corrupt Senators, and the media and would win, by the nineties, seemed absurd or a fantasy. The corporate interests were just too strong in nineties America for anything more ambitious than forcing them to make some slight changes in institutional behavior.

Seemingly, the only suitable stance with regard to politics for American films seemed to be either irony or satire. Therefore in the nineties the political films ranged from a roman à clef of President Bill Clinton's 1992 campaign, *Primary Colors* (1998), to the cynical imputation of war as a strategy to divert attention from White House scandals, *Wag the Dog* (1997), and a radical, hip-hop-inspired political farce, *Bulworth* (1998).

Based on political journalist Joe Klein's pseudonymous novel, *Primary Colors* went over much of the same ground that Chris Hegedus and D. A. Pennebaker's powerful documentary *The War Room* covered back in 1993, with two notable additions. The first was that the witty, incisive script was written by Elaine May and directed by Mike Nichols, who as a comedy team in the late fifties and early sixties built a reputation as brilliant satirists of contemporary manners and morals.

The other was that *Primary Colors* places Bill and Hillary Clinton, a.k.a. Jack and Susan Stanton (John Travolta, Emma Thompson), at the film's center.

Travolta is almost perfect as the Clinton double, Jack Stanton, the governor of a Southern state running for the presidency. His politically astute and seductive Stanton has the raspy accent, the body language, the empathetic handshake, the populist touch, and the gift for self-destruction that his real-life counterpart has. In a similar fashion, Thompson captures Hillary's seriousness, efficiency, aggressiveness, and willingness to turn a blind eye to her husband's indiscretions. They operate with a single will when it comes to electing Jack Stanton president. It's that overarching ambition and Stanton's lack of self-discipline that touch and sometimes destroy the people around them.

Primary Colors may not have the psychological complexity of an *All the King's Men* (1949) (Robert Rossen's film about Huey Long), but it is a lively, often wittily incisive portrait of contemporary American politics. In contrast, *Wag the Dog* moves into blackly comic Strangelove territory. Its premise is that a sex scandal in the midst of a presidential campaign sends all the president's men and women scurrying to provide damage control. They come up with a sardonic, self-assured spin-meister, Conrad Brean (Robert De Niro), who decides to stage a war to divert attention from the president's problems. To aid him he reaches out to the archetypal, narcissistic Hollywood producer, Stanley Motss (Dustin Hoffman), because, as Brean says, "War is show business."

Wag the Dog provides a clear-eyed view of spin control, focusing on Hollywood's gift for manipulating the popular imagination and the public's willingness to be seduced. It was also the basis for a comparable use of spin as an attack weapon. During the Clinton impeachment process, when the president ordered the bombing of Iraq for defying the UN and failing to disarm, a number of congressional Republicans ignored plausible justifications for the bombing and simply denounced the administration for using a "wag the dog" strategy.

If *Wag the Dog* can be viewed as a synonym for the uses of spin, Warren Beatty's political farce *Bulworth* was a model for Hollywood-style radicalism. The disillusioned and suicidal J. Billington Bulworth (Warren Beatty) is the symbol of the sixties left liberal who now makes platitudinous speeches that attack "welfare cheats" and do obeisance to "family values." In despair, Bulworth takes out a 10-million-dollar life insurance policy, and then arranges for a hit-man to kill him.

Freed from the necessity of political caution, Bulworth attacks the Democratic Party's most loyal constituencies, telling Hollywood Jews "it's funny how lousy your stuff is, I guess the money turns everything to crap." And after a night at a black after-hours club, dancing, listening to rap music, snorting cocaine, and becoming infatuated with a beautiful black hit-woman, Bulworth is transformed into a comic version of Norman Mailer's "white negro" hipster, using hip-hop rhythms and rhymes to attack corporate dominance of politics and even advocating socialism.

Of course, Bulworth's suddenly becoming a scourge of mainstream politics turns him into a popular hero and, echoing the sixties association of truth-telling with martyrdom, an assassination victim. Beatty's homily – that a popular politician speaks truth to power at his or her peril – is undeniable. What is dubious about the film is the sentimental thesis that the only source of authenticity, vitality, and salvation in America lies within the black inner-city ethos, since every other stratum and group is tarnished by an insidious, avaricious money culture.

Given Hollywood's usual bland political perspective, a film like *Bulworth* that attacks capitalism can be seen, by comparison, as an ambitious, politically radical work. However, its critique of American society tends to degenerate into ultra-left sixties romanticism and nostalgic calls to action from a homeless Rastaman (the Marxist and black nationalist writer Amiri Baraka), "Don't be a ghost! You got to be a spirit."

It goes without saying that the views of American politics in nineties films are very different from the sublimely decent Jefferson Smith's patriotic appeal to American democracy and small-town virtues in Capra's film. The perspective of a film like *Wag the Dog* on the American political system epitomizes, as much as any other film genre, the change in the nature of American films during the last three decades of the twentieth century. The old landmarks, institutional and moral, that had made the film industry such a potent source of dreams, values, and behaviors in the period before World War II no longer carry much weight, and there are no longer constraints (with the powerful exception of commercial ones) about what can be depicted and said.

In the place of a Capra, who by 1946, in his Christmas classic *It's a Wonderful Life*, needs the intervention of an angel to achieve a happy ending, or of a generally optimistic film like *The Best Years of Our Lives*, there have been a few exceptional films that are genuinely critical of American society or that project a profoundly dark view of the human condition, like Coppola's *Godfather* films or Scorsese's gloriously hallucinatory view of New York in *Taxi Driver* (1976).

Scorsese's vision of the nightmare city is more psychological and aesthetic than political and social. *Taxi Driver*'s complex central figure, Travis Bickel (Robert De Niro), is an alienated cab driver, who drives all night through streets filled with junkies, pimps, and 12-year-old hookers. He is a man "who carries bad ideas in his head," and with an arsenal of weapons wants to clean the "open sewer" of its scum. The film is neither an endorsement of vigilante justice nor a social critic's angry, despairing portrait of the squalor and destructiveness of urban life. Scorsese's interest is more in the dark ambience of film noir, and in projecting his own fantasies, demons, and view of the world where tormented men strive for some form of personal redemption.

However, for every Scorsese film, in which violence is an integral part of the director's and his characters' vision of the world, there are innumerable other works that are just gratuitous exercises in pop nihilism. In these films characters are killed with little sense of reality or narrative logic, as if they are human objects being blown away or drivers in demolition derbies where mayhem is the norm. In fact, many of these works seem to have merely inverted Hollywood's notion of closure, and substituted the bloody, murderous climax for the happy ending.

During the last few decades Hollywood has permitted much greater freedom of subject matter, not only in the treatment of sex and violence, but even in its depiction of race. (There were no Spike Lees or John Singletons regularly making films until the late eighties.) Today's Hollywood executives are clearly more liberal and sophisticated than the old moguls. However, though a belief in good's inevitable victory over evil, and doing obeisance to the old certainties about love, marriage, family, and nation, no longer hold in contemporary Hollywood, most of the films produced remain impersonal, star-driven, high-concept works that are aimed at reaching a teenage audience.

Even the vaunted independent film industry, where such directors as John Sayles, Charles Burnett, Hal Hartley, and Nancy Savoca made films totally free of Hollywood formulae, has begun to behave not much differently than the studios. The independents' new-found success was achieved as much by deal-making, media manipulation, or playing hardball as by talent. The independents' greatest success took place at the 1998 Oscars where Miramax's (the most powerful and shrewdly market-oriented of the independent studios) stylish period piece, *Shakespeare in Love*, won for best picture over *Saving Private Ryan*. There are obviously still many independent directors that see film as an expression of a personal style and vision, but there are probably just as many who have less interest in conveying something they can't say within the system than in using their films as a path to the fame and the wealth that can flow from remaining in the Hollywood mainstream.

Hollywood may crack a bit, but it doesn't crumble. It may substitute seductive, evil characters like Hannibal Lecter to build films around for sweet, virtuous ones like *It's a Wonderful Life*'s George Bailey, and project a much darker and more pessimistic vision of human nature and everyday life than the films of the forties ever did. Also, the structure of the movie industry is now much looser and more decentralized. Still, there isn't much difference between the recent sandals-and-toga hit *Gladiator* (except for more elaborate special effects) and the *Ben-Hur*s and *The Robe*s of the fifties. It's Stephen Spielberg, Ridley Scott, and George Lucas, all talented commercial directors, who dominate the industry, not great American auteurs like Robert Altman and Martin Scorsese. Some of the details may change, but Hollywood's primary goal is still to make films that maximize profits by being morally and intellectually unambiguous, easily accessible, predictably linear, star-centered (for example, Tom Hanks), and tending to tie up all the loose ends at the film's conclusion. For all the changes, Hollywood remains Hollywood.

References and further reading

Agee, James. *Agee on Film: Reviews and Comments*. Boston: Beacon Press, 1966.
American Film Institute. *America's 100 Greatest Films*. Los Angeles: American Film Institute, 1998.
Biskind, Peter. *Easy Riders, Raging Bulls: How the Sex-Drugs-and-Rock 'n'Roll Generation Saved Hollywood*. New York: Touchstone, 1998.
Brodie, Fawn M. *Richard Nixon: The Shaping of his Character*. New York: W. W. Norton, 1981.
Byron, Stuart. "*The Searchers*: Cult Movie of the New Hollywood." *New York Magazine* (March 5, 1979): 45–8.
Grimes, William. "What Debt Does Hollywood Owe to Truth?" *New York Times*, May 5, 1992: C15, 22.
Gussow, Mel. "A Child (and an Adult of War): A Military Historian Puts a Vivid Cast on World War I." *New York Times* (July 3, 1999): B9.
Hobsbawm, Eric. *The Age of Extremes: A History of the World, 1914–1991*. New York: Vintage Books, 1994.
Hodgson, Godfrey. *America in Our Time*. New York: Vintage Books, 1976.
Kass, Judith. *Robert Altman: American Innovator*. New York: Popular Books, 1978.

Littman, Barry R. *The Motion Picture Mega-Industry*. Boston: Allyn and Bacon, 1998.

Mailer, Norman. "Footfalls in the Crypt." *Vanity Fair* (February 1922): 124–9, 171.

Patterson, James. *Grand Expectations: The United States, 1945–1974*. New York: Oxford University Press, 1996.

Petras, James. "The Discrediting of the Fifth Estate: Press Attacks on JFK." *Cineaste*, 19.1 (1995): 1–15.

Polonsky, Abe. "*The Best Years of Our Lives*: A Review." *Hollywood Quarterly* (April 1947): 91–2.

Reeves, Richard. *President Kennedy: A Profile of Power*. New York: Touchstone, 1993.

Summers, Anthony. *Not in Your Lifetime: The Definitive Book on the JFK Assassination*. New York: McGraw-Hill, 1998.

Weintraub, Bernard. "Nixon Family Assails Stone Film as Distortion." *New York Times* (December 19, 1995): C18.

Wills, Garry. "Dostoevsky Behind a Camera: Oliver Stone Is Making Great American Novels on Film." *Atlantic Monthly* (July 1997): 96–101.

Chapter 7

The Beauty and Destructiveness of War: A Literary Portrait of the Vietnam Conflict

Pat C. Hoy II

The literature of war holds a mirror to our bestiality, alerts us to our most primitive urges, warns us of the inextricable link between hubris and destructiveness – shows us clearly that we pay an enormous price for who we really are. In the war stories themselves, we glimpse not only our destructiveness but also our political failures and the paucity of our ideas; war stories reveal our best-kept secrets. But we also find there in those stories signs of grandeur: willing sacrifice for the welfare of others, deep love for comrades, redemptive acts of mourning, the revelation of character, the knowledge of what it means to be responsible, the acknowledged ache of loneliness. War literature catches us at our worst and at our best. And when the literature itself is good, when it captures the essence of war, it spares no one – neither civilian nor soldier – because it speaks of our deepest primordial urges.

In *The Soldiers' Tale*, one of the most comprehensive accounts of war ever written (especially of war from the soldiers' point of view), Samuel Hynes tells us that the "story of the Vietnam War is a cautionary tale for our time, the war story that can teach us most" (177). Hynes is right; it is a war that we Americans have still, as a nation, not come to terms with, a war whose lingering impact on the relationship between the soldier and the state has been largely unexamined. Hynes wants us to know that it was one of our most brutal wars, one in which our soldiers were much younger than in previous wars and much more inclined to undisciplined killing. The short, 13-month tours, the availability of drugs, the failure of leadership on many levels, the lack of support on the home front, all left the individual soldier isolated, abandoned to his own devices, his own immature and often unformed judgments about what to do; he did not generally feel that he belonged to a larger community, to a concerted war effort organized and executed for the common good. According to Hynes the hundreds and hundreds of war narratives that he examined (memoirs, letters, journals) confirm these impressions.

They also confirm a change in the language of the war, perhaps a change in the male psyche and its response to war – a change that Hemingway revealed as long ago as *A Farewell to Arms*. Frederick Henry finds "abstract words such as glory, honor, courage . . . obscene beside the concrete names of villages, the numbers of roads, the names of rivers, the numbers of regiments and the dates." Hynes, not under the influence of Hemingway, wants us to see that Vietnam war stories do not accommodate the language of romance and are not built on the foundation of abstract principles associated with the inflated values of those big words.

One of the soldier's tales that Hynes examines is from Philip Caputo's *A Rumor of War*. The particular detail under scrutiny is Caputo's account of the death of Captain Frank Reasoner, a man I knew more than 40 years ago when we were cadets at West Point. In his analysis, Hynes is interested in the "way the narratives use the traditional language of military values, the Big Words like 'courage' and 'duty' and 'heroism.' Those words survive, but without a clear moral base; they are simply words for extraordinary kinds of behavior" (212–13). He is concerned less about what this shift says of the soldier than he is about the way soldiers in this particular war tell their stories. To demonstrate his point Hynes turns to what Caputo calls "'the hero's' death of Captain Reasoner":

> We split a beer and talked about the patrol he was taking out in the afternoon. His company was going into the paddy lands below Charlie ridge, flat, dangerous country with a lot of tree lines and hedgerows. Reasoner finished his beer and left. A few hours later, a helicopter brought him back in; a machine gun had stitched him across the belly, and the young corporal who had pulled Reasoner's body out of the line of fire said, "He should be covered up. Will someone get a blanket? My skipper's dead." (213)

"How flat and workmanlike that sounds," Hynes tells us, "just a story of a Marine going out to do his job and coming back dead. But then there is the touch of tenderness for the dead captain: 'he should be covered up . . . My skipper's dead.' The emotional links between soldiers, and between officers and their men, are difficult to render, because though attachments between men in war can be strong – stronger than peacetime friendships – they are mostly inarticulate. Caputo does it delicately here" (213–14). Caputo's description of what actually happened during the firefight is just as flat, and then he tells us, finally, "They gave Frank Reasoner the Congressional Medal of Honor, named a camp *and* a ship after him, and sent the medal and a letter of condolence to his widow." Just like that. No fanfare. No hype. No glory.

In closing his assessment of the Vietnam War, Hynes draws an important parallel between Vietnam veterans and what he calls the *victims* of other wars – victims of the Holocaust, the bombing of Hiroshima, and the brutal Japanese prisons. "Collectively, [the narratives] describe what happens to men when war takes them so far beyond the limits of ordinary human behavior that they can't find their way back" (221). That story places Vietnam veterans with the *victims*. Hynes knows, of course, and acknowledges that this story, which has become a part of the "after-myth" of the war, was true of some soldiers' experiences, but that many others returned home to live relatively uncomplicated lives.

Hynes's assessment of these war narratives and the war in general rings true of my own experience in Vietnam and of the literature of that war that still compels me. But there is more to learn from the best of the memoirs and from a few novels and short stories about war's seductiveness and the obsessions that arise out of armed conflict. The literature, and a few important films, tell us in dramatic ways what sends a nation's people out into the fray and what havoc war wreaks on those who fight and then come home.

Norman Mailer captures two important aspects of America's involvement in the war in *Armies of the Night: History as a Novel, the Novel as History* and *Why Are We in Vietnam?*. Each of these works is a tour de force, an attempt to create a new form for containing and showcasing the nation's response to the war. *Armies* covers the 1967 anti-war march on the Pentagon. Mailer is the hero-fool of the first section of the book (the novel), a drunken wise man who more often plays at being the jester. He is suffering from delusions of grandeur, imagining himself the general leading those armies of the night – the consciousness-raising voice of protest. His vision of Washington is Whitmanic, reminiscent of the Whitman of *Specimen Days* who, imagining the grand sweep of history and his place in it, watches the convergence of forces on the nation's capitol.

The entire first section of the book is written to establish Mailer's central place in the history that will follow; in the second section he is the mastermind who provides the historical and philosophical analysis of the march and his place in it. In the second half of the book, the novel becomes the foundation for history – Mailer on Mailer if you will, fashioning a new image for the nation. The gist of this analysis is that America is on the verge of something revolutionary, something never before experienced in its history. The book is a call to arms, or a call to minds and bodies, to resist the war and to understand, with Mailer's help, of course, how he and other brave souls have created this apocalyptic moment of reckoning.

The unwieldy persona of *Armies* finds his place in yet another guise in *Why Are We in Vietnam?*. The narrator operates in concert with a young Dallas Texan who is a hipster, a Texas version of what Mailer had celebrated in 1957 as "The White Negro," a risk taker tuned to psychopathic brilliance who refuses to live in the world of corporate America, boxed in by the rules and denied the life of his body. This young man, D. J., has a wild theory that he has a transistor up his anus that puts him in touch with the electromagnetic forces of the universe, so that he is at times privy to both God and the Devil. His language is most often obscene but hip, and he is at odds throughout the novel with his father, Rusty, a corporate tycoon of some stature in the plastics business in Dallas. The central conceit of the novel is a recollected hunting trip that father and son had taken to an Alaskan mountain range to hunt for grizzly bear.

Rusty goes to hunt for trophy. D. J., along with his friend Tex, goes for the purifying experience of the hunt itself. Mailer creates a monstrous, but compelling, version of Faulkner's "The Bear," developed in such a way that the greed of the father and those who attend him (the "medium assholes" of his corporation) reveals America's dirtiest corporate secrets. This conceit gives Mailer a chance to bring to fictional life his ideas about the hipster, the importance of living at risk, and the possibility of becoming attuned to the mysterious forces at work in the universe. The hunting guide and D. J.'s friend Tex are there to remind us of a better way of being in relation to nature. What we see staged during the hunt is a propensity for Rusty and his corporate minions to dominate nature with technology; we see too a guide who is shrewd enough to play the father for money while reminding him of his corrupt ways. The boys turn out to be the only ones on the hunt willing to strip themselves bare to confront the challenges of the wilderness; their act of divestiture confirms their blood-brother relationship and speaks to the deep male urge to hunt and face danger. Vietnam is not mentioned until the last page of the novel, but we know long before that moment that we are seeing played out before us a misuse of power emblematic of US foreign policy and our conduct of the Vietnam war.

Tim O'Brien, back from the war, takes us into it so that we can begin to know what it was like actually to be in Vietnam. His is no symbolic, indirect method. He wants us to feel the war, wants us to know what it did to him and his fellow soldiers. He even instructs us, in a fictive mode, about how to tell the stories, what to listen for, how they ought to affect us. "In a true war story," O'Brien claims, "nothing is ever absolutely true." And there is no moral – at least not on the surface. "In a true war story, if there's a moral at all, it's like the thread that makes the cloth . . . You can't extract the meaning without unraveling the deeper meaning." The truth, the lesson, finally, has nothing to do with a moral abstraction. Whether we get it or not, whether the story works, "comes down to gut instinct," he argues. "A true war story, if truly told, makes the stomach believe."

After O'Brien had written *If I Die in A Combat Zone* ("my effort at relating an experience that happened to me, as I would tell a friend") and *Going After Cacciato* ("my effort at literature") – and before he wrote *The Things They Carried* – he spoke in an interview of the distinct difference between "writing purely from memory" (tied to "real stuff") and writing with a "sense of playfulness that isn't possible in non-fiction." Naive as those distinctions between autobiography and fiction sound for a writer of O'Brien's genius, they tell us how he was approaching and thinking about his own early work, as well as how he distinguished himself from others who, in his mind, were merely writing autobiography and calling it fiction.

But in *The Things They Carried*, O'Brien began to loose the ties that had bound him to the "real stuff" and to that clean distinction between nonfictive autobiography and the more playful fictive mode where the writer is free to pursue a "single *idea* of a character" without having to worry about "a lot of physical stuff." The facts, I suppose. Reality, perhaps. For O'Brien, Cacciato is "memorable because the reader can fasten on this idea of a guy who's run away from the war." But in *The Things They Carried*, O'Brien seems momentarily to have lost interest in the idea of a single character; he's on the scent of memory and imagination and the craft of his own fiction.

Confounding his earlier categories, O'Brien himself shows up as a character in *The Things They Carried*, as do the other members of his infantry platoon from Vietnam, but we are continually given a version of the truth – a story about what happened – only to find in a subsequent chapter that the narrator (also presumably O'Brien) has made up an event, distorted the "physical stuff," crafted the material, created a character out of whole cloth, told a lie in the interest of some kind of Truth larger than the truth of any given moment, any given event. Often, what's clearly masquerading as fictive truth-telling also sounds like a good essay, ringing with a fascinating kind of certainty. O'Brien on O'Brien. The writer helping us see what he wants us to see, but managing also to hit us in the gut.

The most compelling thing about the stories is the way they move in and out of one another, the way one version is affected by another version. But there are moments of reversal and grandeur within individual stories, moments when we experience the confusion of the men we are observing, and moments too when we experience O'Brien's confusion years after the war. One of the most intriguing of those moments occurs near the end of "How to Tell a True War Story." Then narrator, presumably O'Brien, is relating the story of Curt Lemon's death:

> In the mountains that day, I watched Lemon turn sideways. He laughed and said something to Rat Kiley. Then he took a peculiar half step, moving from shade into bright sunlight, and the booby-trapped 105 round blew him into a tree. The parts were just hanging there, so Dave Jensen and I were ordered to shinny up and peel him off. I remember the white bone of an arm. I remember pieces of skin and something wet and yellow that must've been the intestines. The gore was horrible, stays with me. But what wakes me up twenty years later is Dave Jensen singing "Lemon Tree" as we threw down the parts.

This is certainly not Caputo giving us the report of Captain Reasoner's death, but it is very close: flat, matter of fact. The death, the body parts, the gore, the order to "shinny" – all a part of a day-to-day combat mission. Then come the word *horrible* and the recollection of the singing. So the story ends with something like "my skipper is dead," but this ending is not about loss, not about camaraderie. Instead we are reminded of the strangeness of the moment, the bringing together of the gore picking and the singing. With O'Brien as storyteller, we have no idea whether this is actually what happened; we know only that, according to the terms of this story about telling war stories, the imperative is to make us feel.

Right after telling the story about Lemon's death, O'Brien tells another story and then says immediately, "That's a true story that never happened." Then he begins again, as if he has not already told us about Lemon's death:

> Twenty years later, I can still see the sunlight on Lemon's face. I can see him turning, looking back at Rat Kiley, then he laughed and took that curious half step from shade into sunlight, his face suddenly brown and shining, and when his foot touched down, in that instant, he must've thought it was the sunlight that was killing him. It was not the sunlight. It was a rigged 105 round. But if I could ever get the story right, how the sun seemed to gather around him and pick him up and lift him high into a tree, if I could somehow recreate the fatal whiteness of that light, the quick glare, the obvious cause and effect, then you would believe the last thing Curt Lemon believed, which for him must've been the final truth.

There is much to say about the storyteller's seeming desire to transfigure a death, to somehow get inside Lemon's mind so that what Lemon left this life remembering was something about "cause and effect," something about the way that "fatal whiteness" lifted him up into the tree. But there is something of greater importance going on too. This retelling is not just about O'Brien trying to come to terms with that moment of death; there is something here of beauty – a beauty that, according to O'Brien, rides along on the crest of horror during war.

Hear O'Brien earlier in this longer story:

> The truths are contradictory. It can be argued, for instance, that war is grotesque. But in truth war is also beauty. For all its horror, you can't but gape at the awful majesty of combat. You stare out at tracer rounds unwinding through the dark like brilliant red ribbons. You crouch in an ambush as a cool, impassive moon rises over the nighttime paddies. You admire the fluid symmetries of troops on the move, the harmonies of sound and shape and proportion, the great sheets of metal-fire streaming down from a gunship, the illumination rounds, the white phosphorus, the purply orange glow of napalm, the rocket's red glare. It's not pretty, exactly. It's astonishing. It fills the eye. It commands you. You hate it, but your eyes do not. Like a killer forest fire, like cancer under a microscope, any battle or bombing raid or artillery barrage has the aesthetic purity of absolute moral indifference – a powerful, implacable beauty – and a true war story will tell the truth about this, though the truth is ugly.

Yes, it will. We have seen it in America in our own time. We saw it as the Twin Towers collapsed, and we could not take our eyes off the reruns, could not reconcile our minds to the spectacle and the horror that lay behind it. We still play the images over and over in our minds, unable to break our fascination with the stolen, unspeakable glimpse of beauty that manifests itself with absolute moral indifference. It frightens and fascinates and horrifies us. There is more.

At Harvard where I taught after retiring from the US Army, one of my students wrote a stunning essay about beauty. He suggested that the house of cards his uncle used to build for him held one long and enduring fascination – the chance to pull the card that would destroy the house. "The only good way to get a sense of the delicate precision involved in creating it," Gian wrote, "was to touch it gently, to try to alter it ever so slightly, and have it crumple to nothing." There was not anything malicious about pulling the card, but there was something powerful about it, something lasting in the stolen glimpse of beauty that revealed itself only in the moment of destruction.

I know now that Gian Neffinger was onto a mystery beyond the reach of his experience. I had never been able to understand the scene in the movie *Patton* when Old Blood and Guts stands on the battlefield in Italy, gazing out over the smoking debris, the charred bodies – the carnage that is war – and exclaims with passionate conviction, "God, I love it." That was a scene against which I once measured my fitness to command a combat division and came up short. I didn't have it in me to be sanctified by my own destructiveness.

I suspect now that Patton must have seen in all that carnage a touch of beauty such as a man sees reflected in the face of a woman transformed momentarily by his love. In her radiance, he glimpses himself. For a fleeting moment, she is a part of his handiwork. But as she awakens again to her own independence, he cannot bear what he sees – the loss, the beauty of that intoxicating togetherness. That's her allure and war's. She and war allow a man to taste the complexity of his own power-making – Venus and Mars and Pygmalion all at once, creating a reality no mortal can bear for long and few can live without. The intoxication can be habit-forming and destructive and beautiful.

If we divorce the carnage of Patton's battlefield from an elusive idea about that carnage – Patton's own grand conception of himself as a charismatic, historical figure with a sacred mission – we have left only the fact of carnage itself. In that unadorned fact, no one but a psychotic can see beauty. It is altogether too ghastly to look at. But we know that the consequence of the soldier's deed and a nation's deeds can never be disentangled from the ideas that motivated them. So, in the final analysis, it is the purity of the idea itself that determines how we view the carnage. We redeem such destruction only through acts of mind – long before the deed is done or long after, depending on our predisposition.

Once, in Vietnam, I stood in the aftermath of a battle and observed the carnage of war. I helped train the soldiers who won the battle, but I had played no part in the fighting itself. I flew to the scene in my helicopter after the fighting was over and saw the carnage and the satisfaction on the soldiers' faces. My work had been done long before the battle, and satisfaction came to me privately as I stood watching those soldiers recover through the saving rituals they performed together – burying the dead, policing the battlefield, stacking ammunition, burning left-over powder bags, hauling trash, shaving, drinking coffee, washing, talking as they restored order and looked out for one another's welfare. They were bound up in the throngs of community, and at that precise moment the communal satisfaction was its own pure reward.

But, as sweet as that victory was, my satisfaction remains tainted. Those men had done the soldiers' dirty job in a war that will probably never end – for them or for this nation. The Vietnam War has not been and will not be transfigured by a purifying idea. The men and women who fought there will forever be haunted by the fact of carnage itself. The ones who actually looked straight into the eyes of death will scream out in the middle of the night and awake shaking in cold sweat for the rest of their lives – and there will be no idea, nothing save the memory of teamwork, to redeem them. That will not be enough. That loneliness is what they get in return for their gift of service to a nation that sent them out to die and abandoned them to their own saving ideas when they came home.

O'Brien takes up the task of storytelling as a way of telling us that there is no redeeming idea for that war in Vietnam – that it was indeed what it was, a brutal, unnecessary war. And it did indeed leave men lonely and confused, many for a lifetime. It left them not knowing what to do with their experiences; it left them searching for Truth, knowing full well that they will never find a satisfying version of it.

In a later novel, *In the Lake of the Woods*, O'Brien focuses again on a single character. This novel is not about the effect of war on a platoon of men; it is about lingering, destructive effects of war. Like Cacciato before him, John Wade, a failed politician, runs from the war, but he's been doing it for twenty years, thousands of miles from the combat zone. Until his race for the US Senate, Wade manages to put the war in the back of his mind. His success stems from a childhood interest in magic that initially helped him survive the alcoholic abuse and neglect of a suicidal father, and later helped him survive in Vietnam, where he was known as "Sorcerer." Across all those years, illusion worked its way deep into Wade's soul, and the mirrors that he played with in his head to shift the nature of reality came to reflect only his own emptiness.

The effect of this novel is to turn us into detectives. We're supposed to be worrying about the Wades who, while vacationing in Minnesota in the wake of his political defeat, disappear – first Katherine, then Wade himself. But the chapters devoted to various "hypotheses" about Katherine's disappearance and those devoted to "evidence" serve only to arouse our curiosity about O'Brien's macabre vision. They do little to make us care about the Wades. This is a novel that could just as well be autobiography.

The mirrors O'Brien puts in Wade's head, and the way in which he uses them to change our sense of the nature of reality, have as much to do with O'Brien as with Wade: the proof is in the intricate structure of the novel that actually mirrors the mirroring in Wade's head. We're pulled not into the Wades' lives but into the magical recesses of O'Brien's mind where he continually sifts the grains of truth, or causes us to, until we fall prey to our own deepest urge to bring all the parts of the Wades' story together so that we can see clearly, see the truth – about them, about Vietnam, about life. But by O'Brien's own design, we are led to see that there is no truth. No truth at all. Only our individual, shifting perspectives.

That's the illusion anyhow. It takes a while to see through it, to see that O'Brien's quite got his mind made up about a number of things, no matter what he might lead us to believe. He gives it all away, finally, outside the frame of the novel, or inside if you will. Wherever. Inside and outside working together. Anywhere is fair territory because O'Brien has constructed his life and his art that way. He invites us into both and insists that the lines between them are invisible. He gives himself away in interviews, in the *New York Times*, in the novel's footnotes, in the ironies that eventually turn back on themselves to reveal what's inside haunting O'Brien himself.

One of the things O'Brien seems most certain about is that he went to Vietnam because of love, and when he came home, he was silent about what he saw and what he did because he could not "bear the prospect of rejection: by my family, my country, my friends, my hometown. I would risk conscience and rectitude before risking the loss of love." Following his conscience, wrestling with his own moral daemon, gives way to expediency, but up to this day, O'Brien sticks to love as his explanation. Even Vietnam itself "was partly love," he tells us, love as absence – a heightened sense of longing for what you need and want but haven't got.

Like O'Brien, John Wade went to Vietnam "in the nature of love . . . Not to hurt, not to be a good citizen or a hero or a moral man. Only for love. Only to be loved." But, of course, nothing is ever quite so simple as it seems. Wade also went for political reasons, which can amount to the same thing as love if you can get the mirrors in your head arranged just so. With the mirrors in place, you can do what John Wade did about the facts of the war: "he tricked himself into believing it hadn't happened the way it happened." You can actually kill a fellow soldier or an innocent civilian, and make it seem as if it didn't happen – all in the name of love or politics or whatever you abandon the truth for.

Even after a war like Vietnam, the people back home will eventually love you because you went and came back. Because you served. They too will confuse what you did with a more palpable ideal. Or at least they will until they find out the truth – that you were at My Lai, that you played some part in the massacre of all those innocent civilians – women, children, old men, animals. This matter of love is even more complicated for Wade and (as we will see) for O'Brien. In the early days of his courtship, Wade follows his intended around, snoops on her to find out everything he can about her. Knowing becomes a form of possession, and John Wade convinces himself it's love. Love makes obsessiveness palpable. There is destruction in the beauty of the affair.

O'Brien, in a *New York Times Magazine* article published just before the release of *Lake*, tells the story of going back to Vietnam in February 1994 to visit the area of operations where his platoon had pursued the enemy 25 years earlier; they were operating in the vicinity of My Lai, in an area the soldiers called Pinkville. O'Brien went back there with his girlfriend, but by the time he returned home and finished the article in June, he had lost Kate and become suicidal. Too much of the piece is about his obsession over that loss. He knows that he's done some "bad things to stay loved," but he doesn't seem to understand that what he means by love, others think of as obsession. On one level, the article is a *cri de coeur*, a wailing lament from a man who's got the mirrors in his head working all too well about the war itself, and then again, not well at all about love.

The difference between love and obsession comes down, perhaps, to those two snakes that John Wade saw on the road to Pinkville, "each snake eating the other's tail, a bizarre circle of appetites that brought the heads closer and closer." To Wade, his love for Katherine feels "like we're swallowing each other up, except in a *good* way," and he wants to get home to "see what would've happened if those two dumbass snakes finally ate each other's heads." Elsewhere in the novel, we're told that "John Wade wanted to open up Kathy's belly and crawl inside and stay there forever. He wanted to swim through her blood and climb up and down her spine and drink from her ovaries and press his gums against the firm red muscle of her heart. He wanted to suture their lives together." All in the name of love.

This obsessiveness works for a while. Kathy's needs seem somehow attuned to her husband's, even though she loathes the public game of politics. She is relieved, quietly radiant, about Wade's election loss. But in the wake of defeat, she begins to know that Wade will never be able to be honest with her about what happened in Vietnam; that always, there will be secrets. He can't tell her the truth, and truth will not leave him alone. As the old war wound festers, the mirrors keep refracting the truth, interfering with the psyche's healing.

It is not that O'Brien and Wade do not know the truth about that war or what they did in it. But they do not know how to live with what they know. When O'Brien talks straight out about the war, and especially about My Lai, he tells the awful truth. And when he imagines what happened to Wade in the midst of the massacre, he makes us see what we might not otherwise see in all that testimony from Calley's trial, or in the analysis done by General Peers in the Commission's report. It is not just that O'Brien quotes verbatim from those records; he puts Wade in the midst of a historical moment and elongates it, puts him there with a host of characters, both fictional and real, and he stretches the moment out so that we see what Wade saw and what they all did – the bloodshed, the brutality, the absurdity. And he reminds us in subtle ways that abuse like that happened on smaller scales in other wars and might very well happen again.

What O'Brien says about My Lai is convincing because he is so careful not to overstate his case; he is so careful to reveal how that "wickedness soaks into your blood and heats up and starts to sizzle." Even though he finds what happened at My Lai repugnant and even though his own unit did not "cross that conspicuous line between rage and homicide," he understands how it happened, especially in "a war without aim, [where] you tend not to aim. You close your heart."

When O'Brien elongates that historical moment in the novel, he complicates our sense of Wade because there in the midst of the brutality, where morality and civilized restraint virtually disappear, there is only one character who refuses to take part in the killing. Wade is more that soldier's comrade than he is the others' comrade. Wade kills twice – an old man, who has in his hands a hoe that looks like a weapon, and PFC Weatherby, who has been slaughtering innocent civilians all during the massacre. At a moment when Wade stands in the ditch where the bodies are being dumped, up to his knees in gore, PFC Weatherby comes to the edge and begins to smile as Wade looks up. Small wonder that a relatively moral man in a despairing fit of rage might blow Weatherby away. Wade does. But he cannot go on to tell the truth about what happened. He tucks the killing away.

There in the aftermath of the battle, Wade thinks of "the future," thinks about politics and can't bring himself to take a courageous stand. Twenty years later that silence costs him his political career, but long before that day of defeat, the "inconvenient squeeze of moral choice" got the best of him. Later, he would not be able to deal with the truth, either inside his head, or with those he loved. And that failure cost him everything. Truth matters in O'Brien's fictive world.

One other point. In O'Brien's world, evil and the spirit seem bound together. The spirit world is not a place a man turns to for solace. It's a place haunted by goblins and inhabited by dead men who "just don't *die*." The spirit is what gets into our heads and will not let us forget the evil that we do. O'Brien wants us to see the evil, wants us to hear what it sounds like going round in our heads, wants to make us taste its bitterness. He is concerned that "evil has no place . . . in our national mythology." "We erase it," he claims. "We use ellipses. We salute ourselves and take pride in America the White Knight, America the Lone Ranger, America's sleek laser-guided weaponry beating up on Saddam and his legion of devils."

In this novel of ideas, O'Brien evokes what may be the most evil moment in America's history – that day in March in 1968 when those 400 or so Vietnamese men, women, and children were murdered in cold blood. And he reminds us in the *NYT* article that only one man out of the thirty charged, one ridiculously inept and immoral young lieutenant, would ever be convicted. Even he only "spent three days in a stockade and four and a half months in prison." The others walked free, and the nation never took heed, never felt the horror . . . the utter horror. Never felt its complicity.

In this war story, O'Brien reawakens us to the horror of that national tragedy, and he awakens us as well to the lingering effects of that war on the lives of his characters and on himself. But we are left finally with only a head full of ideas and a deep awareness of how the obsessiveness of love can trick us into thinking too well of ourselves and can leave us bankrupt in spirit. But there is nothing of the other side of love, nothing of the redeeming nature of the spirit. My head spins and reels from O'Brien's ideas, but I do not feel in my gut what I ought to feel, would feel, had I heard a true war story, or even a satisfying love story.

At the end of his memoir, *In Pharaoh's Army: Memories of the Lost War*, Tobias Wolff gives us a glimpse of his own homecoming after a year as an adviser to the Vietnamese army. Joining the American army had been essential to Wolff's "idea of legitimacy" because the men he had respected as he was growing up, and most of the writers he looked up to, had all served. He also wanted to become "respectable" in a way that his father had not been. Serving was the "indisputable certificate of citizenship and probity."

Yet, when Wolff came back from Vietnam, he spent a week alone in a "seedy" San Francisco hotel room feeling not "freedom and pleasure" as he had expected but "aimlessness and solitude." It wasn't the US Army he missed; there was a more troubling condition that he saw reflected in his own "gaunt hollow-eyed" image. Without his army headgear, he seemed "naked and oversized . . . newly hatched, bewildered, without history." "Broodingly alone," he knew that he could not re-enter the "circle" of his family, and so he avoided its members: "It did not seem possible to stand in the center of that circle. I did not feel equal to it. I felt morally embarrassed."

Outside that family circle Wolff had trouble holding up his end of a conversation; he said embarrassing and hostile things without awareness of what he was doing, and his laugh sounded "bitter and derisive" even to himself. "Lonesome as I was," Wolff writes, "I made damn sure I stayed that way."

Wolff's memoir is the most balanced, unapologetic account of the war I have read. We hear his reasons for going, see him through his preparation, and experience the beauty of his stories of friendship, as well as his stories of corruption. Often friendship and corruption go hand in hand. His portrait of a Harvard-bred foreign-service officer reveals Wolff's own susceptibility to that man's privileged life, privilege that expressed itself in lavish, courtly parties leading to evenings of debauchery in Saigon and in a kind of cultured fluency with

Vietnamese life that could hold even the Vietnamese captive. But Wolff could see past the charm, finally, into the man's deeper character, and what he found enraged him. What he found was that Pete's "demonstration of mastery" of the Vietnamese way of life required that others in his presence be stripped of mastery, "made helpless, reduced to spectators." Wolff's is an unusually clear portrait of civilians who preyed on the war's career benefits without having their reputations tarnished by association.

In Pharaoh's Army is so perfectly crafted that in the end we are left questioning the literal truth of Wolff's stories. But we end up rethinking what O'Brien has already taught us, that literal truth matters less than the truth a polished story can reveal.

Wolff's account of the fateful Tet offensive in 1968 might just as well stand for the war itself. It works offhandedly through a host of clichés – about destroying villages to save them, about the indiscriminate slaughter of civilians, the incompetence of the South Vietnamese army, the absurdity of war, any war – and yet his account never mentions these clichés. In Wolff's details, we see where such clichés might have come from, but he skips over the superficial, making us look directly at the complications so often masked by simplification. Listen as Wolff reflects, reconfiguring and assessing the Tet offensive he had survived:

> How about the VC? I used to wonder. Were they sorry? Did they love their perfect future so much that they could without shame feed children to it, children and families and towns – their own towns? They must have, because they kept doing it. And in the end they got their future. The more of their country they fed to it, the closer it came.
>
> As a military project Tet failed; as a lesson it succeeded. The VC came into My Tho and all the other towns knowing what would happen. They knew that once they were among the people we would abandon our pretense of distinguishing between them. We would kill them all to get at one. In this way they taught the people that we did not love them and would not protect them; that for all our talk of partnership and brotherhood we disliked and mistrusted them, and that we would kill every last one of them to save our own skins. To believe otherwise was self deception. They taught that lesson to the people, and also to us. At least they taught it to me.

In this assessment Wolff honors the enemy's shrewdness, looks into its motives and effectiveness. What he does is uncharacteristic of what we did during that protracted war. Jonathan Shay in *Achilles in*

Vietnam: Combat Trauma and the Undoing of Character reminds us over and over that the devaluing and dehumanizing of the enemy that was so much a part of the experience of Vietnam contributed to severe combat trauma and the long suffering it effects. Such devaluations contributed as well to our defeat. We never actually learned what it might cost to win the hearts and minds of those people. We seemed not to have it in us to understand them. They were, Shay's patients told him time and again, just "gooks" – not shrewd, indefatigable warriors.

Robert Olen Butler's haunting, poignant stories in *A Good Scent from a Strange Mountain* do what war books rarely do: they bring us face to face with the people we fought for and the people we fought. In Vietnam it was hard to tell the difference.

Most of Butler's characters are Vietnamese Americans living in southern Louisiana on "flat bayou land" that resembles the country they left behind. They are, nevertheless, uneasy culture straddlers struggling for assimilation – some too easily becoming "one of us," others clinging to a past they do not fully understand. Through them we see the effects of war, long past the putative end of hostilities.

The men fare less well than the women, but the differences are slight. In "Love," a diminutive Vietnamese man struggles to hold on to his beautiful wife. As an "agent handler" during the war, he could call for firepower to destroy rocket locations. "The United States Air Force would come in and blow those coordinates away," he tells us. "You can see how this might be a great help to a seemingly wimpy man with a beautiful wife."

After the war, in America, his wife falls again for another Vietnamese, this time "a former airborne ranger, a tall man, nearly as tall as an American." The little man elicits help this time from a "black man with a fire of a different kind." Doctor Joseph's voodoo concoction ultimately sends the little fire-bringer up a tree "in a fit of rage," and even though he injures himself in a fall, his strange bomb finds its mark. Recovering in a hospital room, the man tells his wife stories about the "ways the Vietnamese were becoming a part of American society." She sits by his bedside, ministering silently to his needs, listening.

Other men in Butler's stories yearn for and often rediscover the importance of the fire-bringer's madcap persistence. In "Crickets" a Vietnamese father tries to reach his American-born son through a game from his "own childhood in Vietnam." But his son shows no lasting interest in crickets fighting to the death. Besides, America produces only the "very large and strong" charcoal crickets that are "slow and . . . become confused." Missing are the small, brown "fire crickets" that were "precious and admirable" among the kids in Vietnam.

Even American men who seemed to bring the fire back from Vietnam lose it on the home front. "Letters from My Father" recounts the disappointment of a war child whose American father finally rescues her and her mother from Ho Chi Minh City. But after a year in Louisiana with her father, she yearns for the man she finds in a packet of his old letters, written on her behalf "when he was so angry with some stranger he knew what to say."

In "The American Couple" a Vietnamese American wife on vacation with her husband in Puerto Vallarta discovers as she watches him in a mock battle with another veteran that there is "passion still inside him." The men, she figures, had "shared something once, something important – rage, fear, the urge to violence, just causes, life and death. They'd both felt these things in the same war. And neither of them wanted to let go of all that." Observing them, she realizes that she had "embraced this culture with such intensity that it isolated [her] from him, made it impossible for him to find a way to touch [her] anymore." But Vinh in his grey suit, studying spreadsheets, flying here and there with his leather briefcase, is also American. America subverts their passions.

These stories pointing past the war are matched by others looking back long before it, recalling the old ways. The confrontational narrator of "A Ghost Story" challenges us to listen to his tale of Miss Linh, a beautiful young woman who had "passed into the spirit world." Miss Linh once saved a Vietnamese major from the Viet Cong only to crush him later in her jaws. The narrator, insisting on the truth of that story, tells his own. He too encountered Miss Linh. On the last day of the war as he ran for asylum in the US Embassy, she saved him once from instant death and then again, giving him access to a "limousine with American flags." But as he drove away in the vehicle that would take him to safety in America, he "looked out the window and saw Miss Linh's tongue slip from her mouth and lick her lips, as if she had just eaten [him] up." He reminds us in closing that "indeed she has."

There are other ghost stories, each powerful and distinct in its own right – "Open Arms" about a Viet Cong deserter who awakens in a fellow countryman from the South all that he need ever remember about a wife who abandoned him for a cripple during the war; "Relic" about a wealthy Vietnamese American who acquires one of the shoes John Lennon wore the day he was murdered and discovers with that shoe on his foot something of the "lightness" of a martyr's death; and "A Good Scent from a Strange Mountain" about a man's enlightening "visitation" from his old friend Ho Chi Minh who helps him clarify his own obligation to establish harmony in the Vietnamese family before he dies.

Looking in on these stories from the outside, we see a touch of lunacy: ludicrous plots, bizarre games; far-fetched men and women their Southern neighbors might consider "tetched." But inside the stories, inside the lives Butler creates, we experience loss and need. We learn about the suffering that comes from desire, and just for an instant we look into things so deep we can't deny them.

Those still searching for justification for our very earliest involvement in Vietnam can find it in *South Wind Changing*, Jade Ngoc Quang Huynh's compelling narrative that recounts with quiet resignation what happened to him and his family after America negotiated the peace with honor. Not only do we see what it was like to be a young South Vietnamese boy caught in a village during Tet, subjected to Viet Cong brutality on the ground and American firepower from the sky, we see as well what it was like to be incarcerated in a communist labor camp, forced to subsist for a year on bugs, rodents, and stolen vegetables, and forced to endure torture and indoctrination until he was finally able to escape, ending up eventually in America.

Huynh's only crime in Vietnam was that he was an intellectual, a student at the university following the war. His captor offered this explanation for imprisonment: "Because you are educated. When you're educated you have knowledge that will stop us from controlling you, and you're one of the people who could start a revolution against us, against our government, against the Communist Party and those like myself." We see here no confirmation of the wisdom of our government's Domino Theory, but we do see what once upon a time, long ago, our nation believed it was combating. The world has changed since then, and so have we. But we are only beginning to confront the limitations of our power in this new world.

We should, perhaps, never forget that America forged its might out of decency and honor, and if it is to survive intact, it must revisit often the scene of its own undoing in Vietnam. We the people must go back to see how it was that our own crippling hubris led us far beyond the bounds of reason, causing us to send young boys to die in the tall grass, for far too long. The literature takes us back there, reminds us of the awful and sometimes beautiful seduction of war, makes us keenly aware of the costs of our own obsessiveness. It tells us much of what we need to know to preserve the sacred link between the citizenry and its government, the link that ties citizen to soldiering and soldier to state. If we do not reforge and strengthen that link, I suspect that the circling ghosts of those 58,000 dead men and women will know no rest. Their peace and ours depends on such resolve.

References and further reading

Beidler, Philip D. *American Literature and the Experience of Vietnam.* Athens, GA: University of Georgia Press, 1982.

Butler, Robert Olen. *A Good Scent from a Strange Mountain.* New York: Holt, 1992.

Franklin, H. Bruce, ed. *The Vietnam War: In American Stories, Songs, and Poems.* New York: Bedford-St Martin's Press, 1996.

Hendin, Herbert, and Ann Pollinger Haas. *Wounds of War: The Psychological Aftermath of Combat in Vietnam.* New York: Basic Books, 1984.

Huynh, Jade Ngoc Quang. *South Wind Changing.* Saint Paul, MN: Graywolf Press, 1994.

Hynes, Samuel. *The Soldiers' Tale: Bearing Witness to Modern War.* New York: Viking-Penguin, 1997.

McNamara, Robert S. *In Retrospect: The Tragedy and Lessons of Vietnam.* New York: Random-Times, 1995.

Mailer, Norman. *The Armies of the Night: History as a Novel, the Novel as History.* New York: Signet, 1968.

Mailer, Norman. *Why Are We in Vietnam?* New York: Putnam, 1967.

Newman, John, et al., eds. *Vietnam War Literature: An Annotated Bibliography of Imaginary Works about Americans Fighting in Vietnam.* 3rd edn. Lanham, MD: Scarecrow Press, 1996.

Norman, Michael. *These Good Men: Friendships Forged from War.* New York: Crown, 1989.

O'Brien, Tim. *In the Lake of the Woods.* New York: Penguin, 1994.

O'Brien, Tim. *The Things They Carried.* New York: Viking-Penguin, 1991.

Olson, James S., and Randy Roberts. *Where the Domino Fell: America and Vietnam, 1945–1995.* 3rd edn. Naugatuck, CT: Brandywine Press, 2000.

Shay, Jonathan. *Achilles in Vietnam: Combat Trauma and the Undoing of Character.* New York: Atheneum, 1994.

Wolff, Tobias. *In Pharaoh's Army: Memories of the Lost War.* New York: Vintage, 1994.

Chapter 8

Postmodern Fictions

David Mikics

> The Tolstoy Museum is made of stone – many stones, cunningly
> wrought . . . The amazing cantilever of the third level has been much
> talked about. The glass floor there allows one to look straight down and
> provides a "floating" feeling. The entire building, viewed from the street,
> suggests that it is about to fall on you. This the architects relate to
> Tolstoy's moral authority. (Barthelme: 52–4)

Donald Barthelme's story "At the Tolstoy Museum," from his *City Lights*
(1970), is a fitting place to begin a consideration of American postmodern fiction. In the lines I have quoted as my epigraph, Barthelme
mocks the prizing of form in high Modernism, the "cunningly wrought"
structures of a Joyce, an Eliot, a Woolf – or an Elizabeth Bishop, whose
poem "The Monument" Barthelme here echoes. The "moral authority" that Tolstoy conveyed through old-fashioned didactic messages
became, in the Modernist aesthetics of these authors, a property of
form itself: form as a puzzle to be solved by the heroic reader or, as
Barthelme remarks in another story from *City Life*, "The Glass Mountain," a "beautiful enchanted symbol" to be strenuously attained
(Barthelme: 69).

   In high Modernism, the more intricate a work's form was, the
more it declared its superiority to the mere commercial products of
mass culture. But with the advent of postmodernism, the idolizing of
form became a museum exhibit rather than a living practice, as it was
for the Modernists. After Modernism, Barthelme suggests, for a writer

to claim too exalted a role for his or her art is to risk unwitting self-parody, a pretentious top-heaviness that threatens to crush the reader, with the text itself "suggest[ing] it is about to fall on you."

The familiar literary-historical fable I have just told, with Barthelme's help, is true in its way. It is often present in postmodern texts themselves, as part of their claim that their authors practice a more sardonic and knowing style of priest-craft than that of the high moderns, one somehow liberated into a new skepticism about art's (lack of) privileges in the contemporary world. But the fable overlooks what is most crucial about American postmodern fiction: its return to the encyclopedic ambitions of Modernism, a return that happily suggests an overcoming of, rather than a surrender to, skepticism about the powers of literature.

My argument for a postmodernism that measures itself against the monumental ambitions of Modernist authors will be based largely on the works of the two most significant American postmodern novelists, Thomas Pynchon and Don DeLillo. Pynchon and DeLillo make high claims for their work that stand against the skepticism voiced by the witty and melancholy Barthelme. And Barthelme himself, notably in *The Dead Father* (1975), engaged a high Modernist myth, that of Freud's *Totem and Taboo*, in a way that was not merely parodic or skeptical, but that bore witness to the myth's desperate and noble persistence even in the face of its obvious absurdity.

First, it will be helpful to define the cultural phenomenon of postmodernism in its most common or dictionary definition. In order to do so, I turn to an account by Fredric Jameson in an essay from 1984. Jameson is describing postmodernist architecture, but his remarks, as he indicates, apply to literature, music, and visual art as well. "Postmodernist buildings," writes Jameson, "celebrate their insertion into the heterogeneous fabric of the commercial strip and the motel and fast-food landscape" of contemporary America. Instead of claiming the characteristic radical Modernist separation between the sleek, monumental space of the International Style and its degraded mass-cultural surroundings, an environment which these new buildings speak against by their very presence, postmodern architects submerge their work in the jumbled sea of contemporary popular styles. Similarly, in literature, Jameson adds, the high Modernism that positioned itself as a "realm of authentic experience over against the surrounding environment of philistinism, of shlock and kitsch, of commodification and of *Reader's Digest* culture" has yielded to postmodernist literary forms that embody or blend with this environment, rather than highhandedly quoting from it, as the Modernists did (Jameson, "Politics of Theory": 112). Postmodern texts often practice a kind of collage or sampling that seems to deny the heroic originality that Modernism prized. These works deliberately confuse their own expressive powers with the streams of words or images that make up contemporary life, so that it is unclear whether they are incorporating, or being incorporated by, their ambient cultural surroundings.

Jameson begins his essay by noting that the idea that we live in a postmodern culture assumes that there has been a historical break between an earlier form of capitalism and its current configuration. Earlier, capitalism required a grand legitimizing narrative, the story of Enlightenment progress whose linear and momentous character could be supported by the idea of the (cultural or economic) breakthrough, the decisive reconfiguration that changes everything. Now, as Jean-François Lyotard famously remarked in *The Postmodern Condition* (1979), capitalism has become a set of energies that interconnect and recombine without rhyme or reason, and without any need to be legitimated by the old Enlightenment narrative of progress.

According to Lyotard, the demise of this grand narrative brings the dawn of a new freedom, the freedom of the superficial, so that we, like money itself, can enjoy the pleasures of merely circulating. This new era of information technology, of images exchanged and consumed in dizzying profusion, was described by Jean Baudrillard as a constant moving spectacle, a play of surfaces and ecstatic intensities that renders the question of authenticity irrelevant. For both Lyotard and Baudrillard, the arrival of this vast newness is accompanied by anxiety, since the old truths have been replaced by a limitless and vertiginous openness. But finally, in their reading, the anxiety merely proves the definitive transformation of our existence, the irresistible thrill of the new. The description, in Baudrillard and Lyotard, of postmodernity as a liberated realm of superficiality stands behind the celebration of what Jürgen Habermas has called "affirmative postmodernism," the happy bricoleur's reliance on whatever fragments float around us in the colorful consumerist wasteland (or garden, if one prefers). But in the works of our best postmodernists, I will argue, "affirmative postmodernism," which I have linked to a skepticism about art's powers in the contemporary environment of postmodernity, has been defeated. Instead, these writers' ambitions equal those of the high Modernists.

I am not denying that postmodernism is often inhabited by a skepticism about its own strength; but I am suggesting that the strongest

189

forms of postmodern writing, among them the works of Pynchon and DeLillo, have successfully opposed such skepticism. When Jameson approvingly describes a postmodernism that "renounc[es] the high modernist claim to radical difference and innovation," he applauds a kind of authority that sounds more like a loss of authority, a shrinking back into the chance context supplied by the "surrounding commercial icons and spaces" (Jameson, "Politics of Theory": 112). (I will have more to say about Jameson later on, since in his major work, *Postmodernism*, he does make a strong claim for postmodern authority, in contrast to the essay I am citing now.) Is this new work no more than "a patchwork of deceits, borrowings, deceptions," as William Gaddis conceives the style of carpenter's Gothic, that low American pastiche, in his *Carpenter's Gothic* (1985) (27)? Such conniving modesty stands in radical contrast to the Modernist Tolstoy Museum – and to those of a writer like Gaddis, who produced *The Recognitions* (1955), the enormous, and enormously complex, novel that stands behind much of American postmodern fiction, while echoing the vast ambition of Joyce's and Faulkner's Modernism.

In postwar Europe and the Americas, late Modernism refined itself relentlessly in the work of international masters like Celan, Beckett, Borges, Duras, and Robbe-Grillet, and its prestige increased even as it more and more seemed too rarefied and strenuous to jump with the liberationist America of the sixties. In his influential essay "The Literature of Exhaustion," published in the *Atlantic* in 1967, John Barth admired the terse, compact marvels of late Modernism, the texts of Beckett and Borges – the unspoken contrast being Barth's own big, somewhat messy entertainments. But it is at least arguable that Barth's novels, notably *The Sot-Weed Factor* (1960, rev. 1967) and *Giles Goat Boy* (1966), with their many playful flourishes and extravagancies, were a truer response to the carnivalesque sixties than the spare, sleek works of the other two Bs, Beckett and Borges. In envying Beckett (and, in the art world, Ad Reinhardt) the refined, wry desperation of having nothing left to say, Barth mistook his own strength, which had nothing to do with the purity of silence and everything to do with the endless, contentious gab that distinguishes what Emerson called "this our talking America."

Our contemporary literature of exhaustion is the school of Raymond Carver, the legion of minimalist short story writers who purvey a slender economy of chicness and efficiency in place of the larger, talkier claims of postmodernists like John Barth or Ishmael Reed, who in many ways paved the way for Pynchon's and DeLillo's expansive confrontations with history. Both Barth and Reed engaged American history and legend in its broadest contours. In *The Sot-Weed Factor*, Barth reimagined colonial Maryland in an anachronistic, polyglot manner that forecasts Pynchon's *Mason & Dixon*. And in *Mumbo Jumbo* (1972), Reed outlined the peculiar secret tradition of Neohoodooism, depicting African American culture as a wild, improvised essence always lurking beneath, and resisting, the bland conformity of American life (Mikics).

In my view, critics have erred by trying to define postmodernism as a contrast to the Modernism of the 1920s. In America, at least, the works of those most often named postmodern – William Burroughs, Ishmael Reed, Thomas Pynchon, Robert Coover, and Don DeLillo, along with Barth and Barthelme – represent a return to Modernism after, and in reaction against, the existential impulse of American fiction in the 1950s (an impulse satisfied but also parodied in Jake Horner, the ascetic protagonist of Barth's *The End of the Road* [1958, rev. 1967]). After arguing this point, I will conclude by focusing on recent works by the two writers who have made the strongest case for American postmodern fiction, producing novels that rival, in their density, ambition, and encyclopedic grasp, the best achievements of high Modernism: Pynchon and DeLillo. Pynchon's *Mason & Dixon* (1997) and DeLillo's *Underworld* (1997) introduce an elegiac tone in place of the paranoid sublimity conveyed in the most truly monumental work so far produced by American postmodern fiction, Pynchon's *Gravity's Rainbow* (1973). If one takes *Gravity's Rainbow* as the paradigmatic summit of American postmodernism, the later works of Pynchon and DeLillo represent a kind of post-postmodernism, cooler and more melancholy, at times ripe with a sense of decline.

A brief detour will first be necessary, to consider the formal definition of postmodernism (in contrast to the historical definition offered by Lyotard, Baudrillard, and Jameson, which explains postmodernism as a symptom of or response to late capitalism). Some of the ideas commonly associated with "postmodern" as a formal structure include: a metafictional breaking of the frame, including stories within stories and direct addresses to the reader; transgression of the boundary between fiction and nonfiction; magical realism, or the use of the fantastic within a realist or low-mimetic narrative world; reference to "marginal," "minor," or subcultural places and practices; and finally, perhaps most of all, the free use of citation, as if all previous literature were in fact a museum – or a refrigerator ripe for plundering, not just after midnight, but in broad daylight. Postmodernists frequently seem to write in a world in which literary history is already over, and meaningful innovation is no longer possible (even as the realization that this is the case marks, to their minds, an innovation). As Andrei Codrescu jokes, whereas Pound exhorted writers to "Make it new," the gurus of postmodernism instead seem to advise, "Get it used" (Codrescu: 2).

The bag of literary tricks I have just described was well explored centuries ago, by Apuleius, Ovid, Rabelais, Fielding, Sterne – and maybe Homer, Hesiod, and the Bible as well. Those critics who generate a concept of the postmodern based solely on the formal characteristics I have listed must avoid investigating these older texts, because, if they did, their easy periodization would dissolve just as easily. Writers and literary movements have sometimes, in the past, felt that they have seen, and survived, the end of literature, and discovered a new creativity in this exhaustion. At times, too, they have proclaimed the political significance of the act of literature. There has not until now, however, been to my knowledge a critic who has broadened the definition of "historically *engaged*" literature in as carefree and wishful a fashion as Linda Hutcheon, currently one of the most frequently cited commentators on postmodernism. Hutcheon attributes to the works she prizes, and to postmodernism as such, a political engagement. Politics, to her, means "foreground[ing] the inescapable contextualizing of the self in both history and society," and suggesting "that any meaning that exists is of our own creation." Accordingly, postmodernism à la Hutcheon "question[s]" "the commonly accepted values of our culture (closure, teleology, and subjectivity)," even while realizing that this "questioning is totally dependent on that which it interrogates." These two emphases, on the foregrounding of historical context and on the self's meaning-making projects (two aspects of narrative that, it is safe to say, have existed approximately since the beginning of time), somehow, in Hutcheon's treatment, enable the postmodern subject to question "commonly accepted values" and to resist big bad totality while also admitting that the totality is irresistible, an "inescapable contextualizing" of the self. Hutcheon leaves her readers with the impression that postmodern writers indulge in a ceaseless interrogation, both freewheeling and fraught, in order to mark their superiority to the "closed symbolic systems" that Eliot, Joyce, and Pound supposedly favored (Hutcheon: 52, 84, 42–3, 78).

"Closure, teleology, and subjectivity" bad; "problematizing" good: if only political consciousness were so simple. Hutcheon's theory of postmodernism takes to new heights the current impulse of critics to justify themselves by showing that the works that they study, and therefore they themselves, are "somehow progressive or liberating" (Kershner: 76). Hutcheon accomplishes this aim by tagging every book she happens to like with an attractive jargon term like "questioning" or "problematizing." Her case illustrates the perils of seeing in the formal features of the text, in the general strategies that most sophisticated fictions use, proof of political wholesomeness and advanced historical consciousness.

My main guide to the meaning of postmodernism as a concept will be a historical critic rather than a formalist one like Hutcheon: Jameson, whose book *Postmodernism* has recently been shrewdly assessed by Stephen Helmling. Helmling positions Jameson's idea of postmodernism within the cultural history of postwar America, beginning with the popularity of existentialism in the 1950s as an anti-conformist means of social critique. Existentialism relies on the questing hero's confrontation with the absurd, with a morbid or chaotic state of things. It prizes the hero's Promethean effort to break through this absurdity to a meaning that will be true for him, and that can only be achieved by some grand action of the individual (however paradoxical or cryptic that action might seem to the outside or straight world). This existential pattern holds true of Ralph Ellison's landmark *Invisible Man* (1952), as well as the works of Saul Bellow, Philip Roth, Norman Mailer, J. D. Salinger, Flannery O'Connor, and others – the postwar writers who tend *not* to be called postmodern.

Those who *are* postmodern confront, according to Helmling, not an absurd universe but a completely administered one, in which meaning, instead of the hoped-for reward of the quester, appears to be a prison or totalized enclosure. As Gianni Vattimo has pointed out, under postmodernism the narrativization of absolutely everything, the colonizing of the world by discourse, paradoxically means that the world has become unreadable, a totality that is omnipresent and overwhelming (Vattimo: 92, 108–9). In Jameson's postmodernism as Helmling describes it, our sheer desire for the unrepresentable, which signifies potential escape from the suffocation that this totalized, systematized world imposes, blends with a desire to represent, to echo or mirror, this totality, and with an anxiety about our incapacity to convey its forceful enormity (Helmling: 25).

In other words, for Jameson, postmodernism incarnates the sublime, its unleashing of "joyous intensities" being simultaneously a celebration and a violent expression of anxiety about the source and true shape of these intensities, the "lawless libidinalism" of capital (Helmling: ii). In

Jameson's reading, capital itself, having outstripped the rational impulse of capitalism to control and routinize outcomes in some predictable, manageable way, is the sublime. For Jameson capital is also, therefore, the true subject of history, having taken the place of the proletariat, which by this time is no longer the coherent world-historical entity that it was for Marx and Engels.

We can see the theme of the totalized, sublimely incomprehensible universe not just at the apex of American postmodernism, Pynchon's *Gravity's Rainbow*, but also in the influential works of Gaddis, particularly *The Recognitions* and *JR* (1975). In Gaddis as in Pynchon, the labyrinthine or unreadable nature of the administered universe takes over as a subject from the crucial theme of the existentialist-influenced writers, the heroic struggle of an individual in the face of the absurd, the lack of meaning that surrounds him. These American postmodernists posit not a lack but a sublime superabundance of meaning, whose ambient, all-encompassing character both frightens and excites. For postmodern American fiction, the French *nouveau roman*, with its interest in a laconic purification of quest, was a dead end, a laboratory of warmed-over existentialism at once too overwrought and too coldly hip for these shores. (Paul Auster, in his stilted austerity the most French of American novelists, offers a light version of the *nouveau roman*.)

American postmodernism, then, beginning with *The Recognitions* and William Burroughs's *Naked Lunch* (1959), represents a return to the expansive character of high Modernism, and a break from the existentialism of the fifties. But this was a return with a difference. The most familiar example of American high Modernism in its encyclopedic form, Dos Passos' *USA* (1937), looks positively genial in its dialogic ease next to the fierce, parodic voices that inhabit the texts of Burroughs, Gaddis, Pynchon, and DeLillo. In these later writers, Dos Passos's Whitmanesque solidarity with the chaotic variousness of the masses, expressed by his pastiche of styles and his catalogue of divergent individuals, is replaced by a chaos that gives life to paranoia, the insistent haunting of narrative by invisible forces (Pynchon's "They" in *Gravity's Rainbow*).

Burroughs gives us a vision of the universe as a nightmare underworld ruled, even constituted, by an artificial or undead substance from which, it seems, there is no escape. The vampiric substance is, of course, junk, narcotics. In Burroughs, junk stands for the fact of a total, administered universe whose effect is to turn any sign of life into rigid caricature, an artificial animation that replaces life with the durable eternity of the undead. Just as Burroughs's first novel, *Junkie* (1953), accomplishes an emptying out of the hardboiled novel, with its protagonist flattened to a simple receptor and describer of sensations, so in *Naked Lunch* the Modernist phantasmagoria narrows itself to an extreme point. In place of the rich quotidian variety of *Ulysses*, *Mrs Dalloway*, and *USA*, Burroughs offers an overloaded thinness or shrillness.

In Burroughs, junk is revealed as synonymous with capital itself (à la Jameson) and with sublime, ecstatic experience. His unwelcome revelation exposes human meaning as addictive consumption, a moment of desperate need when "everyone finally sees what's at the end of his fork" (Burroughs's explication of *Naked Lunch*'s title).

Burroughs, with his exploitation of random detritus, including the "cut-up" or random collage technique of composition pioneered by his friend Brion Gysin, explores the double significance of the term *junk* in a way that will influence later postmodernists' interest in remnants, the leftover and excremental sectors of the world. These "sorts, scraps and fragments" (as Woolf puts it in *Between the Acts*) constitute a secret unity, an occult network or (as in DeLillo) underworld. It is no accident that Pynchon, in *The Crying of Lot 49* (1966), a novel preoccupied with a secret organization named WASTE, gives Hemingway's chant of Nada (from "A Clean, Well-Lighted Place") the tang of junk-culture leftovers in place of Hemingway's ascetic, stylish despair. In a cruel joke, Pynchon names the desolate husband of the novel's heroine, Oedipa, Mucho Maas. The depleted Mucho, a former used-car dealer, has nightmares featuring "Just this creaking metal sign that said nada, nada, against the blue sky. I used to wake up hollering" (Pynchon, *Crying of Lot 49*: 144). The sign signifies, of course, the National Automobile Dealers' Association. Get it used, indeed.

The children of Burroughs have not always been fortunate in their legacy. Kathy Acker's taste for grotesque rant in *Empire of the Senseless* (1988) and *Blood and Guts in High School* (1984) is reminiscent of Burroughs at his worst; her earlier *Kathy Goes to Haiti* (1978), like Burroughs's *Junkie*, cultivates a more ascetic tone in its simultaneous fulfillment and voiding of existential quest. But Burroughs at his best, for example in his later novels *Cities of the Red Night* (1981) and *The Western Lands* (1987), reaches toward a visionary gnosticism, the sublime intuition of a cryptic energy flowing beneath, or through, the dead world.

One of Burroughs's most famous routines, the talking asshole of *Naked Lunch*, was taken up and transformed by Pynchon in *Gravity's*

Rainbow, and the transformation is instructive. Pynchon has always been fascinated by cartoon-like, animate objects. *Mason & Dixon* features a talking dog, a humongous animate Gloucester cheese, a voluble mechanical duck, a quivering, seductive disembodied ear, and so on. The modernist ancestor of these entities is Leopold Bloom's soap in *Ulysses*. "A capital couple are Bloom and I," the Soap sings in the Nighttown chapter, "He brightens the earth, I polish the sky." Similarly, Pynchon's joshing, sophomoric male couples go back to the Buck Mulligan–Stephen Daedalus relationship in *Ulysses*, and *Mason & Dixon*'s conjunction of scientific measurement and storytelling finds its origin in Joyce's Ithaca chapter. But Pynchon turns to Burroughs rather than Joyce when he gives us, in *Gravity's Rainbow*'s opening pages, a wartime secret weapon: the memorable monstrosity of a giant, slobbering adenoid, which has engulfed its former owner, Lord Blatherard Osmo, and now "suddenly *sshhlop*! wipes out an entire observation post with a deluge of some disgusting orange mucus in which the unfortunate men are *digested* – not screaming but actually laughing, *enjoying* themselves" (Pynchon, *Gravity's Rainbow*: 15).

Pynchon's gigantic adenoid resembles a friendlier version of Burroughs's talking asshole. "Did I ever tell you about the man who taught his asshole to talk?," Burroughs's character Doc Benway asks.

> This man worked for a carnival you dig, and to start with it was like a novelty ventriloquist act. Real funny, too, at first . . . After a while the ass started talking on its own . . . Then it developed sort of teeth-like little raspy incurving hooks and started eating. He thought this was cute at first and built an act around it, but the asshole would eat its way through his pants and start talking on the street, shouting out it wanted equal rights. It would get drunk, too, and have crying jags nobody loved it and it wanted to be kissed same as any other mouth. Finally it talked all the time day and night, you could hear him for blocks screaming at it to shut up. (Burroughs: 120–1)

The asshole, of course, wins, generating a viscous tissue that covers and suffocates its host's body.

Pynchon's adenoid, like Byron the Bulb, an animated, adventurous light bulb who appears later on in *Gravity's Rainbow*, is infinitely cuter than Burroughs's talking asshole. The asshole seems to stand for a certain obsessive interest, throughout *Naked Lunch*, in the corporate or mindless – the undead – character of being. Burroughs here reflects on his own temptation to let a single gag swell and grow until it swallows his text's dignity and coherence, smothering its host in a nightmarish instance of the mathematical sublime. The asshole, like junk, like capital (in Jameson's reading), like America itself, becomes a monster whose dimensions are too vast and inconceivable for it to be tamed by any reasonable discourse. Pynchon's adenoid, by contrast, is rapidly sent on its way, a cartoon monster, to make way for the next number in the show. Nevertheless, Pynchon's sense of his own text as monstrous and all-encompassing owes something to Burroughs. *Gravity's Rainbow* itself "seems to be some very extensive museum, a place of many levels, and new wings that generate like living tissue – though if it all does grow toward some end shape, those who are here inside can't see it" (Pynchon, *Gravity's Rainbow*: 537).

One of *Gravity's Rainbow*'s crucial cartoon-like episodes, clearly influenced by R. Crumb as well as Burroughs, occurs when its hero Tyrone Slothrop, questing after his lost blues harmonica, journeys down a toilet in Boston's Roseland ballroom in 1940, a scene that features the shoeshine boy Red Little, later known as Malcolm X. Prominent in the Roseland episode are Slothrop's reflections, as he navigates the nightclub's subterranean sewage pipes, on his Harvard classmate "Jack Kennedy, the ambassador's son":

> Say where the heck is that Jack tonight, anyway? If anybody could've saved that harp, betcha Jack could . . . for the sake of tunes to be played, millions of possible blues lines, notes to be bent from the official frequencies, bends Slothrop hasn't really the breath to do . . . not yet but someday . . . well at least if (when . . .) he finds the instrument it'll be well soaked in, a lot easier to play. (Pynchon, *Gravity's Rainbow*: 65)

Given the racial matrix of this episode (Malcolm and his fellow shoeshiners are at the point of gang-raping Slothrop just before he slips away and escapes into the toilet), the phrase "notes to be bent from the official frequencies" must hark back to Ellison's *Invisible Man*, whose famous last line proclaims, "Who knows but that, on the lower frequencies, I speak for you?" The nervous, conclusive boldness of Ellison's Jack-the-Bear is an existential gesture, his invisibility to white America signaled by, among other things, his attachment to the blues, a music too low-down to be heard on the "official frequencies."

After his long existential quest, Ellison's hero at the end of *Invisible Man* has broken through to a momentous place, become the fulcrum of a new, huge pressure: he resides beneath white America, as the embodied summation of blackness's durable challenge to a society that has chosen not to hear or see it. Ellison's figure of an unheard, elusive frequency becomes, in Pynchon's hands, not a message sent out to America, but instead a comic reflection on the status of America's lost heroes: if anyone could have played that harp (whether to avert or to swing with the cataclysms of the sixties is unclear), it would have been promising young Jack Kennedy, now lost to us. The soaking of Slothrop's harp as it travels down the toilet in the Roseland Ballroom becomes an image for the saturation of Pynchon's text by history. As Slothrop swims after the lost harp, he sees historical traces, his friends' excrement bearing the imprint of their distinct personalities. Here are "patterns thick with meaning," Pynchon, or Slothrop, tells us, "Burma-Shave signs of the toilet world, icky and sticky, cryptic and glyptic" (Pynchon, *Gravity's Rainbow*: 65).

But the Roseland harp–toilet episode, with its suggestion of a link between "shit, money, and the Word" (Pynchon, *Gravity's Rainbow*: 28), bears on a history more significant than that of Slothrop's Harvard pals. The buoyant male camaraderie, as so often in Pynchon, masks a historical fear. On his way down the toilet, Slothrop and, by implication, the white college boy elite he represents encounter a black enemy lurking beneath Slothrop's hipster enthusiasm for African American style (the blues harp). Much later in *Gravity's Rainbow*, Pynchon, meditating on the phrase "Shit 'n' Shinola," returns us to the Roseland episode: "Well there's one place where Shit 'n' Shinola do come together, and that's in the men's toilet at the Roseland Ballroom, the place Slothrop departed from on his trip down the toilet . . . Shit, now, is the color white folks are afraid of. Shit is the presence of death" (Pynchon, *Gravity's Rainbow*: 688). In a maneuver reminiscent of Ishmael Reed's *Mumbo Jumbo*, the polar character of America, its obsessive opposition between white and black, innocence and evil, master and slave, life and death, here finds itself exposed, at least for a few seconds, in the fictive conjunction of Red Little and Jack Kennedy. The dark underside of triumphant whiteness becomes, just barely, visible: "Did Red suspend his ragpopping just the shadow of a beat, just enough gap in the moire there to let white Jack see through, not through to but through through, the shine on his classmate Tyrone Slothrop's shoes[?]" (Pynchon, *Gravity's Rainbow*: 688). The moment of historical consciousness is a brief one, only scarcely or hypothetically allowed to "white Jack."

Pynchon's relentless fooling, like the rag-popping routines of the future Malcolm X, half-conceals an apocalyptic gravity. As Louis Mackey writes, Pynchon's "undergraduate defenses against seriousness are an embarrassed and self-conscious way of talking about grave and momentous things, and a preterition of sorts," a passing-over of those lost ones barred from salvation. Here Pynchon "implies the solemnity of the matter only negatively by means of the gross incompetence of the manner" (Mackey: 59). The solemnity of the matter being, in *Gravity's Rainbow*, modern mass death in its anonymity, the work of World War II.

The preterite, as Pynchon calls them in *Gravity's Rainbow*, are those who have been singled out to be passed over, chosen to be excluded: in postwar America, the Jews of the Holocaust, the segregated and lynched African Americans, and anything associated with Vietnam, from American veterans to the murdered masses of Southeast Asia. As Mackey makes clear, Pynchon's whole project gestures toward the preterite at the same time as it wards off the disaster they represent – an ambivalence that fits Jameson's definition of postmodern sublimity. Slothrop, very late in his toilet journey, glimpses the reality of the air-raid shelters, the novel's opening image of the preterite. In a similar way, we see through the harsh caricatural glee of Pynchon's tone, which is like the bright shine on Jack Kennedy's shoes, to an underlying deadly seriousness, the facts of history: slavery and its aftermath; Nazism. These facts point us toward an underworld of the preterite, and a wished-for communion with them that can only take place in unreality.

The preterite, elusively linked together, may form a sort of evanescent secret society. As James Nohrnberg notes in an important essay on *The Crying of Lot 49*, Pynchon engages in not just a "researching of things past and lost," but also a vision of the paraclete, the comforting work of the holy spirit that unites, at least tangentially and momentarily, the community of the forgotten (Nohrnberg: 158). Pynchon's interest in joining the lost ones to one another is comparable to that of Toni Morrison in *Beloved* (1987), currently the most canonized or institutionally favored of contemporary American novels. Both Pynchon and Morrison work through a traumatic history that can neither be ignored nor assimilated, and that continues to exist in troubling, ghostly form. (In Morrison's case, this history is embodied in the persistent afterlife of the slave child Beloved, murdered by its mother.)

The long transition from *Gravity's Rainbow* to Pynchon's later masterpiece, *Mason & Dixon*, can best be understood through a comparison of the two books' beginnings. *Gravity's Rainbow* begins with what appears to be British soldier Pirate Prentice's dream of an evacuation during a V-2 strike but "it is already too late," "it's all theatre": the evacuation becomes an effort "to try to bring events to Absolute Zero . . . and it is poorer the deeper they go . . . ruinous secret cities of poor" (Pynchon, *Gravity's Rainbow*: 3). The tendency toward absolute zero, annihilation or blank poverty, is the form that sublimity takes in *Gravity's Rainbow*. "Each" of the evacuees, Pynchon continues, "has been hearing a voice, one he thought was talking only to him, say, 'You didn't really believe you'd be saved. Come we all know who we are by now. No one was ever going to take the trouble to save you, old fellow'" (Pynchon, *Gravity's Rainbow*: 4). This reflection introduces Pynchon's theme of the preterite, of being passed over rather than saved. The trauma of war expresses itself as an obliteration of heroic existential action; instead, something is done *to* us. In Pynchon's negative religion, accordingly, the preterite are the register or blank screen on which history is projected.

The bare, solitary voice imagined by each evacuee in Prentice's dream modulates, as he awakes, to jocular *Kameradschaft*. The evacuees are transformed into Pirate's actual "comrades in arms" who "look just as rosy as a bunch of Dutch peasants dreaming of their certain resurrection in the next few minutes" (Pynchon, *Gravity's Rainbow*: 4). What follows is the warm shelter of the banana breakfast that Pirate prepares for his hungover companions, complete with musical interludes and stage patter: a solidarity of overacted sophomoric high jinks, shielding us against the annihilation that will reign throughout the rest of *Gravity's Rainbow*.

Mason & Dixon, an errand into a rich and elaborate wilderness, heads in the opposite direction from *Gravity's Rainbow*, which went "beyond the zero" to touch an absolute bareness and an absolute destruction. Whereas *Gravity's Rainbow* is largely concerned with London during the Blitz, when all of daily life was overshadowed by the blunt deathly presence of the V-2 rocket, the later novel is the story of the mostly peaceable partnership between a surveyor and an astronomer, Jeremiah Dixon and Charles Mason, commissioned in 1764 by the Royal Society to settle a boundary dispute between Pennsylvania and Maryland. But Mason and Dixon, whose first joint project involved a trip to South Africa to observe the transit of Venus, find themselves "doom'd to re-encounter thro' the World this public Secret, this shameful Core," the existence of slavery, just as the line they draw will, we know, divide slave states from free states (Pynchon, *Mason & Dixon*: 412). Mason and Dixon gradually sense in the presence of racism and colonial exploitation an invisible, ineluctable force structuring all their adventures.

The course of this revelation is, however, casual, in keeping with *Mason & Dixon*'s picture of history as "a great disorderly tangle of Lines, long and short, weak and strong, vanishing into the Mnemonick Deep" (Pynchon, *Mason & Dixon*: 339). In contrast to the silent, anxious opening of *Gravity's Rainbow*, the "progressive *knotting into*" that characterizes the Londoners' evacuation into bomb shelters, with the passage "under archways, secret entrances of rotten concrete that only looked like the loops of an underpass" (Pynchon, *Gravity's Rainbow*: 3), the beginning of *Mason & Dixon* gives us not an approach to the fearful preterition of those threatened with death, but instead a *Wunderkammer* offered, festively, to the living. All of *Mason & Dixon*'s remarkable first paragraph deserves admiring study, but here I will cite only the description of "a sinister and wonderful Card Table which exhibits the cheaper sinusoidal Grain known in the Trade as Wand'ring Heart, causing an illusion of Depth into which for years children have gaz'd as into the illustrated Pages of Books . . . along with so many hinges, sliding Mortises, hidden catches, and secret compartments that neither the Twins nor their Sister can say they have been to the end of it" (Pynchon, *Mason & Dixon*: 5–6). The children look and look their infant sight away, to paraphrase Elizabeth Bishop (Pynchon also seems to be remembering book 1: 508ff of Wordsworth's *Prelude*, where the poet remembers his childhood "home-amusements," games played around the table or beside the fire).

This table, stationed in the living room of the LeSpark family in post-revolutionary Philadelphia, and cherished by the niece and nephews of Pynchon's storyteller, the Revd Wicks Cherrycoke, in the Christmas season of 1786, furnishes, of course, an image of *Mason & Dixon* itself, that book of marvels with its many "hidden catches and secret compartments." Yet Pynchon's book, like the table, generates a mere "illusion of Depth," spinning fantasies that prove vulnerable to a historical ruthlessness: slavery and colonialism as emblems of the powers of the void, analogous to the brutal scientific reduction epitomized by the V-2 rocket in *Gravity's Rainbow*, and by the Pavlovian researches of its infamous Ned Pointsman. In what has already become the novel's most famous passage, Mason meditates on the idea of America:

Does Britannia, when she sleeps, dream? Is America her dream? – in which all that cannot pass in the metropolitan Wakefulness is allow'd Expression away in the restless Slumber of these Provinces, and on Westward, wherever 'tis not yet mapp'd, nor written down, nor ever, by the majority of mankind, seen, – serving as a very Rubbish-Tip for

> subjunctive Hopes, for all that may yet be true, – Earthly Paradise, Fountain of Youth, Realms of Prester John, Christ's Kingdom, ever behind the sunset, safe till the next Territory to the West be seen and recorded, measur'd and tied in, back into the Net-Work of points already known, that slowly triangulates its Way into the Continent, changing all from subjunctive to declarative, reducing Possibilities to Simplicities that serve the ends of Governments, – winning away from the realm of the Sacred, its Borderlands one by one, and assuming them unto the bare mortal world that is our home, and our Despair. (Pynchon, *Mason & Dixon*: 345)

This passage immediately follows Mason and Dixon's interview with white settlers who have perpetrated a notorious massacre of Indians, and its dreaminess represents a swerve away from the cruel reality of colonialism that is so present in Pynchon's novel, from its early South African episode on. *Mason & Dixon*'s sustained and wonderful fantasizing somewhat guiltily takes the place of an elegy for what has been left out or left behind: the preterite, those who, like the murdered Indians, have been excluded from America's promise.

The "bare mortal world" produced to "serve the ends of Governments" keeps returning in Pynchon's prose: a world that has an eighteenth-century origin, but that clearly evokes the administered universe of the end of the twentieth century. Beneath *Mason & Dixon*'s exponential growth of fantasy lies the suggestion of an emptiness as complete, as bare, as anything to be found in the Zone of *Gravity's Rainbow*.

Like Pynchon and Burroughs, Don DeLillo occupies himself with Their plans for us, with the paranoid knowledge that the "Simplicities that serve the ends of Governments" must be hidden in a narrative as compound, twisted, and multiply plotted as the Warren Commission report (which DeLillo once suggested would have been Joyce's next novel had he survived *Finnegans Wake* and moved to Iowa City). Both *Mao II* and *Underworld* evoke the paranoia given expression in DeLillo's earlier novels, especially *White Noise* (1985) and *Libra* (1988), the latter his remarkable account of Lee Harvey Oswald. As DeLillo's character Lenny Bruce, sounding rather like DeLillo himself, remarks during the Cuban missile crisis, a major focus of *Underworld*, "The true edge is not where you choose to live but where they situate you against your will. This event is infinitely deeper and more electrifying than anything you might choose to do with your own life" (DeLillo, *Underworld*: 505). This is living in the administered universe, its ultimate form the "replacement of human isolation by massive and unvaried ruin" (507).

DeLillo's *Underworld* is a novel about waste and science and nostalgia, about avant-garde art and the nuclear family; it encompasses the second half of the American twentieth century in a various cast of characters, from gangsters to bohemians. The novel starts from the "shot heard round the world," Bobby Thomson's homer against Ralph Branca in the final, deciding game of the 1951 Dodgers–Giants pennant race. Like many of DeLillo's opening scenes, this one is a tour de force. *Underworld* begins with a set piece of historical fiction starring Frank Sinatra, J. Edgar Hoover, Toots Shor, and Jackie Gleason, all of them at the Polo Grounds, watching the game.

For DeLillo's characters, the Bobby Thomson homer signifies some-thing momentous because it precedes postmodernism, the era in which everything is replayed endlessly (DeLillo, *Underworld*: 98). Yet the baseball's odd journey also becomes, in true postmodern style, a thread of near-endless connection and reconnection. In *Underworld*, the base-ball memorabilia collector Marvin voices his "dot theory of reality": "All knowledge is available if you analyze the dots" (DeLillo, *Under-world*: 175, 176). Such analysis shows us the power of technology to "make reality come true" (177). Whereas classic paranoia gives up reality in favor of certainty, here is a new, more impressive paranoia, a technological paranoia that *builds* reality. In this connection DeLillo espouses the Italianate concept of "*Dietrologia*. It means the science of what is behind something. A suspicious event. The science of what is behind an event" (DeLillo, *Underworld*: 280).

The central romantic couple of *Underworld*, Albert and Klara, offer a bourgeois idyll to stand against this universal suspicion and fright:

> [Albert] Bronzini lay beaming in the massive bath, a cast-iron relic raised on ball-and-claw feet, only his head unsubmerged. Salt crystals fizzed all around him. His wife leaning against the door frame, Klara, with their two-year-old affixed to her leg, the child repeating words that daddy issued from the deeps. "Tangerine," Albert said. This was happiness as it was meant to evolve when first conceived in caves, in mud huts on the grassy plain . . . Albert himself in the hot bath, back from the hunt, returned to the fundamental cluster. (DeLillo, *Under-world*: 681–2)

DeLillo's hero Albert, the king of the castle, at home in his bath talking to wife and child, here plays the majestic bourgeois father. His status is validated by a sense of age-old continuity dependent on his mantra: "Tangerine." The word *tangerine*, an exotic Keatsian beaker full of the warm south (Tangier), is like the baseball in its journey, a

Joycean object soaked with friendly resonance, closer to Bloom's soap than Slothrop's harp. The word confirms the persistence of primitive feelings of home, "happiness . . . first conceived in caves, in mud huts on the grassy plain." Private life now looks like an unshifting piece of a larger design, a way to anchor the vastness of *Underworld*'s encyclopedic detective story.

But DeLillo ends by letting his book float free, rejecting the eternal centripetal comfort concentrated in Albert, Klara, and their baby. At the end of *Underworld* Albert and Klara are replaced by a rival, much odder couple, who have never before met. The nun Sister Edgar finds herself "hyperlinked at last" to J. Edgar Hoover, like her a main character in DeLillo's massive novel:

> "Everything is connected in the end. Sister and Brother. A fantasy in cyberspace and a way of seeing the other side and a settling of differences that have less to do with gender than with difference itself, all argument, all conflict programmed out. Is cyberspace a thing within the world or is it the other way around? Which contains the other, and how can you tell for sure?" (DeLillo, *Underworld*: 826–7)

Death means being online, bodiless. *Underworld* finally rests in its concluding evocation of the world-wide web, an echo of Pynchon's paraclete, a vision of comfort extended to the most numerous possible collective.

DeLillo's vision of cyberspace as paradise delivers to us, with an easy double click, the archetypal postmodern utopia best described by Slavoj Žižek. Žižek speaks of the possibility that "radical virtualization – the fact that the whole of reality will soon be 'digitalized,' transcribed, redoubled in the 'Big Other' of cyberspace – will somehow redeem 'real life,' opening it up to a new perception" (Žižek, *Plague of Fantasies*: 164). The new perception is of a reality in the making, whose illusory, unfinished character, which in "actual" life we are made to forget, we might now be able to remember. The new virtualization promises a release from the world of totalitarian pretense depicted by both Pynchon and DeLillo, from the paranoid structure in which we believe only *that the other believes that we believe*. This hall-of-mirrors effect is exposed by a German nun near the end of *White Noise*, who tells the novel's hero that the nuns' role is to "pretend to believe these things" – "the devils, the angels, heaven, hell" – for the sake of "the others who spend their lives believing that *we* still believe" (DeLillo, *White Noise*: 318).

In the final lines of *Underworld*, DeLillo follows the word *peace*, as he earlier followed *tangerine*, but this time he addresses the underworld beneath the computer screen, tracing the word's emergence into pulsing, pensive light. If Slothrop's toilet journey was purgatorial, this new path appears, by contrast, Edenic:

> a word that carries the sunlit ardor of an object deep in drenching noon, the argument of binding touch, but it's only a sequence of pulses on a dullish screen and all it can do is make you pensive – a word that spreads a longing through the raw sprawl of the city and out across the dreaming burns and orchards to the solitary hills. "Peace." (DeLillo, *Underworld*: 827)

Here, in his vision of the world-wide web as the work of the holy spirit, DeLillo sustains the elusive sacred space of epiphany or pentecostal community that we have also seen in Pynchon. The conclusion of *Underworld* invokes the end of the archetypal high Modernist masterpiece, *The Waste Land*, with its chant of "shantih" or "peace," as well as Keats's "Ode to a Nightingale" in which "thy plaintive anthem fades / Past the near meadows, over the still stream, / Up the hill-side; and now 'tis buried deep / In the next valley-glades." In DeLillo, the word of peace is "only a sequence of pulses on a dullish screen," but it fills the space that William Gass memorably invoked in "In the Heart of the Heart of the Country" (1967), and that Pynchon designated as central in his great early story "The Secret Integration" (1964), the white-noise emptiness of American suburbia. "The Secret Integration" is set in a neutral, whites-only, nuclear-familial part of the Berkshires. Pynchon writes: "Everything in the place was out in the open, everything could be seen at a glance; and behind it, under it, around the corners of its houses and the safe, gentle curves of its streets, you came back, you kept coming back, to nothing; nothing but the cheerless earth" (Pynchon, "The Secret Integration": 158). The passage evokes an originary American openness, the powerful blank of Emerson's transparent eyeball in "Nature," or Stevens's "Bare night is best. Bare earth is best," from "Evening Without Angels" – only to expose this openness as a lethal poverty of situation, rather than the force-field of imagination that it was for Emerson and Stevens.

DeLillo's *Mao II*, like Pynchon's *Gravity's Rainbow*, experiments with the specter of a sublimity bigger than the modest, responsible act of writing, even as it depends on this act: on the authorial precision that captures the elusive, that sees behind and between the lines. The entire enterprise of *Underworld* is such a detection, a fine tracing of connections. But in *Mao II*, writerly work itself comes into question: is the novelist's craft an adequate answer to the postmodern world of total spectacle and total violence? The metallic, inhuman world that flickers by us like the cat described in *Mao II*, "a lunar shrug of muscle and fur" (DeLillo, *Mao II*: 90), is capable of shaking off the writerly finesse that invokes it. Accordingly, as a kind of meditation on the superseding of writing itself, *Mao II*'s hero, novelist Bill Gray, finds himself involved with terrorists. Gray, a reclusive cult figure apparently meant to evoke both Pynchon and Gaddis, remarks, "Beckett is the last writer to shape the way we think and see. After him, the major work involves midair explosions and crumpled buildings" (157). The novelist has been replaced by the terrorist, the individual by the mass man or woman, the traditional wedding by, in *Mao II*'s opening scene, the massive nuptials at Yankee Stadium, with thousands of devotees paired off at random by Reverend Sun Myung Moon. Marriage, previously the emblem of the private life, has attained the sublimity of a meteor that crashes into the earth, "a catastrophe, a total implosion of the future" (DeLillo, *Mao II*: 80).

But *Mao II* ends with a fragile victory of individual, careful art over the new universe of mass, "televisual" existence suggested by the novel's paired icons of Chairman Mao and Reverend Moon. On the last page of *Mao II* the photographer Brita, lover of now-dead novelist Bill Gray, stands watching a lonely wedding in that archetypal war zone, Beirut. The happy couple is saluted by a tank that swivels its gun turret "like a smutty honeymoon joke," and hears, not the expected guns, but rather a camera's flashbulbs popping. Brita, isolated on her balcony, "crosses her arms over her body against the chill and counts off the bursts of relentless light. The dead city photographed one more time" (240–1). Like Pynchon's Oedipa Maas in *Lot 49*, Brita finds herself exposed, a target for all manner of forces beyond her control. Yet this vulnerability insures her, keeps her where she should be. No existential quester, she is instead just a lucky survivor, whom the forces of destruction have unexpectedly passed over.

Both Pynchon and DeLillo turn away from the massive and intense work of constant transgression that animates Burroughs, Acker, or the British writer J. G. Ballard in *Crash* (1973). In a recent book, *The Fragile Absolute*, Žižek comments that, in postmodernism, the use of transgressive shock that distinguished Modernism has now become a familiar commodity: "the transgressive excess loses its shock value and is fully integrated into the established artistic market" (Žižek, *The*

Fragile Absolute: 25). Žižek continues by stating, apropos of the post-modern use of excremental trash as art object, the skeptical question that this artistic practice itself asks: "Is not every element that claims the right to occupy the sacred place of the Thing by definition an excremental object, a piece of trash that can never be up to its task[?]" (Žižek, *The Fragile Absolute*: 26).

Such postmodern skepticism doubts not just the capacity of any object, however refined or transformed, to fill the sacred place reserved for art. It also doubts that the sacred place can itself be sustained, suspecting that the true destiny of the sacred or sublime status of art is to diminish in value, to become a mere commodity (rather than a reflection on commodification that, through this reflection, retains its superiority, as in Peter Bürger's theory of the avant-garde). The result of the sort of extremist skeptical postmodernism that Žižek describes is that the sublime that distinguished the Modernist achievement threatens to vanish, surrendering to the fear that sublimity itself may suddenly be revealed as trash, as the meaningless or excremental echo of a dead tradition. Yet such diminishing can always be reversed, it seems; sublimity remains possible, judging by the examples of DeLillo and Pynchon.

In the light of Žižek's analysis, we can link the sublimity of *Gravity's Rainbow* with its famous obscenity, as proclaimed by the trustees who refused to give it the Pulitzer Prize, despite the judges' unanimous vote in its favor. The trustees found *Gravity's Rainbow* turgid, obscene, and unreadable – itself an echo of the reception accorded to *Ulysses* and *Naked Lunch*. Unreadability here stands for a sublimity that proves itself by threatening to collapse into the grotesque, the caricatural, the obscene.

The noisiness, the near-overwhelming volume, of American postmodernism, from *The Recognitions* and *Naked Lunch* on, reads like the shocked reflection of a mindless, ceaseless totality: the sublimity Jameson sees in late capitalism, which has turned the systematic into an unimaginable, systematized chaos. But what is most significant in *Gravity's Rainbow*, as in the other texts I have examined here, is not its use of loud, transgressive effects to convey the sense of this chaos, but rather its quieter evocation of the preterite, the lost ones. The elegiac coloring of *Mason & Dixon* was there all along in Pynchon. Like DeLillo, Pynchon gathers together the fragments that remain after the work of destruction, rather than simply admiring, or standing frightened before, the sublime character of this destruction. Not everything has been annihilated, they seem to tell us, nor has it been preserved only as a deathly and eternal collector's item, a tribute to our paranoia. History is not over: but this is a sense we can only reach by looking back into it (with wondering), as well as behind it (with suspicion). In *Underworld* DeLillo defines dietrologia as "the science of what is behind something. A suspicious event. The science of what is behind an event" (280). Dietrologia follows, supplements, dietrologia.

References and further reading

Barth, John. "The Literature of Exhaustion." (Originally published in *Atlantic* [August 1967].) In *On Contemporary Literature*. Ed. Richard Kostelanetz. 2nd edn. New York: Avon and Discus, 1969.

Barthelme, Donald. *City Life*. New York: Farrar, Straus and Giroux, 1970.

Barthelme, Donald. *The Dead Father*. New York: Farrar, Straus and Giroux, 1975.

Baudrillard, Jean. *The Ecstasy of Communication*. Trans. Bernard and Caroline Schutze. Ed. Sylvere Lotringer. Brooklyn, NY: Autonomedia, 1988.

Bürger, Peter. *The Theory of the Avant-Garde*. Trans. Michael Shaw. Minneapolis: University of Minnesota Press, 1984.

Burroughs, William. *Naked Lunch*. New York: Grove Press, 1959.

Codrescu, Andrei. *American Poetry since 1970: Up Late*. New York: Four Walls Eight Windows, 1987.

Coover, Robert. *Pricksongs & Descants*. New York: Dutton, 1969.

DeLillo, Don. *Mao II*. New York: Viking Penguin, 1991.

DeLillo, Don. *Underworld*. New York: Scribner's, 1997.

DeLillo, Don. *White Noise*. (Originally published 1985.) Ed. Mark Osteen. New York: Penguin (Viking Critical Library), 1998.

Gaddis, William. *The Recognitions*. New York: Harcourt, Brace, 1955.

Gaddis, William. *Carpenter's Gothic*. New York: Penguin, 1985.

Habermas, Jürgen. "Modernity – An Incomplete Project." In *The Anti-Aesthetic*. Ed. Hal Foster. Port Townsend, WA: Bay Press, 1983. 3–15.

Helmling, Stephen. "Failure and the Sublime: Fredric Jameson's Writing in the '50s." *Postmodern Culture* 3.10 (May 2000).

Hogue, Lawrence. *Race. Modernity. Postmodernity*. Buffalo: State University of New York Press, 1996.

Hutcheon, Linda. *A Poetics of Postmodernism*. New York: Routledge, 1988.

Huyssen, Andreas. *After the Great Divide*. Bloomington: Indiana University Press, 1986.

Jameson, Fredric. "The Politics of Theory: Ideological Positions in the Postmodernism Debate." (Originally published in *New German Critique* 33 [Fall 1984]: 53–65.) In *The Ideologies of Theory: Essays 1971–86*, vol. 2. Minneapolis: University of Minnesota Press, 1988.

Jameson, Fredric. *Postmodernism*. Durham, NC: Duke University Press, 1991.

Kershner, R. B. *The Twentieth Century Novel: An Introduction.* Boston: Bedford Books, 1971.

Lyotard, Jean-François. *The Postmodern Condition: A Report on Knowledge.* Trans. Brian Massuni. Minneapolis: University of Minnesota Press, 1988.

Mackey, Louis. "Paranoia, Pynchon, and Preterition." (Originally published in *Substance* 30 [Winter 1981].) In *Modern Critical Interpretations: Thomas Pynchon's Gravity's Rainbow.* Ed. Harold Bloom. New York: Chelsea House, 1986. 53–68.

Mikics, David. "Postmodernism, Ethnicity, and Underground Revisionism in Ishmael Reed." In *Essays in Postmodern Culture.* Eds Eyal Amiran and John Unsworth. New York: Oxford University Press, 1993. 295–324.

Morrison, Toni. *Beloved.* New York: New American Library, 1987.

Nohrnberg, James. "Pynchon's Paraclete." In *Thomas Pynchon: A Collection of Critical Essays.* Ed. Edward Mendelson. Englewood Cliffs, NJ: Prentice-Hall, 1978. 147–61.

Pynchon, Thomas. *The Crying of Lot 49.* (1st edn 1965.) New York: Perennial Library, 1986.

Pynchon, Thomas. *Gravity's Rainbow.* New York: Penguin, 1973.

Pynchon, Thomas. "The Secret Integration." In *Slow Learner: Early Stories.* Boston: Little, Brown, 1984. 139–93.

Pynchon, Thomas. *Mason & Dixon.* New York: Henry Holt, 1997.

Reed, Ishmael. *Mumbo Jumbo.* New York: Bard Avon, 1972.

Tanner, Tony. *City of Words: American Fiction. 1950–1970.* New York: Harper and Row, 1987.

Vattimo, Gianni. *La società transparente.* 2nd enlarged edn. (1st edn 1989.) Milan: Garzanti, 2000.

Žižek, Slavoj. *The Plague of Fantasies.* London: Verso, 1997.

Žižek, Slavoj. *The Fragile Absolute.* London: Verso, 2000.

Chapter 9

Gay and Lesbian Writing in Post-World War II America

Mary Jo Bona

Introduction

Since the early 1950s, American gay and lesbian writers have conveyed variety and intelligence in their works despite an early atmosphere of enforced conformity. Considered a censorious and repressive decade, the 1950s in America nonetheless produced daring literary works by both gay men and lesbians. While it might seem a convenience to divide American homosexual writing neatly into pre- and post-Stonewall generations (before and after the rise of gay liberation in 1969), such divisions tend to overlook the resistance of writers during the decades of the 1950s and 1960s. In the United States after 1950, Joseph McCarthy's House Un-American Activities Committee (HUAC) classified homosexuals along with communists as dangerous, claiming that they were at risk of blackmail and therefore potential subversives who should be ostracized from government or made subject to punishment through incarceration.

During such difficult times, lesbian and gay writers continued to write stunningly revealing works, including James Baldwin's novel *Giovanni's Room*, and Jeannette Howard Foster's pioneering bibliography of fiction and poetry in the United States, *Sex Variant Women in Literature*, both published in 1956. On the cultural front, the 1950s also saw the radical beginnings of both gay and lesbian movements, represented by the Mattachine Society developed by Marxists in the early 1950s and the Daughters of Bilitis, a lesbian organization, whose periodical, the *Ladder*, reviewed lesbian writers. Although both groups retreated into "respect-ability" (for example, by focusing on assimilation within a dominant heterosexual world), according to historian John D'Emilio, they set the stage for future tensions in twentieth-century lesbian and gay history between radical liberationist and liberal reformist politics.

Representing a culmination of many forces throughout the postwar period (especially the black and student movements of the 1960s), the uprising on June 27, 1969, at the Stonewall Inn Bar in Greenwich Village ushered in the contemporary American gay and lesbian move-ment. The Stonewall was a gay bar and a private club in Greenwich Village. The police had raided other gay bars in the area, and came to the Stonewall with a search warrant, authorized to investigate ostens-ible reports of illegal selling of alcohol. Refusing to be routed by one more police raid, the two hundred or so working-class patrons – gay men, butch lesbians, and drag queens – initiated a grassroots libera-tion movement. A riot was staged and continued the following night. These riots came to be known as the Stonewall Rebellion, and marked the first gay riots in history (Faderman: 194–5). Gay liberation was born and the Gay Liberation Front, modeled on civil rights rhetoric and the liberation struggles in Vietnam and Algeria, interrogated struc-tures of power in a heterosexual and patriarchal society (Duberman: 217). The ongoing themes within the literature at this time included coming out, sexual exploration in the city and/or in pastoral places of retreat, and sexually transgressive writing, including material on pornography and sadomasochism.

Unfortunately, continued criticism of and resistance toward homo-eroticism was exacerbated by the AIDS crisis, beginning in the 1980s. Certainly the epidemic moved gay literature beyond coming-out stories and sexual adventures. At the same time, however, the illness, which initially struck homosexual men, refueled the mythology estab-lished in the nineteenth century that linked homosexuality with ill-ness and death. The considerable body of testimonial AIDS literature, however, put names and faces to those suffering from the disease, and many gay artists sought in their works to educate an initially indifferent public. The assimilation of the idea of AIDS into the main-stream was wrought by strategic activist movements such as the AIDS Coalition to Unleash Power (ACT-UP) and the staggering number of writers who died from this disease. No longer the sole preserve of the gay community, literary responses to AIDS continue to grow and change. The introduction of drug treatments, such as protease inhibi-tors, that may slow the production of the virus in the body had the effect of shifting the focus of literature from an emphasis on states of crisis to the more subtle and universal problems of living with the disease.

Gay and lesbian writing continued to flourish in the 1990s. Both traditional gay and lesbian presses – Alyson, Naiad, Seal, and the former Firebrand – and academic presses – Columbia University Press's "Between Men/Between Women" series, Duke University's "Series Q," New York University Press's "The Cutting Edge" series – devote time and energy to publishing works by and about homosexuality. In the 1980s and 1990s, gay and lesbian publishing extended into the central regions of the United States with the publications of literary journals such as the *James White Review* (Minneapolis) and *Common Lives/Lesbian Lives* (Iowa City). With the boom in postmodern lesbian and gay scholarship and queer theory, the literature by gays and lesbians finds a home in college classrooms and academic fields of study. In keeping with the aims of postmodernism, recent literature and critical analysis of the literature of lesbians and gays shift away from a unified and definable idea of sexual identity and move toward a more expansive understanding of sexual expression.

Gay Writers: 1950s–60s

The typical description of 1950s America as a repressed, conformist, and humorless decade often fails to account for the racial unrest and the radical beginnings of civil rights movements. James Baldwin's writing career began in the last years of legislated racial segregation in America and his works, both nonfiction and fiction, explore the difficulties faced by blacks in a hostile society. Baldwin introduced homosexual themes in *Go Tell It on the Mountain* (1953) and *Giovanni's Room*, exploring troubled adolescence in the former and the shame associated with homosexuality in the latter. His early departure from standard American and African American literary conventions – including depictions of interracial love affairs – helped pave the way for subsequent generations of gay writers well before the Stonewall riots of 1969. Another prolific writer, Gore Vidal, traverses a wide range of themes and subjects, including the early focus on a gay man in *The City and the Pillar* (1949) and his controversial and Wildean achievement in *Myra Breckinridge* (1968). Impudent and egotistical, Myra, formerly Myron, is a homosexual male turned female through surgery. Vidal explores the relationship between sex and power, overturning popular and stereotypical ideas about gender identity, anticipating queer writers and transgender theorists by more than two decades.

The complex and innovative works of James Purdy often tell the story of tragic passion for gay men, a conventional theme of the period. While *Malcolm* (1960) put Purdy on the literary map (it was adapted as a play of the same name by Edward Albee), *Eustace Chisholm and the Works* (1968) explores the consequences of repressing gay desire and the internalized homophobia that causes the destruction of the protagonist. Purdy continues these themes in later fiction in the 1970s and 1980s as well (*Narrow Rooms*, 1978; *Garments the Living Wear*, 1989). John Rechy, best known for his novel of male prostitution, *City of Night* (1963), managed to sign a publishing contract with the then unknown Grove Press, which subsequently printed his first five novels and a nonfiction documentary on male prostitution. (Grove Press has since become a mainstream publisher.) Considered a leading Mexican American writer, Rechy's first sensational novel provides a close-up view of the dangerous and lonely profession of male prostitution and uses the cadences of the blues and the movement of rock and roll to capture the story.

Two major postwar playwrights, Tennessee Williams and Edward Albee, exhibit gay visions in their work, albeit obliquely during the 1950s and 1960s. Critics of Williams have traced homosexual resonances in famous plays such as *The Glass Menagerie* and *A Streetcar Named Desire*, examining the effects of living in the closet and the punishment for pursuing alternative sexualities. Williams's long-uncollected short stories, mostly written during the late 1940s and mid-1950s, including "One Arm" and "Hard Candy," examine more overtly gay male desire, beauty, and, a staple of Williams's work, the wounded body. (Williams's stories were collected and published in 1985; Gore Vidal wrote the introduction.)

Throughout much of his early career, Edward Albee's writing suffered from the homophobic biases of critics. Albee's first play, *The Zoo Story* (1960), is regarded as establishing in American writing an absurdist vision of relationships. Exploring the debilitating nature of the American family, Albee's *Who's Afraid of Virginia Woolf?* (1962) was an instant critical success, but nonetheless met with vitriolic responses from some critics, who accused the playwright (who was discreet about his homosexuality) of misrepresenting decent, straight Americans by attributing his own "perverse" behavior to them (Sinfield: 228). Critic Alan Sinfield reminds readers that the theater was not a supportive environment for a gay playwright, especially if, as in the case of Albee, he criticized prevailing American ideology. Displeasing both straight and gay critics, playwright Mart Crowley's *The Boys in the Band* (1968) was produced off-Broadway and became an instant sensation, running for three years and filmed in 1970. Like a more explicitly gay version of Albee's *Who's Afraid of Virginia Woolf?*, *The Boys in the Band* presents gay men inhabiting a single set, revealing uncomfortable truths about themselves. Crowley, however, represents the standard gay motifs of the time, depicting characters like the closeted homophobe, the hyper-masculine cowboy, and the quasi-tragic gay man. Despite its use of types, Crowley's play sets the stage for influential gay playwrights of the 1970s.

Several other notable playwrights – including Robert Patrick and Lanford Wilson – were pioneers of openly gay drama in the 1960s, working in venues such as the off-Broadway Caffé Cino. Produced in 1964, Patrick's *The Haunted Host* and Wilson's *The Madness of Lady Bright* overtly portray contemporary gay men's lives (including a trans-vestite man in Wilson's play). Both playwrights continued to produce plays into the 1990s; Patrick's *The Haunted Host* in fact experienced a successful New York revival in 1991, with playwright Harvey Fierstein appearing in the play.

Poets of the 1950s and 1960s confronted rejection from the main-stream media. "The Homosexual in Society," a now-famous essay published in 1944 by Robert Duncan in the journal *Politics*, was one of the first written works to speak candidly on homosexual writers. While Duncan's commentary portrayed homosexuals as a minority group subject to bias, he believed that they should nonetheless seek acceptance within the larger culture. Duncan authored many volumes of poetry, including *Bending the Bow* and *My Mother Would Be a Falconess*, both published in 1968. While Duncan had a reputation as a "Beat" poet, his verse was more traditional and formal than that of his con-temporary, Allen Ginsberg. Ginsberg's 1955 classic, "Howl," is perhaps the most famous post-World War II poem written in English. Like Whitman before him, Ginsberg populates his long lines of free verse with those marginalized from society, those "angelheaded hipsters" who oppose the materialism, militarism, and repressive Christianity of the Cold War era. Making his homosexuality the basis of his poetic aesthetic, Ginsberg became an important figure in the Beat move-ment of the 1950s and the most socially active gay poet of the 1960s and 1970s. He and Duncan also wrote powerfully about the terror of the Vietnam War. James Merrill may be the most technically intricate and esoteric of the gay poets during the post-World War II period.

Merrill's poetic trilogy, combined into *The Changing Light at Sandover* (1982), is regarded as a major poetic work, employing traditional terza rima and incorporating gay relationships.

Gay Writers: 1970s–80s

Gay writers emerged and flourished during the coalescence of the gay and lesbian movement after the June Stonewall riots. One of the leaders of the gay literary movement during the 1970s was Felice Picano. The author of several novels, short stories, and poetry, Picano founded the first gay publishing house in New York City, SeaHorse Press, collaborated with two small gay presses to form Gay Presses of New York (GPNY), and edited an early landmark anthology called *A True Likeness: Lesbian and Gay Writing Today* (1980). Following three commercially successful novels, Picano published *The Lure* (1979), a coming-out story and a classic thriller set in Manhattan. Founded in New York in 1979, the Violet Quill, a gay writers' club, included such members as Picano, Robert Ferro, and Andrew Holleran. This circle of writers helped create a post-Stonewall era in which homosexuality was placed at the center of literary focus.

One of the most distinguished members of this explicitly identified gay writers' group was Edmund White, author of works in many genres, including biography (*Genet*, 1994), the novel (*Nocturnes for the King of Naples*, 1978), the sex manual (*The Joy of Gay Sex*, co-authored with Charles Silverstein, 1977), the travelogue (*States of Desire*, 1980), and the autobiographical novel (*A Boy's Own Story*, 1982, and *The Beautiful Room is Empty*, 1988). Moving from the surreal, dream-like fantasy of his first novel, *Forgetting Elena* (1973) (set on a fictional Fire Island), to the more realistic social observations of his autobiographical fiction, beginning with *A Boy's Own Story*, White explores his quest for identity as a gay man. White's autobiographical novels lead the gay narrator away from his Midwestern family, through college years, to New York and his participation in the Stonewall Riot.

As in much of gay fiction, White's coming-out-novels portray both a literal and psychological move away from the family of origin. In contrast, Robert Ferro's novels are firmly tied to the biological family, including extended family members. In two of his autobiographical novels, *The Family of Max Desir* (1983) and *Second Son* (1988), Ferro emphasizes that not all families are nuclear or shaped by Anglo-American mores.

While the novels examine homosexual integration within the Italian American family, Ferro insists that such homosexual relationships are consistent with ethnic family values. Another member of the Violet Quill, Andrew Holleran, captured the attention of mainstream critics and readers with his 1978 *Dancer from the Dance*, a novel epitomizing post-Stonewall gay literature in its portrayal of disco life in Manhattan and on Fire Island. Considered by some critics a gay *Great Gatsby*, Holleran's novel depicts the gay ghetto of promiscuity; like Gatsby, the protagonist of *Dancer* suffers the terrible realization of the fragility and illusory nature of beauty. In this world, traditional family culture is antithetical to frenetic gay life, though his second novel, *Nights in Aruba* (1983), more pointedly depicts the conflict of the protagonist between homosexual freedom in New York and closeted family life in Florida.

Perhaps the most playful and popular representation of family is drawn in the fictional commune of Armistead Maupin's *Tales of the City* sequence of novels (1978, 1980, 1982, 1984, 1987, 1989), set in San Francisco. Maupin's series examines the changing milieu of San Francisco, from the excessive freedoms of the 1970s to the tragic consequences of the AIDS era. Quite appealing is Maupin's creation of Anna Madrigal, landlady and surrogate "mother" figure to the collection of tenants – gays and straights – that inhabit her apartments at 28 Barbary Lane. Providing an inviting alternative to the family of origin, Maupin nonetheless recreates nostalgic ideas about family in his novels.

Like playwright Lanford Wilson, who began his career off-Broadway and was known for his departure from conventional themes and forms, playwrights Christopher Durang and Harvey Fierstein also met with early success in small theaters. Durang's plays expanded the genre of satire in his caustic portraits of the nuclear family (*The Marriage of Bette and Boo*, 1973), of the Hollywood industry (*A History of American Film*, 1978), and of Roman Catholic ideology (*Sister Mary Ignatius Explains It All For You*, 1979). Well known for his plays *Torch Song Trilogy* (1982) and *Safe Sex* (1987), Harvey Fierstein began his productions in off-off-Broadway theater, but moved quickly to Broadway and to positive reviews. Presenting homosexuals as seeking the same satisfactions as nongay people – a place to live, a decent job, and a companion – Fierstein sometimes met with critics who disliked the traditionalism of his plays. However, the playwright's emphasis on commitment and responsibility is fully integrated within his portrayal of the often marginalized lives of drag queens. Both Durang's 1987

Laughing Heart and Fierstein's *Safe Sex* incorporate the cultural and political situation of AIDS in the United States. In order to highlight the scathing misuse of religious orthodoxy, Durang articulates the inhumanity of homophobia in a satiric skit in which a fundamentalist God decides that homosexuals, Haitians, and hemophiliacs will get AIDS. In three one-act plays, Fierstein's *Safe Sex* explores the difficulties of intimacy in the time of AIDS.

The AIDS Crisis

The preoccupying concerns of post-Stonewall gay literature – the exploration of gay identity, male friendships, and sexual exploration – were fractured by the epidemic of AIDS in the 1980s and 1990s. While the focus on AIDS in writing may itself be coming to an end in the new millennium, during the early years of the crisis, gay writers began writing prolifically, focusing on health, the tragedy of AIDS, the accompanying pervasive state of mourning in the gay community, and the limited power of art to capture accurately or fully the horrors of the disease. Artistic priorities often shifted dramatically to reflect the urgency of the crisis. Poet, novelist, and memoirist Paul Monette commented, for example, that he'd rather be remembered for loving well than for writing well, and for "being a witness to the calamity that has engulfed my people." His distinguished writing career and outspoken AIDS activism allowed Monette to contribute importantly to the visibility of AIDS as a national issue in mainstream venues. Written in response to his lover Roger Horwitz's AIDS diagnosis, Monette's harrowing book of poems *Love Alone: 18 Elegies for Rog* (1988) and his memoir *Borrowed Time* (1988) examine the mourner's inconsolable grief during the illness and death of AIDS of a loved one. Monette's novel *Afterlife* (1990) expands on the topic of illness to include a fictional story about AIDS "widowers" and emphasizes the necessities of personal activism. *Becoming a Man: Half a Life Story* (1992) explores with humor and compassion the struggles of growing up gay, the suffocation of living in the closet, and living with AIDS, from which the writer himself died in 1995.

Nonfiction writer Randy Shilts produced the first influential commentary on the AIDS crisis in his investigative historiography, *And the Band Played On* (1987). Several other post-Stonewall writers turned to the topic of AIDS with increasing frequency. For example, Andrew Holleran's essays in the gay journal *Christopher Street* are collected in his third book, *Ground Zero* (1988), which, in part, focuses on the limitations of art in capturing the savage nature of what Holleran calls "the plague." Sam D'Allesandro, Christopher Davis, David Feinberg, and Ethan Mordden are just four of many gay writers who contributed AIDS stories to George Stambolian's *Men on Men* series (anthologies of short stories, beginning in 1986). Despite Stambolian's 1991 death from AIDS, David Bergman continues to edit the series and recently published the 2000 edition of *Men on Men*.

Like Robert Ferro, Felice Picano, and Andrew Holleran before him, Christopher Bram comes out of a tradition of urban gay male writing in which the central issues of gay male life become the focus of his fiction. With his 1989 *In Memory of Angel Clare*, however, Bram moves beyond the perennial gay theme of "coming out" in order to explore with humor and social perspicacity the reactions, by his grief-stricken lover and a circle of Manhattan friends, to the death of a beloved filmmaker from AIDS.

African American novelist Samuel R. Delany, perhaps one of the most innovative science fiction writers since the early 1960s, also considers contemporary issues, including AIDS. In 1975, Delany published *Dhalgren*, a technical tour de force, compared by critics to James Joyce's *Finnegans Wake*, and considered a pioneering work of New Wave science fiction. Offering sympathetic depictions of alternative sexualities, Delany's *Neveryon* series (1976–87) incorporates erotic portrayals of mastery and enslavement, and innovative depictions of gender and sexuality. Additionally, in "The Tales of Plagues and Carnivals" (Appendix A of *Flight From Neveryon*, 1985), Delany uses the topic of AIDS to depict the disease in persons of color and the homeless and to chronicle more largely the apocalypse in a city like New York. Delany expands on these themes in *The Mad Man* (1994) by depicting the protagonist (a black gay man without AIDS) replicating degrading sexual experiments and defending promiscuous sex during the time of AIDS. Delany's writings make connections between several disparate areas in contemporary culture – between African and white American, gay and straight, science fiction and avant-garde.

Playwrights also convincingly made AIDS writing an influential and necessary American literary subject in the United States in the 1980s and 1990s. Plays about AIDS during these decades dramatize the magnitude of the epidemic. As Alan Sinfield notes, as in poetry and other prose works, such plays seek to represent the human reality of the illness, and its attendant concerns regarding loss, stigma, and impending death. These dramas thus helped to draw the attention of the wider community to the gravity of the disease. The first play about AIDS, Robert Chesley's *Night Sweats* (1984), was quickly followed in 1985 by William Hoffman's *As Is* and Larry Kramer's *The Normal Heart*. Each of these plays gave special urgency to the AIDS crisis. Called by one critic the paradigmatic AIDS drama, Hoffman's *As Is* details one man's journey to discover the self-love that is required when one is diagnosed with AIDS. Employing images of the Holocaust (as do other playwrights, including Kramer and Tony Kushner), Hoffman represents the extremity of pain and fear produced by imminent death.

The linking of AIDS and activism fuels the career of Larry Kramer. While his 1978 novel *Faggots* angered the gay press because of its satirical critique of gay promiscuity, by the 1980s, when the novel was reissued, lifestyle changes within the community had acquired increased urgency. Both AIDS activist and writer, Kramer in his play *The Normal Heart* traces the early years of the illness, chronicles the often foiled attempts of activists to get increased governmental funding, and tells the story of one man's involvement in the formation of the Gay Men's Health Crisis. While not all gay activists cared for Kramer's attack on promiscuity (regarded in the immediate post-Stonewall decade as fundamental to gay liberation), his work as the founder of ACT-UP in 1987 and his numerous essays on the crisis (published as *Reports from the Holocaust: The Making of an AIDS Activist*, 1989) profoundly politicized the gay response to AIDS in America.

Perhaps more than any other work of gay writing, Tony Kushner's two-part play *Angels in America: A Gay Fantasia on National Themes* (1992, 1993) brought the trauma of AIDS and the realities of gay American life in the 1990s to mainstream viewers. Among its lengthy cast of characters, *Angels in America* includes a historical figure from 1950s America: Roy Cohn, chief counsel to Senator Joseph McCarthy, chair of HUAC. A vehement anti-communist crusader, Cohn also outwardly asserted his hatred for homosexuals while denying his own homosexuality. Set in New York City during the mid-1980s, *Angels in America* portrays Roy Cohn, the conservative lawyer and former aide to Joseph McCarthy, refusing to accept the fact that he has been diagnosed with AIDS. Other characters include Joe Pitt, a Mormon homosexual who leaves his wife, and Prior Walter, an openly gay man with AIDS, who is the recipient of a prophetic vision about America. Compared to classic American plays such as *A Streetcar Named Desire* and *Death of a Salesman*, Kushner's play suggests that, like the pioneers who settled in America, homosexuals have courageously traversed an unmapped terrain.

As demonstrated by Paul Monette's *Love Alone*, the genre of poetry supremely captures the language of loss. Not surprisingly, then, many gay poets turned to the topic of AIDS during the height of the crisis. An early example of the elegiac strain in such poetry is Robert Boucheron's 1985 *Epitaphs for the Plague Dead*, in which a variety of persons, including a baby who contracted the virus before birth, offer their own epitaphs in individual monologues. An exploration of a meeting between a heterosexual man, his dying brother, and his brother's male lover, in "How to Watch Your Brother Die" (from *Poems for Lost and Un-lost Boys*), brought recognition to Michael Lassell in the same year. Several of Lassell's later poems, especially the section "Rendezvous with Death," published in *Decade Dance* (1990), explore the tragic consequences of the epidemic. Mark Doty describes his collections *My Alexandria* (1993) and *Atlantis* (1995) as an effort to examine the inseparability of desire and loss. Doty's elegiac poems mourn the horrific consequences of AIDS as an experience of "seeing blood everywhere"("Fog"), but temper the resulting fear with lyrical elegance and an unsentimental belief in redemption.

Like the work of Samuel Delany in prose, African American poets such as Melvin Dixon and Essex Hemphill articulate the struggles of black gay men who are living through the agonies of AIDS-related illnesses. Melvin Dixon, whose poems have appeared in the ground-breaking anthology of African American AIDS writing, *Brother to Brother: New Writings by Black Gay Men* (1991), make visible the particular difficulties of African American gay men living with the disease. Many of the poems in *Brother to Brother* figure prominently in Marlon Riggs's critically acclaimed film *Tongues Untied* (1991). Essex Hemphill, editor of *Brother to Brother* (who carried on the work of trailblazing anthologist Joseph Beam), also recognizes the relationship between homophobia, racism, and AIDS. A pervasive motif in the literature of black gay writers is the fraught relationship between the individual black gay man and certain segments of the larger African American community. In "Cordon Negro," however, Hemphill's admission that he is dying "twice as fast / as any other American" indicts the larger United States culture as a source of racism, homophobia, and medical neglect.

Gay Writers: Late 1980s–90s

While the topic of AIDS continues to inform the literature throughout the 1990s, it is often incorporated into family narratives along with other subjects and themes. Often unwelcome in their biological families, gays and lesbians at times militantly refused to portray the traditionally nuclear, American family in which normative heterosexuality is assumed. Nonetheless, the topic of family is often of concern to gay writers, who represent it in diverse and complicated ways. A place of neglect, homophobia, social control, struggle, and even genuine joy, the redefinition of family continues to be a source of abiding concern for recent gay writers who are reflecting and inventing family configurations in their work. Writers of this generation include, for example, Randall Kenan, Michael Cunningham, and David Leavitt.

Randall Kenan, a black writer from the South, is nontraditional in the sense that his 1989 novel, *A Visitation of Spirits*, does not focus on the available tropes of gay writing since Stonewall. The "coming-out" narrative, the migration to the big city, and the illness narrative are absent in this story of Horace Cross's life in rural North Carolina, which ends in his suicide, recalling the pre-Stonewall tales of the tragic homosexual. Kenan, the biographer of James Baldwin (*James Baldwin*, 1994), is said in this novel to have rewritten Baldwin's *Go Tell It On the Mountain* (1953) in his examination of the limitations of certain segments of the African American community and church and in his depiction of the supernatural experiences of its protagonist. Kenan's second book, a collection of 12 short stories entitled *Let the Dead Bury Their Dead* (1992), also focuses on the lives of blacks in Tims Creek, North Carolina, employing the magic realism apparent in his earlier work. Another Southern American writer, Allan Gurganus, who achieved commercial success with *The Oldest Living Confederate Widow Tells All* (1989), writes reflexively about whiteness and identity in his 1990 collection *White People*, which, like Kenan's work, is situated in the South.

With the publication of his second novel, *Home at the End of the World* (1990), Michael Cunningham explores the untenable nature of an alternative family structure, which consists of two men (one gay, one straight) and a woman who bears a child with the straight man, but ultimately opts for single motherhood. By exploring themes of family, friendship, commitment, and AIDS-related illness, the author places homosexuality within the larger context of American life, refusing to ghettoize the gay experience. In a similar manner, David Leavitt integrates gay themes into the larger fabric of affluent, white, traditional American family life. Critics agree that no gay writer of the post-AIDS generation has received more attention than Leavitt, whose stories in *Family Dancing* (1984) portray relationships between parents and children. Leavitt's first novel, *The Lost Language of Cranes* (1986), depicts the complexities of "coming out" within the family when one of the members doing so is the gay son's father. *Equal Affections* (1989), Leavitt's second novel, expands on this theme of multiple coming out within families by introducing both a lesbian daughter and a gay son, whom the traditional family must learn to accept.

While much of the literature by gay men in the 1990s attempts to portray in a realistic manner the complexities of gay life in a hetero-sexual world, other writers, uninterested in depicting gays in tradi-tional, mainstream American families, use postmodern techniques to explore graphic same-sex erotic behavior, including sexual violence. One such writer is Dennis Cooper. While Cooper's first collection of poems, *Tiger Beat*, was published in a banner year for white, gay males – 1978, the year that also saw Edmund White's *Nocturnes for the King of Naples*, Holleran's *Dancer from the Dance*, and Kramer's *Faggots*, his later novels, *Closer* (1990) and *Frisk* (1991), explore the connections between desire and death, creating disengaged male protagonists and depicting sadomasochistic themes. *Martin and John*, Dale Peck's 1993 debut novel (first published in the United Kingdom as *Fucking Mar-tin*), upsets traditional linear narrative in favor of multiple narrative patterns, including a story of a self-destructive young man whose lover dies of AIDS. Both writers embark on a thematic and narrative course that differs from the post-Stonewall literature that celebrates gay sexuality.

Lesbian Writers: 1950s–60s

Lesbian writing, like gay writing, did not achieve cultural visibility until the late 1960s and early 1970s. Nevertheless, a novel that had a profound influence on lesbian thought in America was British writer Radclyffe Hall's *The Well of Loneliness* (1928), arguably the most influ-ential lesbian novel of the twentieth century. Defining lesbianism within the perimeters of nineteenth-century discourses of sexologists, Hall subscribed to a definition of lesbians as a "third sex," tragic and maimed sexual inverts. Despite the self-loathing of Hall's protagonist, the author believed that homosexuality was natural, her protagonist was noble, and lesbianism incontrovertibly existed.

Ann Bannon's five lesbian "pulp" novels, the Beebo Brinker series, spanning the years 1957–62, might be said to rewrite the fate of protagonist Stephen Gordon in *The Well of Loneliness*. Bannon is one of the few women who wrote overtly about lesbian experiences during the 1950s (even though Bannon is a pseudonym). The author inaugurates two staple features of lesbian and gay fiction: the migration to the big city and the process of coming out. The fifth novel in the series, *Beebo Brinker* (1962), which chronologically appears first in the sequence, explores a young woman from the Midwest who jubilantly enters the subculture of the Greenwich Village bar scene. Beebo Brinker, a handsome and self-assured butch woman, is nonetheless adversely affected by her choice to live and dress as she does. In this way, Bannon offers an accurate portrait of the social pressures placed on women in the 1950s and the difficulties for women who did not abide by traditional heterosexual norms.

For Anita Cornwell, being black, a woman, and lesbian shape many of her short stories and essays. Forthright in her lesbian feminism, Cornwell's early essays appeared in the *Ladder*, the magazine launched by the 1950s lesbian organization, Daughters of Bilitis. Cornwell's analysis of racism in the feminist movement and homophobia in certain segments of the black community challenges the heterosexist bias of both groups. Cornwell was an early, outspoken radical lesbian, anticipating the lesbian feminist movement of the 1970s.

Another writer of the 1950s who incorporated gay characters into her fiction is Patricia Highsmith, who began a long-running series of suspense novels with *The Talented Mr Ripley* (1955), which subsequently became a cult classic among gay male readers and explored the psychological complexity of a serial murderer. Using the pseudonym Claire Morgan, Highsmith published her one lesbian novel, *The Price of Salt* (1952), that sold nearly one million copies in the United States in 1953. With her lesbian characters' lives ending in neither madness nor death, Highsmith's portrayals were created in pointed contrast to the hundreds of lesbian pulp novels of the 1950s and 1960s, which generously depicted suicide, despair, and insanity. That Highsmith portrays a lesbian who loses custody of her child after she chooses a female lover powerfully attests to the author's prescience in anticipating the concerns of feminists and lesbians in the 1970s and beyond.

Patience and Sarah, Isabel Miller's (Alma Routsong's) 1969 historical romance, recounts the lives of two lesbians in the 1820s who decide to live together in upstate New York, in a green world that permits these nineteenth-century heroines to express their own unconventional behavior, including cross-dressing. Because of its characterization of lesbians as strong and happy, *Patience and Sarah* challenged the predominant view of lesbians as the self-hating, suicidal, and tragic creatures of the pre-Stonewall era. As a result of Miller's overturning of conventional sex and gender prescriptions, her novel enormously influenced the burgeoning lesbian community of the 1970s.

Lesbian representation in the theater during this period was minimal. Lillian Hellman's *The Children's Hour* (1934), with its negative portrayal of lesbianism, was revived on Broadway in 1952 and San Francisco in 1957 during the height of the McCarthy era. But it was Lorraine Hansberry's Broadway play, *The Sign in Sidney Brustein's Window* (1964), that created a gay male character whose artistic creativity (he is a playwright) and political commitments offer a radical view of human complexity. For Hansberry, issues of race and sexuality are woven into the larger fabric of social justice and world peace. Hansberry's highly acclaimed first play, *A Raisin in the Sun* (1959), focuses exclusively on a black family whose dignity is threatened by institutionalized racism in America. While no overt depiction of lesbianism appears in the play, Hansberry's depiction of the daughter, Beneatha, who is discontented with her options as a woman, suggests the importance to the playwright of expanding opportunities for women and blacks alike. A supportive contributor in the 1950s to the lesbian periodical the *Ladder*, Hansberry supported gay liberation well before it became a political movement in America.

Megan Terry developed transformational theater in which actors change from one character into another, depending on specific circumstances. An active playwright for over 40 years, Terry's early plays such as *Ex-Miss Copper Queen on a Set of Pills* (1963) met with success on off-off-Broadway venues. Regularly focusing on feminist themes, Terry's plays revolve around issues of gender and choice; her acclaimed play *Approaching Simone* (1970), for example, examines the life of French mystic Simone Weil, who chooses starvation and self-exile in order to achieve enlightenment. Terry's interest in gender transformation allows her to incorporate cross-gender casting in her plays, compelling the audience to revise traditional definitions of gender and sexuality.

Several prolific lesbian poets emerged in the 1950s and 1960s and continued long writing careers into the latter part of the century. They are Muriel Rukeyser, May Swenson, May Sarton, and Adrienne Rich. In her tribute to a female sculptor, Rukeyser writes "What would happen if one woman told the truth about her life? / The world would split open." Author of numerous books of poetry (and prose, children's books and translations), Rukeyser writes poems that engage both private and public spheres, revealing her leftist leanings and her dedication to exploring the silenced area of women's experience: sex, menstruation, erotic passion, and mother–daughter relations. In her 1968 book of poems *The Speed of Darkness*, Rukeyser writes, "I am working out the vocabulary of my silence," anticipating the concerns of feminist lesbians of the 1970s and 1980s.

Like Rukeyser, May Swenson belongs to a generation of poets who risked being exiled because of sexual choices. Swenson's poetic career, however, spanned 40 years. When her love poems were collected in 1991 (*The Love Poems of May Swenson*), her work had already appeared in one of the early lesbian anthologies, *Amazon Poetry* (1975), which allowed earlier poems to be placed in a lesbian context. Early collections of poetry, *Another Animal* (1954) and *Cage of Spines* (1958), reveal Swenson's wide range and interests, including the physical processes of the natural world. Expertly combining her knowledge of the natural world with domestic love, Swenson's later poems such as "Poet to Tiger" are playful portraits of female lovers at home.

Accomplished in many genres, May Sarton is perhaps best known for her courageous novel, *Mrs Stevens Hears the Mermaids Singing* (1965), a pre-Stonewall novel about the awakening of lesbian identity. Sarton's many published journals such as the 1968 *Plant Dreaming Deep* examine the creative writer's work amidst the quotidian tasks of domestic life. While her earlier poetry was formal in meter and style, Sarton increasingly wrote less strictly closed-form verse about such topics as loss and love.

Perhaps no other woman poet (and author of nonfiction) in the second half of the twentieth century achieved such distinction as Adrienne Rich. Recognizing her responsibility as a poet to the community, Rich has insisted throughout her 50-year literary career that poetry must be forceful enough to change lives. Possibly the most widely read of America's lesbian poets, Rich's role as a public figure and a writer has included making audible women's voices, investigating the silences of lesbians and gays, women of color, and working-class writers who struggle in anonymity. Her award-winning first collection of poetry, *A Change of the World* (1951), represented Rich's most observantly traditional poems, both in form and theme. Perhaps anticipating a commitment to a radical, lesbian feminist vision of politics and poetics, Rich published *Snapshots of a Daughter-in-Law, 1954–1962* (1963), in which she observes "A thinking woman sleeps with monsters." *Diving into the Wreck: Poems, 1971–1972* (1973) reconceptualizes the patriarchal meanings of myths, striving to locate the core of their meanings, for Rich is devoted to "the wreck and not the story of the wreck / the thing itself and not the myth."

Described by critics as her coming-out book, Rich's *The Dream of a Common Language* (1978) includes perhaps the most famous of lesbian poetic sequences, "Twenty-One Love Poems." Rich employs the language of lesbian love in an effort to rethink traditional sonnet sequences and the central narrative antecedent of such sequences, the love story of *Tristan und Isolde*: "though the chronicle of the world we share / it could be written with new meaning / we were two lovers of one gender, / we were two women of one generation." Throughout the 1980s and 1990s, Rich's poetry and essays embraced the themes of multiple oppressions in subsequent collections such as *An Atlas of a Difficult World* (1991), *Dark Fields of the Republic* (1995), and *Midnight Salvage* (1999).

Lesbian Writers: 1970s–80s

Lesbian writers emerged in the 1970s as politically active producers of a literature that expressed their concerns and hopes. With publications like Jill Johnston's 1973 *Lesbian Nation*, lesbians defined a community unto themselves, a sanctuary in which women were free to develop an alternative reality separate from heterosexual norms, but more culturally visible than the world of bars and private homes necessary for lesbians in the 1950s and 1960s. *Rubyfruit Jungle*, published in 1973 by Daughters Inc. (a pioneering feminist publisher), made Rita Mae Brown the most widely read United States lesbian writer to date. A runaway best-seller, *Rubyfruit Jungle* portrays a young heroine, Molly Bolt, who overcomes her illegitimate birth and impoverished background to develop a strong, lesbian identity. Like a classical picaro, Molly Bolt displays an audacity and cleverness that enable her to overcome many obstacles. Molly's triumphs illustrate both the American literary tradition of radical individualism and that staple feature of gay and lesbian writing, the coming-out story.

Co-founder (with attorney Parke Bowman and author Bertha Harris) of Daughters Inc., June Arnold was instrumental in publishing the works of Rita Mae Brown, Elana Nachman (Dykewomon), Monique Wittig, and Bertha Harris. Arnold's two novels from the 1970s, *The Cook and the Carpenter* (1973) and *Sister Gin* (1975), examine issues revolving around lesbian women living communally, a fictionalized rendering of the political vision of "Lesbian Nation." In particular, *Sister Gin* deals with issues of ongoing importance to feminist writers such as violence against women, homophobia, race, and aging. In her influential and extremely popular 1974 novel, *Riverfinger Women*, Elana Dykewomon explores such issues as social ostracism, queer identity, and outlaw status. Unabashedly portraying violence, prostitution, and sadism, Dykewomon creates a heroine who does not succumb to the despair and desperation frequently seen in earlier novels. In this way, both Arnold and Dykewomon anticipate, both in narrative style and in content, the experimental concerns of lesbian writers in the 1980s and 1990s.

Bertha Harris remains one of the most innovative prose stylists of the 1970s, influencing the creative development of lesbian writers of the 1980s and 1990s, including Dorothy Allison. Inspired by the Metropolitan Opera broadcasts in the post-World War II era, Harris incorporates into her fiction recurring operatic tropes such as tumultuous sexual passion, violence, and family dysfunction. Uninterested in making lesbian literature in any way acceptable to mainstream culture, Harris explains that lesbians and literature achieve greatness by being "unassimilable, awesome, dangerous, outrageous, different: *distinguished*." *Confessions of Cherubino* (1972), Harris's second novel, examines the dangerous relationship between desire and madness. *Lover* (1976) has been compared to Djuna Barnes's *Nightwood* in its unconventional storytelling, its web of relationships (replete in Harris's case with a list of dramatis personae), and its skillful language and striking imagery. Expressing her desire to see lesbian fiction develop into a wholly new genre, Harris has offered experimental writers of the 1980s and 1990s virtuoso examples of what this writing might look like.

Several other writers from the 1970s created fictionalized landscapes in which women in power and communal existence are central. For example, Joanna Russ's third novel, *The Female Man* (1975), is a classic tour de force of science fiction, and has been compared to Virginia Woolf's *Orlando*, which is considered its spiritual predecessor. *The Female Man* portrays four genetically identical protagonists who inhabit parallel time frames and exist in four different lives, including a utopian lesbian planet. In an effort to focus on the problems of patriarchy, Russ examines how women respond to a heterosexist culture, expanding the genre of science fiction writing both formally and thematically. Part of the New Wave of science fiction writers – including Samuel Delany – Joanna Russ's stream-of-consciousness style and feminist themes enriched the genre of science fiction and lesbian writing.

Inhabiting both science fiction and utopian genres, Sally Gearhart's *The Wanderground* (1978) also explores communities where lesbians are central to society. According to Bonnie Zimmerman, three locations of community – the bar, the country commune, and the matrilineal family – express the lesbian separatist impulse envisioned by Johnston's *Lesbian Nation*. Gearhart's novel associates the city with male violence and invasion and the country with female nurturance and cooperation. The Hill Women live peaceably with nature, reinforcing Gearhart's utopian ideals. One of the earliest novels in the post-Stonewall era that introduces ecofeminism and women's spirituality, *The Wanderground* became a classic of speculative lesbian fiction.

Ann Allen Shockley's 1974 novel, *Loving Her*, portrayed her major character as a young black mother who awakens to lesbian desire. A landmark novel, *Loving Her* examines the intersections between sexuality, race, and gender, as it traces a black female pianist who falls in love with an affluent white woman. Shockley's depiction of interracial relations between women challenged both the color prejudice within some black communities and the homophobia within a heterosexist culture, anticipating the themes explored by African American lesbian writers such as Audre Lorde and Becky Birtha. Shockley's later novel, *Say Jesus and Come To Me* (1982), explores the homophobia that pervades certain segments of the predominantly heterosexual Southern black community. Using satire to expose the black male oppression of women and the racism of white women in the feminist movement, Shockley reinforces the centrality of lesbianism to women's communities.

In the 1970s, lesbian theater companies were founded and often enacted feminist strategies such as raising consciousness, revising traditional images of women in myth and literature, and celebrating lesbian sexuality. Companies such as Medusa's Revenge (New York), the Lavender Cellar (Minneapolis), and the Red Dyke Theater (Atlanta) possessed varying goals, but each focused on women's independence from male domination. The first major openly lesbian playwright, Jane Chambers, portrayed lesbian characters in two well-known plays, *A Late Snow* (1974) and *Last Summer at Bluefish Cove* (1980). Chambers herself has said of her reasons for writing: "much of my work is set in minority or ethnic subcultures. I am not writing about social injustice – I am writing about specific people who happen to be victims of that injustice" (quoted in Malinowski: s.v. "Chambers"). Using the conventions of dramatic realism, Chambers explores lesbian characters developing mature, reciprocal relationships.

Peggy Shaw and Lois Weaver created the Women's One World festivals in 1980 and gave lesbian performances at the WOW Café in the East Village in 1982. According to critic Kate Davy, playwright and performance artist Holly Hughes liberated lesbian and feminist theater from the "good-girl syndrome." In particular, Hughes's *The Well of Horniness* (1983) playfully spoofs Hall's classic novel of lesbian despair, using camp and satire to explore lesbian issues in the late twentieth century. Responding to the experiences of race and culture, Cherrie Moraga's first play, *Giving Up the Ghost* (1986), examines Chicana oppression and lesbian invisibility.

As many critics have pointed out, the 1970s produced a bountiful harvest of lesbian poetry and alternative presses and journals to support the work of lesbian writers. A short list of poetry volumes include Judy Grahn's *Edward the Dyke* (1971), Pat Parker's *Child of Myself* (1972), Robin Morgan's *Monster* (1972), Audre Lorde's *From a Land Where Other People Live* (1973), Marilyn Hacker's *Presentation Piece* (1974), Joan Larkin's *Housework* (1975), Susan Griffin's *Like the Iris of an Eye* (1976), and June Jordan's *Things That I Do in the Dark* (1977). Literary journals such as *Sinister Wisdom* and *Conditions* present creative and analytical work from lesbians of different background and experiences. Equally influential has been the *Journal of Homosexuality*, which includes essays from medical and cultural perspectives on homosexuality and gay men and lesbians.

Poet and nonfiction writer Judy Grahn best bridges the pre- and post-Stonewall worlds in her unflagging commitment to the gay rights movement of both eras. In all of her work, Grahn seeks to uncover the mythic origins of gay and lesbian culture and to make poetry a viable forum for working-class people. Such collections as *Edward the Dyke* (several poems appeared in the *Ladder*) and *The Work of a Common Woman* (1978) explore gay and lesbian existence and the ways in which sexuality is connected to other identities such as gender, race, and class. In her long poem "A Woman is Talking to Death," Grahn examines the interrelations between races, classes, and sexual orientations, depicting a fatal motorcycle accident involving a white man, a black driver who will suffer the cruelties of the police force, and the white lesbian who fails to intervene effectively. Examining cultural documents, myths, and etymology, *Another Mother Tongue* (1984) attempts to recuperate a suppressed history of gay culture. Similarly, Grahn's literary criticism, *The Highest Apple* (1985), connects Sappho with eight poets from the nineteenth and twentieth centuries, including Adrienne Rich and Audre Lorde.

Perhaps one of the most formally challenging poets of the post-World War II era is Marilyn Hacker. A pre-eminent writer of closed forms – villanelles, sestinas, sonnets, and pantoums – Hacker early established herself as a poet of many cultures, including Jewish American, urban, expatriate, and lesbian. In her New York years in the 1960s, Hacker captured the ominous beginnings of liberation: "The file clerks took exams and forged ahead. / The decorators' kitchens blazed persimmon. / The secretary started kissing women, and so did I, and my three friends are dead" ("Nights of 1964–1966").

In her third book, *Taking Notice* (1980), Hacker explicitly establishes her lesbian identity, and links herself with Adrienne Rich's "Twenty-One Love Poems," employing Rich's lines as an epigraph to her own poems: "two women together is a work / nothing in civilization has made simple" (XIX). Hacker herself writes, "if I lost myself in you I'd be / no better lost than any other woman" ("Taking Notice"). Indeed, such loss is explored again in Hacker's poetic sequence, *Love, Death, and the Changing of Seasons* (1986). Recalling thematically the sonnet sequence of Shakespeare, Hacker's poems follow a modified Italian form, and, by using colloquial language and enjambments, she gives the verse a breathless and turbulent quality. However wild and rampant, the erotic for Hacker is subsumed by the domestic chores of daily life: "I'd like to throw my laundry in with yours. / I'd like to put my face between your legs."

Drawing from the traditions established by such African American writers as Lorraine Hansberry and Audre Lorde, Pat Parker was instrumental in shaping some of the themes distinctive to lesbian writing: long-repressed feelings of women, gay and lesbian queerness, and violence against women. In one collection, *Movement in Black* (1978, with a foreword by Audre Lorde and an introduction by Judy Grahn), Parker illustrates her forthright depiction of lesbian sex and "Black Queerness," in an effort to shape the complexities of black, lesbian identity in America.

Audre Lorde's expansive literary career and activism have produced several books of poetry and essays, along with hybrid narratives such as her "biomythography," *Zami: A New Spelling of My Name* (1982). Lorde's embracing of multiple identities – black, woman, lesbian, mother, librarian, activist, and writer – has been instrumental in defining the self as fluid and lesbian communities as inhabiting "the very house of difference." *The Black Unicorn* (1978), a poetry collection, illustrates Lorde's commitment to creating African-based images and traditions that affirm lesbian identity and replace Greco-Roman mythology with West-African female creation figures. Similarly, in *Zami*, Lorde constructs a collective identity from a cross-cultural community of African women by embracing her mother's West Indian homeland, symbolized by Carriacou, the island of black women, and Zami, "a Carriacou name for women who work together as friends and lovers." Within this mythic narrative, Lorde recalls her childhood in Harlem before World War II and lesbian life in 1950s Greenwich Village, fusing several cultures in her work. Lorde's personal battles with cancer and mastectomy are captured in her prose collection, *The Cancer Journals* (1980). In 1992, Lorde died from the liver cancer she had lived with for over a decade.

Lesbian Writers: 1980s–90s

Adrienne Rich's powerful essay "Compulsory Heterosexuality and the Lesbian Existence" (1980) firmly established lesbianism as a theory as well as a practice within feminism. Audre Lorde's long choral poem "Need" (*Chosen Poems*, 1982) also anticipated postmodern concerns by refusing to stabilize identity, opting instead for a collective voice that is necessary for survival. Later writers in the 1980s and 1990s conducted open experiments in genre, identity, and sexual politics, destabilizing any essential relationship between lesbianism and feminism.

As Kathleen Martindale has pointed out, as in earlier foundational feminist texts, the anthology, the collection, and mixed-genre work centrally shape the writings of lesbians. The groundbreaking publication that, though not exclusively lesbian, highlighted the proliferation and diversity of lesbian writing in the 1970s, and anticipated further experimentalism in form and content in the 1980s and 1990s, is *This Bridge Called My Back: Writings by Radical Women of Color* (1981). One of the small women's presses that was founded in an attempt to give visibility to lesbian and feminist writers, Persephone Press published the first edition of *This Bridge*, along with such key works as *The Wanderground*, *Zami*, and *Nice Jewish Girls*. Edited by two self-identified Chicana American writers, Gloria Anzaldua and Cherrie Moraga, *This Bridge* articulated in essays, fiction, and poetry the heretofore underrepresented voices of women of color. Calling attention to racism within the feminist movement, this anthology paved the path for future writers to expand the concept of feminism and to incorporate multiple identities. Gloria Anzaldua's own dedication to creating mixed-genre writings is represented by her 1987 *Borderlands – La Frontera:*

The New Mestiza. Bringing together the histories of Mexicans living on the United States border, interspersing her poetry and prose with Spanish and English, Anzaldua expands the complexity of marginalized identity be it national, racial, linguistic, or sexual. Likewise, Moraga's *Loving in the War Years: Lo que nunca paso por sus labios* (1983), is constructed as a generic montage, uniting autobiography, essays, and poetry to explore the sources of Moraga's lesbianism.

The focus on generic experimentation continued in the prose works and poetry of lesbian writers in the 1980s and 1990s. Much of the writing of Chicana, Native American, Jewish, black, Asian, and white ethnic minorities examines the importance of cultural heritages and the rituals peculiar to them. Insisting on the necessity of developing their own written history, many lesbians from minority groups incorporate multiple sensibilities, based on such inflections as race, culture, class, and sexuality. For example, literary scholar, poet, and novelist Paula Gunn Allen reinterprets Native American traditions from a lesbian perspective by developing a myth-laden account of the past and a feminine connection to power and spirit. In her novel, *The Woman Who Owned the Shadows* (1983), and her critical work, *The Sacred Hoop: Recovering the Feminine in American Indian Traditions* (1986), Allen has recovered a complex understanding of traditional and contemporary sexualities. Equally recuperative has been Native American poet Beth Brant's anthology, *A Gathering of Spirit: Writing and Art by North American Indian Women* (1983), in which the work of Chrystos, Vicki Sears, Allen, and others appears.

Exploring multiple identities has not been limited to writers of color. Minnie Bruce Pratt, a European American poet from a middle-class background, incorporates her many identities – lesbian, poet, mother, Southerner, activist – in two volumes of her poetry, *We Say We Love Each Other* (1985) and *Crime Against Nature* (1990). Pratt's poems offer ways to resist hostility and violence from a punitive society intolerant of difference. Using song, repetition, and what Pratt calls "maps," the poet traces the development of her identities, including her outlaw status as a lesbian mother who loses custody of her sons.

Lesbian literature has never lacked first-rate poetry, and its prose artists have recently demonstrated innovative techniques, experimenting in form and content. Five pre-eminent writers in this category are Valerie Miner, Dorothy Allison, Rebecca Brown, Carole Maso, and Sarah Schulman. Valerie Miner's novels, short stories, and nonfiction explore the relations between personal lives and political struggles, beginning with the novel *Blood Sisters* (1981), which details the failed sisterhood of women of the Irish Republican Army. Miner's emphasis on literary collaboration – what she calls "imaginative collectivity" – highlights her unconventional narrative technique in such a work as *Movement* (1982), a novel-in-stories in which vignettes of other women are written that depict the protagonist's emergence as a feminist. Miner's novels in the 1990s increasingly emphasized working-class families, as in her retelling of Shakespeare's *King Lear* from Cordelia's point of view in *A Walking Fire* (1994), set in a working-class family in America.

Bastard Out of Carolina (1992) catapulted Dorothy Allison into the literary limelight. This first novel explores domestic abuse from the perspective of an adolescent narrator who is raped by a terrifying stepfather. Allison's depiction of Southern roots recalls the novels of Rita Mae Brown and Blanche McCrary Boyd, but unlike theirs, Allison's characters are both socially despised and violence prone. Writing in a strictly realist vein, Allison refuses to exploit issues of incest and violence in her work, illuminating instead the powerful status of her young protagonist. While she does not focus directly on the topic of lesbianism, Allison writes narratives, as she puts it, "in which lesbians live." For example, Allison's second novel, *Cavedweller* (1998), incorporates another adolescent protagonist whose cave explorations become a larger metaphor for her sexual self-excavation.

Like Miner and Allison, Rebecca Brown's narrative gifts do not conform to the typical lesbian genres of romance, coming out, and detective fiction. Brown successfully published her first short story collection, *The Evolution of Darkness* (1984), in London with the then acquisitions editor Jeanette Winterson, a British novelist of far-reaching imagination. *The Terrible Girls* (1986), a novel-in-stories, has been compared by Joan Nestle to Djuna Barnes's *Nightwood* in its subversive erotics. Like Jeanette Winterson in her subsequent *Written on the Body*, Brown uses sex-unspecified narrators and constructs a narrative around the topics of obsessive desire, loss, and redemption. Written from the point of view of an AIDS homecare worker, *The Gifts of the Body* (1994) explores the lives of dying patients in their last weeks and hours.

Also escaping the strictures of typical lesbian genres, Carole Maso's innovative narratives make her one of the most experimental, and, to use her own description, "reckless" novelists of the 1990s. Beginning with her first novel, *Ghost Dance* (1986), Maso explores the ethnic roots (Armenian and Italian) of the protagonist's family, whom she loses at the beginning of the narrative and whom she redeems through the language of ritual and memory. Employing lyrical metaphors and sensual prose, Maso extends her experiment with language in her second novel, *The Art Lover* (1990). Featured here is a double narrative on family, a nonfiction section in which Maso interrupts the family narratives and incorporates her own eulogy for the death of her friend from AIDS, and a montage of pictures, articles, details of paintings, sign-language cards, and mathematical symbols. Maso's virtuosity is demonstrated in her lesbian protagonist's own recounting of her descent into madness (and her concomitant loss of language) in *The American Woman in the Chinese Hat* (1994), and in her lyrical tour de force *Ava* (1993), which recounts in fragments and images one woman's last day of life. Both intoxicating and dangerous, desire in Maso's *Aureole* (1996) and *Defiance* (1998) is always connected to the intensity of language and its relation to the body.

Novelist, playwright, and essayist Sarah Schulman best serves as a link between the social activism prevalent in the 1970s and the literary lesbian avant-garde of the 1990s. One of the founders of the direct action political group Lesbian Avengers, Schulman redefines traditional lesbian genres in each of her six novels and insists on the necessary relation between politics and art. In her first novel, *The Sophie Horowitz Story* (1984), Schulman introduces a lesbian sleuth who fails both as a detective and as a reporter, reinforcing the author's belief that lesbian writing needs to reach beyond lesbian formula fiction. Taking her second novel's title from Jack Kerouac's *On the Road*, Schulman's *Girls, Vision, and Everything* (1986) traces the urban adventuring of Lila Futuransky, who reads a male Beat writer's excursions in the absence of a practical and interesting lesbian literary tradition.

As in all of Schulman's work, *After Dolores* (1988) is set in New York City and explores the lesbian protagonist's isolation after being left by her lover for another woman. The unnamed narrator's adventures as a detective neither liberate nor enliven her; she ultimately remains unfulfilled. *People in Trouble* (1990) is Schulman's most overtly political novel, as it responds to the crisis of AIDS and the imperative that the artist must transcend the act of creating art by taking social responsibility. Remarking herself that *People in Trouble* is more about neglect and homophobia than about AIDS, Schulman's satiric portrayal of a romantic triangle of a lesbian, a married woman (who cross-dresses), and her husband illuminates the problem of disengagement from social issues. Like Maso and Rebecca Brown, Schulman demonstrates the narrative potential of the AIDS epidemic in the 1990s.

Conclusion and Other Voices

Throughout the post-World War II era, gays and lesbians successfully experimented in form and developed dissident voices. Whether they employed traditional or unconventional genres and themes, lesbian and gay writers discovered the language they needed to illuminate the sexual and social identities of homosexuals in American culture. Philip Gambone (*The Language We Use Up Here*, 1991) and Stephen McCauley (*The Object of My Affection*, 1987) write fiction in which homosexuality is woven into the fabric of the characters' lives.

David Feinberg's involvement in ACT-UP inspired his two novels, *Eighty-Sixed* (1989) and *Spontaneous Combustion* (1991), which depict a gay character who must learn how to live with AIDS. The short stories of Ethan Mordden (collected in *I've a Feeling We're Not in Kansas Anymore, Buddies*, and *Everybody Loves You*) function as a trilogy by using the same narrator and redefining the theme of family by focusing on a post-Stonewall world of male friendship. Another writer of short stories, Norman Wong (*Cultural Revolution*, 1994), interweaves several generations of immigrants within tales about the conflicts between Old World parents and rapidly assimilated children. Rafael Campo's poetry, all published in the 1990s, painfully portrays the continuing homophobic culture that causes feelings of alienation for a young gay man: "One lover held the other's hand. / The other / Man was me. I watched as if I hovered / Far above the scene" (*The Other Man Was Me: A Voyage to the New World*, 1994).

In keeping with a commitment to collective subjectivity, lesbian writers continue to produce mixed-genre work. Joan Nestle, co-founder of the Lesbian Herstory Archives in 1972, recounts butch–femme practices in the 1950s in *A Restricted Country* (1987). A self-identified sex radical, Nestle, in her essays, stories, and poems, resexualized lesbian theory and practice. Likewise, Pat Califia's erotic fiction (*Macho Sluts*, 1988) purposefully depicts consensual sadomasochistic practices, expanding the aesthetic boundaries of lesbian literature. Leslie Feinberg's work on transgendered subjects examines the overlapping communities of gay and lesbian cultures in her novel *Stone Butch Blues* (1993) and mixed-genre work *Transgender Warriors: Making History from Joan of Arc to Ru Paul* (1996). Lesbian writers such as Sapphire (*Push*, 1996) and Rachel Guido deVries (*Tender Warriors*, 1986) explore issues of racism and violence within the family. Cartoonists Alison Bechdel (*Dykes to Watch Out For*, 1986) and Diane DiMassa (*Hothead Paisan:*

Homicidal Lesbian Terrorist, 1991) introduce unconventional lesbians – dykes and hotheads – to popular culture, thereby challenging the more mainstream romances of popular lesbian fiction.

Gay and lesbian writers after World War II present a remarkable variety in their works. The medical profession in the early twentieth century pathologized homosexuality, which encouraged negative portrayals of gays both in the public mindset and in literature. The censorious decades of the 1950s and 1960s, however, produced a body of gay and lesbian notable writing that nonetheless remained invisible to the general public, even though political activism preceded the 1969 Stonewall riots. Gay and lesbian writers before Stonewall began affirming homosexual identity while recognizing the problematic freedom of the outlaw status. Certainly the 1969 Stonewall riots heralded an emergence of gay and lesbian voices previously inaudible to the larger public. The literature produced in the years directly following Stonewall emerged from a distinctive gay and lesbian political movement, which developed independent bookstores, journals, writers' associations, and publication houses. Gay and lesbian writers of the late twentieth and early twenty-first centuries are increasingly prolific and artistically liberated, producing both traditional works and postmodern experiments.

References and further reading

Abelove, Henry, Michele Aina Barale, and David M. Halperin, eds. *The Lesbian and Gay Studies Reader*. New York: Routledge, 1993.

Allen, Carolyn. *Following Djuna: Women Lovers and the Erotics of Loss*. Bloomington: Indiana University Press, 1996.

Clum, John M., ed. *Staging Gay Lives: An Anthology of Contemporary Gay Theater*. Boulder, CO: Westview Press, 1996.

Davidson, Cathy N., and Linda Wagner-Martin, eds. *The Oxford Companion to Women's Writing in the United States*. New York: Oxford University Press, 1995.

D'Emilio, John. *Sexual Politics, Sexual Communities: The Making of a Homosexual Minority in the United States, 1940–1970*. Chicago: University of Chicago Press, 1983.

D'Emilio, John. *Making Trouble: Essays on Gay History, Politics and the University*. New York: Routledge, 1992.

Duberman, Martin. *Stonewall*. New York: Dutton, 1993.

Duberman, Martin, Martha Vicinus, and George Chauncey, Jr, eds. *Hidden From History: Reclaiming the Gay and Lesbian Past*. New York: Meridian, 1989.

Faderman, Lillian. *Odd Girls and Twilight Lovers: A History of Lesbian Life in Twentieth-Century America*. New York: Penguin, 1991.

Farwell, Marilyn R. *Heterosexual Plots and Lesbian Narratives*. New York: New York University Press, 1996.

Foster, David William. *Chicano/Latino Homoerotic Identities*. New York: Garland Press, 1999.

Lilly, Mark, ed. *Lesbian and Gay Writing: An Anthology of Critical Essays*. Philadelphia: Temple University Press, 1990.

Malinowski, Sharon, ed. *Gay and Lesbian Literature*. Vol. 1. Detroit: St James Press, 1994.

Martindale, Kathleen. *Un/popular Culture: Lesbian Writing After the Sex Wars*. Albany, NY: State University of New York Press, 1997.

McRuer, Robert. *The Queer Renaissance: Contemporary American Literature and the Reinvention of Lesbian and Gay Identities*. New York: New York University Press, 1997.

Morse, Carl, and Joan Larkin, eds. *Gay and Lesbian Poetry in Our Time: An Anthology*. New York: St Martin's Press, 1988.

Murphy, Timothy F., and Suzanne Poirier, eds. *Writing AIDS: Gay Literature, Language, and Analysis*. New York: Columbia University Press, 1993.

Pastore, Judith Lawrence, ed. *Confronting AIDS through Literature: The Responsibilities of Representation*. Urbana: University of Illinois Press, 1993.

Pendergast, Tom, and Sara Pendergast, eds. *Gay and Lesbian Literature*. Vol. 2. Detroit: St James Press, 1998.

Pollack, Sandra, and Denise D. Knight. *Contemporary Lesbian Writers of the United States: A Bio-bibliographical Critical Sourcebook*. Westport, CT: Greenwood Press, 1993.

Sinfield, Alan. *Out on Stage: Lesbian and Gay Theater in the Twentieth Century*. New Haven, CT: Yale University Press, 1999.

Summers, Claude J. *The Gay and Lesbian Literary Heritage*. New York: Henry Holt, 1995.

Woodhouse, Reed. *Unlimited Embrace: A Canon of Gay Fiction, 1945–1995*. Amherst: University of Massachusetts Press, 1998.

Woods, Gregory. *A History of Gay Literature: The Male Tradition*. New Haven, CT: Yale University Press, 1998.

Zimmerman, Bonnie. *The Safe Sea of Women: Lesbian Fiction, 1969–1989*. Boston: Beacon Press, 1990.

Chapter 10

Identity and the Postwar Temper in American Jewish Fiction

Daniel Fuchs

I have a vivid memory of a day in the spring of 1954 when a professor in the Columbia College English Department told me that the distinguished literary critic Lionel Trilling was Jewish. I could not tell what affected me more, surprise that this genteel and apparently gentile man was a Jew or exhilaration that if Trilling was Jewish then anything was possible. Trilling was the only professor to have asked me, "What is your Christian name?" And he wrote an impressive High Church critical prose that a teenage undergraduate from the Bronx contemplated with a sense of intimidated wonder. The author of the novel *The Middle of the Journey*, Trilling would not have been taken by my provincial emotionality. He had written in 1944, a time of particular Jewish vulnerability, that the American Jewish community is "sterile," partly because it reflects a history of "exclusion," which he thinks of as a willing parochialism. Though it was "a point of honor" to affirm his Jewishness as a "citizen," it had nothing to do with his being a writer. "I should resent it," he made clear, "if a critic of my work were to discover in it either faults or virtues which he called Jewish" (Trilling: vii, n. 1).

In saying so Trilling was expressing a sentiment that virtually any *Partisan Review* Jewish intellectual would have then echoed. In the Modernist, Marxist orbit, some had been resistant to engaging in the war against Hitler; few were especially involved in the fate of the

Jews during World War II. On the home front, former Marxists and Trotskyites saw Judaism as a form of bourgeois smugness; Freudians considered it a form of bourgeois neurosis. Though Trilling's early fiction deals with Jewishness, it soon becomes a dead end. Yet Trilling's protestations to the contrary notwithstanding, *The Middle of the Journey* can be seen as a classic production of the secular Jew. But first it must be seen for what it primarily is, a dramatization of the conflict between liberalism and its enemies. The novel is didactic; its deepest emotion is ideational.

One of the main points about the postwar temper as manifested in Jewish writers is that it represented, in Leslie Fiedler's phrase, an end to innocence, an end to radical utopianism. In Trilling's novel John Laskell is the hero of disillusion, the Crooms are the illusioned radicals, and Gifford Maxim is the ex-communist turned Christian. The "middle" of the title refers to Laskell's liberal stance between left and right as well as to mid-life crisis – Laskell is 33, Dante's age at the beginning of his journey. Laskell's brush with death because of illness is endlessly elaborated but is important in that it shows the conditionality of life, which the Crooms prefer not to recognize. For them, there is nothing that cannot be changed. There is no marginal character who is not innocent, a victim of society. Therefore, they fail to see the negative qualities of Duck Caldwell, a ne'er-do-well whose vulgarity and aggression lead to the death of his heart-diseased daughter as she stumbles in the reading of a poem, a death by culture-envy. Other than that of class oppression, the Crooms recognize no guilt. Maxim recognizes only guilt; hence his view of Herman Melville's "Billy Budd" as a tragedy of theology rather than of justice. Between disbelief in conditionality (the Crooms) and belief only in conditionality (Maxim), Laskell opts for the liberal middle, responsibility. (The title of the French translation of the novel is *Les Responsibles*.) So the emotional highlight of the book, Laskell's final confrontation with the Crooms and Maxim, is didactic. If Laskell, in his wisdom, suffers from the liberal malady, passivity, he converts it into intellectual activity. And if his Keatsian rose shows him half in love with easeful death, he overcomes that temptation to forge an ego. Nothing is more typical of the postwar temper than this frame of mind, in which cultural Stalinism, the original political correctness, is denigrated and the individual elevated. (The scenario is rather Freudian: Laskell overcomes illness, a death-wish, and a brief neurotic episode, to arrive at a genital calm and a forceful ego.) What may be considered Jewish about Trilling as a writer is his focus on responsibility, the liberal virtue. Liberalism is not Judaism, yet most Jews are liberal. Such are the confusions of assimilation.

The most popular novel of the fifties was written by another assimilated Jew, J. D. Salinger. One might say that Salinger is Jewish American in that you can never tell he was. (He is half Jewish, half Irish.) Yet if there is one major contribution that American Jewish writers made it was the comedy of suffering. Here in affluent, affable America, suffering could be funny, especially in an age of self-regard. It is in this sense that Salinger's small masterpiece, *Catcher in the Rye*, can be considered a Jewish book. Of course, you do not have to be Jewish to be a comic sufferer. Vladimir Nabokov's *Lolita* and J. F. Powers's *Morte d'Urban* are notable illustrations from the period. But the frequency with which the literature of comic suffering occurs in Jewish fiction, including such masterworks as *Herzog* and *Portnoy's Complaint* – not to mention the films of Woody Allen, which show the popularity of pickled herring – would seem to indicate that it is an especially Jewish thing. Jews have been familiar with the role of suffering servant since biblical days. Golden America and the disintegration of the romantic ego brought the comedy. The main contour of Salinger's career, from psychological comedy to religion, might be seen as a Jewish one. Salinger is Jewish American in that he is Zen Buddhist! From *Catcher in the Rye* to *Franny and Zooey* to *Seymour*, Salinger's most notable fiction becomes increasingly otherworldly. But nowhere does Salinger become Jewish in any obvious sense. And Salinger is not at all Jewish in his characters' refusal to grow up, to take on the responsibility of full genital ego. He remains an instance of one kind of American Jewish writer at mid-century, assimilated to the point of Jewish exclusion.

Where Trilling and Salinger in their very different ways were deidentifying Jews in their fiction, Saul Bellow, Bernard Malamud, and Philip Roth, in their different ways, were identifying ones. Yet the latter three all say that they are American writers who happen to be Jewish. Although they mainly write about characters who are Jews, they want to be judged as novelists in the tradition of the novel. They aspire to artistic eminence. Like Trilling, like Salinger, they want to reach a general American audience, indeed an international one. Bellow, for one, resists being known as a Jewish writer to the degree that he is wary of being categorized as merely a Jewish writer. Like the great majority of Americans at mid-century they may best be characterized by individual rather than religious identity. Even when the element of self becomes soul, as it does in Bellow and Malamud, it is the reaching for individual awareness more than transcendent connection or belief that is dramatized. Would Shakespeare want to be known as "that Christian writer"?

During the discussion session after a lecture I had given at a University of Haifa symposium on Bellow, an Israeli asked me the inevitable question, "Is Bellow a Jew first or an American first?" I gave him the answer I have just given. But I could just as well have asked this kibbutznik – the kibbutz is generally known for its socialist rather than its religious identity, indeed the tension between secular and religious Jews in Israel well beyond the kibbutz can be substantial – "Are you a Jew first or an Israeli first?" In Israel the following joke came to mind. A woman is sitting on a bus talking to her son in Yiddish. The people in the bus look at her. She continues to talk to him in Yiddish. Finally, someone turns around and says, "Why are you talking to your son in Yiddish? You're in Israel now." She answers, "Because I don't want him to forget that he's a Jew." All nations, even the nation of priests, are witness to what Hegel called the secularization of spirituality. For Jews, who came late to the party, the Holocaust was a precipitating factor.

The Adventures of Augie March was Bellow's breakthrough novel from the point of view of reversing Modernist aestheticism and the sense of alienation and victimization that much twentieth-century literature embodied, including his own. It was a breakthrough into anti-Modernism, a real switch. Bellow found a style answerable to the energies of everyday life and an antiheroic hero who was amiable rather than alienated. This picaresque novel gives us a distinctly nonideological hero. The thirties is the time that comes after the twenties, tougher times, but not inhibiting much of the energetic immigrant rhythm. Augie is more concerned with female structure than class structure. And his one stint as a union organizer serves to expose union corruption.

A major contribution of the Jewish writers was the dramatization of a plausible positivity, often in the form of ethical comedy. *Augie March* was a popular success as well as, generally, a succès d'estime. The need to affirm – Herzog's middle name is Praise God, Elkanah – is a Jewish specialty. God's creation is good. The fifties were, amidst everything else, desperate for the myth of moral agency. The revival of an energetic realism satisfied an apparent craving for the affirmation of ordinary life. Bellow was resisting what he called the unearned pessimism of Modernism, but there were those who viewed Augie March as an illustration of unearned optimism. Because Augie undercuts his own optimism, beginning with even the first sentence of the novel, the buoyancy and level-headedness of the prose are one of the triumphs of the fifties.

In *Augie March* Bellow writes lyrically of America in his first and last sentences, a rarity in twentieth-century American fiction. More typically, America was a place to escape from, as in the expatriate twenties. *Augie March* ran parallel to the *Partisan Review* symposium on "Our Country and Our Culture" where, mainly, former Stalinists and Trotskyites said that America was not so bad a place. Compared to what? The Jewish writers and intellectuals were, then, politically as well as aesthetically affirmative, with endless modifications.

Yet, for many, the fifties were the worst thing that ever happened to us: McCarthy–Rosenbergs–conformity–gray-flannel-suit–counterfeit, raced the litany of complaint. What with Korea, the Soviet Union getting the bomb, the Cold War, there was a reactive hysteria, about which so much has been said. But other things happened in the fifties as well. GIs, who knew mainly the Depression and World War II, were given a new lease on life with the GI Bill, which many were still enjoying. The historic Marshall Plan (1947–52), as much generosity as self-interest, was reviving Europe. The momentous Montgomery bus boycott started the civil rights movement. The Ivy League schools, some more gradually than others, raised the quota bar to minorities (some had done so decades before), particularly, it seems, to Jews, who served as the vanguard of the movement in this respect. It is possible to argue that this democratization of the elites will be a more important and enduring legacy of the fifties than McCarthy and Rosenberg. The sense of possibility involved more than elites. For the first time, according to pollsters, most Americans identified themselves as middle-class. The prosperity of the period was not accidental. There were many full of talent, energy, and aspiration functioning within a workable society who rendered the negative cartoon suspect.

Was *Augie March* a travelogue for timid intellectuals, as the then radical Norman Mailer put it? Weren't Einhorn, Grandma Lausch, Augie's bumpy love-life justifications of the revival of realism? But if *Augie March* was a triumph it was no reason to stand still. Bellow's works stand in a kind of dialectical relationship to each other. If he was positive in *Augie March* he was negative in *Seize the Day*. Yet both works are marked by a belief in what Augie calls the axial lines of life, often realized in the former, desperately but convincingly reached in the final scene of *Seize the Day*. Bellow's scathing portrait of capitalism as a spiritual category, Dostoyevsky-style, finds closure in the oldest of Jewish gestalts, transcendence through suffering. The juxtaposition of "oral" Tommy and "anal" Dr Adler, of naive Tommy and the petty bourgeois Tartuffe Dr Tamkin, of desperate Tommy and his financial-organizer estranged wife, make for painful comedy. The darkness is so real that it nearly eclipses the comedy.

Henderson the Rain King is a release from the near claustrophobia of *Seize the Day*. Like Augie's, Henderson's "I" expresses a personal lyricism. This time, though, the voice is middle-aged, funny and exasperated, desperately hopeful; Henderson is in search of experience adequate to his desire. A rich Wasp, even if an epigone, Henderson can afford to air out his miseries by traveling through Africa, where his American Faustian urge to do some technological good only backfires. What Africa can do for him, it seems, is give him the wisdom of nature, the pride of the lion. But Africa turns out to be another adventure in comic suffering. The lion's-den scene is at once a celebration and *reductio ad absurdum* of Romantic iconography. Vitalism gives way to Judeo-Christian moral abstraction as God is beseeched. Henderson's allegiance to Dahfu, the African wise man who sounds much like a post-Freudian analyst, is transcended by an allegiance to soul. Henderson considers himself mediumistic and is given to prayer, an archaic impulse perhaps but contemporary in that he pleads to be preserved from the unreal.

Herzog is another Bellow protagonist who finds himself beseeching God, and with his marital difficulties you can see why. *Herzog* gives us a deeper and funnier *de profundis* than even *Henderson the Rain King*. Those who say that Herzog is too much of a narcissist miss the point that Herzog is trying to find a way out of his narcissism. The lyrical, funny first person gives us a humorous perspective on the actual third person events. The present comments on the past and yearns for a future. In this epistolary novel, letters greatly intensify the "I" and connect in a crucial way to the comic climax of the book. The letters begin in gloom and end in release, always with a comic counterpoint complicating both. The climactic scene in the novel, a mock murder scene, supplies the pivotal tonal shift. The humanist Jew Herzog, of course, will not kill Gersbach, the man who cuckolds him. Not that he likes him or his wife, far from it, but as he sees Gersbach performing his child's ablutions with care, the patterns of civilization overtake the claims of barbarism. Gersbach may deserve death, but life is better than death, restraint better than murder. No, it is not Gersbach personally who makes Herzog relent, but the fact that any man subdued to benign custom is not killable. Herzog is renewed by a traditional moral restraint, once again a Jewish climax.

The other most vivid aspect of *Herzog* is Herzog's relation to Ramona. Here too the sensibility is Jewish in that Herzog resists, hard as it is to do, the sexual utopia promised by Ramona for some higher, axial sense of usefulness. Herzog is a comic idealist who must have moral seriousness. In this sense Herzog is the culminating American Jewish novel of the postwar era. For most Jewish writers the early to mid-sixties are far closer to the fifties than they are to the late sixties. *Mr Sammler's Planet* is a late sixties book, but also a Holocaust survivor book, in which the voice of traditional humanism is shaken if not shattered. In this world sexuality has evolved as the greatest force. Dionysus is prominent and what most people call morality is a still, small voice.

Before going on to Bernard Malamud and Philip Roth, for reasons both chronological and dialectical, the work of Norman Mailer in this period will be considered. Although Mailer spent his youth in one of the most securely Jewish neighborhoods in Brooklyn and even used to have his mother over for Friday night (I hesitate to say Sabbath) dinner well into his mature years, he is the most actively deidentifying of our Jewish writers. Trilling and Salinger pretty much ignored Jews as such in their mature work, but Mailer actively subverts them. He has said that the one thing not to call him is a nice Jewish boy from Brooklyn. Not much chance of that.

The well-known *The Naked and the Dead* is Mailer's first novel, naturalistic but with romantic undercurrents that undermine naturalism, which is a literature of conditionality. It is a political novel as much as it is a war novel set in the Pacific theater in World War II. The political dialogue between General Cummings and Lieutenant Hearn, dramatically focused in the pick-up-my-cigarette-butt scene, gives us a struggle between fascism and liberalism. Croft is the fascist or at least sadistic egomaniac on the enlisted level and Valsen is the liberal. Although an officer, Hearn resents the way the other officers treat the privates. In the narrative, Hearn and Valsen are effectively destroyed in the power struggle. Since liberalism is powerless against fascism, a radical alternative is implied.

Because he is a liberal and because of his dark facial features, the Wasp Hearn at one point fancies himself a Jew. The real Jews in the novel, Goldstein and Roth, are two of the many victimized privates, but with a difference. Both feel the anti-Semitism of their compeers. But what Mailer is really interested in is their personal limitations. Roth is a college boy, a CCNY *klutz*, and a *kvetch* to boot, complaining about army this and army that even when it may not be justified. In the anti-climactic climax of the novel, the meaningless and failed ascent of Mount Anaka, his physical incompetence is a contributing factor to his death. In Private Roth, the Jew is a half-educated geek who cannot get it up. Goldstein is a very different case. Competent, married, in love with his children, patriotic, he is, in Mailer's view, insufferably square. He is a good man for a physical emergency and performs heroically in this regard, but he is unaware of his victimization by the system. In short, he is middle-class, or even worse, aspires to be. Goldstein and Roth do what Mailer thinks Jews do – both sublimate. Mailer wants something more.

What does he want? He has said that the character in the novel for whom he had the most secret admiration was Croft – sadistic, sonofabitching Croft. Sergeant Croft has aggression, which includes sexual aggression. In this respect he transcends General Cummings, whose sexually aggressive impulses merely mask homosexuality. Croft presages Mailer's hipster, the white Negro, who acts on the morality of impulse. Mailer is moving toward the sexual politics that will, before too many years, replace Marxism.

Where in *The Middle of the Journey* Trilling shows part of the general repudiation of radicalism in the postwar period, Mailer's *Barbary Shore* gives us a sympathetic if agonized account. Mailer posits a moral equivalence between Stalinism and capitalism through the fallen radical McLoed and the intimidating, sadistic Hollingsworth, a McCarthy era FBI agent. Though there is blood on McLoed's hands, he tries to redeem himself through Trotskyite faith. Sexuality in this novel is a reflection of political hysteria, violent and desiccated. There is nothing Jewish in this Brooklyn boarding-house novel, except, perhaps, Mailer's apparently ineradicable sympathy for the failing left.

The Deer Park was Mailer's next novel and it meant much to him. He reportedly was very pleased when, at a White House gathering, JFK asked him about it and not *The Naked and the Dead*. His war novel was somewhat derivative and exhibited a flat style. *The Deer Park* was original and attempted a more ambitious style, though it was not until *An American Dream* that Mailer went for baroque. *The Naked and the Dead* and *The Deer Park* are similar in strategy in that they both attempt an indictment of fascist America through delineation of one of its segments, the army and Hollywood. Mailer cheats a bit using the army in this way in that it is an institution inherently authoritarian; his Hollywood is a more plausible account of the authoritarian, in this case, McCarthyism. Teppis, the studio's big brother, plays the role that Cummings played in the earlier novel, the fascist who wins. Eitel (I-tell) is the confused, cowardly liberal, a victim of HUAC (the House

Un-American Activities Committee). In Teppis and Eitel, Mailer presents the Jew as villain. The rebel psychopath, Marion Faye, is the novel's Croft. He is the hipster, Mailer's first white Negro, though far more self-conscious in his romantic Satanism. Considering the desiccated relationships of everyone else, Mailer creates a certain sympathy for him. Eitel's former lady friend Elena says that the one way Marion is like him is that when Marion is engaging in dirty sex he thinks it is going to blow up the world. This is the first mention of Mailer's idea of the apocalyptic orgasm. Mailer, in short, has switched from a political to a sexual radicalism.

Of all of Mailer's deidentifying strategies this is the most prominent. Its clearest exposition occurs in his essay "The White Negro," a glorification of the morality of impulse, however destructive that impulse may be. An age of apocalypse – Mailer lists the concentration camps, the bomb, and "slow death by conformity" (Mailer: 312) – justifies apocalyptic orgasm, the sexual aggression necessary, indeed appropriate, to survival. Political justifies personal violence. In a notorious passage Mailer justifies the murder of a storekeeper by violent hipsters on the grounds that they are destroying the institution of private property and "daring the unknown" (321). So Mailer has decided to settle for revolution as gesture. As Jean Malaquais has said in the discussion appended to the essay, his hipster is an attempt to resurrect the myth of the proletariat. In his glorification of impulse Mailer becomes the anti-Jew. He could not see that the next major wave of American conformity would be the infantile. And he did not see that his lurid revolutionary bore little resemblance to the rather passive, stoned ethic of the hipster.

During the fifties Mailer engaged in an all-out assault on the middle, which he sees as a deadly conformity rather than an accommodating civility. *Advertisements for Myself* is one of his most important books, largely because it contains three vivid short works, "The White Negro" and the stories "The Man Who Studied Yoga" and "The Time of Her Time," addressed to this point. "The Man Who Studied Yoga" is a satiric account of bourgeois conformity, with its nostalgia for radicalism and its current attachment to psychoanalysis or at least psychobabble. A four-room flat in Queens, a ten-year marriage, children, a hack writer hiding a wish to be a novelist – can anything be more expressive of the dead center of dullness? Can a porno movie save them, elicit the liberating orgy? Let us hope not.

Denise Gondelman is the female lead of one of Mailer's best fictions, "The Time of Her Time." She is attractive, educated, in analysis, haughty, engaged to a Jewish pre-law at Columbia College, and virginal. Clearly, this girl needs help. Enter Village stud of working-class origins Sergius O'Shaughnessy, the "I" narrator, as he was as a character in *The Deer Park*, where his sexual escapades with the capricious movie star Lulu lead him a merry chase. The self-styled "Messiah of the one-night stand" (447) breaks the ice with Denise with a sadistic flourish – "you dirty little Jew" (464), slap – as he turns her every which way. Apocalyptic orgasm indeed! Bourgeois smugness and totalitarian psychoanalysis exploded in one swell foop. Well, at least for a minute.

In this last story Mailer finds a voice adequate to his aggression. The voice becomes more elaborate in *An American Dream*. Rojack is another portrait of the hipster. He too acts on immediate impulse in this case to the point of criminal psychopathology. He strangles his wife and throws her out of the window. After all, she crudely questioned his manhood and literally went for his sexual jugular. We are somewhat distanced from the white Negro. In no way can Rojack be considered an extension of the proletariat. And Mailer the sexalogue has moved from the rebel without a cause to the rebel with one. Moreover, Rojack has worked within the system, has even been elected to Congress, and is a professor of psychology. And, most conventional of all, he is much married. His current wife was a castrator and, given her social background, a representative of the corrupt power structure itself.

Marriage for Rojack is not just a form of alienation but a form of war. As it is for wife Deborah whose incestuous victimization brings with it a revenge against men. Drawn by the magic at the top and its contempt for the mediocre middle, Rojack soon enough discovers the depravity of her powerhouse father. A pop *Crime and Punishment, An American Dream* reverses Dostoyevsky's moralism by giving us crime without punishment. Mailer presumably is really interested in certain states of mind and not murder, but these states of mind come somehow only after murder. Mailer's hero is one-eighth Jewish. This is an irrelevance. Mailer can rest assured that no one will confuse Rojack or any of his other heroes with a nice Jewish boy.

Herzog came out in 1964, *An American Dream* in 1964 and 1965 (serialized). Their appearance generated an excitement that, with the exception of Philip Roth's *Portnoy's Complaint* and Thomas Pynchon's *Gravity's Rainbow*, has not appeared in the literary community since. Bellow and Mailer showed that the culture of the postwar period contained its own contradiction. The humanist and the sexalogue are opposed. This can be vividly seen in comparing the murder scenes of these novels. Mailer's murder scene is a dramatization of negative transcendence, an antinomian ascent by descent, romantic immoralism writ large. It is lurid, bloody, final, and rewarding to the murderer, even sexually rewarding, since after killing his wife, he has sex with her maid! It is a scene that begins and ends in eroticism. Bellow's murder scene begins in revenge and ends in restraint. The mesmerizing benignity of ordinary custom holds sway. Murder is not an option but a joke. Herzog comes to a moral not a sexual exhilaration, a positive if modest transcendence. Bellow shows what is most typical of American Jewish fiction of the postwar period, the sway of the ordinary. In this sense he is thematically of the postwar period. Mailer illustrates the power of rebellion and is thus more attuned to the late sixties, another period. Mailer was lauded for a while but became disillusioned by what he called left hard-ons.

Most of Bernard Malamud's best fiction comes out in the fifties and is as representative of that decade as it is of Jewish qualities. *The Assistant* appears in 1957 but is an attempt to capture the thirties immigrant milieu, to recapture qualities of Jewishness that no longer clearly existed. This attempt to seize the evanescent past is a result of the increasingly secularized, increasingly assimilated fifties. It is why in *The Assistant* and in *The Magic Barrel*, whose characters live in a similar time-warp, Malamud's Jewishness has a precious quality. So, in *The Assistant*, Morris Bober, in explaining to the inquiring Frank Alpine what suffering means to a Jew, answers, "I suffer for you . . . you suffer for me" (98). If it is extremely unlikely that any Jewish storekeeper ever said that to a gentile employee, it is nonetheless memorable as a poetic formulation of moral life. As has often been said, Malamud at his best presents us not with realism but with a sort of moral mythology. His best effects are those of an intense lyricism. For the big, open, contemporaneous world, the world of social fiction, one reads Bellow or Roth (who do other things as well). Not that *The Fixer* and *Dubin's Lives* do not have these qualities, but Malamud rarely achieves the distinction of his postwar period work. So if these works seem precious in the sense of curiously affected, they are equally precious as value.

In *The Assistant*, the economic pressures on Morris are such that he finally yields to the temptation of burning his store for the insurance money. Luckily, he is too much the *schlimazel* to handle the fiery celluloid and is saved. Even Morris yields to temptation but, mainly, Morris and Frank Alpine take life from their moral avatars, Moses and St Francis. Morris lives by the law, humanely, the law being synonymous with the good heart, as the rabbi says at his funeral. Frank, miscast as a burglar and confused rapist of Morris's daughter Helen, is fascinated by suffering. Becoming a Jew is his redemption. He bears the pain of circumcision, which may be seen as a triumph of superego over id. Frank becomes a Son of the Covenant, a man of stern morality. He takes on Morris's burden. And Morris's daughter, Helen, is still there.

In most of the stories of *The Magic Barrel* Malamud stays old-fashioned ethnic, paradoxically appealing to the outside world by avoiding it. Ethnicity serves as a stay against fifties homogeneity, the all-consuming and all-consumering present. Moreover, World War II revived the reality of categories like good and evil. Belief was taken seriously by many, including Heschel, Maritain, and Niebuhr. The appeal of the Jewish writers in America was, in part, the need for roots, even if the need was sometimes more apparent than the roots. Still, there was far more rootedness to T. S. Eliot's rootless Jew than he perceived.

"The First Seven Years" is another story about a no-longer-young man trying to win a shopkeeper's daughter. This time the man is Jewish, the daughter loves him, but the father, Feld, has better hopes for his girl than the bald, bookish refugee Sobel. He wants a college boy. Despite her love of reading, he could not provide that sort of education for her. Miriam isn't impressed with the young man he has introduced to her. It turns out educated means accountant and Miriam rejects his materialism. When he finds out Sobel's intentions, the astonished Feld rejects him, only to be taken by the assistant's grief at being rejected. In a variation on the biblical story, Sobel has been working for five years for the girl of his dreams and almost does not get her. Feld relents. For reasons of modesty – she is only 19 – Feld will have him work for two years and then she will be his. The heavy-hearted Feld need not have bothered to come to the store early the next day. Sobel was already there "pounding leather for his love" (16). Eros, builder of arch supports!

Malamud's immigrant Jews evoke an idea of community through redemptive suffering, wry though this may be. In "The Mourners," Kessler, a miserable and dirty old man, is chucked out on the street with his belongings when the smell from his apartment becomes too much. He is brought back upstairs by his Italian neighbor and her two sons, who take pity. "What did I did to you," weeps Kessler to landlord Gruber (23). Gruber, who is, after all, Jewish, thinks of offering to put the old man in a nursing home. But Kessler's mourning is so rending that it occurs to Gruber that the man is mourning for him – "it was he who was dead" (25). Such is Gruber's perception of the event. There is a moment in these stories that involves a transcendent giving. Gruber makes a *talis*, a prayer shawl, of Kessler's sheet and becomes a mourner. I mourn for you, you mourn for me in the community of suffering.

"The Last Mohican" is a variation on the giving theme. Fidelman, failed painter and present art student, is plagued by the ever-needy, ever-demanding *schnorrer* Susskind. The not exactly wealthy art student can never seem to give him enough. There is the Joint Distribution Committee, there is repatriation to Israel, but no, Susskind (the name, ironically, means sweet child) insists on salvation through Fidelman. Denied Fidelman's suit, Susskind steals his briefcase, including the Giotto chapter he has been working on. In a dream Fidelman sees a Giotto painting in which a saint is handing a knight "in a thin robe his old gold cloak" (181). Fidelman has the answer to his previous question, "Am I responsible for you then, Susskind?," to which the latter had answered that he was, "Because you are a man. Because you are a Jew" (166). So he runs to give Susskind his suit and receives back his briefcase. But the Giotto chapter has been burned. "The words were there but the spirit was missing," says the somehow knowledgeable Susskind as he flees. "All is forgiven," Fidelman shouts and we are supposed to believe in this climactic goodness (182). There is never enough of giving, a moral for an increasingly acquisitive culture grown subtle in the morality of self-interest.

Malamud's moral aesthetic rests on a stylized Jewish identity. But suffering is a mess, Jewish history a mixed blessing. Henry Levin of "The Lady of the Lake" would like to forget the whole thing and takes to calling himself Henry R. Freeman. He is an American, not a Jew. Alas, he falls for a young woman whose Holocaust experience means everything to her, whose pride is her Jewish identity. This former resident of Buchenwald will not marry someone who cannot share her meaningful past. "I treasure what I suffered for," she says, a true Malamud heroine (132). She is not a son but a daughter of the Covenant.

Marriage made or broken is often the moment of truth in Malamud's fiction of the fifties. In his world it is, ideally, responsibility made flesh. In this respect Malamud spoke to a wide fifties audience, which believed in the accessible ideal of married normalcy. As the divorce courts of the seventies attest, this is one more ideal buffeted by reality. Yet people remarry, so even here maybe it was not the ideal but the particular enactment. Given his stylized milieu, Malamud is still dealing with marriage brokers in his fifties fiction. Appearing in passing in "The First Seven Years," the marriage broker takes center stage in "The Magic Barrel." Sex in Judaism is not inhibited in a Puritan way, but it is, traditionally, holy, involving marriage and leading to reproduction. Marriage brokers in the fifties were a rarity, except in Orthodox communities. Hence Leo Finkle and Salzman.

A rabbinical student at Yeshiva University, Leo Finkle does not love God, because, except for his parents, he does not love man. When he does fall in love he does so with a picture of someone who has deeply suffered, who gives him an impression of "evil." He finds this "good: good for Leo Finkle" (209). She is Salzman the matchmaker's daughter, whom the father considers "an animal. Like a dog" (212). Could Leo convert her to goodness, himself to God? "The idea alternately nauseated and exalted him" (213). For, in embracing her, he is embracing life, a reality of innocence and experience, as her white dress and red shoes indicate. Leo momentarily thinks of the colors in reverse, as she waits like a fallen woman under the street lamp. He notices, however, the "desperate innocence" of her eyes and pictures, in her, "his own redemption" (214). Leo's Jewishness, then, is a romantic appropriation of the traditional. Yet once again insight into suffering brings redemption. Suffering crystallizes identity in Malamud's best work.

This variation of the more traditional religious theme is an indication that Malamud may be feeling too much the heroism of giving and selflessness. Frank Alpine may be, finally, too painful a case. And Fidelman may be involved in a parody of solicitude. Should one continually give to an egregious *schnorrer* like Susskind? There is something hokey about such goodness (and something implausible about setting Susskind up as a critic of Giotto).

The radical break between the first Fidelman story and the rest may indicate Malamud's unease with it. The erotic replaces the altruistic in his character as it does to some degree in Malamud's imagination. In "Still Life," a ravenously sex-hungry, uxorious Fidelman falls into sex almost fortuitously as he happens to dress as a priest in a self-portrait. This elicits penitential guilt in his elusive Italian lover, whose story includes incest and murder. She can function as an artist and a love only under the aegis of Christian guilt. Eroticized, Fidelman surprises himself with a moral though not a Jewish world as he pumps his difficult *inamorata* to her penitential cross. By the next Fidelman story, the picaresque takes over. The Jew becomes, of all things, pickpocket, art thief, immoralist. Judging from the frequency of these stories Malamud seems to have found them liberating. We get an idea of Fidelman's predicament when, involved in a copy-and-switch scheme, he kisses the hands, thighs, and breasts on Titian's *Venus of Urbino*, murmuring, "I love you." Fidelman is given to a tawdry eroticism, a tumble with an unattractive model, a memory of his sister stepping into the tub. Trapped in a criminal element, he is victimized by an art theft gone awry. The later Fidelman stories, though not without flashes of moral earnestness on the part of the would-be artist, are even more strained examples of comic eroticism taking over the life of a failed artist. Fidelman is a dead end.

But his pursuit of the erotic is not. *Dubin's Lives*, which Malamud intended to be something like a summa, is its ultimate expression. Malamud in the fifties may be considered the most Jewish of the Jewish writers. He now defines the truly significant in terms of erotic life. This is a sign of the times and a difference between the fifties and the seventies. Though even "The Magic Barrel" was seen as a way out of oppressive moral restraint, classic Malamud is more typically given to heroes who can creatively repress, heroes of conscience. That the self cannot be understood without the erotic is not exactly news in fifties Malamud. But is the self to be understood primarily as a function of the erotic? The 56-year-old Dubin seriously entertains this idea. D. H. Lawrence, in Dubin's view, answers yes. And Lawrence is his culture hero. But since Dubin has as much trouble with his biography of Lawrence as with his erotic life, the answer may be no. In a nightmare, Dubin is confronted by a vituperative, anti-Semitic Lawrence who curses him as a Jew antagonistic to the male principle. Dubin thinks of Jewishness as a sense of obligation and met his gentile wife through a "personal" in which she expressed the desire for a marriage-minded man who is "responsible" (46). He even sees his subsequent adultery as a reward for being good. He remains responsible to his wife in his own way. He defines the Jew in America, circa 1979 – Dubin is a man who will not commit adultery in his wife's bed! Dubin is what Lawrence is not, ambivalent. That his young lover, Fanny of course, thinks of sharing Dubin with his wife is a wish fulfillment. Displaced by Fanny's young man, Dubin leaves her house for his, "holding his half-stiffened phallus in his hand, for his wife with love," a half-cocked ending if there ever was one (362). Dubin is too much the Jew for a pagan game. No erotic transcendence for him. And he never breaks the matrimonial bonds. Suffering amorphously, Dubin is through much of the novel weightless, gutless, feckless, and fuckless. He embodies the lack of moral clarity that inspired Malamud to create his fifties period milieu in the first place. This is Malamud's brilliant world, where characters can picture their own redemption.

The period we are mainly dealing with, about 1946 to 1964, coincides with Philip Roth's bar mitzvah and his turning 31, one might say his symbolic and real manhood. Roth is of the next generation, the one to come of age after the war, not during the Crash, the Depression, and World War II. For this reason Roth deals with affluence rather than poverty. Nor does he deal with the American immigrant experience, his parents having been born in America. Irving Howe, whose best-selling *World of Our Fathers* defined the immigrant Jewish heritage for a multitude of American readers, has considered Roth cut off from the roots of Jewish feeling, but it would seem that Howe is making that contingent upon intensity of contact with the immigrant experience. With Roth's emphasis on family, even on the extended family of Israel, with his unique grasp of Jewish Newark and his close grasp of Jewish suburbia, with his self-lacerating comedy of suffering, one would be hard pressed to think of a writer who more Jewishly expresses the reality of the post-Howe generation of assimilated American Jews. Howe is like the Jewish lady in the Israel joke who will not stop talking Yiddish to her son because she does not want him to forget that he is a Jew. Surely Roth's development as a writer undermines Howe's contention that Roth is "never a writer deeply absorbed by experience for its own sake," that he is after some of his early stories reduced to *kvetching*, which Irving Howe, writing in *World of Our Fathers*, defines as "a sterile humor" (596f).

But *kvetching*, in my understanding, is more accurately rendered as "unjustifiable complaint." Roth's complaints are generally justified, not only in their social and moral ambience, but by their frequent transformation into brilliant comedy. In art, as Howe has said in conversation, performance may be its own justification. Howe recognizes that what he considers Roth's deficiency regarding traditional Jewish values need not be fatal if American values are put in their place. Without even considering the first, can anyone doubt at this point in Roth's career his American values? You cannot, for example, make people laugh unless you share their values. And even if Roth reverses the classical Molièrean pattern by flaying the typical and sympathizing with the eccentric, he does so in a community of self-regard.

Howe's distinction between Jewish and American values has little currency for a writer who insists that he is an American writer who happens to be Jewish. So though Roth often writes about Jewish characters, the context is American. This is true from the beginning. "Goodbye, Columbus," in the volume of the same name, is a social portrait of suburban Jewish America as seen through the eyes of a young man from urban Jewish America. Judaism as religion is given only satiric treatment. Neil Klugman finds himself praying or at least making a little speech to himself in St Patrick's Cathedral as his love gets a new diaphragm. "If we meet You at all, God, it's that we're carnal, and acquisitive, and thereby partake of You," he reflects, in what is not a particularly Jewish moral or locale. A confused Klugman wonders if God can provide Patimkin heaven. Impossible. Brenda's parents discover the diaphragm, which she subconsciously wished them to find. Having to choose between her lover and her parents, she chooses the parents, little though they mean to her. "Goodbye, Columbus" is a sort of domesticated, fifties, Jewish *Gatsby*. Poor boy, rich girl, dreaming, heartbreak. Daisy Buchanan too chooses respectability, but she chooses between lovers. Both heroines wilt, but the triumph of family piety, empty in this case, is Jewish. The story ends with Klugman going back to work on the Jewish New Year, a holy day. So Roth's hero breaks with Jewish tradition, defined here as bourgeois provincialism. Klugman is a stick, the satire a bit obvious, but particularly in its evocation of social surfaces and an athletic America, it will do nicely.

Another story in the volume equally evocative of the fifties, and the only one to have become a household word, at least in Jewish households, is "Eli, the Fanatic." Whether or not the level of satire meets with Howe's approval, Roth has touched on an ambivalence in the character of Eli Peck, as his name indicates. Eli is short for Eliyahu or Elijah, Peck is his changed, assimilated name, Wasp-sounding. Roth prepares us for his conversion *to* the Jews by making him a sensitive man who has had two nervous breakdowns. The Protestant and Jewish calm of Woodenton is pierced by Eli's heartfelt affinity with Jewish suffering. The assimilated lawyer out to keep the Yeshiva in line becomes the penitential Jew, and the assimilated lawyer is what he is doing penance for. "You are us. We are you," he says, suggesting the traditional community of Jewish concern (Morris Bober was, shall we say, more catholic). This takes precedence over Eli's lightweight suburban friends, of whom he nonetheless thinks, "I am them. They are me" (265). Roth here gives us sympathetic, quixotic, hilarious comedy, siding with the eccentric. Roth is in this story a master of the socially incongruous.

In *Letting Go*, his novel about the fifties, Roth is the realist rather than the satirist. It is in the literary rather than the vernacular tradition that Roth favored in his first book. Vaguely Jamesian, with a focus on consciousness, it is a work of psychological realism. James's characters are alluded to a number of times in the text, particularly Isabel Archer. She seems to be a symbol of failed marriage, as she is, toward the end of *Letting Go*, an exemplar of obligation. Early marriage was part of fifties mores and, in Paul and Libby Hertz, Roth gives us one of the most painful marriages in literature. Even so, Roth is capable of superb, excruciating dialogue reflecting, for example, the breakdown of belief as it mirrors personal breakdown. Libby's hysteria is one of the best things in the book. In this novel of lost illusions, Paul is to duty what Gabe is to feeling. But Gabe, the Roth surrogate, is, like Neil Klugman, a tepid conception. His amorphousness helps to transform the novel into a beached whale. His last-minute selflessness, in the style of James's Lambert Strether of *The Ambassadors*, is a desperate attempt to act on feeling. The best flat portrait in the novel is that of Bigonness, the conniving unionist. In his utter lack of sentimentality about labor, Roth reflects another fifties quality. That Roth could have sustained himself through so dreary a tome was an indication that here is a writer who can do anything.

In Roth's writing up to *Portnoy's Complaint* libido is generally a form of imprisonment. His small masterpiece was published in 1969 and has a freedom and wildness Roth possesses to some degree thus far in only some of the comic stories of *Goodbye, Columbus*. Portnoy's desire is to put the id back in Yid, a sentiment more typical of the late sixties than of the postwar period. Portnoy is a child of the fifties, the 1950 valedictorian of Weequahic High and an editor later in that decade of the *Columbia Law Review*. He remembers Pumpkin, the psychologically sound all-American girl, with her naturally streaming early fifties hair, one of a number of indications in Roth that the fifties might be an embodiment of normalcy when it was not its inversion. Portnoy is what is not nice about the nice Jewish boy, with his parents, his guilt, his furtive sexuality, issuing eventually into a rebellious troilism where he cannot quite navigate through such pagan traffic. *Portnoy* is a landmark in the Jewish comedy of self-exposure.

The comic agony of erotic salvation is mined eight years later in the underrated *The Professor of Desire*. It shows again that, with the possible exception of some of the late social novels, Roth is at his best in the wild mode, though here that mode is tempered by an almost Chekhovian bitter-sweetness. Like Byron, David Kepesh is studious by day, dissolute by night. Unlike Byron, Kepesh has an analyst. A problem is that he is Jewish so that where id should be there ego is. Although he thinks of the fifties as "that woebegone era in the history of pleasure" (92), our sexual gourmet also thinks about "the libidinous fallacy" (94). The professor critic is taunted by his swinging, megalomaniac, Jewish friend Baumgarten – "Virtue, virtue, who's got the virtue? Biggest Jewish racket since Meyer Lansky in his prime" (131). But after a number of women, including ex-wife Helen, an energetic and cantankerous sexual athlete, Kepesh seems to find calm as well as voluptuousness in Claire, Clarissa as he sometimes calls her, her name invoking light, clarity. "My obstructed days are behind me – along with the unobstructed ones," he declares harmoniously (169). But as fate? love? Kafka? would have it, Kepesh soon becomes impotent. His analysis proves to be interminable. Kepesh remains a Jewish Dionysus, one part Priapus, one part depression.

Zuckerman takes over from Kepesh when Roth realizes that the persona of artist rather than scholar gets closer to the bone, even the funny bone. The coincidence of comedy and subjectivity is Roth's métier, showing superbly in the Zuckerman trilogy masterwork, *The Anatomy Lesson*.

In *The Ghost Writer*, the first volume of the trilogy published as *Zuckerman Bound*, Roth gives us, centrally, a portrait of Malamud (Lonoff) and, tangentially, one of Bellow (Abravanel). He emphasizes Malamud's residually Jewish qualities and thinks of him as the most famous literary ascetic in America. Lonoff grants authority to the prohibitive and thereby gives young Zuckerman "visions of terminal restraint" (14). Lonoff represents "Sanity, Responsibility, and Self-Respect" (15), the capital letters paying due deference to moral abstraction, a Jewish, anti-Modernist trope. Yet Lonoff's troubled marriage and his open flirtation with, of all people, the still living Anne Frank shake the abstractions. The audacious story line almost succeeds. What does succeed is this further step in the literature of the bachelor impatient to assume the world.

By *Zuckerman Unbound* he has assumed it. The novel is post-*Carnovsky* (*Portnoy's Complaint*). Zuckerman is a celebrity living in the paradoxical glare of hermetic luxury. As if to set some critics straight, he lucidly describes his motivation for writing *Carnovsky*: "You set out to sabotage your own moralizing nature" (305). The book was not an apology for Dionysus. Zuckerman's life seems always to involve contradiction. Like Thomas Wolfe, he left home for Art only to find that he had taken home with him. Has his celebrity cost him his heart? He feels no grief at his father's death. He does feel guilt. Did his father actually call him "bastard" on his deathbed, his final word? Or is it, Zuckerman sardonically notes, a writer's wishful thinking, "If not quite the son's" (380)? His rivalrous brother is there to assure him of patricide – "You killed him, Nathan" (397). Loyalty, responsibility, restraint, the brother inveighs, "Jewish morality, Jewish endurance, Jewish wisdom, Jewish families – everything is grist for your fun machine" (397). In the eyes of this solid bourgeois the artist's cannibalizing life is essentially guilt and sterility. His brother is not man enough to see that Zuckerman, himself a conscience-ridden Jew, is in partial agreement. Rather, his brother goes on about how he knows what it is to have a child and, he tells Zuckerman, "You don't, you selfish bastard, and you never will" (399). No family – this is the ultimate Jewish curse. Neither son, husband, nor brother, Zuckerman finds himself unbound. Will he bring the Promethean fire of art?

The final novel of the trilogy, *The Anatomy Lesson*, shows us that Zuckerman is far from indifferent to his brother's accusations. He is, in fact, decimated by guilt, not having completed a page since his father's presumptive dying rebuke. He is in a writer's depression: "he had nothing left to write, and with nothing to write, no reason to be" (416). He finds himself, literally, in traction. Not that he does not manage intercourse, fellatio, and cunnilingus from a supine position with the help of a thesaurus under his head. Zuckerman's static position is balanced in the narrative by the speedy movement of obsessive rage. When it is not directed at himself it is directed at the critic Milton Appel (Howe), to whose generation Zuckerman owes much of his aggressive marginality and independence – the style of literary Jews like himself, who came of age in the fifties. Zuckerman reflects that "to be raised a post-immigrant Jew in America was to be given a ticket out of the ghetto into a wholly unconstrained world of thought ... Alienated? Just another way to say 'set free'!" Does this imply a severance from Jewish consciousness? No. There is a "thrillingly paradoxical kicker," for Zuckerman: "A Jew set free from Jews – yet only by steadily maintaining self-consciousness as a Jew" (480). In his own mind Zuckerman is not an effective apostate but a Jew.

What Zuckerman finds most disturbing is that Appel does not see this. Moreover, Zuckerman thinks that Appel loathes the bourgeois Jews he seems to be defending "now that the Weathermen are around, and me and my friends Jerry Rubin and Herbert Marcuse and H. Rap Brown" (505). Zuckerman assures us that as an undergraduate at the University of Chicago in the fifties he "savagely reviewed beat novels in *The Maroon"* (585). Though Appel does not do this, Zuckerman feels down deep that the critic obtusely classifies him with the crazies and the morality of impulse people. Yet it is not much of a leap to Zuckerman's cogent criticism of the critic. He shrewdly objects that Appel seems to have read *Carnovsky* "as a manifesto of the instinctual life. As if he'd never heard of repressed, obsessive Jews" (505f). This position does not prevent Zuckerman from experiencing the hospital ministrations of sex priestess Gloria Galanter, who visits him with vibrating dildo, K-Y Jelly, a length of braided rope, and a talented and adventurous finger. After all, goes her maternal wisdom, "A child is sick . . . you bring toys" (526). That Gloria is married is no obstacle to anyone. Zuckerman, against his will, almost, speculates on Dionysian rites and the physically afflicted in ancient days. Gloria and the wise and disillusioned Jaga are the most memorable sketches from his harem. Jaga touches a nerve in describing writers as "warm ice" (538), interested in women primarily as material. Zuckerman ruefully admits as much but can only plead being possessed and the therapeutic out that "the only patient being treated by the writer is himself" (540). With answers like these, maybe Appel has something.

The irony of Zuckerman's life is that perfecting the writer's iron will "began to feel like the evasion of experience . . . like the sternest form of incarceration" (586). Zuckerman is bound by his art. "Once one's writing," he contends, "it's all limits. Bound to a subject. Bound to make sense of it. Bound to make a book of it" (609). Roth circles the square here in that the life of aesthetic impulse is inseparable from the life of obligation. He becomes totally absorbed in the life of art in a Jewish way. He may have fooled Appel, but he does not quite fool the students who submit a questionnaire to the patient whose mouth is literally if not metaphysically shut by a fall. They ask, "Do you feel yourself part of a rearguard action, in the service of a declining tradition?" This apropos of postmodernists like Barth and Pynchon. Even with his mouth wired shut Zuckerman is the liberal Jewish humanist. If it were not perhaps he would have bitten them.

The Anatomy Lesson crystallizes the trilogy into formidable stature and, in its debt to *Herzog*, brings us back to 1964. In tempo, in tone to some degree, in its epistolary style, in its first person/third person narrative making at once for sympathy and intensity and for comic and social distancing, in its lovable, reflective, lunatic protagonist who remembers his erotic life as he seeks to transcend it for a higher wisdom, in its beleaguered Jewish quality, Roth's novel owes much to Bellow's masterwork. Stretching chronology, one might say that in these two works a good measure of postwar Jewish sensibility is contained.

In *Zuckerman Bound* Roth carries the comedy of self-regard to an exhausting end (only to reach comic heights again in *Operation Shylock*). At first, as in *Portnoy*, this comedy was a way of breaking out of the postwar bourgeois doldrums, and to a degree it remains so in *Zuckerman Bound*. In a totally different vein, however, the postwar period engages Roth in some of his most striking recent fiction. In this fiction, ironically, the postwar period bails him out of the narcissistic doldrums. "I've had my story," says Zuckerman in *I Married a Communist*. We now get a Balzacean narrative which seeks to examine character through segments of social history. *I Married a Communist* presents the depredations of the McCarthy era through the eyes of young Nathan Zuckerman (class of 1954) and, decades later, his great high school English teacher, who narrates the story of his flamboyant brother Ira, a communist who rises from the Party to a disastrous marriage to a one-time movie star now settling for daytime radio. Her book, entitled *I Married a Communist* (a turn on Claire Bloom's name-naming account of her marriage to Roth), decimates an already shaky relationship and assures election of a right-winger to Congress. Young Zuckerman is something of a left-winger who is eager to shed his bourgeois Jewish identity. Religion, for him, is the opiate of the masses. He "didn't care to partake of the Jewish character . . . [he] wanted to partake of the national character" (39). In the end he inevitably partakes of both, assuming, as does his Jewish teacher, the postwar style, an anti-utopian, ethical cast of mind. His nonagenarian teacher warns the already old, now ascetic, artist against "the utopia of isolation" as well (317). For Zuckerman adulthood has meant orphanage and he shares his teacher's stoicism as he admires his endurance. His teacher once paid the price of refusing to cooperate with HUAC and later pays the price of his liberal inclinations by staying on in Newark – his wife was murdered in a mugging. The teacher laments "the myth of your own goodness – the final delusion" (318). Zuckerman bleakly concludes, "There's the heart of the world. Nobody finds his life. That is life" (319). One wonders at this point about the reality of identity, Jewish or otherwise.

American Pastoral, which came out in 1997 a year before *I Married a Communist* but deals with the late sixties as well as the postwar period, is a novel which would seem to counter this bleakness. It is highlighted by one of Roth's finest character portraits, Swede Lvov, a former star high school athlete who carries on his family's lucrative glove business. Roth shows compassion for what he once ridiculed in Ron Patimkin, for example. In Swede, Roth succeeds in portraying a good ordinary man, a difficult task. Swede embodies responsibility, rectitude, superego, chastity even. And he loves America. (Zuckerman appears to be particularly elated at his marrying out.) As social novelist Roth develops a sense of figures of masculine virtue: Murray Ringold, the wise, sympathetic high school teacher, if not Ira Ringold, the once idealized, spectacular, unstable, radical brother, and Swede Lvov. In *American Pastoral* Roth presents a bourgeois family lovingly perceived. "What on earth," this hard book concludes, "is less reprehensible than the life of the Lvovs" (423). That life is devastated by their daughter, Merry, who is radicalized by social unrest and, even more, by the hypocrisy of the American administration during the Vietnam War (which also disturbed many middle-class protesters). She is moved to blow up a post office, killing an innocent man in doing so. "Inspired" (258), she plants two other bombs, killing three more people. She has expressed her violent hatred of America. She eventually becomes an Eastern religious ascetic, living in dire poverty, guilty about taking the life of plants by eating them.

American Pastoral, one of Roth's finest achievements, does not sit well with some critics on the left, who remember the energy of the late sixties without remembering its dangers, without, in some cases, ever having considered them. They fault Roth for short-changing the period, as if it were the novelist's obligation to be sociologically exhaustive. It is quite enough to brilliantly record the savage impact of one late-sixties revolutionary on one family. It is true that Zuckerman, dreaming his realistic chronicle, equates this radicalism with infantilism, that he denigrates Merry's reading of Marx, Marcuse, Malraux, Frantz Fanon, that he loathes the radical literary critic wife of an old friend for playing "the old French game of beating up on the bourgeoisie," as a guest puts it (383). These are, to say the least, plausible positions, not to mention the basic political (not artistic) immunity in such matters that a novelist has. Indeed, some of Zuckerman's most brilliant perceptions are anti-radical perceptions, the description of Rita Cohen's Isro (Jewish Afro) hairdo, for example; it says "I go wherever I want, as far as I want – all that matters is what I want!" (134). Perception like this transcends politics.

Some of the deepest emotion in Roth occurs when he reconciles himself with the middle-class world he is no longer a part of, in *American Pastoral* and in *Patrimony*, for example. Rarely in fiction does fact rise to such a loving eloquence as Roth's description of the manufacturing of gloves. Roth is describing the process of civilization. His superego nostalgia, a nostalgia for the fifties, cannot be simply attributed to his own narcissism. Swede is an alter ego. Moreover, he and his family are faulted for living by "the utopia of a rational existence" (123) The Lvovs are in the end subject to Roth's late pessimism, dramatizing as they do a disintegrated innocence, a deracinated sense of obligation. Yet the dominant tone is elegy, just as it was rage in *I Married a Communist*. Such is Roth's late encounter with the era that gave him mature consciousness.

American Jewish fiction, then, shows us deidentifying writers (Trilling, civilly; Salinger, indifferently; Mailer, aggressively) and identifying writers (Bellow, Malamud, Roth). Yet with the exception of much of early Malamud, all of these writers dream American dreams, anxiety as well as wish fulfillment. Cynthia Ozick wishes to dream Jewish dreams. Doing so involves a journey into normative Judaism far longer than any of these writers is willing to take. Quoting *The Ethics of the Fathers*, writing about Rabbi Akiva and the destruction of the Temple, writing fiction with titles like " The Pagan Rabbi" and "Levitation," and essays entitled "America: Toward Yavneh" and "Toward a New Yiddish," attacking Harold Bloom for idolatry and Lillian Hellman for Holocaust denial in the case of Anne Frank, Ozick represents a significant zeitgeist shift. She admires Bellow, Malamud, and Roth as writers, even Jewish writers, but feels a lack. So, probably, do they, but normative Judaism is not a direction they care to pursue. Of course, Ozick herself can be a traditional writer only at a remove. But if she is the first (or one of the first; Hugh Nissenson and Arthur Cohen got there at about the same time) to be a writer of Judaism, she will not be the last.

The rise of ethnicity, the turn to religion, the reflection of history (for example, the Holocaust, Israel), individual temperament – these all give rise to a new generation of fiction writers whose variations on tradition or the lack of it is reflected even in the titles: Steve Stern's *Lazar Malkin Enters Heaven*, Rebecca Goldstein's *Mazel*, Thane Rosenbaum's *Elijah Visible*, Melvin Jules Bukiet's *While the Messiah Tarries*. Ironically, this turn occurs at a time when Jewish assimilation has been so much of a success that, for many, particularly "minorities," Jews are regarded as part of the Wasp establishment – to the extent that such a thing exists. As the marriage statistics show, Jews being in bed with Wasps is not just a metaphor. Of course, this may itself be a major reason for the turn. In any case, with the exception of some of Ozick's stories, it remains to be seen whether a more intense concentration on Jewishness can produce the level of art attained by Bellow, Malamud, and Roth.

I recall browsing in shops of the Mea Shearim or Orthodox section of Jerusalem to no avail. I finally asked a Chassid in black caftan and sidelocks where I could pick up some objets d'art or artifacts. He had trouble understanding what I was looking for. Between his English and my Yiddish we were in some difficulty. Finally, I got through. He knew what I meant. *"Tchatchkis,"* he said, the Yiddish word conveying a bemused contempt for the merely aesthetic, for art and artifacts. This incident made me think that if the moderate swing to religious themes in contemporary American Jewish fiction were to become an extreme shift to the totally religious it would undo itself. One would dispense with mere literature and focus only on the revealed word of God. It is neither probable nor desirable that the breakthroughs of the Enlightenment be reversed.

References and further reading

Howe, Irving. *World of Our Fathers*. New York: Simon and Schuster, 1976.

Mailer, Norman. *Advertisements for Myself*. New York: Berkley Medallion, 1966.

Malamud, Bernard. *The Assistant*. New York: Signet, 1957.

Malamud, Bernard. *The Magic Barrel*. New York: Farrar, Straus and Cudahy, 1958.

Malamud, Bernard. *Dubin's Lives*. New York: Farrar, Straus and Giroux, 1979.

Roth, Philip. *Goodbye, Columbus*. New York: Meridian, 1960.

Roth, Philip. *The Professor of Desire*. New York: Bantam, 1978.

Roth, Philip. *Zuckerman Bound*. New York: Farrar, Straus and Giroux, 1985.

Roth, Philip. *American Pastoral*. New York: Vintage, 1997.

Roth, Philip. *I Married a Communist*. New York: Vintage, 1998.

Trilling, Lionel. Comments in "Under Forty." Symposium. *Contemporary Jewish Record* vii.1 (February 1944): 16f.

Chapter 11

Fire and Romance: African American Literature Since World War II

Sterling Lecater Bland, Jr

Fiction is of great value to any people as a preserver of manners and customs – religious, political, social. It is a record of growth and development from generation to generation. No one will do this for us; we must ourselves, develop the men and women who will faithfully portray the inmost thoughts and feelings of the Negro with all the fire and romance which lie dormant in our history, and, as yet, unrecognized by writers of the Anglo-Saxon race.

> Pauline E. Hopkins, *Contending Forces: A Romance of Negro Life North and South* (1900)

The world changed a great deal in the years between the conclusion of World War II in 1945 and the dawn of the twenty-first century. For African American literature, examinations of this change have traditionally been reflected in discussions about the relationship between black writing and politics, culture, and the unyielding influence of memory and the past. Those alterations, however, have been informed by a series of adjustments that acknowledged traditional influences and relationships while simultaneously calling into question the assumptions situated at the very basis of change. Basic perceptions of African American subjectivity shifted, the composition and boundaries of the African American literary canon were renegotiated, and the influences of gender, class, and sexual orientation acknowledged. The symbiotic relationship between the world's changes and black literature is felt nowhere more profoundly than in the constantly increasing audience for black writing in the decades following World War II.

The Great Depression of the 1930s serves as the point of transition from the Harlem Renaissance into the period of literary naturalism that characterized a great deal of African American novel writing throughout the 1940s. Harlem Renaissance-era writers like Langston Hughes, Jessie Redmon Fauset, Zora Neale Hurston, Claude McKay, and Alain Locke adopted a vision of black progress and creativity that was self-consciously revisionist in the ways it sought to reconsider commonly held notions of African American life and the validity of its cultural contributions. The Renaissance had venerated black self-determination and the validity of African American cultural contributions. The varied facets of the New Negro movement were closely intertwined with organizations like the National Association for the Advancement of Colored People (NAACP) and the Urban League. These organizations produced magazines (the *Crisis* and *Opportunity*, respectively) that provided writers with outlets for producing their work and focused on the very themes that informed their work: issues of economic self-determination, racial equality, gender, and political empowerment that consumed the attention of most black social and political organizations. Though grounded in the realities of the cultural moment, the ideals of the Harlem Renaissance were large and encompassing. In *The New Negro* (1925), the anthology compiled by Alain Locke that defined the aspirations of the movement, Locke argues:

> In this new group psychology we note the lapse of sentimental appeal, then the development of a more positive self-respect and self-reliance; the repudiation of social dependence, and then the gradual recovery from hyper-sensitiveness and "touchy" nerves, the repudiation of the double standard of judgment with its special philanthropic allowances and then the sturdier desire for objective and scientific appraisal; and finally the rise from the social disillusionment of race pride, from the sense of social debt to the responsibilities of social contribution, and off-setting the necessary working and common-sense acceptance of restricted conditions, the belief in ultimate esteem and recognition. (10–11)

Because of the reliance Harlem Renaissance writers placed upon wealthy white patrons for support, much of the cultural momentum inscribed in the movement was slowed by the stock market crash in 1929 and the economic downturn that characterized much of 1930s

America. The effects of the Great Depression served as the ideological basis for the flow of African American literary production in the years during and immediately following World War II.

By 1937, Locke's sense of hope and idealism about the New Negro movement had dissipated considerably. In an essay entitled "Spiritual Truancy," which was a review of Claude McKay's *A Long Way from Home* that appeared in the *New Challenge* in 1937, Locke castigates McKay in particular and the New Negro movement in general for failing to offer "a wholesome, vigorous, assertive racialism" capable of interpreting "the folk to itself, to vitalize it from within" (85). Rather than addressing itself to "the people themselves" the Renaissance pandered "to the gallery of faddist Negrophiles" (84).

> The task confronting the present younger generation of Negro writers and artists is to approach the home scene and the folk with high serious-ness, deep loyalty, racial reverence of the unspectacular, unmelodramatic sort, and when necessary, sacrificial social devotion. They must purge this flippant exhibitionism, this posy but not too sincere racialism, this care-free and irresponsible individualism. (84)

Locke's emphasis on collective consciousness and the needs of the group over the desires of the individual are reflected in an essay by Richard Wright entitled "Blueprint for Negro Writing" that appeared in the same issue of the *New Challenge*. Locke's obvious dissatisfaction with the direction taken by New Negro writers is echoed in Wright's opening paragraph:

> Generally speaking, Negro writing in the past has been confined to humble novels, poems, and plays, prim and decorous ambassadors who went a-begging to white America. They entered the court of American Public Opinion dressed in the knee-pants of servility, curtsying to show that the Negro was not inferior, that he was human, and that he had a life comparable to that of other people. For the most part these artistic ambassadors were received as though they were French poodles who do clever tricks. (53)

Wright's manifesto, arguably his strongest statement about liter-ature and the role of the black writer, goes on to reject what he sees as the bourgeois impulses of the majority of black writers in favor of a Marxist critique of literature and culture that sees the writer as a "purposeful agent" who has the responsibility of depicting black life "in all of its manifold and intricate relationships" (Wright, "Blueprint for Negro Writing": 59). In short, the black writer "is being called upon to do no less than create values by which his race is to struggle, live and die" (59).

> Hence, it is through a Marxist conception of reality and society that the maximum degree of freedom in thought and feeling can be gained for the Negro writer. Further, this dramatic Marxist vision, when consciously grasped, endows the writer with a sense of dignity which no other vision can give. Ultimately, it restores to the writer his lost heritage, that is, his role as a creator of the world in which he lives, and as a creator of himself. (60)

Wright's *Native Son* (1940) is, by many accounts, the literary event that deeply influenced the direction of African American literature for over a decade. Writing during a period in which he was profoundly influenced by Marxist ideology and the theories of the Chicago School of Urban Sociology, Wright produced a novel infused with urban realism and naturalistic effect convincingly arguing that Bigger Thomas, a black youth who lives in the poverty of Chicago's South Side slums during the Great Depression, who murders the daughter of his wealthy white employer, and rapes and murders his girlfriend, is actually the victim of an overly determined social environment that turns Bigger into the very monster that society dreads. In an essay explaining the basis and composition of Bigger Thomas's character, entitled "How 'Bigger' Was Born," Wright argues that "The birth of Bigger Thomas goes back to my childhood, and there was not just one Bigger, but many of them, more than I could count and more than you suspect" (Wright, *Native Son and "How 'Bigger' Was Born"*: 506).

Wright's comments about characterization suggest for Bigger a broadly representative function that eclipses the particularity of his experiences, in favor of an allegorical quality suggesting that Bigger's pathologies are potentially reflected in blacks everywhere, who are similarly controlled by unseen social, economic, psychological, and political activities sharply restricting their possibility of social and personal advancement. As Wright indicated in "Blueprint for Negro Writing," the novel combines aesthetic attributes with the socially catalyzing potential of literary protest. Though Wright continued to publish until his death in 1960, his early work, particularly the breakthrough accomplishment of *Native Son*, is commonly regarded as being his most influential (Rowley: 125–265; Walker: 105–202).

The success of *Native Son*, of course, was unprecedented. It sold over 200,000 copies in its first three weeks of publication and was selected as a Book-of-the-Month Club main selection. It was the first novel written by a black author to receive this distinction. But Wright's literary ascendancy and the obvious influence he has had on writers of his generation and beyond should not entirely overshadow the work of his contemporaries or the complexity of the literary moment. What is clear, however, is that Wright's unflinching portrayal of the black urban landscape and his decision to link social determinism with naturalistic description serves as an important and useful way of addressing a gathering of writers disparate in style and literary output. His influence has been widely acknowledged. Wright clearly shaped the direction of black novel writing in the years following World War II and may even be seen as laying the bedrock of the Black Arts movement's attempts to join aesthetic concerns with the atmosphere of social protest, civil rights, and Black Nationalism that defined 1960s America (Joyce: 29–74; Drake: xvii–xxxiv; Kent, *Blackness and the Adventure of Western Culture*: 76–97).

According to Bernard Bell in *The Afro-American Novel and its Tradition*, African Americans published 37 novels in the 1940s (Bell: 185). Of these, the finest suggest direct literary links to the themes and techniques expressed in Richard Wright's early work: William Attaway's *Blood on the Forge*, Chester Himes's *If He Hollers Let Him Go*, and Ann Petry's *The Street*. When William Attaway (1911–86) published his first novel, *Let Me Breathe Thunder* (1939), he was hailed as a promising young writer. Attaway had met Richard Wright in 1935 when they both worked on the Federal Writers' Project *Illinois Guide Book*. In reviews of the novel appearing in the *New York Times Book Review* and *New York Herald Tribune Books*, reviewers approvingly cited Attaway's naturalistic influences and his obvious literary debts to Ernest Hemingway and, especially, John Steinbeck's *Of Mice and Men* (1937). Attaway's far-reaching second novel, *Blood on the Forge* (1941), draws on his own experiences as part of the Great Migration from Mississippi to Chicago, Illinois. The novel focuses on a wide variety of laborers (including black sharecroppers, white farmers, ethnic minority immigrants, company representatives, and union organizers) whose lives are affected by a number of shifts in Northern industrial power. One of the things that seems clear, and was noted by Ralph Ellison in his review of the novel, is the sense of pessimism characterizing the book and permeating its conclusion (Ellison, "Transition": 87–92). Although Attaway implicitly seems to recognize the potentially transformative power of labor organization, the novel's conclusion pessimistically chronicles the inability of workers adequately to adapt to the changes caused by the post-World War II industrial environment. Attaway's literary reputation rests almost entirely on the critical response to these two novels. Though he subsequently turned his attention to writing books about music and writing radio, television, and movie scripts, Attaway shares with Wright an awareness of the dangers of a capitalist system for individuals who are socially and psychologically unprepared for its demands (Garren: 3–7; Bone: 132–40; Margolies, *Native Sons*: 52, 63–4; Bell: 167–71; Accomando: 30–1).

Like Richard Wright, Chester Himes (1909–84) sees American culture as an environment that is relentlessly hostile to blacks in general and especially antagonistic to black men. In Himes's literary world, society demands of black men a willingness to give themselves over to social and institutional versions of racism that are emasculating and psychologically repressive. For Himes, that racially repressive atmosphere, combined with a number of humiliating stereotypical assumptions about black men, creates a social space that makes physical violence and other antisocial behavior an obvious response. To a large extent, these themes are present throughout the work Himes produced during his long and distinguished literary career.

Roughly speaking, Himes's writing can be divided into several broad areas: the naturalistic writing, much of it drawn from personal experience, that defines the novels he published between 1945 and 1955; the Harlem detective novels that brought him widespread notoriety; and the autobiographical writing he produced later in his career.

It is important to realize that, for Himes, from a relatively early age, race was something he experienced from within his family as well as from without. Himes's mother had descended from house servants, was very fair, and undoubtedly had white ancestors. Her husband was dark-skinned and had a lineage that stretched back to the slave fields. According to Himes, their relationship was fraught with the residual power effects of slavery. He saw an unresolved desire of white women (and those black women who perceived themselves as having the reflected glow of prestige of being descended from those who worked in the master's home rather than the master's fields) to control black men. As such, Himes saw his father as overly passive and acquiescent to white people and even to his own wife. Himes translates the discord he felt in his parents' relationship into a more ubiquitous, free-floating conflict between black men and white women in his writing (Fuller; Williams, "My Man Himes"; Reckley, "Chester Himes": 90).

Himes's work is often seen in direct relation to the writing Richard Wright produced in the early and middle portion of his career. Himes's language was direct, uncompromising, and often colloquial. The novels he produced in his first decade of publication exhibited the naturalistic qualities that remained a part of his writing throughout his life. The naturalist influence was so pervasive in his writing that, even in the 1970s, John A. Williams was able to hail Himes as "the single greatest naturalistic American writer living today" (Williams, "My Man Himes": 27). Those novels (*If He Hollers Let Him Go* [1945], *Lonely Crusade* [1947], *The Third Generation* [1947], *Cast the First Stone* [1952], and *The Primitive* [1955]) suggest the ways cultural assumptions about race impair black masculine well-being. By the early 1950s, Himes, like fellow African American expatriate writers Richard Wright and James Baldwin, turned to Europe as a place of refuge from the sting of American racial injustice. Though he already had a substantial readership in France that was devoted to his naturalistic work, Himes published a series of Harlem-based detective novels that were financially and artistically successful: *For Love of Imabelle* (1957), *The Real Cool Killers* (1959), *The Crazy Kill* (1959), *The Big Gold Dream* (1960), *All Shot Up* (1960), *Cotton Comes to Harlem* (1965), *The Heat's On* (1966), and *Blind Man With a Pistol* (1969). Himes's work with the detective genre is, by his own admission, not innovative.

> American violence is public life, it's a public way of life, it became a form, a detective story form. So I would think that any number of black writers should go into the detective story form . . . They would not be imitating me because when I went into it, into the detective story field, I was just imitating all the other American detective story writers, other than the fact that I introduced various angles which were my own. But on the whole, I mean the detective story originally in the plain narrative form – straightforward violence – is an American product. So I haven't created anything whatsoever; I just made the faces black, that's all. (Williams, "My Man Himes": 49).

But Himes's detective novels carried forward many of the themes he had addressed in his earlier fiction: racial bigotry, the impossibility of achieving the American Dream for black Americans, and the simultaneous cultural attempts to emasculate and hypersexualize black men (Soitos: 124–8). Like Wright's, Himes's later work, a two-volume autobiography entitled *The Quality of Hurt* (1972) and *My Life in Absurdity* (1976), continued to chronicle what he saw as the absurd relationship between racism, powerlessness, and rage (Glasrud and Champion: 203–10; Bell: 171–8; Fuller: 4–22, 87–8; Bone: 157–9, 173–6; Margolies, *Native Sons*: 87–101).

Ann Petry's (1911–97) interests are as much about a feminist vision of the complicated roles black women are required to play in society as they are about the deterministic qualities of racial, social, and economic degradation. Richard Wright's Bigger Thomas and Chester Himes's Bob Jones (the protagonist of *If He Hollers Let Him Go*) are battered by a debilitating rage created by their confrontation with the barriers contrived by the society in which they live. Their anger is fueled by an understanding of the oppressive desperation society creates in all blacks who seek social and economic advancement. Conversely, many of the characters at the center of Petry's work exhibit a middle-class consciousness that is far removed from the underclass and working-class consciousness upon which Wright and Himes focus. In her three novels, *The Street* (1946), *Country Place* (1948), and *The Narrows* (1953), Petry exhibits a willingness to move beyond naturalistic depictions of urban life to a more subtle analysis of American society as it is defined and influenced by race, class, gender, and expectations rooted deep in the foundation of the American Dream.

In *The Street*, for example, Lutie Johnson lives on 116th Street in Harlem, New York, during World War II. She is a black single mother who is doggedly determined to achieve the American Dream. The novel consists of Lutie's education about a system that purports to reward hard work and self-sacrifice while actually reinforcing the very divisions that separate hardship from prosperity. By the conclusion of the novel, she has realized the impossibility of ever achieving her dream. Like *Native Son*, to which *The Street* is often compared, the story ends in violence and hopelessness. Lutie's life is devastated by a series of forces she can neither see nor entirely comprehend. It is clearly a novel of social criticism that shifts the focus away from a troubled individual blindly driven to antisocial activity by fear and anger, and instead focuses squarely on the limiting elements of a dominant culture that are imposed on an aspiring black middle class.

To some extent, the novel's often-repeated similarities to *Native Son* seem facile. Wright's novel, after all, is about a young man who kills one woman and rapes and murders another. At the conclusion of *The Street*, Lutie Johnson beats a man to death who has physically threatened her in an attempt to take advantage of her need for money. Though he comes to embody all of the resentment and frustration Lutie feels about the forces that keep her from her dreams, his threat to her, initially, at least, is physical. This is a subtle but important rewriting of the *perceived* threat that Bigger Thomas feels from the two women whom he kills (Alexander: 140–7; Bone: 157, 180–5; Bell: 178–83; Ervin, "Ann Petry": 570–2).

Petry's decision in *Country Place* to focus on white characters signals both a willingness in black writers to extend beyond the relatively narrow confines allowed by protest literature in general, and economic determinism in particular, in favor of forms and characterizations that provided black authors with the chance to comment on the human experience. Hence *The Narrows*, the third novel Petry published in the years immediately following World War II, is fittingly about the pervasive influence of time and place, the relationship between a black man and the white woman who is the heir to an industrial fortune in a small Connecticut town, and the need to adjust to change or face profound disappointment.

In the 1930s, Dorothy West (1907–98) was editing *Challenge*. This journal, which West had founded and financed with her own money, was her attempt to revitalize black writing and "recapture, in the mid-thirties, the literary vitality of the Harlem Renaissance which had not survived the Depression" (Daniel: 494). Practically speaking, her journal also served as a bridge between West's aesthetic circle of Alain Locke and James Weldon Johnson and the emerging influence of Chicago naturalistic realist writers artistically guided by Richard Wright. The journal's conservative, nonpolitical stance drew the criticism of Chicago writers like Wright and Margaret Walker. This undoubtedly led to West's decision in 1937 to rename the journal *New Challenge* and collaborate with Wright as associate editor. The collaboration was fraught with disagreement between the two and the new journal was plagued by inadequate funding. It ceased publication after its first issue. In the years between 1926 and 1940, Dorothy West had contributed a number of short stories to Harlem Renaissance literary magazines. In 1945, she turned her attention to the composition of her first novel, *The Living Is Easy* (1948), which signaled in the period in which it was published the rise of an influential group of post-World War II black female authors and critics that included Ann Petry, Gwendolyn Brooks, Margaret Walker, and, approximately a decade later, Paule Marshall (Griffin: 766–7; Jimoh: 475–81).

By the end of the 1940s, the naturalism that critics had previously hailed for its ability convincingly to convey the urban experiences of black characters had run its course. Writers like Ralph Ellison and James Baldwin began to feel confined by the literary rules naturalism and urban realism imposed. As early as 1946, though the essay was not published until 1953, Ralph Ellison questions, in "Twentieth-Century

Fiction and the Black Mask of Humanity," the usefulness of naturalism: "How is it then that our naturalistic prose – one of the most vital bodies of twentieth-century fiction, perhaps the brightest instrument for recording sociological fact, physical action, the nuance of speech, yet achieved – becomes suddenly dull when confronting the Negro?" (83).

James Baldwin's critique of protest writing in his 1949 essay "Everybody's Protest Novel" is equally keen:

> All of Bigger's life is controlled, defined by his hatred and his fear. And later, his fear drives him to murder and his hatred to rape; he dies, having come, through this violence, we are told, for the first time, to a kind of life, having for the first time redeemed his manhood. Below the surface of this novel there lies, as it seems to me, a continuation, a complement of that monstrous legend it was written to destroy. (18)

The ambivalence both Ellison and Baldwin came to feel about their literary relationship to Wright is clearest in their first novels, the importance of which defined the literary tone and direction of critical attention throughout much of the 1950s.

Ellison's realization of the limitations of sociological writing and his intense desire to chart a new course for himself is clear. To some extent, his literary dispute with Wright is as much about audience as it is about literary form. In "Richard Wright's Blues," Ellison suggests that the avenues available for black writers to explore are substantially narrowed when the black writer instinctively writes to a white audience. For him, even audiences that purport to "know" American blacks are screened from the realities of black experiences:

> Why then have Southern whites, who claim to "know" the Negro, missed all this? Simply because they, too, are armored against the horror and the cruelty. Either they deny the Negro's humanity or feel no cause to measure his actions against civilized norms; or they protect themselves from their guilt in the Negro's condition – and from their fear that their cooks might poison them, or that their nursemaids might strangle their infant charges, or that their field hands might do them violence – by attributing to them a superhuman capacity for love, kindliness and forgiveness. (141–2)

In short, for Ellison, black writing that exclusively addresses itself to its audiences' limited assumptions about black life requires black writers needlessly to argue for the very existence of black humanity and culture.

After growing up in Oklahoma City, Oklahoma, Ellison studied for several years at the Tuskegee Institute before relocating to New York City in 1936. Though his initial intention was only to work in New York during the summer and return to Tuskegee to complete his senior year, he decided to remain in New York. Jobs were scarce, but like many other writers of the time, he eventually found work writing for the Federal Writers' Project of the Works Progress Administration. More importantly, perhaps, he met many writers, like Langston Hughes and Richard Wright, who by 1937 was editing *New Challenge* and subsequently encouraged Ellison to pursue a writing career of his own (Jackson: 132–60). Though his earliest writing reflects some of Wright's influences, Ellison soon began to move toward a vision of African American identity that integrated a broad variety of aspects of American culture, black American culture, and the frontier mentality that characterized what had been, until seven years before Ellison's birth, the Oklahoma Territory in which he was raised (Busby: 1–20, Jackson: 1–22, Nadel: 1–62). In his introduction to *Shadow and Act*, Ellison notes:

> One thing is certain; ours was a chaotic community, still characterized by frontier attitudes and by that strange mixture of naïve and sophisticated, the benign and malignant, which makes the American past so puzzling and its present so confusing; that mixture which often affords the minds of the young who grow up in the far provinces such wide and unstructured latitude, and which encourages the individual's imagination – up to the moment "reality" closes in upon him – to range widely and sometimes even to soar. (51)

Invisible Man (1952), which was the only novel Ellison published during his lifetime, exemplifies Ellison's desire to assimilate disparate influences and characteristics into a literary vision of racial integration. Ellison's thoughts on the idea of assimilation, for which he was extensively criticized in the 1960s and 1970s by Black Arts movement writers, gradually shifted. Ellison had moved toward the idea that society was best served by acknowledging and encouraging a pluralistic, rather than an integrationist, outlook. His thoughts on the novel reflect his critique of integrationist thinking. In "The Novel as a Function of American Democracy," which appears in his collection of essays *Going to the Territory*, Ellison argues that:

> The state of our novel is not healthy at the moment. Instead of aspiring to project a vision of the complexity and diversity of the total experience,

> the novelist loses faith and falls back upon something which is called "black comedy" – which is neither black nor comic, but a cry of despair. Talent, technique and artistic competence are there, but a certain necessary faith in human possibility before the next unknown is not there. (764)

Invisible Man, comprised of realist, absurdist, surreal, and folkloric elements, tells, in miniature, the mythic quest of the unnamed narrator to discover his identity. From a more expansive perspective, the novel is an allegorical rendering of African Americans who are required by social convention contradictorily to "move without moving" (Ellison, *Invisible Man*: 59) by being promised social freedom while at the same time being restrained by society (Bell: 193–215; Eichelberger: 25–57; Jackson: 432–44; Kent, *Blackness*: 152–63; Moses: 273–82). The narrator's experiences throughout the novel are chaotic and ambiguous. Though he desperately wants to negate the influence of history and the past, he is continually called upon to revisit that past. By the conclusion of the novel, the narrator has temporarily withdrawn from a world that he cannot fully understand and that refuses to see him as anything but a representative figure. He says: "I am an invisible man. No, I am not a spook like those who haunted Edgar Allan Poe; nor am I one of your Hollywood-movie ectoplasms. I am a man of substance, of flesh and bone, fiber and liquids – and I might even be said to possess a mind. I am invisible, understand, simply because people refuse to see me" (Ellison, *Invisible Man*: 3).

The novel's cryptic final words, "And it is this which frightens me: Who knows but that, on the lower frequencies, I speak for you?" (Ellison, *Invisible Man*: 581) suggests Ellison's desire for his reader to see the narrator's experiences as being broadly representative of black presence and experience in America (Curtin: 281–311). Ellison refers to this in "Perspective of Literature" from *Going to the Territory* as the "symbol of guilt and redemption" that characterized the role of black Americans when they "entered the deepest recesses of the American psyche and became crucially involved in its consciousness, subconscious, and conscience" (778). The narrator's experiences are suggestive of the hopes and limitations inscribed in the human condition.

James Baldwin's (1924–87) literary influences from both Wright and Ellison are clear. In his essay "Alas, Poor Richard," published after Wright's death in a collection of essays entitled *Nobody Knows My Name: More Notes of a Native Son* (1961), Baldwin makes clear the influence Wright had on him:

But when we met, I was twenty, a carnivorous age; he was then as old as I am now, thirty-six; he had been my idol since high school, and I, as the fledgling Negro writer, was very shortly in the position of his protégé. This position was not really fair to either of us. As writers we were about as unlike as any two writers could possibly be. But no one can read the future, and neither of us knew this then. We were linked together, really, because both of us were black. I had made the pilgrimage to meet him because he was the greatest black writer in the world for me. In *Uncle Tom's Children*, in *Native Son*, and, above all, in *Black Boy*, I found expressed, for the first time in my life, the sorrow, the rage, and the murderous bitterness which was eating up my life and the lives of those around me. His work was an immense liberation and revelation for me. He became my ally and my witness, and alas! my father. (252–3)

Similarly, Baldwin notes in his comments about Ellison from the essay "Autobiographical Notes" in *Notes of a Native Son* (1955):

But in the work of Faulkner, in the general attitude and certain specific passages in Robert Penn Warren, and, most significantly, in the advent of Ralph Ellison, one sees the beginnings – at least – of a more genuinely penetrating search. Mr. Ellison, by the way, is the first Negro novelist I have ever read to utilize in language, and brilliantly, some of the ambiguity and irony of Negro life. (9)

Clearly, Baldwin was as drawn to Modernism and realism as he was to naturalism and black folklore. Baldwin, however, expanded both theme and structure. In the novels he published between 1953 and 1963 (*Go Tell It on the Mountain* [1953], *Giovanni's Room* [1957], and *Another Country* [1963]), he suggests a recurring sense of shared experiences for blacks that created a fabric of continuity and cohesion to black life. In "Many Thousands Gone," Baldwin sees this disregard of relationship and shared experience as reflecting Wright's greatest weakness as a writer (27). In *Go Tell It on the Mountain*, the community Baldwin depicts is entirely black. Rather than focus on the inequalities between the races, Baldwin addresses the inhibiting qualities of what he sees as the basis that defines black life in America: religion, the family, and the influence of the past (Bell: 224; Kent, *Blackness*: 139–51; Leeming: 84–9). *Giovanni's Room* entirely eliminates the issues embodied in blackness by centering the novel on the actions of white characters living in Europe. Baldwin replaces the isolating qualities of blackness with bisexuality and its implications in American society concerning identity, self-approval, and masculinity. Baldwin saw an analogous relationship between race and sexuality in American culture. For Baldwin, the country actively denied both blacks and homosexuals a place in American society. Like blacks, homosexuals must actively make places for themselves or risk being determined by a culture that neither recognizes nor accepts them (Johnson: 399–416; Kaplan: 27–54; Leeming: 122–9; Ross: 13–55).

Wright's *Native Son* was published a year before the United States entered World War II, and was composed at the conclusion of the Great Depression. This was the beginning of the increasing ability of socialist organizations successfully to win growing numbers of blacks by equating the struggle of African Americans for equality with the labor movement's struggle for workers' rights (Crossman: 115–62). Baldwin's work during this period is similarly influenced by a social climate that had been, since the years following the conclusion of the war, leaning toward integration. The Supreme Court upheld *Brown v. the Topeka Board of Education* in May 1954. The Reverend Dr Martin Luther King, Jr, organized the Montgomery bus boycott in December 1955, and students staged a sit-in at the Woolworth lunch counter in Greensboro, North Carolina, in 1960 (Bell: 188–9). It seems only natural, then, that the emphasis on collectivity to which Baldwin aspired was characterized as much by the relationship of the individual to collective experience as it was by the influence of various kinds of collective guilt on individual lives (Sylvander: 27–66).

Ralph Ellison and James Baldwin clearly cast long shadows across the body of African American narrative forms like prose fiction and essays produced during the middle decades of the twentieth century. There were, however, diverse other voices that are significant in the work they rendered and the forms in which they chose to work.

Gwendolyn Brooks's (1917–2000) poetry, along with the poetry written by those of her generation who have come to be most highly admired – Margaret Walker, Melvin Tolson, and Robert Hayden – addresses the experiences of blacks, with one ear absorbing the rhythms and cadences of black vernacular and the other ear listening to scholarly techniques and the Modernist pressure to make old forms new. Throughout her life, Gwendolyn Brooks maintained close connections to the South Side Chicago experiences that shaped her life and influenced the conception of her earlier work: *A Street in Bronzeville* (1945), *Annie Allen* (1949), *Maude Martha* (1953), and *The Bean Eaters* (1960) (Melhem: 16–131). To some extent, these works provide a kind of literary connection between the generation of poets whose work, in terms of theme and technique, is often associated with the academy and those writers whom Brooks inspired (many of whom she later actively encouraged) who are traditionally associated with the Black Arts movement in Chicago. In terms of form, Brooks's work makes use of ballads, sonnets, lyrics, narratives, the blues, and free verse while simultaneously infusing these forms with strikingly vivid characters who often reside in hopeless areas in underprivileged black communities. Some of her work is deceptively simple; other work, like *Annie Allen*, remarkably dense and nuanced. Brooks's work was always conscious of individuals and the world in which they lived (Hansell: 71–80; Kent, "Aesthetic Values": 30–46; Smith, "Paradise Regained": 128–39; Tate: 140–50).

By the 1960s, Brooks's work reflected the sense of purpose and possibility many blacks felt as the successes of the civil rights era expanded and the country was forced to confront the burdens and legacies of its racialized past. As the decade wore on, some of the sense of hope and possibility was replaced with anger, frustration, and, eventually, revolt. In April 1967, Brooks participated in the second Fisk Writers Conference, which brought her into contact with Black Arts movement writers like LeRoi Jones (who later became Amiri Baraka) and John Oliver Killens. The conference changed Brooks's thinking. By 1967, the energy for change that earlier had been associated with the fight for civil rights was being transferred to the Black Power movement. What Brooks found at the conference was a determination to articulate a unique black aesthetic that combined politicized goals and artistic control over the images defining black life. It was this revised concept of the mutual supportiveness of politics and art that Brooks took with her when she returned home to Chicago and established black writing workshops that nurtured the talents of writers like Don L. Lee (Haki R. Madhubuti). Her appointment as poet laureate of Illinois in 1968 brought her a prominent stage from which to encourage the work of younger writers by giving readings and sponsoring workshops. Brooks's work effectively broke barriers between the poet and the audience by making poetry a meaningful form of personal expression (Kent, *Blackness*: 104–38, "Gwendolyn Brooks": 11–24, *Life of Gwendolyn Brooks*: throughout).

Like Gwendolyn Brooks, Margaret Walker (1915–98) was fortunate in having a professional life that spanned countless literary movements and several genres (poetry, prose fiction, and essay). And like Brooks, Walker was able to reorient herself to shifting aesthetic demands while simultaneously remaining in touch with the ideas, images, and materials around which her work continued to be oriented. Walker's introduction to the literary world began in 1936 when she was assigned as a junior writer to the Federal Writers' Project of the Works Progress Administration in Chicago, where she worked with a group including Nelson Algren, Fenron Johnson, Frank Yerby, and Richard Wright on the *Illinois Guide Book*. Wright and Walker worked together fairly closely in a three-year literary friendship in which he helped her revise her work for publication and she, after his relocation to New York, contributed a great deal of the research necessary for the completion of *Native Son*. Their friendship abruptly ended in 1939 due to a misunderstanding between the two (Fabre: 195; Giovanni and Walker: 88; Walker: 107–8).

Walker's first collection of poetry, *For My People* (1942), grew out of the master's thesis she prepared at the University of Iowa. The tone of social protest used extensively in *For My People* is replaced in her novel *Jubilee* (1966) by an expanded vision of history centering on the antebellum era, the American Civil War, and Reconstruction. The novel fuses folklore and the oral tradition with intensely realistic depictions of slavery. Though it was influential, critics saw the book as little more than a black writer's reworking of the myths of the antebellum South that were popularized and sustained by Margaret Mitchell's best-seller, *Gone with the Wind* (1936). Walker's literary output after the publication of *Jubilee*, including essays, poetry, and a biography of Richard Wright, provide for her a place in the continuum of black writers from poets like Gwendolyn Brooks, whom she first met in the 1930s when they both lived in Chicago and were becoming active on the literary scene, to Sonia Sanchez and Nikki Giovanni, with whom she collaborated in a literary conversation entitled *A Poetic Equation: Conversations between Nikki Giovanni and Margaret Walker* (1974). Each writer, though generationally separated, discusses her life as a writer whose work is called upon to confront and examine racism, the relationship between black women and men, and the social status of blacks in America. Like Gwendolyn Brooks's, Walker's ability to communicate to a broad and diverse readership is clear.

The same has not traditionally been the assessment of the work by her contemporary poets like Melvin Tolson (1898–1966) and Robert Hayden (1913–80). Each of these writers is widely acknowledged to have found ways to connect the black vernacular with the innovations developed by Modernist poets like T. S. Eliot, Ezra Pound, Wallace Stevens, Hart Crane, and William Carlos Williams. The most influential work of Tolson (*Rendevous with America* [1944], *Libretto for the Republic of Liberia* [1953], and *Harlem Gallery: Book I, The Curator* [1965]) and of Hayden (*Heart-Shape in the Dust* [1940], *Figure of Time* [1955], *Words in the Mourning Time* [1970], and *The Night-Blooming Cereus* [1975]) shimmers with technique and literary allusion that incorporates the modernism espoused by the New Critics with the themes of social injustice, cultural heritage, and the influence of the past that other black poets (and prose writers) of their generation were exploring. Less sympathetic assessments of their writing point toward their technical sophistication as indicating that their mature work is overly academic and complicated, of relevance to a narrow audience willing and able to place it in the Modernist tradition with which it is so closely associated, and somehow out of touch with the directions younger generations of black poets envisioned their poetry as being able to go in.

Tolson and Hayden's work clearly sees Modernist innovations as creating new possibilities for the black poet to use in expanding the boundaries of black experience, in ways that extended how national and international audiences experienced and understood black culture. For Tolson, at least, the stylistic nuance of a work like *Harlem Gallery: Book I, The Curator* very successfully combines Modernism's formal elements with the vernacular rhythms of Harlem life that both define a black artist and call into question the black artist's larger purpose in American society (Farnsworth, *Melvin B. Tolson*: 227–70). Some of the criticism Tolson experienced from the generation of poets who emerged during the Black Arts movement can be traced to what many in the movement saw as the poetry's inaccessibility (Farnsworth, *Melvin B. Tolson*: 136–51; Flasch: 19–133). Hayden's poetry in his later works is crafted around an appreciation of symbolist tradition, one that allows him consciously to move from particular racial experiences toward a vision of humanity that emphasizes the commonality of human pain, despair, and aspiration against the seemingly insurmountable reality of the human condition (Fetrow: 39–60, 124–41; Williams, *Robert Hayden*: 37–143).

The effects of the events of the 1960s on the American psyche are incalculable. To recite the litany: John F. Kennedy, Jr, was elected president; the limits of diplomacy were tested during the Bay of Pigs and the Cuban Missile Crisis; the conflict in Vietnam escalated; James Meredith enrolled as the first black student at the University of Mississippi; groups like the Southern Christian Leadership Conference (SCLC), the Congress of Racial Equality (CORE), and the Student Nonviolent Coordinating Committee (SNCC) were formed to end segregation and advance the cause of civil rights (with CORE and SNCC adapting to the increase in social and governmental resistance by becoming increasingly militant during the course of the decade); John F. Kennedy, Jr, Malcolm X, Medgar Evers, Martin Luther King, Jr, and Robert F. Kennedy were assassinated; the Civil Rights Act and the Voting Rights Act were both eventually passed; the Black Panther Party for Self-Defense and the National Organization of Women (NOW) were organized; student protests against the military's engagement in Vietnam proliferated; urban riots, indicative to some of an impending black revolution, broke out in a number of cities including Watts, California (1965), Detroit, Michigan (1967), and Newark, New Jersey (1967); and Richard Nixon, whom John F. Kennedy, Jr, had defeated in the 1960 election, was elected president in 1968.

By the middle portion of the decade, an influential group of writers and political activists, led among others by Amiri Baraka (who, at the time, was known as LeRoi Jones), Gwendolyn Brooks, Ed Bullins, Alice Childress, Charles Fuller, Addison Gayle, Jr, Nikki Giovanni, Maulana Karenga, Haki R. Madhubuti, Larry Neal, Carolyn M. Rodgers, Sonia Sanchez, and Askia M. Touré speculated about the social, political, and literary possibilities of aesthetic considerations coupled with active political participation by the black working class. Their work coalesced into the movement that became known as Black Arts. In his essay "The Black Arts Movement," Larry Neal defines the spirit and aspirations of the movement:

> The Black Arts Movement is radically opposed to any concept of the artist that alienates him from his community. Black Art is the aesthetic and spiritual sister of the Black Power concept. As such, it envisions an art that speaks directly to the needs and aspirations of Black America. In order to perform this task, the Black Arts Movement proposes a radical reordering of the western cultural aesthetic. It proposes a separate symbolism, mythology, critique, and iconology. The Black Arts and the Black Power concept both relate broadly to the Afro-American's desire for self-determination and nationhood. Both concepts are nationalistic. One is concerned with the relationship between art and politics; the other with the art of politics.

In short, the movement sought to produce a body of art by and for black audiences, that was unapologetically politically engaged, activist, and dramatically conscious of the connections between race and class (Kent, *Blackness*: 183–202; Moses: 123–37; Redmond: 294–417). Equally importantly, it disavowed the integrationist impulse that had characterized the civil rights agenda and called for black art to detach itself entirely from the flow of Western thought in an effort to forge a new, Afrocentric world-view.

Addison Gayle, Jr, in his introduction to *The Black Aesthetic*, sees black artists as being at war against society. For Gayle, critical methodologies like "the Aristotelian Critics, the Practical Critics, the Formalistic Critics, and the New Critics" (xxii) are inherently weak because they interrogate art solely on the basis of its beauty rather than on that of its ability to transform ugliness into beauty:

> The Black Aesthetic, then, as conceived – is a means of helping black people out of the polluted mainstream of Americanism, and offering logical, reasoned arguments as to why he should not desire to join the ranks of a Norman Mailer or a William Styron. To be an American writer is to be an American, and, for black people, there should no longer be honor attached to either position. (xxii)

The Black Arts movement had forged itself in the shadow of conflict in Vietnam and a litany of domestic conflicts. By the mid-1970s, it had descended into a series of internal and external conflicts that almost assuredly cost the movement its sense of cohesion and mission and led to the end of its formal activities. The movement splintered from within as its most influential members disagreed about how best to focus its revolutionary impulses. Some participants continued to view race as the only true battleground. Others, like Amiri Baraka, expanded their thoughts away from a strict nationalist platform and toward a Marxist-Leninist viewpoint that saw class warfare as the true foundation of racialized struggle. In his essay "The Latest Purge: The Attack on Black Nationalism and Pan-Afrikanism by the New Left, the Sons and Daughters of the Old Left," Haki R. Madhubuti sees leftists as undermining black nationalism in an attempt to further their own agenda:

> The Black Nationalist-Pan Afrikanist movement is now under attack from the white left, to the extent that they . . . have infiltrated two of the most influential black organizations: Afrikan Liberation Support Committee and the Congress of Afrikan People. Less than a year ago, both of these organizations were Nationalist and Pan Afrikanist . . . Now . . . they are both pushing for the "world socialist revolution" and both feel that at some point in the future, black people in the West must align themselves with the white workers to make the revolution. But the saddest part of their new thrust is that they see black people as

the *vanguard* for the "world revolution" . . . [as] the front line not for our own *liberation*, but for the liberation of the world: white people, yellow people and perhaps black people. The problem with this is that if we are the vanguard for the world revolution, we are bound to get wiped out for the interests of others and not even for the interests of ourselves. (46)

Conversely, Baraka and his organization, the Congress of Afrikan People, had come to believe that "the liberation of the black masses in the United States is impossible without the total annihilation of capitalism" (Baraka: 9; Fox: 11–37). From without, the movement, along with many other leftist organizations, was scrutinized by the Nixon administration's counterintelligence activities (COINTELPRO), which were carried out by the Federal Bureau of Investigation, the Central Intelligence Agency, the Internal Revenue Service, and the Department of Justice against radical activities. The country's decline into economic recession in the late 1970s further eroded the influences of the Black Arts and Black Nationalist movements.

As the Black Nationalist political movement exerted diminishing pressure on the national agenda in the 1970s, a number of writers used the assumptions of the Black Arts movement to expand the creative possibilities of black writers. The black aesthetic relied on an experimental combination of techniques that emphasized vernacular orality, folk culture, public performance, accessible political rhetoric, an engagement with African history and subjects, and a tone that was frequently revolutionary, polemical, and confrontational. For all that it brought to black literature – and its influences were many – the Black Arts movement also brought with it a prescriptive set of assumptions about blackness and the role of the artist that many writers ultimately found limiting at best, if not outright wrong.

The diverse gathering of writers who began or expanded their literary output in the late 1960s and 1970s all reflect a desire, conscious or unconscious, to expand the boundaries of theme, form, genre, culture, sexual orientation, history, gender, class, politics, and nation. These boundaries had either been hidden by benign neglect or actively silenced by critics marching in what some perceived as lockstep with a narrow vision of blackness and black experience.

Historical perspective provides the luxury, perhaps illusory, of assigning a kind of thematic and stylistic coherence to what is otherwise an unruly and disparate gathering of writing. Sheer numbers complicate matters. In the twenty-first century, the number of black novels produced has risen exponentially from the 37 published in the decade between 1940 and 1950 (Bell: 185). The current yearly production of black fiction, poetry, nonfiction prose, and drama is, by comparison, staggering. It would be a mistake to attempt to organize this work around a particular writer or singular literary objective. What is clear, however, is that there is, broadly speaking, an evolving series of themes and literary forms around which the most influential writers of the current generation have repeatedly oriented themselves.

Henry Louis Gates, Jr, drawing on the work of Harold Bloom, theorized in *The Signifying Monkey* (1989) that black writers, and particularly black male writers, drew upon and reacted against the generations of writers who preceded them. This "signifyin(g)," which Harold Bloom describes in his work as an "anxiety of influence," suggests for Gates a flow of literary influence in which a particular writer actively writes in reaction to the writing that has preceded him or her. In commenting about the work of Ishmael Reed, for example, Gates notes that:

> Reed has criticized, through Signifyin(g), what he perceives to be the conventional structures of feeling that he has received from the Afro-American tradition. He has proceeded almost as if the sheer process of the analysis can clear a narrative space for the next generation of writers as decidedly as Ellison's narrative response to Wright and naturalism cleared a space for Leon Forrest, Ernest Gaines, Toni Morrison, Alice Walker, James Alan McPherson, John Wideman, and especially for Reed himself. (Gates: 218; see also Clark: 65)

The decades following the 1960s produced a re-emergence of black women's writing that has been critically well regarded and commercially successful. This is certainly not the case for much of the writing produced by black women in the decades following World War II. An assorted gathering of writing by black women, all of whom were influenced by the 1960s, emerged in the 1970s and 1980s, notably including: Sherley Anne Williams's *Dessa Rose* (1986), *Peacock Poems* (1985), and *Working Cotton* (1992); Gayle Jones's *Corregidora* (1975) and *Mosquito* (1999); Lucille Clifton's *Good News about the Earth* (1972); Maya Angelou's *I Know Why the Caged Bird Sings* (1970); Paule Marshall's *The Chosen Place, the Timeless People* (1969) and *Praisesong for the Widow* (1983); and Toni Cade Bambara's *Gorilla, My Love* (1972), *The Sea Birds Are Still Alive* (1977), and *The Salt Eaters* (1980). In short, this highly selective sample of prose, poetry, and drama shifts the literary perspective by looking inward to the experiences contained within the black community, rather than looking outward at the historically troubled relationship between black and white communities.

The experiences of women, as mothers, daughters, wives, and lovers who inhabited worlds that were as much spiritual as they were social and sexual, were brought forward. The mutually sustaining relationship between black women and men has also served as a point of interest for these writers. Their work in the decades following the 1960s set the stage for the work of contemporary writers like Terry McMillan (*Disappearing Acts* [1989], *Waiting to Exhale* [1992], *How Stella Got Her Groove Back* [1996]) and Anna Deveare Smith (*Piano* [1989], *Fires in the Mirror* [1993], *Twilight – Los Angeles, 1992 on the Road* [1994], *Talk to Me* [2000]) (Smith, "Literary History": 458–9; Washington: 3–15).

Alice Walker's (b. 1944) Womanist outlook, an activist view that joins black feminism with the needs of humanity, exemplifies the possibilities of this expanded perspective. Walker's poetry, prose, and fiction speak in very specific ways to the experiences of black women in environments characterized by oppression, desperation, and transcendent faith. It is, however, Walker's abilities as a writer that allow her to create worlds in which the experiences of her primary characters, who are almost always black women, illuminate human experience beyond limits traditionally defined by class and race.

Walker produced diverse and provocative, creative works in the 1970s, but it is her epistolary third novel, *The Color Purple* (1982), that many critics have seen as being her most successful, because of its ability to combine in Celie, the main character of the novel, the concerns and perspectives of her earlier women characters. Its epistolary style allows Walker to see Celie in both subjective and objective terms. Through Celie's letters, the novel addresses, among other issues, the silencing of black women whose lives are defined by the physical and psychological limitations imposed upon them by the men around them. The novel transcends the trap of becoming ideological propaganda and successfully illuminates the complex relationship that exists between sexuality, self-acceptance, female friendship, and self-identity.

Walker was awarded a Pulitzer Prize and an American Book Award in 1983 for *The Color Purple*. Both the novel and Steven Spielberg's film (1985), whose screenplay was based on the novel, have been immensely successful and influential. Neither, however, has been without critics, often male, who have felt the story inaccurately depicts the realities of life for African Americans. Walker's subsequent novels *The Temple of My Familiar* (1989) and *The Way Forward Is with a Broken Heart* (2000), and her nonfiction *In Search of Our Mothers' Gardens* (1983), *Warrior Marks* (1993), and *Anything We Love Can Be Saved* (1997), have ambitiously confronted racism, spiritual truth and illumination, environmentalism, nuclear proliferation, cultural diversity, and female genital mutilation. Her most recent work, in short, continues to reverberate with the Black Art movement's emphasis on the importance of combining art and activism (Byrd: 363–78; Christian, "Alice Walker": 258–71; Christian, "Alice Walker: The Black Woman Artist as Wayward": 457–77; King: 413–15).

Gloria Naylor's (b. 1950) first novel, *The Women of Brewster Place* (1982), won the American Book Award for best first fiction in 1983, the same year Alice Walker's *Color Purple* was awarded a Pulitzer Prize and an American Book Award. The overlap of these public acknowledgments from the literary establishment is notable because, like Walker, Naylor writes from a position rooted in black womanhood while simultaneously transcending that rubric in favor of a broader awareness of American literature. Like Walker, Naylor has centered in *Linden Hills* (1985) and *Bailey's Café* (1992) on the stories of strong black women. Where Walker has received a certain amount of criticism, especially in *The Color Purple*, for what some regard as a narrow depiction of African American life, Naylor seems especially aware of the complex nature of black life in America. Her novels employ the stories of characters from a variety of socioeconomic, political, sexual, and generational positions. The worlds she creates on Brewster Place, in Linden Hills, in Bailey's Café, and Willow Springs, the island off the coast of Georgia and South Carolina on which the action of *Mama Day* (1988) takes place, reflect this multiplicity of experience.

Naylor clearly sees black experiences, though separated by any number of economic and social divisions, as ultimately being interconnected. In a technique acknowledging William Faulkner's influence on her writing, Naylor links the various microcosms of which she writes by involving characters from earlier novels in subsequent ones. Perhaps her greatest contributions to African American literature have been her interest in expanding the narrative palate available to writers and her willingness, like Toni Morrison and Gabriel Garcia Marquez, to acknowledge and incorporate the influence of the spirit world on that of everyday experience (Andrews: 1–25; Christian, "Gloria Naylor's Geography": 348–73; Collins: 680–5; Metting: 145–68; Yohe: 306–8).

Toni Morrison's (b. 1931) influence on American arts and letters, and on the dialogue of African American culture, is incalculable. She is the 1993 winner of the Nobel Prize in literature. Morrison, arguably more completely than any writer of her generation, has managed to combine many of the attributes of the post-World War II literary climate with the experimentalism of the Black Arts movement. For her, the experiences of blacks in America, and particularly the legacy of slavery, serve as a kind of metaphor for the human experience. Because of this, memory and the past are recurring themes, to some extent, in virtually all of her fiction and much of her non-fiction writing. In an interview from 1977, just after the publication of *Song of Solomon* (1977), Morrison was questioned about the overall intentions of her writing. Her response is particularly illuminating:

> My attempt, although I never say any of this until I'm done . . . is to deal with something that is nagging me, but, when I think about it in a large sense, I use the phrase "bear witness" to explain what my work is for. I have this creepy sensation . . . of loss. Like something is either lost, never to be retrieved, or something is about to be lost and will never be retrieved. Because if *we* don't know it (what our past is), if we women don't know it, then nobody in the world knows it – nobody in our civilization knows it . . . But if we women, if we black women, if we Third-World women in America don't know it, then it is not known by anybody at all. And I mean that. Then nobody knows it. And somebody has to tell somebody something. (Samuels and Hudson-Weems: 139)

Morrison's fiction creates a series of communities in which her characters are unable to grow and develop because of tension between community, family, and self-development. The world to which she bears witness is one in which the responsibility of individual characters is balanced against the physical and emotional violations perpetrated by the community around them. Morrison's focus shifts away from the insulated, individual experiences in her earliest novels, *The Bluest Eye* (1969) and *Sula* (1973), to map a terrain of self-discovery and epic resonance, in novels like *Song of Solomon* (1977) and *Tar Baby* (1981), emphasizing individual growth, self-acceptance, and a deeper understanding of communal history.

Song of Solomon was awarded the National Book Critics' Circle Award in 1977 and was the first Book-of-the-Month Club main selection written by a black author since Richard Wright's *Native Son* in 1940. In *Beloved* (1987) and *Paradise* (1998), Morrison more directly confronts the pervasive influence of memory and the past in African American life. These novels, with their seamless movement between the real and the supernatural, the past and the present, address the dual influences of memory and violence.

Beloved is based on the true story of Margaret Garner, a black woman who chose to kill her own children rather than allow them to endure a lifetime of slavery. It is the story of Sethe Suggs, who, during an escape attempt, decides to kill her children rather than let them be returned to slavery. Sethe is only able to kill Beloved, her youngest daughter. Beloved returns in the flesh as a 20-year-old girl who haunts her mother and sister and is able to consume Sethe's thoughts, almost to the point of killing Sethe, with the "rememory" of slavery. Beloved is eventually decisively driven from Sethe by an exorcism performed by neighbors. It is the insistence of memory and the value of community to which Morrison bears witness. She concludes the novel by noting:

> Disremembered and unaccounted for, she cannot be lost because no one is looking for her, and even if they were, how can they call her if they don't know her name? Although she has claim, she is not claimed. In the place where long grass opens, the girl who waited to be loved and cry shame erupts into her separate parts, to make it easy for the chewing laughter to swallow her all away.
>
> It was not a story to pass on.

The title of Morrison's eighth novel, *Love* (2003), is an explicit reference to 1 Corinthians: 12–13: "For now we see in a mirror dimly, but then face to face. Now I know in part; then I shall understand fully, even as I have been fully understood. So faith, hope, love abide, these three; but the greatest of these is love." The novel is saturated with the memory of Bill Cosey. Cosey, who is already dead when the novel opens, had been the owner of the Cosey Hotel and Resort during its prime in the 1930s and 1940s, when the resort was frequented by America's black elite. By the 1960s, the resort's appeal had begun to decline under the turbulence created by black activism and increased competition from large, international hotel chains. The hotel was finally closed and abandoned when Cosey died in 1971 at the age of 81.

The novel itself is an ensemble piece narrated by a number of women consumed by the persistence of Cosey's memory 30 years after his death. With that as its backdrop, the novel largely centers on Heed the Night Johnson, whom Cosey took as his second wife when she was only 11 years old (Cosey was 52 at the time), and Christine Cosey, who was Bill Cosey's granddaughter and Heed's best friend before the marriage. Heed and Christine, who are now in their sixties, have lived together since 1975 in the house on Monarch Street that Cosey had owned. The animosity they have come to feel for each other deepens as they relentlessly work, in the absence of a will, to attempt to gain the inheritance from Cosey's estate. (Only "L," the novel's sometimes alive, sometimes dead, omniscient narrator, who had worked as a cook at Cosey's hotel, seems definitively to know what made Heed and Christine first turn against each other when they were only 12.) Heed believes that Cosey wrote his will on a hotel menu, now lost, that she hopes to find and use to remove Christine from the house.

At one level, the novel is about the ongoing dispute between Heed and Christine and the influence of the man whose actions changed the direction of both of their lives. The novel is generationally juxtaposed between the broad, expansive, romanticized world that Cosey created and inhabited, and the claustrophobically dilapidated world that Heed and Christine are forced to inhabit because of Cosey's faults. From a fuller perspective, however, the novel is an extended rumination on the true nature of love. This seems to be reflected in Morrison's depiction of the innocent, childlike love that Heed and Christine experience before the arrival of Bill Cosey's destructively sexualized version of love. The novel suggests a redemptive possibility of returning to that kind of love as the two women reconsider the meaning and consequences of their shared past.

Morrison's literary and cultural criticism has also been influential. In *Playing in the Dark* (1992), which is composed of three essays, she engages the issue of race as it is explored in the fiction of canonical American writers including Mark Twain and Ernest Hemingway. Her edited volumes *Race-ing Justice, En-Gendering Power* (1992) and *Birth of a Nation'hood* (1997) examine the intersections of race, gender, and power in the Anita Hill/Clarence Thomas Senate confirmation hearings and the O. J. Simpson trial. Morrison's literary reputation, of course, rests most fully on the themes she revisits in her seven novels. It is there that she has been able to create dramas in which recognizable African American figures in recognizable settings struggle for wholeness and identity in communities that are often hostile and unforgiving (Carmean: 81–104; Harding and Martin: 87–110; Heinze: 55–101; Matus: 103–20; Mobley: 295–7; Peach: 102–25; Kubitschek: 115–38; Samuels and Hudson-Weems: 1–9, 94–138).

The expansion of opportunities for black women writers has occurred contemporaneously with an expansion of literary forms and genres for black women and men. Writers balance the influences of the past against the effects that past produces. These writers include Ishmael Reed (*Mumbo Jumbo* [1972], *Japanese by Spring* [1993]), Ernest Gaines (*Autobiography of Miss Jane Pittman* [1971], *Gathering of Old Men* [1993], *Lesson Before Dying* [1993]), Alex Haley (*Autobiography of Malcolm X* [1965], *Roots* [1976]), Charles Johnson (*Oxherding Tale* [1982], *Middle Passage* [1990]), Audre Lorde (*Zami* [1982], *Our Dead Behind Us* [1986]), Colson Whitehead`(*The Intuitionist* [1999], *John Henry Days* [2001]), and John Edgar Wideman (*Brothers and Keepers* [1984] and the Homewood trilogy, consisting of *Hiding Place* [1981], *Sent for You Yesterday* [1983], and *Damballah* [1988]).

The 1960s produced a number of speculative works that presented alternative realities. Sam Greeley's *The Spook Who Sat by the Door* (1969), for example, imagines a black CIA agent secretly planning an urban revolution. *The Man Who Cried I Am* (1967) by John A. Williams speculates on the potential for government-sponsored black genocide. In the hands of a writer like Ishmael Reed, in *Flight to Canada* (1976), imaginative speculation leads to a conflation of modern society with the antebellum South. Samuel Delany (*Captives of the Flame* [1963], *Empire Star* [1966], *The Mad Man* [1994]), Octavia Butler (*Kindred* [1979], *Parable of the Sower* [1993], *Parable of the Talents* [1998]), and Steven Barnes (*Street Lethal* [1983], *Gorgon Child* [1989], *Fire Dance* [1993]) are perhaps the best-known African American writers currently working in the area of speculative fiction. Each has used his or her fiction as a place to examine the interworkings of myth and legend, psychology, and social commentary in multiracial, multisexual societies (Govan: 683–7; Saunders: 50–3).

Black detective and crime fiction clearly traces its post-World War II influences to Chester Himes. But in the hands of Walter Mosley (*Black Betty* [1994] and the Easy Rawlins mysteries, including *Devil in a Blue Dress* [1990], *White Butterfly* [1992], *Gone Fishin'* [1997]) and Barbara Neely (*Blanche on the Lam* [1992], *Blanche Among the Talented Tenth* [1994]) the genre has experienced a substantial renaissance. Detectives range from the classic hardboiled like Walter Mosley's Easy Rawlins, who is a World War II veteran who has migrated to

Los Angeles following the war and who becomes a detective because his race allows him access to areas of urban society not available to white detectives, to Barbara's Neely's Blanche White, who is a black woman who solves crimes while working as a servant to a white family. Though different in style and attitude, the detective figures reflect an insightful awareness of black vernacular culture (Bailey: 3–24; Soitos, *Blues Detective*: 3–92, "Crime and Mystery Writing": 182–4).

The black theater, led by the success of Lorraine Hansberry's *A Raisin in the Sun* (1959) and followed by Amiri Baraka's Obie Award winning play *Dutchman* (1964), which tells a metaphoric story of racial relations in a play about the murder of a black man aboard a subway train by a blonde woman, has provided a consistent space for African American playwrights to examine family, identity, collective memory, and the effects of politics on the lives of individuals. Charles Gordone, in 1970, was the first black recipient of the Pulitzer Prize for drama, for his play *No Place to Be Somebody* (1970), which is about a black hustler metaphorically searching for his own identity in his quest for place. Charles Fuller won the Pulitzer Prize, the New York Drama Critics Circle Award, and the Outer Critics Circle Award for *A Soldier's Play* (1981), about murder and racial unrest in a military camp. August Wilson has emerged as the best-known black dramatist. He has been the recipient of the Drama Critics Circle Award for *Ma Rainey's Black Bottom* (1982), a Pulitzer Prize for *Fences* (1987), and a Tony Award, a New York Drama Critics Circle Award, an Outer Critics' Circle Award, a Drama Desk Award, and a second Pulitzer Prize for *The Piano Lesson* (1998). His work explores generational conflicts, the pervasive nature of the past, and the pressures experienced by black families (Peterson, Jr, *Early Black American Playwrights*: 3–24, "Drama": 228–34).

The expansion of black writing has had other consequences as well. The ability of black writers to find their own voices has expanded the audiences and literary possibilities for white American women writers, as well as writers associated with Native American, Indian, Asian, Chicano, Latino, gay, lesbian, and transgendered communities. Contemporaneous with the unparalleled expansion of black literary expression has been that of influential critical analysis that effectively draws on psychoanalytic, poststructuralist, Marxist, historicist, and feminist ideas, in ways that have deepened the understanding of the literature in the context of individual texts' reference to and revision of one another. In a larger context, these approaches examine the ways these texts collectively speak to the larger world-view of Western literature.

In short, contemporary African American literature has, perhaps consciously, become increasingly trans-disciplinary. From this perspective, culture and the literature it produces are the articulation of a constantly shifting social dynamic defined by changing relationships of class, gender, race, and political and economic influence. Thus, literary critics like Molefi Kete Asante (*The Afrocentric Idea* [1987], *The Painful Demise of Eurocentrism* [1999]), Houston A. Baker, Jr (*Singers at Daybreak* [1974], *Blues, Ideology, and Afro-American Literature* [1984], *Turning South Again* [2001]), Barbara Christian (*Black Feminist Criticism* [1985]), Henry Louis Gates, Jr (*Black Literature and Literary Theory* [1984], *Signifying Monkey* [1988]), Donald B. Gibson (*Politics of Literary Expression* [1981]), Arnold Rampersad (*Slavery and the Literary Imagination* [1989], *The Life of Langston Hughes* [1986]), Valerie Smith (*Self-Discovery and Authority in Afro-American Narrative* [1987], *Not Just Race, Not Just Gender* [1998]), Robert B. Stepto (*Afro-American Literature* [1979], *From Behind the Veil* [1991], and Claudia Tate (*Domestic Allegories of Political Desire* [1992], *Psychoanalysis and Black Novels* [1998]) all interrogated the ways African American literature questioned itself; and while they did so, cultural critics examined the ways African American literature considered the culture from which it arose (Ervin, *African American Literary Criticism*: passim).

Cultural theorists and critics expanded the work of a generation of literary commentators, many of whom benefited from the agitations of Black Nationalists and their sympathizers, who demanded the creation of black studies programs at colleges and universities nationwide and helped move black writing more completely into the canon of American literature. A number of influential thinkers like Cornell West (*Breaking Bread* [1991], *Race Matters* [1993]), Derrick Bell (*And We Are Not Saved* [1987], *Faces at the Bottom of the Well* [1992], *When Race Becomes Real* [2002]), bell hooks (*Outlaw Culture* [1994], *Teaching to Transgress* [1994], *Where We Stand* [2000]), Patricia Williams (*Alchemy of Race and Rights* [1991], *Seeing a Color-Blind Future* [1998]), Shelby Steele (*Content of Our Character* [1990], *Dream Deferred* [1998]), and Stephen Carter (*Reflections of an Affirmative Action Baby* [1991], *Emperor of Ocean Park* [2002]) have used the increasingly inclusive relationship between African American literature and the contemporary canon as an opportunity to move the discussion of race beyond its literary confines. They have been able successfully to use race as the foundation of a larger discussion of American culture.

References and further reading

Accomando, Christina. "William Attaway." In *The Oxford Companion to African American Literature*. Eds William L. Andrews, Frances Smith Foster, and Trudier Harris. New York: Oxford University Press, 1997. 30–1.

Alexander, Sandra Carlton. "Ann Petry." In *Dictionary of Literary Biography. Vol. 76: Afro-American Writers, 1940–1955*. Eds Trudier Harris and Thadious M. Davis. Detroit: Gale Research, 1988. 140–7.

Andrews, Larry R. "Black Sisterhood in Gloria Naylor's Novels." *CLA Journal* 33 (September 1989): 1–25.

Bailey, Frankie F. *Out of the Woodpile: Black Characters in Crime and Detective Fiction*. Westport, CT: Greenwood Press, 1991.

Baldwin, James. "Autobiographical Notes." In *James Baldwin: Collected Essays*. Ed. Toni Morrison. New York: Library of America, (1955) 1998. 5–9.

Baldwin, James. "Everybody's Protest Novel." In *James Baldwin: Collected Essays*. Ed. Toni Morrison. New York: Library of America, (1955) 1998. 11–18.

Baldwin, James. "Many Thousands Gone." In *James Baldwin: Collected Essays*. Ed. Toni Morrison. New York: Library of America, (1955) 1998. 19–34.

Baldwin, James. "Alas, Poor Richard." In *James Baldwin: Collected Essays*. Ed. Toni Morrison. New York: Library of America, (1961) 1998. 247–68.

Baldwin, James. "Nobody Knows My Name: A Letter from the South." In *James Baldwin: Collected Essays*. Ed. Toni Morrison. New York: Library of America, (1961) 1998. 197–208.

Baraka, Amiri. "The Congress of Afrikan People: A Position Paper." *Black Scholar: Journal of Black Studies and Research* 6.5 (1975): 2–15.

Beaulieu, Elizabeth Ann. "Melvin Tolson." In *The Oxford Companion to African American Literature*. Eds William L. Andrews, Frances Smith Foster, and Trudier Harris. New York: Oxford University Press, 1997. 731–3.

Bell, Bernard W. *The Afro-American Novel and its Tradition*. Amherst: University of Massachusetts Press, 1987.

Bishop, Jack. *Ralph Ellison*. New York: Chelsea House, 1988.

Bone, Robert A. *The Negro in America*. Revised edn. New Haven, CT: Yale University Press, 1965.

Busby, Mark. *Ralph Ellison*. Boston: Twayne, 1965.

Byrd, Rudolph P. "Spirituality in the Novels of Alice Walker: Models, Healing, and Transformation, or When the Spirit Moves So Do We." In *Wild Women in the Whirlwind: Afra-American Culture and the Contemporary Literary Renaissance*. Eds Joanne Braxton and Andrée Nicola McLaughlin. New Brunswick, NJ: Rutgers University Press, 1990. 363–78.

Carmean, Karen. *Toni Morrison's World of Fiction*. Troy, NY: Whitson, 1993.

Christian, Barbara. "Alice Walker." In *Dictionary of Literary Biography. Vol. 33: Afro-American Writers after 1955*. Eds Thadious M. Davis and Trudier Harris. Detroit: Gale Research, 1984. 258–71.

Christian, Barbara. "Alice Walker: The Black Woman Artist as Wayward." In *Black Women Writers (1950–1980): A Critical Evaluation.* Ed. Mari Evans. Garden City, NY: Anchor Press/Doubleday, 1984. 457–77.

Christian, Barbara. "Gloria Naylor's Geography: Community, Class, and Patriarchy in *The Women of Brewster Place* and *Linden Hills.*" In *Reading Black, Reading Feminist: A Critical Anthology.* Ed. Henry Louis Gates, Jr. New York: Meridian, 1990. 348–73.

Clark, Keith. *Black Manhood in James Baldwin, Ernest J. Gaines, and August Wilson.* Urbana, IL: University of Illinois Press, 2002.

Collins, G. Michelle. "There Where We Are Not: The Magical Real in *Beloved* and *Mama Day.*" *Southern Review* 24 (1988): 680–5.

Crossman, Richard, ed. *The God That Failed.* Chicago: Regnery Gateway, (1949) 1983.

Curtin, Maureen F. "Materializing Invisibility as X-Ray Technology: Skin Matters in Ralph Ellison's *Invisible Man.*" *Literature, Interpretation, Theory* 9.4 (April 1999): 281–311.

Daniel, Walter C. "*Challenge Magazine*: An Experiment that Failed." *CLA Journal* 19 (June 1976): 494–503.

Drake, St Clair. *Black Metropolis: A Study of Negro Life in a Northern City.* New York: Harper and Row, 1962.

Eichelberger, Julia. *Prophets of Recognition: Ideology and the Individual in Novels by Ralph Ellison, Toni Morrison, Saul Bellow, and Eudora Welty.* Baton Rouge: Louisiana State University Press, 1999.

Ellison, Ralph. "Transition." *Negro Quarterly* 1 (Spring 1942): 87–92.

Ellison, Ralph. "Richard Wright's Blues." In *The Collected Essays of Ralph Ellison.* Ed. John F. Callahan. New York: Modern Library, (1945) 1995. 128–44.

Ellison, Ralph. *Invisible Man.* New York: Vintage International, (1952) 1995.

Ellison, Ralph. "Twentieth-Century Fiction and the Black Mask of Humanity." In *The Collected Essays of Ralph Ellison.* Ed. John F. Callahan. New York: Modern Library, (1953) 1995. 81–99.

Ellison, Ralph. "'Introduction' to *Shadow and Act.*" In *The Collected Essays of Ralph Ellison.* Ed. John F. Callahan. New York: Modern Library, (1964) 1995. 49–60.

Ellison, Ralph. "The Novel as a Function of American Democracy." In *The Collected Essays of Ralph Ellison.* Ed. John F. Callahan. New York: Modern Library, (1967) 1995. 755–65.

Ellison, Ralph. "Perspective of Literature." In *The Collected Essays of Ralph Ellison.* Ed. John F. Callahan. New York: Modern Library, (1976) 1995. 766–81.

Ervin, Hazel Arnett. "Ann Petry." In *The Oxford Companion to African American Literature.* Eds William L. Andrews, Frances Smith Foster, and Trudier Harris. New York: Oxford University Press, 1997. 570–2.

Ervin, Hazel Arnett, ed. *African American Literary Criticism, 1773–2000.* New York: Twayne, 1999.

Fabre, Michel. *The Unfinished Quest of Richard Wright.* Urbana, IL: University of Illinois Press, (1973) 1993.

Farnsworth, Robert M. *Melvin B. Tolson, 1898–1966: Plain Talk and Poetic Prophecy.* Columbia: University of Missouri Press, 1984.

Farnsworth, Robert M. "Melvin B. Tolson." In *Dictionary of Literary Biography. Vol. 76: Afro-American Writers, 1940–1955.* Eds Trudier Harris and Thadious M. Davis. Detroit: Gale Research, 1988. 164–72.

Fetrow, Fred M. *Robert Hayden.* Boston: Twayne, 1984.

Flasch, Neva Joy. *Melvin B. Tolson.* New York: Twayne, 1972.

Fox, Robert Elliot. *Conscientious Sorcerers: The Black Postmodernist Fiction of LeRoi Jones/Amiri Baraka, Ishmael Reed, and Samuel R. Delany.* Westport, CT: Greenwood Press, 1987.

Fuller, Hoyt W. "Traveler on the Long, Rough, Lonely Old Road: An Interview with Chester Himes." *Black World* 21 (March 1972): 4–22, 87–8.

Garren, Samuel B. "William Attaway." In *Dictionary of Literary Biography. Vol. 76: Afro-American Writers, 1940–1955.* Eds Trudier Harris and Thadious M. Davis. Detroit: Gale Research, 1988. 3–7.

Gates, Jr, Henry Louis. *The Signifying Monkey: A Theory of Afro-American Literary Criticism.* New York: Oxford University Press, 1988.

Gayle, Jr, Addison. *The Black Aesthetic.* Garden City, NY: Anchor Books, 1971.

Gayle, Jr, Addison. *Richard Wright: Ordeal of a Native Son.* Garden City, NY: Anchor Press and Doubleday, 1980.

Giovanni, Nikki, and Margaret A. Walker. *A Poetic Equation: Conversations between Nikki Giovanni and Margaret Walker.* Washington, DC: Howard University Press, (1974) 1983.

Glasrud, Bruce A., and Laurie Champion. "Chester B. Himes." In *Contemporary African American Novelists.* Ed. Emmanuel S. Nelson. Westport, CT: Greenwood Press, 1999. 203–10.

Govan, Sandra Y. "Speculative Fiction." In *The Oxford Companion to African American Literature.* Eds William L. Andrews, Frances Smith Foster, and Trudier Harris. New York: Oxford University Press, 1997. 683–7.

Griffin, Farah Jasmine. "Dorothy West." In *The Oxford Companion to African American Literature.* Eds William L. Andrews, Frances Smith Foster, and Trudier Harris. New York: Oxford University Press, 1997. 766–7.

Hansell, William H. "The Poet-Militant and Foreshadowings of a Black Mystique: Poems in the Second Period of Gwendolyn Brooks." In *A Life Distilled: Gwendolyn Brooks, Her Poetry and Fiction.* Eds Maria K. Mootry and Gary Smith. Urbana, IL: University of Illinois Press, 1987. 71–80.

Harding, Wendy, and Jacky Martin. *A World of Difference: An Inter-Cultural Study of Toni Morrison's Novels.* Westport, CT: Greenwood Press, 1994.

Harper, Michael S. "Remembering Robert Hayden." *Michigan Quarterly Review* 21 (Winter 1982): 182–6.

Harris, Trudier "James Baldwin." In *The Oxford Companion to African American Literature.* Eds William L. Andrews, Frances Smith Foster, and Trudier Harris. New York: Oxford University Press, 1997. 44–6.

Heinze, Denise. *The Dilemma of "Double-Consciousness": Toni Morrison's Novels.* Athens, GA: University of Georgia Press, 1993.

Jackson, Lawrence Patrick. *Ralph Ellison: Emergence of Genius.* New York: Wiley, 2002.

Jimoh, A. Yemisi. "Dorothy West." In *Contemporary African American Novelists: A Bio-Bibliographical Critical Sourcebook.* Ed. Emmanuel S. Nelson. Westport, CT: Greenwood Press, 1999. 475–81.

Johnson, E. Patrick. "Feeling the Spirit in the Dark: Expanding Notions of the Sacred in the African-American Gay Community." *Callaloo* 21.2 (Spring 1998): 399–416.

Jones, Norma R. "Robert Hayden." In *Dictionary of Literary Biography. Vol. 76: Afro-American Writers, 1940–1955.* Eds Trudier Harris and Thadious M. Davis. Detroit: Gale Research, 1988. 75–88.

Joyce, Joyce Ann. *Richard Wright's Art of Tragedy.* Iowa City: University of Iowa Press, 1986.

Kaplan, Cora. "'A Cavern Opened in My Mind': The Poetics of Homosexuality and the Politics of Masculinity in James Baldwin." In *Representing Black Men.* Eds Marcellus Blount and George P. Cunningham. New York: Routledge, 1996. 27–54.

Kent, George E. *Blackness and the Adventure of Western Culture.* Chicago: Third World Press, 1972.

Kent, George E. "Aesthetic Values in the Poetry of Gwendolyn Brooks." In *A Life Distilled: Gwendolyn Brooks, Her Poetry and Fiction.* Eds Maria K. Mootry and Gary Smith. Urbana, IL: University of Illinois Press, 1987. 30–46.

Kent, George E. "Gwendolyn Brooks." In *Dictionary of Literary Biography. Vol. 76: Afro-American Writers, 1940–1955.* Eds Trudier Harris and Thadious M. Davis. Detroit: Gale Research, 1988. 11–24.

Kent, George E. *A Life of Gwendolyn Brooks.* Lexington, KY: University Press of Kentucky, 1990.

King, Debra Walker. "Alice Walker." In *The Oxford Companion to African American Literature.* Eds William L. Andrews, Frances Smith Foster, and Trudier Harris. New York: Oxford University Press, 1997. 413–15.

Kubitschek, Missy Dehn. *Toni Morrison: A Critical Companion.* Westport, CT: Greenwood Press, 1998.

Leeming, David. *James Baldwin: A Biography.* New York: Knopf, 1994.

Locke, Alain. *The New Negro.* New York: Atheneum, (1925) 1992.

Locke, Alain. "Spiritual Truancy." In *New Challenge.* Westport, CT: Negro Universities Press, (1937) 1970. 81–5.

McSweeney, Kerry. *Invisible Man: Race and Identity.* Boston: Twayne, 1988.

Madhubuti, Haki R. "The Latest Purge: The Attack on Black Nationalism and Pan-Afrikanism by the New Left, the Sons and Daughters of the Old Left." *Black Scholar: Journal of Black Studies and Research* 6.1 (1975): 47–56.

Margolies, Edward. *Native Sons: A Critical Study of Twentieth-Century Negro American Authors.* Philadelphia: Lippincott, 1968.

Margolies, Edward. *Which Way Did He Go?: The Private Eye in Dashiell Hammett, Raymond Chandler, Chester Himes, and Ross Macdonald*. New York: Holmes and Meier, 1982.

Margolies, Edward, and Michel Fabre. *The Several Lives of Chester Himes*. Jackson: University Press of Mississippi, 1997.

Matus, Jill L. *Toni Morrison*. Manchester: Manchester University Press, 1998.

Melhem, D. H. *Gwendolyn Brooks: Poetry and the Heroic Voice*. Lexington, KY: University Press of Kentucky, 1987.

Metting, Fred. "The Possibilities of Flight: The Celebration of Our Wings in *Song of Solomon, Praisesong for the Widow*, and *Mama Day*." *Southern Folklore* 55.2 (1998): 145–68.

Milliken, Stephen F. *Chester Himes: A Critical Appraisal*. Columbia: University of Missouri Press, 1976.

Mobley, Marilyn Sanders. "Toni Morrison." In *The Oxford Companion to African American Literature*. Eds William L. Andrews, Frances Smith Foster, and Trudier Harris. New York: Oxford University Press, 1997. 295–7.

Moses, Wilson Jeremiah. *The Wings of Ethiopia: Studies in African-American Life and Letters*. Ames: Iowa State University Press, 1990.

Nadel, Alan. *Invisible Criticism: Ralph Ellison and the American Canon*. Iowa City: University of Iowa Press, 1988.

Nielsen, Aldon L. "Melvin B. Tolson and the Deterritorialization of Modernism." *African American Review* 26 (Summer 1992): 241–55.

O'Meally, Robert G. *The Craft of Ralph Ellison*. Cambridge, MA: Harvard University Press, 1980.

Peach, Linden. *Toni Morrison*. New York: St Martin's Press, 2000.

Peterson, Jr, Bernard L. *Early Black American Playwrights and Dramatic Writers: A Biographical Directory and Catalog of Plays, Films, and Broadcasting Scripts*. Westport, CT: Greenwood Press, 1990.

Peterson, Jr, Bernard L. "Drama." In *The Oxford Companion to African American Literature*. Eds William L. Andrews, Frances Smith Foster, and Trudier Harris. New York: Oxford University Press, 1997. 228–34.

Pettis, Joyce. "Margaret Walker." In *Dictionary of Literary Biography. Vol. 76: Afro-American Writers, 1940–1955*. Eds Trudier Harris and Thadious M. Davis. Detroit: Gale Research, 1988. 173–81.

Reckley, Ralph. "Chester Himes." In *Dictionary of Literary Biography. Vol. 76: Afro-American Writers, 1940–1955*. Eds Trudier Harris and Thadious M. Davis. Detroit: Gale Research, 1988. 89–103.

Reckley, Ralph. "Ralph Ellison." In *The Oxford Companion to African American Literature*. Eds William L. Andrews, Frances Smith Foster, and Trudier Harris. New York: Oxford University Press, 1997. 252–4.

Redmond, Eugene. *Drumvoices: The Mission of Afro-American Poetry: A Critical History*. Garden City, NY: Anchor Press, 1988.

Ross, Marlon B. "White Fantasies of Desire: Baldwin and the Racial Identities of Sexuality." In *James Baldwin Now*. Ed. Dwight A. McBride. New York: New York University Press, 1999. 13–55.

Rowley, Hazel. *Richard Wright: The Life and Times*. New York: Henry Holt, 2001.

Samuels, Wilfred D., and Clenora Hudson-Weems. *Toni Morrison*. Boston: Twayne, 1990.

Sanders, Mark A. "Chester Himes." In *The Oxford Companion to African American Literature*. Eds William L. Andrews, Frances Smith Foster, and Trudier Harris. New York: Oxford University Press, 1997. 356–7.

Sanders, Mark A. "Robert Hayden." In *The Oxford Companion to African American Literature*. Eds William L. Andrews, Frances Smith Foster, and Trudier Harris. New York: Oxford University Press, 1997. 347–8.

Saunders, Charles R. "Blacks in Wonderland." *American Visions* 2.3 (June 1987): 50–3.

Smith, Gary. "Paradise Regained: The Children of Gwendolyn Brooks's *Bronzeville*." In *A Life Distilled: Gwendolyn Brooks, Her Poetry and Fiction*. Eds Maria K. Mootry and Gary Smith. Urbana, IL: University of Illinois Press, 1987. 128–39.

Smith, Valerie. "Literary History: Late Twentieth Century." In *The Oxford Companion to African American Literature*. Eds William L. Andrews, Frances Smith Foster, and Trudier Harris. New York: Oxford University Press, 1997. 456–9.

Soitos, Stephen F. *The Blues Detective: A Study of African American Detective Fiction*. Amherst: University of Massachusetts Press, 1996.

Soitos, Stephen F. "Crime and Mystery Writing." In *The Oxford Companion to African American Literature*. Eds William L. Andrews, Frances Smith Foster, and Trudier Harris. New York: Oxford University Press, 1997. 182–4.

Sylvander, Carolyn Wedin. *James Baldwin*. New York: Frederick Ungar, 1980.

Tate, Claudia. "Anger So Flat: Gwendolyn Brooks's *Annie Allen*." In *A Life Distilled: Gwendolyn Brooks, Her Poetry and Fiction*. Eds Maria K. Mootry and Gary Smith. Urbana, IL: University of Illinois Press, 1987. 140–50.

Tolson, Jr, Melvin B. "The Poetry of Melvin B. Tolson." *World Literature Today* 64 3 (Summer 1990): 395–400.

Walker, Margaret. *Richard Wright, Daemonic Genius: A Portrait of the Man, a Critical Look at his Work*. New York: Warner Books, 1988.

Ward, Jr, Jerry W. "Margaret Walker." In *The Oxford Companion to African American Literature*. Eds William L. Andrews, Frances Smith Foster, and Trudier Harris. New York: Oxford University Press, 1997. 752–3.

Washington, Mary Helen, ed. *Black-Eyed Susans, Midnight Birds: Stories by and about Black Women*. New York: Doubleday, 1990.

Williams, John A. "My Man Himes: An Interview with Chester Himes." In *Amistad. Vol. 1*. Eds John A. Williams and Charles F. Harris. New York: Random House, 1970. 25–93.

Williams, Kenny Jackson. "Gwendolyn Brooks." In *The Oxford Companion to African American Literature*. Eds William L. Andrews, Frances Smith Foster, and Trudier Harris. New York: Oxford University Press, 1997. 98–9.

Williams, Pontheolla T. *Robert Hayden: A Critical Analysis of His Poetry*. Urbana, IL: University of Illinois Press, 1987.

Wright, Richard. "Blueprint for Negro Writing." In *New Challenge*. Westport, CT: Negro Universities Press, (1937) 1970. 53–65.

Wright, Richard. *Native Son and "How 'Bigger' Was Born."* New York: HarperCollins, (1940) 1993.

Yohe, Kristine A. "Gloria Naylor." In *The Oxford Companion to African American Literature*. Eds William L. Andrews, Frances Smith Foster, and Trudier Harris. New York: Oxford University Press, 1997. 306–8.

Chapter 12

Italian American Literature and Culture

Fred L. Gardaphé

While the great body of work that makes up Italian American literary studies began in earnest after World War II, it would not be until the reformation of the American literary canon, in the 1970s and 1990s, that Italian American literature was posited as a field of inquiry. A pioneer in the field, Rose Basile Green, presented an extensive survey of the novels written by American writers of Italian descent in *The Italian-American Novel* (1974). That same year Richard Gambino's *Blood of My Blood: The Dilemma of Italian Americans* explored the psychological impact of the ethnic identity of America's Italians. Gambino's notion of creative ethnicity as an alternative to ethnic chauvinism laid the groundwork for criticism of myths created by and about Italian American culture. Along with anthologies such as Helen Barolini's *The Dream Book* (1985), Ferdinando Alfonsi's *Dictionary of Italian-American Poets* (1989) and Anthony J. Tamburri et al's. *From the Margin* (1991), Gambino's and Green's studies have enabled a distinct cultural tradition to be identified and maintained.

When Frank Lentricchia located the origins of Italian American fiction in Luigi Ventura's 1886 collection of short stories *Misfits and Remnants*, he made us realize that it took nearly 100 years for the identification and appreciation of a literary tradition within Italian American culture. One explanation for this silence lies in the fact that, until recently, Italian American culture has not depended on a literary tradition for a sense of cultural survival. Steeped in oral tradition, Italian American culture is a rich amalgam of both cultures, and never set out to be a culturally visible identity. Most immigrants from Italy came to America with the idea of earning a livelihood and then returning to Italy. Simply, their goal was to do whatever was necessary to improve their lives in this new land. While the experience of this transition would become the basis for the creation of art, it was never intended by these artists that their work be received as Italian American. Rather, influenced by the literature encountered in schools, in libraries, and in bookstores, such writers saw themselves as American writers.

The Italians and the 'Mericans: Becoming American

Early twentieth-century immigrants from Italy to the United States did not immediately refer to themselves as Americans. Most of the early immigrants were sojourners or "birds of passage," primarily men who crossed the ocean to find work, make money, and return home. This experience is well presented in books such as Michael La Sorte's *La Merica: Images of Italian Greenhorn Experience* (1985). In addition to language barriers, these immigrants often faced difficult living conditions and encountered racism. In *Wop! A Documentary History of Anti-Italian Discrimination* (1999), Salvatore LaGumina gathers evidence of this racism from late nineteenth- and twentieth-century American journalism appearing in the *New York Times* and other major publications.

In response to this mistreatment, many of the Italians referred to Americans as "Merdicani," short for "Merde di cane" (dog shit). The word was also used as a derogatory reference by Italians to those who assimilated too quickly and readily into American culture. Most novels published prior to World War II depicted the vexed immigrant experience of adjustment in America: Louis Forgione's *The River Between* (1924), Garibaldi La Polla's *The Grand Gennaro* (1935), Valenti Angelo's *Golden Gate* (1938), Guido D'Agostino's *Olives on the Apple Tree* (1940), Mari Tomasi's *Deep Grow the Roots* (1940), and Jo Pagano's *Golden Wedding* (1943).

In spite of a substantial presence in literature, other than the romantic exotic types epitomized by Rudolph Valentino and the criminals encountered in the gangster films, Italian Americans had little visibility in American popular culture. Norman Rockwell's paintings and illustrations, considered in the 1930s and 1940s to be typically American, never included images of Italians. Even the works of Italian American artists themselves were conspicuously void of direct references to the immigrant experience. Filmmaker Frank Capra, who emigrated from Sicily with his family in 1903, managed to include the Martini family in *It's a Wonderful Life* (1946) as a marginal reference to the poor helped by George Bailey. In the literary arts, becoming an American is the focus of many of the early artists such as John Fante, whose "The Odyssey of a Wop," appeared in H. L. Mencken's *American Mercury*, a popular magazine of the 1930s and 1940s. Fante, a self-proclaimed protégé of Mencken, wrote novels and became a Hollywood screenwriter. His *Full of Life* (1957), a mainstream Hollywood comedy starring Richard Conte and Judy Holiday, was based on his novel of the same title which helped bring this experience into the American mainstream.

Immigrant struggles, beyond trying to make a living and feed self and family, as recounted in such novels as Pietro di Donato's *Christ in Concrete* (1939), John Fante's *Wait Until Spring, Bandini* (1938), Mari Tomasi's *Like Lesser Gods* (1949), and Julia Savarese's *The Weak and the Strong* (1952) and in autobiographies such as Jerre Mangione's *Mount Allegro* (1943), included coping with the prejudice and discrimination which reached extremes in the 1891 mob lynching of innocent Italians who were accused and acquitted of the murder of the New Orleans police chief, and the trial and 1927 execution of Nicola Sacco and Bartolomeo Vanzetti. The literature produced during this period provides great insights into the shaping of American identities and into the obstacles that these immigrants faced in pursuing their versions of the American dream.

The rise of fascism in Italy during the 1920s–40s would have a tremendous effect on the identity and behavior of Americans of Italian descent. This effect would become a prime subject in their literature. Jerre Mangione captured this experience in his memoirs, *Mount Allegro* (1943) and *An Ethnic at Large* (1978):

In my years of becoming an American I had come to understand the evil of Fascism and hate it with all my soul. One or two of my relatives argued with me on the subject because they had a great love for their native land and, like some men in love, they could see nothing wrong. Fascism was only a word to them; Mussolini a patriotic Italian putting his country on its feet. Why did I insist on finding fault with Fascism, they asked, when all the American newspapers were admitting Mussolini was a great man who made the trains run on time? (*Mount Allegro*: 239–40)

Trapped between two countries (their parents' homeland and their own), Italian American writers tended to stay aloof from the international political situation of their time. It wouldn't be until after the fall of Mussolini that Italian Americans would, in any significant way, address fascism in their fiction and poetry. The earliest anti-fascist writings dared to contradict the pro-fascist posture assumed by the American government and such leading figures of the American literary scene as Wallace Stevens, Ezra Pound, and T. S. Eliot, who as proponents of Modernism were also, interestingly enough, if not outright pro-fascist, at least sympathetic to Mussolini's fascism (Diggins: 245). Those Italian Americans who opposed Mussolini from the beginning did so at the risk of being attacked or labeled as communists by the larger American public as well as their own pro-Mussolini countrymen.

One of the earliest Italian Americans to voice his opinion of Italian fascism in his poetry was Arturo Giovannitti, who, with Joseph Ettor, organized the famous 1912 Lawrence Mill Strike. In his poem "To Mussolini" he accuses the Father of Italian Fascism of winning "fame with lies." And he tells *il Duce* that:

> No man is great who does not find
> A poet who will hail him as he is
> With an almighty song that will unbind
> Through his exploits eternal silences.
> Duce, where is your bard? In all mankind
> The only poem you inspired is this.
>
> (72)

In "Italia Speaks," Giovannitti depicts America as a child of Italy who can rescue its mother from "The twin ogres in black and brown [who] have polluted my gardens" (76). Giovannitti composed poems that echo Walt Whitman's patriotic odes during the Civil War. In his "Battle Hymn of the New Italy" we find a synthesis of Giosue Carducci and Whitman, as Giovannitti calls for the Italian people to rise up against Mussolini and Hitler.

Along with Giovannitti, those most prominent anti-fascists whose writing appeared most frequently in American publications were the "fuorusciti," those Italian intellectuals who left Italy and found refuge, more often than not, in American universities: Gaetano Salvemini at Harvard, Max Ascoli at the New School for Social Research, Giuseppe Borgese at the University of Chicago, and Lionello Venturi at Johns Hopkins (Diggins: 140). These "fuorusciti" were responsible for a number of influential anti-fascist publications. Their presence made "the universities one of the few anti-Fascist ramparts in America" (Diggins: 261).

Similar anti-fascist sentiments are found in the fiction of Jerre Mangione. Mangione's interactions with activist Carlo Tresca became the material upon which he would build his second novel, *Night Search* (1965). Based on Tresca's assassination, *Night Search* dramatizes the experience of Michael Mallory, the illegitimate son of an anti-fascist labor organizer and newspaper publisher by the name of Paolo Polizzi, a character based on Carlo Tresca. Through an investigation of his father's murder, Mallory learns to take action, and in doing so, comes to an understanding of contemporary politics.

Mallory very much resembles Stiano Argento, the main protagonist in Mangione's earlier and more strongly anti-fascist novel, *The Ship and the Flame* (1948). Based on his European experiences of the late 1930s, this novel presents a more sophisticated overview of the effects of fascism by creating an allegory for the sorry state of political affairs in Europe prior to America's entry into World War II. Argento is one of a number of characters fleeing fascist and Nazi powers who were smuggled aboard a Portuguese ship carrying other refugees. The ship, run by a fascist-sympathizing captain, is denied entry into Mexico and heads for Nazi-controlled Casablanca. A liberal Catholic, Argento realizes that the prayers his wife urges him to make won't be enough; he risks his life to take control of the situation. His decision to act comes from the guilt he feels about having let the flame ignite the fascist power that virtually destroyed his Sicilian homeland. Mangione, aware of the dilemma of the liberal and the fate of the revolutionary in the pre-World War II period, suggests that while the struggle against fascism can be won through heroic action, there still remains intolerance and persecution of those who think and act differently.

While immigration to the US from Italy slowed between the 1920s and 1940s due to political maneuvers such as the US quota restrictions of 1924, a number of Italian intellectuals were allowed to immigrate to the United States in flight from fascism. Most prominent among those were scientists such as Enrico Fermi, who has come to be called the father of the atom bomb, and writers Arturo Vivante, P. M. Pasinetti, and Nicolo Tucci. Vivante, a physician, contributed frequently to such major publications as the *New Yorker*. His fiction includes a collection of short stories *The French Girls of Killini* (1967), and three novels: *A Goodly Babe* (1966), *Doctor Giovanni* (1969), and *Run to the Waterfall* (1965). Pasinetti came to study in the United States in 1935 from Venice and first published fiction in the *Southern Review*. He earned a

PhD at Yale in 1949 and went on to teach at UCLA. Pasinetti published three novels, *Venetian Red* (1960), *The Smile on the Face of the Lion* (1965), and *From the Academy Bridge* (1970); his work earned him an award from the National Institute of Arts and Letters in 1965. Tucci, who first came as a student, published two autobiographical novels using European settings to depict a liberation from the history that the emigrant experiences created: *Before My Time* (1962) and *Unfinished Funeral* (1964). For these writers, their sense of the literary was significantly shaped by the prominence in 1930s Italy of *Americanisti* such as Elio Vittorini and Cesare Pavese, both translators and influential editors who helped introduce American literature to Italian culture.

Prior to the US entry into World War II Congress passed the Alien Registration Act (the Smith Act) that required all noncitizens over 14 to be fingerprinted and registered at their local post office. At the outset of the war the FBI identified many Italian Americans as dangerous enemy aliens. Due to political pressure, some of the restrictions were removed on Columbus Day, 1942. In all, 10,000 Italian Americans were restricted to certain areas or held in 46 detention camps in Texas, California, Washington, Montana, North Dakota, Oklahoma, New York, and New Jersey. The father of baseball great Joe DiMaggio had his fishing boats and radios confiscated by the government. While such violations were not as severe or pervasive as those enacted against Japanese Americans, they did significantly disrupt the lives of those imprisoned.

A traveling exhibit entitled "Una Storia Segreta" ("A Secret Story") has revealed that many Italian Americans suffered civil rights violations that seriously affected their lives and livelihoods. This collection of oral histories, photographs, letters, and papers, documenting the evacuation and internment of Italian "enemy aliens," was compiled at the lead of Lawrence DiStasi and has been touring the country as a public display since 1994. This revision of history and the giving of voice to those who had suffered in silence place significant pressure for a political response. In 1999, the US House of Representatives passed Resolution 2442 that acknowledged government violations of civil liberties, and in 2000 with the signature of President Bill Clinton, the Wartime Violation of Italian American Civil Liberties Act became Public Law 106–451 that acknowledged the government's misdeeds.

At the outset of the war, Italian immigrants were the largest foreign-born group in the US. One way of proving unquestionable loyalty to the new country was performing military service during World War II. Estimates of the number of Italian Americans serving in the armed forces run from upwards of a half million to a million, numbers in excess of their percentage of the population at the time. Poet Felix Stefanile captures the motivation of the young Italian American in "The Dance at St Gabriel's": "In those hag-ridden and race conscious times / we wanted to be known as anti-fascists, / and thus get over our Italian names." The films of Frank Capra during this period celebrated American democratic ideals. *Mrs Deeds Goes to Town* (1936) and *Meet John Doe* (1941) established a reputation for Capra that would equal Norman Rockwell's for making art that typified American life of the times. From 1935 to 1941 Capra served as president of the Academy of Motion Picture Arts and Sciences. During the war he produced a series of documentary films with the Signal Service Photographic Detachment entitled "Why We Fight" (1942–5). Because of Italy's alliance with the Axis powers, World War II was not a time to assert one's Italian ancestry. If it did one thing, the war turned Italians into Americans. As Ben Morreale recounts in his autobiographical novel, *Sicily: The Hollowed Land* (2000): "The army, the war, was the final assimilation . . . for the second generation Sicilian. It was the good war to which they all willingly sacrificed themselves and it became the source of passionate patriotism for many of the second generation. America, after all, had asked them to serve 'their' country" (186).

Being Americans: Assimilation and (Un)American Activities

Through their participation at home and on the front lines, Italian immigrants had proven they could be good Americans, and the postwar period saw the rise of those new Americans in action. Italians continued to play a major role in what historian Reed Ueda has so aptly called "the cycle of national creation and re-creation through immigration" (4).

After the war, Italians were among the larger groups of foreign or mixed parentage, with 3.3 million people. Like other children of immigrants, Italian American artists reflected the major themes expressed in postwar literature, such as the soldier's return, the generation gap, the sexual revolution, the focus on education, the struggle for civil rights, interest in jazz, the rise of Catholicism, the creation of suburban culture, and the rise of mass culture and the consumer society. As Ueda notes:

> Encouraging the individualist pursuit of pleasure and novel sensation, [American] consumerist mass culture was at odds with certain aspects of their [foreign-born parents'] tradition that emphasized moralistic and ascetic values, the stoical acceptance of self-denial and abstention for the sake of family propriety ... Mass culture became a part of their developing a sense of self as "ethnic" Americans. (108)

Through mass culture Italian America presented two figures who would become "super Americans." Joe DiMaggio and Frank Sinatra were looked on as "secular saints" of sorts and became examples of how important the offspring of Italian immigrants could become in the US. The 1940s and 1950s saw the arrival of more children of immigrants as serious producers of American art. Many of the early writers were returning soldiers and the first of their families to be literate and attend American schools, especially with the help of the GI Bill.

John Ciardi, as poet and critic, added new dimensions to *Italianità* (Italianness) in America in 1965 with his translation of *The Divine Comedy* of Dante, which surpassed the million-copy mark in paperback sales. Author of more than 40 books of poetry and criticism, Ciardi has done more to popularize poetry than perhaps any other American. Born in the United States, Ciardi traveled to Italy during World War II and in 1956 he received the Rome Prize. Some of Ciardi's poetry dealt with current Italian events. "S.P.W.R.: A Letter from Rome," published in the prestigious *Poetry* in 1958, portrays Italian fascism and Mussolini's attempt to recreate the Roman Empire. Ciardi's writing, his work with the *Saturday Review*, and his national radio programs made him a driving force in American poetry and brought him election to the American Academy of Arts and Letters.

Long before the appearance of his first book of poetry, *River Full of Craft* (1956), Felix Stefanile had labored quietly and effectively in the field of American letters. In 1954, with his wife Selma, he founded *Sparrow*, a journal of poetry that is still published nearly 50 years later. His major collections include *A Fig Tree in America* (1970), *East River Nocturne* (1976), and *The Dance at St Gabriel's* (1995). Winner of the John Ciardi Award for lifetime achievement in Italian American poetry, and professor emeritus of English at Purdue University, Stefanile has written some of the most powerful poems depicting life as the child of immigrants caught between two worlds, gathering many of them in *The Country of Absence: Poems and an Essay* (2000).

The prose fiction of the period just after the war focused on the struggle to create and enjoy the American Dream, which often included moving up and out of urban "Little Italys." George Panetta, with *We Ride a White Donkey* (1944), *Jimmy Potts Gets a Haircut* (1947), and *Viva Madison Avenue!* (1957), used humor as a means of dealing with his movement from a Little Italy to the advertising world of Madison Avenue. In *The Bennett Place* (1948), Michael DeCapite begins moving away from the Italian American subject to create a novel that focuses on the transition from one social class to another. His early death in a car accident at the age of 43 ended what was proving to be a prominent career as an American novelist. As if picking up where his brother left off, Raymond DeCapite wrote *The Coming of Fabrizze* (1960), a wild tale told in the tradition of Mark Twain about an immigrant who starts his Americanization with shovel in hand and ends up playing the stock market, thus affecting his whole neighborhood. In *A Lost King* (1961), he uses the father–son relationship that is the subject of much of the writing of Italian American men to dramatize the struggle between generations.

Stories that defied the stereotypical happy-go-lucky Italian family began to appear. Two of the earliest novels that recount growing up as a daughter of immigrants are by Julia Savarese and Octavia Waldo. Savarese, a playwright and television writer, wrote *The Weak and the Strong* (1952). This dark account of life in a New York Little Italy deals with an Italian American family's struggle to survive immigration and the Great Depression. Waldo's novel *A Cup of Sun* (1961) is a powerful account of coming of age during the World War II and deals with the traumatic experience of incest. Rocco Fumento's *Devil by the Tail* (1954) defies the idea of the stereotypic "nice Italian family" by dramatizing a young boy's confronting his father's tyranny as he attempts to forge his own identity. Antonia Pola in *Who Can Buy the Stars* (1957) presents a rare view of how a woman becomes a bootlegger in order to provide for her family. Michael DeCapite's first two novels portray the evolution from immigrant to ethnic and the effects that assimilation has on three generations of Italian Americans. In *Maria* (1943), the protagonist is an immigrant woman whose marriage to a local bootlegger was arranged by a broker and ends with her being abandoned. *No Bright Banner* (1944) is the coming-of-age story of an Italian American who uses education to escape the destiny of his ancestors.

While many of the writers were busy capturing the disappearance of the immigrant generation, others continued in the tradition of early radicalism. Government investigations into communism, launched by Senator Joseph McCarthy and the House Un-American Activities Committee, sparked the ire of many Italian American artists.

Entertainers such as Frank Sinatra spoke out: "Once they get the movies throttled, how long will it be before we're told what we can say and cannot say into a radio microphone? If you make a pitch on a nationwide radio network for a square deal for the underdog, will they call you a Commie?? . . . Are they going to scare us into silence?" (quoted in Patterson: 189). Pietro di Donato, a participant in the cultural front of the 1930s who joined the Communist Party the night Sacco and Vanzetti were executed, was an avid supporter of the left and refused Frank Capra's offer to film his classic novel *Christ in Concrete*. In a show of solidarity he worked with blacklisted director Edward Dmytryk to create the film *Give Us This Day* (1949).

A powerful example of the political persecution of this period is found in Carlo Marzani's novel *The Survivor* (1958). Written seven years after he was convicted of "defrauding" the government by concealing a reluctant, one-year membership in the Communist Party, the novel tells the story of Marc Ferranti, a character who is acquitted rather than convicted, as Marzani was, for his political affiliations. A strong sense of the damage inflicted on Italy and his father by fascism leads Ferranti to stand strong against injustice in America, even if his actions are seen as "un-American" or subversive. This is a theme that replays itself consistently throughout the critical writings of Marzani. And nowhere does it come through as clearly as in his memoirs. Marzani's first-hand experience of fascism in Italy disposed him to see the 1947 loyalty oaths for public servants, ordered by Harry Truman, and American Cold War policies as the first steps toward fascism in America. Remembering his father's wish that Italians should have fought fascism in Italy, Marzani dedicated his life to combating it in America.

Because of its dominance during the war, the United States had become a leader in international politics and began using immigration "as a tool for shaping foreign relations to further American self-interest" (Ueda: 42). Postwar restrictions on immigration from Italy were relaxed through such legislation as the War Brides Act (1945), the Displaced Persons Act (1948), the McCarran-Walter Act (1952), and the Refugee Relief Act (1953). One beneficiary was Joseph Tusiani, who immigrated to the United States shortly after the war so that his family could join his father. While his first novel, *Envoy from Heaven*, appeared in 1965, he is perhaps best known for his translations of the poetry of Michelangelo and Tasso. He was the first Italian American to be named vice president of the Catholic Poetry Society of America (1956–68). His "Song of the Bicentennial," written in celebration of America's two hundredth birthday, questions Americanization and its relation to the immigrant's identity: "Then, who will solve this riddle of my day? / Two languages, two lands, perhaps two souls . . . /Am I a man or two strange halves of one?" (*Ethnicity*: 5). Through his poetry Tusiani gives voice to those who preceded his arrival:

> I am the present for I am the past
> of those who for their future came to stay,
> humble and innocent and yet outcast.
> For this my life their death made ample room.
>
> (6)

Another postwar immigrant who would help redefine Italian American literature was Giose Rimanelli. Rimanelli's first novel, *Tiro al piccione* (1950, 1991), the publication of which was supported by Cesare Pavese, is a fictionalized autobiographical account of his early years in Molise and his experiences during World War II in Italy. This novel, translated into English by Ben Johnson as *The Day of the Lion* (1954), received critical praise and became an American best-seller. Six years and a number of novels later, Rimanelli came to America to give a lecture at the Library of Congress, after which he was invited to teach and travel throughout North and South America. Even before moving to America, Rimanelli was beginning to examine the American influence on life in Italy. In his second novel, *Peccato originale* (*Original Sin*, 1957), he gives us the story of a Molisani family and the father's (Nicola) obsession with the dream of coming to America. Early in the 1970s he wrote his first novel in English, entitled *Benedetta in Guysterland* (1993), that parodies the Mafia stories of Mario Puzo and Gay Talese. The novel won an American Book Award.

The continuation of a radical heritage begun by Giovannitti, Sacco and Vanzetti, and New York congressman Vito Marcantonio can be found in the literary innovation of a number of poets. Labor activist Vincent Ferrini carried on the worker-writer tradition using the experience of work and injustice to dignify the world of American workers; these sentiments can be found in his avant-garde poetry: *No Smoke* (1941), *Injunction* (1943), and *Know Fish* (1980). America's Beatniks arose in response to an apolitical complacency that seemed to set in directly after the war. As precursors of the 1960s "hippies," the Beats fused art and politics to raise the American consciousness about the politics of life and the life of humanity. Lawrence Ferlinghetti, Gregory Corso, and Diane di Prima, were key figures during this period and profoundly affected America's literary scene. Ferlinghetti, well known as founder of City Lights Books and Bookstore of San Francisco (the first paperback bookstore in the United States), published Allen Ginsberg's "Howl" (1956), the subject of a precedent-setting censorship trial in the late 1950s. Ferlinghetti also became San Francisco's first poet laureate. His classic "The Old Italians Dying" is a testament to the dying immigrant culture and was first published on the op-ed page of the *Los Angeles Times*. The driving force behind the poetry and prose of Diane di Prima is a gender- and culture-based tension created between men and women and between Italian and American culture. Her *Memoirs of a Beatnik* (1969) was the first major autobiography by an Italian American woman, and the poetry in her *Revolutionary Letters* (1971) acknowledges a strong connection to her grandfather's leftist politics. *Recollections of My Life as a Woman* (2001), a memoir, returns to the troubled times before she left home (when *Memoirs* begins) and struggles to uncover and process the family secrets that have haunted her.

Government investigations into organized crime, led by Estes Kefauver, brought Italians to the attention of millions of Americans through the new and pervasive medium of television. "Television," wrote cultural critic George Lipsitz, "provided a forum for redefining American ethnic, class, and family identities into consumer identities" (47). Plots of such shows as *The Goldbergs*, *Life with Luigi*, and *I Remember Mama* offered purchasing products as a way to assimilate into American culture. However, the only major Italian presence on American television, beyond performers such as Perry Como, Frank Sinatra, Dean Martin, and Connie Francis, were televised Senate hearings on crime and the gangsters on the popular program *The Untouchables*.

Mario Puzo, whose earliest works, *Dark Arena* (1955) and *The Fortunate Pilgrim* (1964), received critical acclaim without financial success, took advantage of the nation's new obsession with the Mafia and wrote *The Godfather* (1969). Not since Pietro di Donato had an American author of Italian descent been thrust into the national spotlight. The timing of the novel's publication (just after televised investigations of Joe Valachi) had much to do with its rapid climb to number one and its long, 67-week stay on the *New York Times* best-seller list. The effect of *The Godfather* was tremendous; since its publication, and especially since its film adaptations in the early 1970s, Italian American novelists have been writing in its shadow.

Gay Talese is a noted journalist and pioneer of the "New Journalism" style of writing nonfiction. His work, which has invited comparisons with Truman Capote and Tom Wolfe, explores some of America's postwar social preoccupations. He explores the Mafia phenomenon through the Bonanno crime family in *Honor Thy Father* (1971). His memoir *Unto the Sons* (1992) captures the forces of history that have shaped modern Italy and America as he tells the story of his father's immigration to the United States.

Ben Morreale's first novel, *The Seventh Saracen* (1959), depicts the return of an Italian American to his ancestral homeland in Sicily. *A Few Virtuous Men* (1973) is a literary thriller about Sicily and what it is like to live on the other side of the Mafia. Its main character is a priest who recounts his life among "Mafiosi." In *Monday Tuesday Never Come Sunday* (1977) Morreale explores America in the 1930s through the eyes of a young Sicilian American protagonist. Set in Brooklyn's Bensonhurst, on a block called "Lu Vaticanu," the novel portrays a young man's coming of age during the tough times of the 1930s.

The war and education in American schools brought Italian American writers into contact with the world outside of Little Italy and opened up their imaginations and creativity to Modernist experiments. More and more the postwar Italian American was making his and her way into and through American universities. Diana Cavallo, a professor of creative writing at the University of Pennsylvania, once worked as a psychiatric social worker, and from these experiences she created her novel *A Bridge of Leaves* (1961). Joseph Papaleo, once the director of creative writing at Sarah Lawrence College, began his writing career by publishing short stories in major periodicals such as *Dial*, *Epoch*, *Harper's*, and the *New Yorker*. His two novels, *All the Comforts* (1967) and *Out of Place* (1970), both deal with the psychological struggle of the second-generation Italian American to find a respectable place for himself in American society. *Streets of Gold* (1974) by Evan Hunter, whose real name is Salvatore Lombino, was an example of the auto-biographical fiction that appeared during this period. Hunter also used the pen name Ed McBain, among others, when writing hundreds of detective and science fiction novels. The fiction produced in the 1960s and 1970s fashioned a number of myths that would be explored, exploited, and challenged by later generations of Italian American writers.

Mythologies of Italian America: From Little Italys to Suburbs

The mythology of Italian America, which would become the foundation of the visual explorations of Italian American life found in Francis

311

Ford Coppola's films *The Godfather* (1972) and *The Godfather Part II* (1974) and in Martin Scorsese's *Mean Streets* (1973), contributed a number of character types to postwar American culture, including the gangster and the uneducated, urban blue-collar worker. Prior to the 1960s, very few American writers of Italian descent had been educated through college. As a group, Italian Americans would not surpass the national average of the college educated until the 1990s; an increasing number of those who were becoming writers would be those who had graduated from college. Political activists Mario Savio, a leader of the Free Speech Movement at the University of California at Berkeley, Daniella Gioseffi (*In Bed with The Exotic Enemy* [1997]), who worked in the civil rights movement, and Father James Groppi, a radical Catholic priest and leading civil rights activist in Milwaukee, Wisconsin, were products of the new awakening of the children and grandchildren of immigrants.

During a time when the very definition of "American" was being challenged and changed, Italian American writers were busy exploring their own American histories. Helen Barolini's novel *Umbertina* (1979) appeared during an American ethnic revival period just after the publication of Alex Haley's *Roots* (1976). *Umbertina* tells the story of four generations of Italian American women, focusing on the immigrant matriarchal grandmother, her granddaughter and her great-granddaughter. *Umbertina* is a novel of self-discovery, a bildungsroman that, while it spans four generations, can be read as the historical evolution of the Italian woman into the American woman, or as the Italian woman becoming a feminist.

America's postwar feminist movement had a strong effect on the daughters of the immigrants. Social activist Eleanor Curtri Smeal became president of the National Organization of Women, and a spirit of similar social action and the redefinition of the American woman became subjects of a number of novels by Italian American women. Dorothy Calvetti Bryant explored a specifically Italian notion of feminism in her novels *Ella Price's Journal* (1972), *Miss Giardino* (1978), and *Anita, Anita* (1993), an historical recreation of the life of the wife of Italian Risorgimento leader Giuseppe Garibaldi. Under the impetus of urban renewal programs, many Italian ghettos throughout major US cities were razed, forcing those residents who couldn't flee to the suburbs to find homes outside their traditionally ethnocentric Little Italys.

Tina De Rosa's *Paper Fish* (1985) tells the story of a young girl who comes of age in a disintegrating "Little Italy." De Rosa's tale achieves a timeless quality through her creation of a world unaffected by any history beyond that of the personal history of the family. The author, who has said she can only imagine the southern Italian culture into which her grandmother was born, disconnects her characters from historical time and suggests that the journey toward self is a continuous quest, uninterrupted by the passing of generations. Through the archetypal figure of the grandmother in *Paper Fish*, the author wants us to understand that the image of Italy will remain inside Carmolina, the novel's protagonist, as long as the memory of her grandmother is kept alive. This experience, the death of place and the inevitable dissolution of an accompanying culture, is recorded by De Rosa, an eyewitness, in a language that she has said was impossible for her ancestors to articulate. Similarly Tony Ardizzone, who turned from student protester to creative writer and professor of creative writing at Indiana University, captured this experience in "Nonna," a short story in his collection *The Evening News* (1986), which won the Flannery O'Connor award. His novels include *Heart of the Order* (1986) and *In the Garden of Papa Santuzzu* (1999), which depicts the immigration of a Sicilian family through different points of view

The shift from urban to suburban ethnicity is the subject of the writing of many young Italian Americans who watched as their families moved from working- to middle-class life. Anthony Giardina's novel *A Boy's Pretensions* (1988) and his collection of short fiction *The Country of Marriage* (1997) exquisitely capture this experience. George Veltri's *A Nice Boy* (1995) explores the impact drug use has on the grandson of immigrants. The myth of Italian identity and its reinvention is the subject of Carole Maso's *Ghost Dance* (1986), a novel that tells the story of a multiethnic third-generation woman who, unlike earlier generations, has the option of picking and choosing from the many traditions that make up American culture. The Italian characteristics the protagonist, Vanessa Turin, does not inherit directly through experiences with her grandparents, she imagines and reinvents to fulfill her needs. Few novels capture so well the effects of the fragmentation that occurs when solid cultural traditions are fractured. Maso's subsequent novels, *The Art Lover* (1990), *Ava* (1992), *The American Woman in the Chinese Hat* (1993), and *Defiance* (1998), explore lesbian themes as central to the American experience and are all daring steps into new forms of narrating fiction.

The myth of the dominance of the macho Italian American man is challenged by many of the Italian American women writers, but none as effectively as Josephine Gattuso Hendin in *The Right Thing to Do* (1988). This critically acclaimed novel of a young woman growing out of the shadow of her immigrant father earned an American Book Award. An author of notable scholarly works on contemporary American writing, and professor of English and Tiro A Segno professor of Italian American writing at New York University, Hendin makes the lively and troubled relationship between father and daughter come alive with humor and power. She vividly presents the drama of a young woman's attempts to make her own way outside of her family and her father's expectations. As the daughter Gina rebels, her father weakens in health; as he moves closer to death, she comes closer to understanding his life and the legacy she will inherit.

The accomplishment of these women writers has been acknowledged and analyzed in scholarship and criticism by Mary Jo Bona, whose *Claiming a Tradition* is the first book-length study devoted solely to Italian American women writers. Bona, also an award-winning poet, provides a context for viewing the work of these women as a unique tradition within the larger framework of American literary history.

Robert Viscusi, one of the foremost critics of Italian American literature and culture, president of the Italian American Writers Association, and director of the Wolfe Humanities Institute at Brooklyn College, has captured what it means to be Italian American, in a time when that identity is challenged as never before, with his novel *Astoria* (1995), winner of an American Book Award. In his imaginary autobiography he presents an extended meditation on the meaning of cultures European and American, mother and madonna, father and padrino (godfather), of one's love of the lost and the lost loves of one's past.

The rise of minority political power during the postwar period is reflected in the novels of the late Robert Ferro, *The Family of Max Desir* (1983), *The Blue Star* (1985), and *Second Son* (1988), that explore the complex relationships among gay Italian Americans, their families, and straight and gay communities. Felice Picano has proven to be one of the most prolific writers of the Italian American gay community through his stories, novels, and literary leadership. Rachel Guido deVries's *Tender Warriors* (1986) and *How to Sing to a Dago* (1995), and Mary Saracino's *No Matter What* (1993) and its sequel *Finding Grace* (1994), speak in lesbian voices that affirm ethnic identity and community inclusion as strongly as they attack the myth of the normal, patriarchal, and heterosexual Italian American family. A collection of autobiographical essays, *Fuori* (1996), and an anthology of writing collected by Giovanna (Janet) Capone, Denise Nico Leto, and Tommi Avicolli Mecca entitled *Hey Paesan!* (1999), attest to the variety of gay and lesbian experiences in Italian America.

While some of the most powerful presences of Italian Americans on the US stage can be found in Tennessee Williams's *Rose Tattoo* and Arthur Miller's *A View from the Bridge*, Italian Americans such as Michael Gazzo, Mario Fratti, and Albert Innaurato have had a great impact on American theater. Gazzo's *A Hatful of Rain* (1955), dealing with drugs and family, emerged from improvisations at the famous New York Actors Studio. Fratti, who immigrated to the US in the 1960s as a respected and established playwright, has been a consistent presence in the New York theater scene with such productions as *The Cage* (1966), *The Victim* (1968), and *Nine* (1982), his stage adaptation of Federico Fellini's film *8¹/₂*. Innaurato, born in 1948 in South Philadelphia, studied at the Yale School of Drama and has written several influential plays, such as *The Transformation of Benno Blimpie* (1973), the Broadway hit *Gemini* (1976), and *Coming of Age in Soho* (1984), that have helped pave the way for a more direct recognition of the realities and fantasies of Italian American culture when the worlds of Little Italy and the Ivy League collide. Joe Pintauro, whose early work as a novelist included *Cold Hands* (1979) and *State of Grace* (1983), has had numerous plays produced off-Broadway and at Long Island venues. *The Moon Dreamers* (1969), by Julie Bovasso, the first Italian American woman playwright, paved the way for such contemporary women playwrights as Jo Ann Tedesco (*Sacraments* [1978]), and Teresa Carilli (*Dolores Street* and *Wine Country*, published in *Women as Lovers* [1996]).

Contemporary poets who have had an impact on American culture include Lewis Turco, whose *A Handbook of Poetics* (1968) and *Poetry: An Introduction through Writing* (1973) established him as a promising young teacher of poetry, fulfilled that promise with *New Book of Forms* (1986), *Visions and Revisons of American Poetry* (1986), and *The Public Poet: Five Lectures on the Art and Craft of Poetry* (1991). He has also amassed a healthy body of his own poetry, from *First Poems* (1960) and *Awaken, Bells Falling: Poems 1957–1967* (1968), to his *Pocoangelini: A Fantography* (1971) and *The Shifting Web: New and Selected Poems* (1989). More formalist than his contemporaries, Turco's work captures the daily life of his past in ways reminiscent of Edgar Lee Masters, as this excerpt from "Mrs Martino the Candy Store Lady" demonstrates:

> Listen to the hum of the
> lemon ice machine, mashing
> sugar, mushing ice, crushing
> the pucker bellies of chubby lemons.

> "Twenty minutes, can you wait?
> twenty minutes for lemon ice,"
> mumbles Mrs. Martino.
>
> (69)

A poet more concerned with the politics than the poetics of ethnicity, Maria Mazziotti Gillan, professor of English and director of creative writing at SUNY-Binghamton, is founder and director of the Poetry Center at Passaic County Community College. She is the editor of *Footwork: The Paterson Literary Review* and co-editor of acclaimed anthologies *UnSettling America* (1994), *Identity Lessons* (1999), and *Growing Up Ethnic in America* (1999). Her collections include *Flowers from the Tree of Night* (1982), *Taking Back My Name* (1989), *Where I Come From: Selected and New Poems* (1995), *Things My Mother Told Me* (1999), and *Italian Women in Black Dresses* (2002). Whether dealing with the emotions of overcoming shame or confronting racism, Gillan's poetry evidences an in-your-face power presented in a deceptively simple diction that creates instant identity with her subjects. "Public School No. 18, Paterson, New Jersey," is typical of Gillan's ability to create accessible poetry: to the women she claims taught her to hate herself, Gillan writes:

> Remember me, Ladies,
> the silent one?
> I have found my voice
> and my rage will blow
> your house down.
>
> (12)

Dana Gioia, who has published *Daily Horoscope* (1986), *The Gods of Winter* (1991), and *Interrogations at Noon* (2001), has positioned himself as one of America's best formalist poets. Many of his lyric poems have been set to music and he has composed the libretto for Alva Henderson's opera *Nosferatu*. Also a translator of Latin and Italian poets, Gioia retired from business to devote his full time to his literary career. In 2002 he was named director of the National Endowment for the Humanities. His subjects range from the personal to the public, from the American to the ethnic. David Citino, a professor of English at Ohio State University (*The Appassionata Doctrines* [1985]) and W. S. DiPiero (*The Dog Star* [1990]) are among the best younger poets. Sandra M. Gilbert, a pioneer of feminist theory and scholarship, has written poetry about her identity as an Italian American in *In the Fourth*

World: Poems (1978), *Emily's Bread: Poems* (1984), and *Blood Pressure* (1988). In "The Summer Kitchen," Gilbert lays out the relationship between her past and her poetry, between the world of women and men, of myth and history:

> In June when the Brooklyn garden
> boiled with blossom
> when leaflets of basil lined the path
> and new green fruitless fingers of vine
> climbed the airy arbor roof,
>
> my Sicilian aunts withdrew
> to the summer kitchen
> the white bare secret room
> at the bottom of the house.
>
> (55)

Jay Parini, whose breadth as a writer includes fiction and biography, produced poetry in *Anthracite Country* (1982) and *Town Life: Poems* (1998) that reflects life in Italy and America. Noted editor and translator Jonathan Galassi's poetry is collected in *Morning Run: Poems* (1988). Rose Romano's *Vendetta* (1992) and *The Wop Factor* (1994) unite the personal and the political in strong poetry. Thom Tammaro's *When the Italians Came to My Hometown* (1995) combines prose and poetry to explore the impact an immigrant past has had on his identity.

Fiction produced in the 1980s and 1990s began recreating the immigrant experience from the perspective of the grandchildren. Among the major texts reflecting this point of view are Gilbert Sorrentino's *Aberration of Starlight* (1980), George Cuomo's *Family Honor* (1983), Michael Anania's *The Red Menace* (1984), Kenny Marotta's *A Piece of Earth* (1985), Jay Parini's *The Patch Boys* (1986) and *The Apprentice Lover* (2002), and Denise Giardina's *Storming Heaven* (1994). Key writers of short fiction who deal with similar themes are Mary Bush (*A Place of Light* [1991]), Anne Calcagno (*Pray for Yourself* [1993]), George Cuomo (*Sing Choirs of Angels* [1969]), John Fante (*The Wine of Youth* [1985]), and Agnes Rossi (*The Quick* [1992]). Flannery O'Connor Awards for short fiction collections have gone to Salvatore La Puma for *Boys of Bensonhurst* (1987) and to Rita Ciresi for *Mother Rocket* (1993) and *Sometimes I Dream in Italian* (2002). Renee Manfredi earned an Iowa Fiction Award for her story collection *Where Love Leaves Us* (1994).

A number of scholars have turned from criticizing to creating literature. A professor of English at Duke University, Frank Lentricchia has created a trilogy of works focusing on his experiences of growing up in a Little Italy in the novellas "Johnny Critelli" and "The Knifemen" (1996), growing out of Little Italy in *The Edge of Night* (1994), and returning to a Little Italy in *The Music of The Inferno* (1999). His playing with the Italian American figure in *Lucchesi and the Whale* (2001) is an experiment in critically driven fiction. In all of the works Lentricchia draws breath from Mario Puzo, Edgar Allan Poe, and James Joyce, and blood from filmmakers Federico Fellini, Martin Scorsese, and Brian DePalma, to create his own approach to familiar themes. For example, in *The Music of the Inferno*, Robert Tagliaferro, an orphan child of unknown racial background, makes a grim discovery shortly after his eighteenth birthday and leaves his hometown of Utica, New York. The young man takes refuge in a bookstore in New York City where he lives like Ralph Ellison's "Invisible Man." His book-learning replaces his family, as he tells us: "In the absence of my father, I acquired knowledge. My knowledge is my memory" (72).

Don DeLillo, who is perhaps the most accomplished living American writer of Italian descent, was born to immigrants. His early life was spent in the urban settings of the Bronx and Philadelphia, where he experienced the type of neighborhoods he writes of in some of his early stories. He attended college at Fordham University. Of his entire body of published work, only two of his earliest stories are set in "Little Italy," and these are the only works that overtly use Italian American subjects as protagonists. In his first novel, *Americana* (1971), the American middle-class values that DeLillo infuses into his protagonist David Bell are the very values that ethnic characters try to rid themselves of to become American. By exploring the "other," DeLillo issues a warning to those who would covet Americanness and attempt to remake themselves in the image and likeness of the stereotypical American. While his writing has earned some of the most prestigious prizes the US offers, including a Guggenheim, a National Book, and the Pen Faulkner Award, it wasn't until *Underworld* (1998) that he created a protagonist of Italian American descent. The natural move for the child of immigrants is away from the world of the parents and toward the larger world of mainstream America. *Underworld* maps these steps from Nick Shay's origins in the Bronx to his later life in Arizona. Along the way DeLillo tells the story of the transition of a Cold War America into a postmodern present.

Perhaps the most eloquent tragicomical Italian American fiction can be found in Anthony Valerio's *Valentino and the Great Italians, According to Anthony Valerio* (1986). In this collection of 22 literary essays, Valerio elevates regular Joes and Josephines as easily (and as wittily) as he levels the stature of such household names as Enrico Caruso, Frank Sinatra, and Joe DiMaggio. He has been called the Philip Roth of Italian American literature. His earlier fiction in *The Mediterranean Runs through Brooklyn* (1982) wove imaginative chiaroscuro flights into Italian American history and his own life. In *Conversation with Johnny* (1997), he pushed even further ahead by tackling two stereotypes that have plagued Italian Americans: the gangster and the lover. In this sometimes parodic, sometimes sardonic, but always entertaining look at crime and culture, Valerio attempts a literary hit on those stereotypes. While he might not eliminate them, he certainly paralyzes both of them long enough for us to see that "the cult of *The Godfather*" is over.

One of the best novels reflecting the working-class experience is Chuck Wachtel's *Joe the Engineer* (1983), which tells the story of Joe Lazaro, a Vietnam War veteran who has returned home ready to enter traditional American working-class life. Wachtel, who is half Italian American and half Jewish American, has portrayed the idea of the hybrid American in his 1995 novel *The Gates*, in which the protagonist, Primo Thomas, is born to an African American father and an Italian American mother.

Postmodern experimental writing in an Italian American vein can be found in Gilbert Sorrentino's later work and the experimental fictions of Mary Caponegro's *The Star Cafe* (1990) and *Five Doubts* (1998). Mark Ciabattari has created two novels that might be considered quintessential postmodern fiction, *Dreams of an Imaginary New Yorker Named Rizzoli* (1990) and *The Literal Truth: Rizzoli Dreams of Eating the Apple of Earthly Delights* (1994), and Dennis Barone's poetry in *Forms/Froms* (1988) and her fiction, *Abusing the Telephone* (1994), *Echoes* (1997), and *Temple of the Rat* (2000), provide evidence that the Italian American experience is varied, plural, and very much capable of reinventing itself as it moves further away from the immigrant experience.

Turn-of-a-New-Century:
An Italian American Renaissance

In 1987, *MELUS*, the journal of the Society for the Study of Multi-Ethnic Literature in the United States, devoted a double issue to Italian American literature. In the winter of 2003 another issue dedicated to

Italian American writing appeared, guest edited by Mary Jo Bona. Today, American scholars, critics, and writers of Italian descent are surfacing on the pages of journals dedicated to Italian American culture. These include *Differentia*, edited by Peter Carravetta, *Italian Americana*, edited by Carol Bonomo Albright, *Voices in Italian Americana (VIA)*, edited by Fred Gardaphé, Anthony Tamburri, Paul Giordano, and Mary Jo Bona, and *Arba Sicula*, edited by Gaetano Cipolla.

Key publishers of Italian American writing include Antonio D'Alfonso's Guernica Editions of Canada and the USA, Bordighera Press, directed by Anthony Tamburri, and Legas Books, founded by Gaetano Cipolla. The Feminist Press has reprinted major works by Italian American women. The State University of New York Press has developed a series in Italian American Culture edited by Fred Gardaphé. Rose Romano, poet, editor, and publisher of malafemmina press, brought gender issues to the forefront through the journal *La bella figura* and its subsequent anthology of the same title.

A number of new publications represent the development of a feminist tradition in Italian American culture. Nourished by stories in the oral tradition of her immigrant ancestors, Marianna DeMarco Torgovnick documents her personal and professional journey toward American assimilation in *Crossing Ocean Parkway: Readings by an Italian American Daughter* (1994). Louise de Salvo identifies a major thrust in contemporary Italian American women's writing in her memoir *Vertigo* (1997):

> I come from a people who, even now, seriously distrust educated women, who value family loyalty. The story I want to tell is that of how I tried to create (and am still trying to create) a life that was different from the one that was scripted for me by my culture . . . through reading, writing, meaningful work, and psychotherapy. (xvii)

Italian American women who have broken the traditional silence around abuse in the family include Mary Cappello, in *Night Bloom* (1998), Flavia Alaya, in *Under the Rose* (1999), and Diane di Prima, in *Recollections of My Life as a Woman* (2001). With *ChiaroScuro* (1999), Helen Barolini uses the essay form to map her journey from traditional Italian American daughter to a rebellious adult, something she accomplishes through an extended stay in Italy. The return to Italy, once again redefining what it means to be a contemporary Italian American, arises in such works as Teresa Maggio's travel memoir, *La Mattanza* (1999).

Contemporary Italian American literature demonstrates a growing literary tradition through a variety of voices. Critical studies, reviews, the publication of anthologies and journals, and the creation of new presses are ample evidence that Italian American culture has gained understandings of its past as it develops a sense of a future. Through organizations such as the American Italian Historical Association, MALIA, formerly the Italian American Women's Collective, and the Italian American Writers' Association, American writers of Italian descent are meeting and exchanging ideas. Together these voices are developing an indigenous criticism and advancing a culture that epitomizes the evolution of Italian American ethnic identity in postwar history.

References and further reading

Barolini, Helen. *The Dream Book: An Anthology of Writings by Italian American Women*. Syracuse, NY: Syracuse University Press, 1985/2000.

Bona, Mary Jo. *Claiming a Tradition: Italian American Women's Writing*. Carbondale, IL: Southern Illinois University Press, 1999.

Capone, Giovanna (Janet) et al. *Hey Paesan: Writings by Lesbians and Gay Men of Italian Descent*. Oakland, CA: Three Guineas Press, 1999.

D'Acierno, Pellegrino, ed. *The Italian American Heritage: A Companion to Literature and Arts*. New York: Garland, 1999.

de Salvo, Louise. *Vertigo: A Memoir*. New York: Dutton, 1996.

Diggins, John P. *Mussolini and Fascism: The View from America*. Princeton, NJ: Princeton University Press, 1972.

DiStasi, Lawrence, ed. *Una Storia Segreta: The Secret History of Italian American Evacuation and Internment during World War II*. Berkeley, CA: Heyday Books, 2001.

Ferraro, Thomas J., ed. *Catholic Lives, Contemporary America*. Durham, NC: Duke University Press, 1997.

Gardaphé, Fred. *Dagoes Read: Tradition and the Italian/American Writer*. Toronto and New York: Guernica Editions, 1996.

Gardaphé, Fred. *Italian Signs, American Streets: The Evolution of Italian/American Narrative*. Raleigh Durham, NC: Duke University Press, 1996.

Gilbert, Sandra M. *Blood Pressure: Poems*. New York: W. W. Norton, 1988.

Gillan, Maria Mazziotti. *Where I Come From: Selected and New Poems*. Toronto: Guernica Editions, 1995.

Giordano, Paul, ed. *Ethnicity: Selected Poems of Joseph Tusiani*. Boca Raton, FL: Bordighera Press, 2000.

Giordano, Paul, and Anthony Tamburri, eds. *Beyond the Margin: Readings in Italian Americana*. Cranbury, NJ: Associated University Presses, 1998.

Giovannitti, Arturo. *The Collected Poems of Arturo Giovannitti*. New York: Arno Press, 1975.

LaGumina, Salvatore J. et al., eds. *The Italian American Experience: An Encyclopedia*. New York: Garland, 2000.

Lentricchia, Frank. *The Music of the Inferno*. Albany: SUNY Press, 1999.

Lipsitz, George. *Time Passages: Collective Memory and American Popular Culture*. Minneapolis: University of Minnesota Press, 1990.

Mangione, Jerre. *Mount Allegro*. New York: Columbia University Press, 1972.

Mangione, Jerre, and Ben Morreale. *La Storia*. New York: HarperCollins, 1992.

Morreale, Ben. *Sicily: The Hallowed Land*. New York: Legas Books, 2000.

Parini, Jay, and Kenneth Ciongoli. *Beyond "The Godfather: Italian American Writers on the Real Italian American Experience"*. Hanover, NH: University Press of New England, 1997.

Patterson, James T. *Grand Expectations: The United States 1945–1974*. New York: Oxford University Press, 1996.

Romano, Rose. *La Bella Figura: A Choice*. San Francisco: malafemmina press, 1992.

Salvemini, Gaetano. *Italian Fascist Activities in the United States*. Ed. and intro. Philip V. Cannistraro. New York: Center for Migration Studies, 1977.

Stefanile, Felix. *The Dance at St. Gabriel's*. Brownsville, OR: Storyline Press, 1991.

Tamburri, Anthony, Paul Giordano, and Fred Gardaphé. *From the Margin: Writings in Italian Americana*. West Lafayette, IN: Purdue University Press, 1991.

Tamburri, Anthony. *A Semiotic of Ethnicity*. Albany, NY: State University of New York Press, 1998.

Turco, Lewis. *The Shifting Web. New and Selected Poems*. Fayetteville: University of Arkansas Press, 1989.

Tusiani, Joseph. *Ethnicity: Selected Poems*. Ed. Paolo Giordano. Boca Raton, FL: Bordighera, 2000.

Ueda, Reed. *Post War Immigrant America: A Social History*. Boston: Bedford and St Martin's Press, 1994.

Vitiello, Justin. *Oral History and Storytelling: Poetics and Literature of Sicilian Emigration*. Lewiston, NY: Edwin Mellen Press, 1993.

Chapter 13

Irish American Writing: Political Men and Archetypal Women

"Polytics Ain't Bean Bag": The Twentieth-Century Irish American Political Novel

Robert E. Rhodes

The US Department of Commerce's 1989 *Statistical Abstracts of the United States* identifies 40,166,000 Americans of Irish ancestry counted by the 1980 Census (41). Many of them are doubtless in politics, although the record will show that many fewer than in the past are in big city politics and political machines identified as Irish. The machines themselves have largely gone the way of the written ballot, at least partly because their functions and faults are now served by government agencies and programs. A rural people in Ireland, most of the immigrants to America in the nineteenth century settled in large cities. Here, simply for survival at first, and later for respectability, and later yet for assimilation and prosperity, many of them entered politics. With their earned political clout – it was never simply conceded – it was inevitable that novelists would tell their story. An early negative definition of Irish American politics provides not only the title of this survey but an insight into the fictional versions of politics. The definition is that of Chicago pub-owner Martin Dooley, creation of Irish American journalist Finley Peter Dunne, who said in 1895, "Polytics ain't bean bag. Tis a man's game; and women an' childer, and prohybitionists'd do well to stay out iv it" (25).

323

The 14 twentieth-century novels of this survey were published between 1902 and 1984. In the nearly 100 years of fictional treatment of events and characters – from 1890 in Joseph Dinneen's *Ward Eight* to 1984 in George V. Higgins's *A Choice of Enemies* – can be seen the growth of Irish American political power and its modulation into something we cannot be sure will continue as identifiably Irish American as were the earlier versions. The action of all 14 novels takes place almost in earshot of one another in the Northeastern United States: one in Albany, three in New York City, three – a trilogy by Thomas Fleming – in an unnamed city that may be a fictionalized Jersey City, one in a city not far from Boston, and seven in Boston, America's most Irish city and where the hardest core of opposition to the Irish existed in the Yankees.

How might we characterize the Irish American political novel? Almost always tensions and conflicts thread their way through these important themes: tribalism and the boss; the father–son relationship; Christ and Caesar; the politics of revenge; idealism gone sour; sin, guilt, and cynicism, and the Irish Americans and newer ethnic minorities. So, why did the Irish get into American politics? And why, as is usually conceded, were they so extraordinarily successful at it? The first question might as well be, how could they have avoided politics? The root cause is that they left Ireland only to find in America what they thought they were escaping: extreme economic deprivation and civil and religious disabilities. These were particularly painful in America because of what the Irish had already suffered at home under the Penal Laws – Catholics being ineligible, for example, to hold certain public offices.

As to why the Irish were successful, the short answer is that they had both motivation and traits or skills that turned motivation into action. In the first place, most of them knew English as did no other immigrant group except the English themselves. They had the gifts of eloquence and audacity and their political genius was in organization, developed at home in their struggle with the British. In addition to the example of a disciplined church, there were, for instance, for the first half of the nineteenth century, groups such as Daniel O'Connell's various Irish Associations, which successfully collected weekly tithes in support of O'Connell's drives for Catholic Emancipation and the Repeal of the Union. Locally, Irish peasants struck at exploitation by landlords through such groups as the White Boys, Hearts of Steel, Captain Rock, and the Blackfeet. Perhaps the best-known example of Irish organized resistance was in the boycott, named after Captain

Charles Boycott, a ruthless land agent whose evictions of tenants led, in 1880, to his employees refusing him all cooperation. Since the law in Ireland was British law, the Irish developed a free-and-easy attitude toward obeying it that they brought to America. Thus as Jake O'Connor says in Thomas Fleming's *All Good Men:* "Politics is a way of life in this city . . . A profession which rose outside the existing structure of the community. It made its own rules, which occasionally involved breaking the law of the land" (99).

Many Irish boast of their descent from kings, and they may well be right, since ancient Ireland was made up of small fiefdoms or kingdoms, each with its own king. As it's put in Joseph Dinneen's *Ward Eight*: "Whenever three Irishmen gathered together, according to ancient custom, they formed a political club. The members of the clan were natural-born joiners. They joined any order open to them, the A.O.H., Friends of Irish Freedom, Foresters, trade unions. United Workmen, councils, guilds, chapters, and lodges" (222). In a way, we might think of the ancient kings and their followers as extended families. Or equally accurately, let's think of them as tribes and of their collective behavior as tribalism – having extreme and intense loyalty to one's own immediate kind and to a chieftain, and possessing a profound sense of territoriality, often of the ward, sometimes of an entire city.

From John T. McIntyre's *The Ragged Edge* (1902), dramatizing events in a brief period sometime after 1891, and Dinneen's *Ward Eight* (1936), covering action from 1890 to 1934, to William Kennedy's *Billy Phelan's Greatest Game*, where the action of 1938 is seen from the perspective of 1978, unswerving loyalty is crucial to solidarity in Irish American politics whether the unit is called the club, the gang, the colony, the ward, or specifically the tribe. This sense of loyalty goes far to explain why betrayal of the tribe is perhaps the most heinous sin an Irishman can commit. Thus, ward boss Tom McQuirk in McIntyre's *The Ragged Edge* – subtitled *A Tale of Ward Life and Politics* – advises two constituents: "Stand in with the party, that's the thing, eh, Mrs. Burns? The right kind o' people never forgets who put them in office. Do what's regular, Tim, that's all I ask; do what's regular; vote to keep the organization together and keep the snide reformers out" (191). " 'Gang!' was their rallying cry," we are told in Dinneen's *Ward Eight*. "The word called in a loud voice by one in distress, brought all members within hearing to his assistance. Gang superseded loyalty to anything or any person, even religion" (41). When Kennedy's Billy Phelan is marked a renegade by the McCall machine, Albany's Broadway, the only world he cares about, is closed to him.

In 1951, in Fleming's *All Good Men*, Jake O'Connor explodes to his ward boss father, "You're tribal. Put a spear in your hand and you'd be indistinguishable from the yahoos that used to fight wars over stolen cows ten thousand years ago in Ireland" (188). Charlie Kinsella in Edwin O'Connor's *All in the Family* explains political popularity as "tribal loyalties" (158), and Emmet Shannon in Edward Sheehan's *The Governor* recalls his father's "raw wounds of tribal memory festering for Emmet to observe" (90). Probably the classic voice of the concept is Frank Skeffington's in O'Connor's *The Last Hurrah* as he explains tribal customs to his nephew Adam:

> my position is slightly complicated because I'm not just an elected official of the city, I'm a tribal chieftain as well. Its a necessary kind of dual officeholding, you might say; without the second I wouldn't be the first . . . I have heard the tribe called by less winning names . . . Still I don't suppose it makes much difference what you call them, the net result's the same. (190)

The most obvious manifestation of the tribal or garrison mentality is in the ward, a small kingdom, and in the ward boss, a petty king who is to the ward what the machine is to the city. The two earliest novels adequately make the point. The action of McIntyre's *The Ragged Edge* is confined to a relatively brief period, and so we get a sense of boss Tom McQuirk's grip on the ward in summary form:

> Politics had been McQuirk's study for years, and he had been an apt scholar. He knew nothing of the profundity of statesmanship, and cared less; he had never made a speech on his feet, and could not had his life depended upon it. But what he did not know of practical politics . . . was not worth knowing. He possessed a genius for organizing; in getting out the full vote he was unexcelled, and he dominated the free men of his district by one of three things: Favour – the expectation of favour – the fear of disfavour. (191)

Dinneen's *Ward Eight* covers roughly 45 years, from 1890 to about 1935, and gives us a detailed picture of perennial ward boss Hughie Donnelly; we see Hughie developing and consolidating his power over nearly five decades and Hughie summarized much as Tom McQuirk is. In 1890, for example, it's Hughie to whom protagonist Big Tim O'Flaherty's parents are taken when they arrive in Boston to learn where they'll live and what job Big Tim's father will take, and to have their names entered in Hughie's Doomsday Book so they'll vote the right way when they become citizens. By way of an early summary, Hughie, says Dineen, "was loved and hated with full Gaelic intensity. He was hated by none in the Irish Colony and by many outside of it. He was respected because he assured the members of his class their livelihoods. He was feared because he could deprive them of work instantly" (22).

Thus, the ward boss is sometimes a politicized version of an authoritarian father; and having noted earlier that the extended family is another way to describe the Irish political tribe, we can return briefly to the family. That various ethnic groups reveal different familial patterns comes as no surprise. Readers of Irish fiction will have discovered that both the mother–son and father–son kinships are particularly important in delineating Irish family relationships. James Joyce's *A Portrait of the Artist as a Young Man* and *Ulysses* are the classic texts for revealing a characteristic close bond between mother and son and a tortuous kinship between father and son. With Eugene O'Neill's *Long Day's Journey into Night* being their best example, readers of Irish American literature discover that the same patterns very often hold true for this ethnic literature. Indeed, no fewer than 11 of the 14 novels surveyed here play variations on the father–son theme.

In her study of "Irish Families" in the collection *Ethnicity and Family Therapy*, Monica McGoldrick cites P. Barrabee and O. Von Mering's conclusion that "probably because of the lack of closeness between the parents, the strongest axis in the Irish family is the mother–son tie" (324). McGoldrick further alludes to an Andrew Greeley study in which he "speculates that Irish sons have a compulsion to please their mothers that is built upon the mother's controlling them by starving them for affection" (324). In an essay that touches on literary manifestations of the theme, Joseph Browne argues:

> Throughout the jeremiad that is Irish history, the Irish man has been persistently degraded and emasculated by poverty and political suppression. This has resulted in a strong matriarchal element in Irish and Irish-American life and has intensified the tendency of a son to turn to his mother for understanding and compassion and to be alienated from his father. Surely Irish-American writers don't hold the patent on the theme of alienated fathers and sons, but the manner and frequency with which they develop it are uniquely Irish-American. (72)

The frequency of the motif in the novels in this survey is illustrative, Browne would doubtless agree, of its preponderance in Irish American literature as a whole. We might note, too, that for the entire canon of Irish American fiction a study of the theme holds promise of perceptions beyond the scope of the present survey.

As a largely male preserve, politics is one arena in which the father–son relationship is fought out, and an underlying reason for the conflict here may also be the patrilinear urge to extend the male line of the family and thus to ensure continued control in politics. On the other hand, sons almost always have ideas of their own about their destinies. An important example is Fleming's *All Good Men*, which has two epigraphs pertinent to the political novels as a group. From Sophocles: "What greater ornament to a son than a father's glory or to a father than a son's honorable conduct?" And from Confucius: "There are three thousand offences punished by the five punishments but the greatest of all of them is to be unfilial." In the novel itself, the major development is son Jake's reluctant initiation into ward politics, occasioned by the plot device of father Ben's going into the hospital for the amputation of a gangrenous foot – symbol, perhaps, of the corruption of ward and city politics, corruption Jake tries to leave behind. Jake begins in extreme alienation: "He only knew that he could not say yes to this man about anything" (18). And fairly early on, Ben can't fathom Jake's wish to stay out of politics, and thinks "a good lawyer, with the organization behind him, could become a millionaire in this city within ten years" (63).

While Ben and Jake eventually reconcile, a surrogate relationship is often the result of father–son differences. In Dinneen's *Ward Eight*, the most important kinship is the surrogate father–son bond between ward boss Hughie Donnelly and Big Tim, the novel's protagonist. Their closeness is an earned closeness, won only after several authoritarian episodes by Hughie and corresponding acts of rebellion by Big Tim. In O'Connor's *The Last Hurrah*, Frank Skeffington's resigned alienation from Frank Junior's amiable passion for nightclub dancing finds compensation in his nephew Adam, surrogate son, whom Frank steers through a crash course in big city politics. In Kennedy's *Billy Phelan's Greatest Game*, the mainspring of the action is the kidnapping of boss Bindy McCall's son, Charlie Boy, and Billy's role in rescuing him. Billy himself hasn't seen his own father in 22 years, but he has a surrogate father in newspaperman Martin Dougherty, whose own son "deserts" him by entering a seminary.

When Ben in *All Good Men* says, "with the organization behind him," he suggests what is so: what ward bosses wield is power. If we consider ideal political power as a means to a particular end, the public good, there are some men in these novels who try to use power properly, more who don't. On the positive side, Kelly Shannon of James D. Horan's *The Right Image*, a genuine reformer, uses his power for admirable ends; indeed, Kelly is so admirable himself – he and his family are cast in an idealized Kennedy mold, playing family lacrosse instead of touch football, for example – one must wonder why he needs image-makers at all. Emmet Shannon of Sheehan's *The Governor* goes to the mat on crucial issues and emerges with most of his principles, and some of his program, intact. Jake O'Connor in Fleming's *Rulers of the City* eventually dedicates himself to leading blacks in his city to win peacefully the victories the Irish had won by raw power.

On the negative side, raw power in these novels leaves the stench of malfeasance. In Horan's *The Right Image*, the term "power" and the concept of power form a leitmotif and are associated with images and image-making. So, Kelly Shannon, reformer, has his image marred because, on the one hand, he can say, "the trouble with the Irish was, they never knew what to do with power once they had it. They never thought of politics as an instrument of social change" (148), while on the other, he winks at how much of his own power is achieved. For example, it appears that his public relations team pretty much runs the Congressional committee that gives Kelly the power to pursue his admirable aims. In short, the end justifies the means.

On the whole, other bosses or politicians don't share Kelly's putative idea of politics as "an instrument of social change," their interest being in dispensing favors to those who've played the game and casting into outer darkness those who haven't. Big Tim O'Flaherty of Dinneen's *Ward Eight* acknowledges he's no reformer; he just wants to achieve power and will then decide how to use it – and based on the lessons he's learned from his surrogate father, Hughie Donnelly, it'll be for patronage, not programs. Similarly, creating a dilemma for many readers who admire him as a man, Frank Skeffington of O'Connor's *The Last Hurrah* seems to be largely innocent of the knowledge that his power might benefit the whole city and instead distributes personal largesse and hands out patronage.

If power and its abuse have not been confined to Irish American politicians, and they haven't, a specific religious dimension usually has. In a 1912 broadside, "Gas from a Burner," James Joyce directed his barbs at Irish individuals and institutions he believed had wronged him. Attacking an unholy alliance between Catholicism, more accurately priests, and politicians, he wrote with obvious relish and irony,

"Oh Ireland my first and only love / Where Christ and Caesar are hand in glove" (660). Held together by their common exile, the other "glue" of Irish American tribalism and hence power was its overwhelming Catholicism, imported intact and destined to undergird political ventures. Interestingly, the relationship between Catholicism and politics doesn't loom as large as Catholicism does in other Irish American fiction. To be sure, we do sometimes find Christ and Caesar hand in glove, in Fleming's *All Good Men*, for example, where "Monsignor Patrick O'Keefe [has been] spiritual director of the Thirteenth Ward for three and a half decades" (73). And there is of course some conventional piety by political figures, as when Mayor Skeffington in O'Connor's *The Last Hurrah* kneels at a bedside for prayers and, on his deathbed, receives his church's last rites. On the other hand, and this is also true of nonpolitical Irish American novels, there is considerable cynicism about, and satire of, the church, particularly the clergy. Negative attitudes toward some religious practices are seen, for instance, in the paraphernalia of devotionalism in Wilfred Sheed's *People Will Always Be Kind*. Brian Casey's Aunt Portia is a fanatical collector of holy cards and very much involved in novenas and accumulating rosaries and scapulars. In Sheehan's *The Governor*, a dozen Irish nuns attendant on the bishop are laden with "the very latest religious junk"; "plastic holy water fountains, cream colored crucifixes that glowed in the dark, [and] pastel Madonnas whose eyes pursued the beholder all over the room" (178). Jake O'Connor's priest brother, Paul, who preaches on politics in order to destroy his ward boss father in Fleming's *All Good Men*, gets his comeuppance by being committed to a mental institution, and Jake himself, in *Rulers of the City*, goes to mass only for political reasons.

The most sustained criticism of the wrong kind of church involvement is in Harry Sylvester's *Moon Gaffney*, a novel that, as a corrective, calls for a Christ and Caesar relationship with a particular end: social action. The novel is dedicated to John C. Cort, Dorothy Day, Philip Burnham, and Emerson Hayes, "all good Catholic radicals," and this alerts us to the education of the protagonist's religious and political sensibilities. A lawyer, Moon Gaffney draws his salary "from a vague appointive job at City Hall" (4), and he goes to a mission "out of a vague concern and the surer knowledge that it would be good politics to be seen at least once" (5). The novel's early pages show Moon defending priests and establish him as one of a group of youngish Catholic bigots – there is no room in their social or church circle for blacks, and they are fiercely anti-communist and anti-Semitic. They are supported by their pastor, Father Malone, who "had taken to talking about what he called 'great men' in Italy and Germany who knew exactly how to deal with Communists" (119). Near the novel's end, Moon, whose education has progressed considerably, says to the fascist Malone, "to tell the truth, I've had a bellyful of the Irish today and I'm pretty sick of them." Malone retorts: "Then this is no place for you . . . No one can sit in my rectory and malign the greatest race God ever put on earth. His own true chosen people and the great repository of the Catholic Faith on earth. You can go now" (255). And Moon does – to involvement with the radical periodical the *Catholic Worker*, and to work as a union lawyer, anathema to his former conservative friends. The novel ends with Moon ready to defend three union members for "alleged violence while picketing"; one is a communist and Moon is told, "all three are Negroes," to which he replies, in the words that end the novel, "You know, . . . I knew that was coming. Sooner or later" (289).

With or without the support of the church, the Irish faced many adversaries in their rise, including other ethnic minorities. Their strongest adversarial relationship was with Yankees and Yankee types, and is best seen in the Boston novels. Sometimes Yankees are the targets of the mildest satire; for example, some Yankee women have names like Margaret Lucille Elderberry, Phoebe-Lou Stubbs, Edna Poate, and Bernice Elkins. And some men have names like Dorcan Phelps in Sheehan's *The Governor* and Otis Ames in Higgins's *A Choice of Enemies*. When Phelps's taciturnity allows him to speak, it's usually about his ancestors, who include 52 clergymen. Phil Kinsella of O'Connor's *All in the Family* explains why the Irish find Yankees figures of fun:

> It all goes back to big daddy Calvin. . . . They don't know it but it does. Oop oop oop: Watch it! Don't have too much fun! You can see it in everything they do – even the way they eat. You ever notice that, by the way? You ought to: it's very interesting. They start out fine. They put everything on their plates very neatly . . . Not too much of anything . . . Then do you know what they do? They mix it all up. Before they put a fork to their mouths they mash everything all together on their plates. One big central ungodly mess, just so nothing will look too good or taste too good. Then they eat. (197–8)

The fun and satire are, of course, the reverse side of Irish envy and enmity, both natural enough, about Yankee position, prestige, and power. Three fictional versions of Boston mayor James Michael Curley illustrate this.

In James Carroll's *Mortal Friends*, Colman Brady, fictional right-hand man to a fictional Curley, rather enviously observes a fictional Abbott Lawrence Lowell, president of Harvard, and compares the two men, Curley and Lowell, concluding that: "Both men were brilliant and confident and enormously successful, yet in the gap between [them] the British Isles and the Free State of Ireland could be buried. It was not that Brady preferred Lowell over Curley, but that he recognized in Lowell something that he had chosen for himself long before" (166).

In O'Connor's *The Last Hurrah*, every Yankee adversary of Frank Skeffington (O'Connor's version of Curley) is a crabbed bigot except lawyer-philanthropist Nathaniel Gardiner, but even Gardiner sees Skeffington's career as a lifelong violation of the law. Skeffington, more in enmity than in envy – and also illustrating the long memories of the Irish against those who have wounded them – finds motivation for success through an example of Yankee parsimony. When his mother first arrived in America, she had been a maid in Amos Force's father's home – Amos himself is a newspaper proprietor – and was fired for "leaving the house with a grapefruit and a small jar of jelly" (59), thus prompting Skeffington's side of the vendetta. Force, for his part, can't abide that the son of a discharged employee of his father has risen to mayor. And so it goes.

Finally, in Sheehan's *The Governor*, Emmet Shannon, a reporter as a young man, writes an article based on yet another fictional Curley, an article significantly entitled "The Politics of Revenge," and portraying Curley "as a tribal hero who had squandered his remarkable talents and devoted a lifetime to settling old scores, a crippled warrior egging on an amused mob of shanty Irish in the sacking of the Yankee Troy" (88).

Sometimes existing side by side with the "politics of revenge," perhaps even part of it, we find that many Irish American politicians begin with some idealism only to end in disillusionment or worse. Their outcomes suggest that their authors, if not the characters themselves, know that a compromise with reality or even a surrender to it is essential for survival, and that there is almost always a souring of ideals. Kelly Shannon in Horan's *The Right Image* has his idealism tainted by the source of his power, and Jake O'Connor's priest brother, Paul, in Fleming's *All Good Men*, enters the political lists against his ward boss father only to be institutionalized for madness, the exact same fate meted out to Phil Kinsella in O'Connor's *All in the Family* when he tries to keep his brother Jimmy, the governor, true to the ideals he campaigned on. And Brian Casey of Sheed's *People Will*

Always Be Kind is an idealist in the civil rights and peace movements of the 1960s, but this is sharply undercut when he's described as a "professional idealist" (291).

All in all, the Fleming trilogy most effectively demonstrates idealism gone astray. Three examples: Red Burke, an honest cop close to Jake O'Connor in *King of the Hill*, is murdered for his trouble. Jake's best friend Larry Donohue is a second example from *King of the Hill*. A perverse idealist, Larry himself labels as "idiocy" his "boyish dreams of sacrifice, of daily martyrdom in pursuit of justice," and adds "that to do good in this world a man must first do evil" (94), which in Larry's case means murdering Red Burke. Thirdly, in *Rulers of the City*, Jake's wealthy wife Paula funds "Community Projects, Inc., the agency that [she] and a team of Harvard-based consultants had persuaded [Jake] to create to bring new politics to the city's neighborhoods" (42). Paula's main mission is with the city's blacks, but, we're told, "ten years of toiling in the service of this gospel had slowly eroded [her] faith," and she thinks blacks' lives are "intricate, incredible tangles of stupidity and personal hatred and frustration and – what shocked her most – self-satisfaction" (189).

Considering the strong sense of sin and capacity for guilt in the Irish psyche, it's surprisingly rare to encounter in these novels any strong sense of wrong-doing by the protagonists, never mind a sense of guilt. On the other hand, having said earlier that religion plays a relatively minor role in the works and that, as often as not, religion when it does appear is usually cynically dismissed, we probably shouldn't be surprised by the lack.

Doubtless, some of this can be accounted for by the tolerant Irish attitude toward the letter of the law. As William V. Shannon writes:

> In the course of [their] struggle for power, the Irish community evolved an attitude of tolerant acceptance of political corruption. This was neither cynicism nor hypocrisy, rather it was close to a straightforward acceptance of graft as necessary and inevitable. Graft was part of the operating compromise between the formal rules of the political system and the facts of life as it was actually lived. (63–4)

The easy acceptance of graft may account for Frank Skeffington's extraordinary deathbed scene in O'Connor's *The Last Hurrah*. There's little doubt that Frank, a thoroughly likeable, even lovable, man, has been up to his neck in one kind of political mischief or another most of his political life. Among those around his deathbed is Roger Sugrue,

Irish American but stuffy enough and assimilated enough to be more Yankee than the Yankees. Believing that Frank is unconscious, Roger says to the others about him: "Knowing what he knows now, if he had it to do all over again, there's not the slightest doubt but that he'd do it all very, very differently!" Skeffington opens his eyes and, from the depths of his pillow, says clearly, *"The hell I would"* – to which his nephew Adam reacts by wanting to cheer. And the monsignor who has administered the last rites puts his stamp of approval on Skeffington by exclaiming, "softly and delightedly, 'Oh grand, grand, grand!'" (353). These expressions of approval may mirror the attitudes of others among the fictional politicians, at least some of whom are not as likeable as Skeffington.

What these novels do have in abundance to make up for the lack of a sense of sin and guilt, contrary to what Shannon has observed of actual politicians, is cynicism, partly, as we've already seen, toward religion, and partly, as again we've already seen, toward religion's handmaiden, idealism. Ordinarily, religion and idealism might have checked and balanced the temptation to abuse power. On the whole, this was not to be in these novels, and we might consider the attitude of Senator Brian Casey, "professional idealist," in Sheed's *People Will Always Be Kind*, who, when asked about his "peace constituency," replies, "fuck the peace constituency" (316).

This attitude often finds its counterpart in the attitudes of fictional Irish Americans in these novels toward other ethnic minorities. The fictional Irish Americans demonstrate their own assimilation into mainstream America by their frequent resistance to others trying to follow the same route. It is usually claimed that the Irish showed the way for other ethnic minorities to organize and to gain power, but on the whole, in the fiction there is little enthusiasm about actually helping others to achieve legitimate goals. Perhaps this is just in the nature of the game. In Horan's *The Right Image*, Kelly Shannon, idealist, does make a real effort to join forces with black Gene Abernathy, who leads a coalition variously called "Cubans, niggers, and spicks" (35) and "black, brown, and tan" (150). And in Fleming's *Rulers of the City*, in action that takes place in 1976, after Jake O'Connor has been mayor for 14 years and presides over a city that is now only 50 percent Irish, Jake has tried to help. Police Commissioner Victor Tarentino has been "deliberately chosen [by Jake] to announce to the city – and to the Irish themselves – that the era of Celtic political domination was over" (76), and Dominick Montefiore chairs a city council that includes a black councilman.

On the other hand, there are also the expected slurs and epithets. As the Irish are "Micks," "bogtrotters," and "shanty Irish," others are "wops," "jigs," "kikes," "niggers," "spicks," "dagos," "Polacks," and "squareheads." In Dinneen's *Ward Eight*, for instance, Norah O'Flaherty, a "bogtrotter" in 1890, bitterly resents the "Eyetalians" who start to move into her ward; then, when Sicilians edge in, the Irish and Italians make common cause against them. Moon Gaffney is well on the road to being radicalized when he takes on the cause of Italians and blacks, but it's at the cost of being eased out of his political base, booted out of his church, and ostracized by his former friends. Finally, Fleming's *All Good Men* has ward boss Ben O'Connor looking back on his career and ahead to what might be. He says to his son Jake:

> I think the organization's more important. What were we before we pulled together? A bunch of crummy ditchdiggers and hod carriers living in cold-water flats ... Sure, I'm American, Irish-American. If that doesn't mean something to you it means something to me. For Christ's sake, you think it don't mean something to the wops, when you yell Italian-American to them. Or the Polacks when you say Polish-American. How the hell did we get where we are but by sticking together and bulletvoting just like they will *if* we give them the chance. (145)

In O'Connor's *The Last Hurrah*, Frank Skeffington is indeed chieftain of his tribe, a diminishing one, but he's canny enough to know that he can't just ignore other ethnic minorities, and he doesn't. However, with even his loose coalition against a Yankee coalition, Skeffington loses his last election, his last hurrah, partly because he has lost the youth vote among his nominal constituents, and partly because, as O'Connor appears to believe, by the mid-1950s there is no longer a real role for a chieftain and a machine to dole out patronage – welfare and employment opportunities – that role having been taken over by government programs and bureaucracies, a reformed civil service, labor unions, and especially the programs of Roosevelt's New Deal. If we put together O'Connor's 1956 version of events and the decline of one kind of Irish American politics with some remarks by Daniel Patrick Moynihan in 1978, we might conclude that the Irish American political novel, to the extent that it's been rooted in one set of actualities, is nearing an end. However, it's at least equally valid to argue that what's happening is not cessation but gradual change. A 1978 article by Frank Lynn entitled "Decline of the Irish-American in New York Politics" offers statistics and analysis of that decline. Moynihan, however, views this development as "the normal sequence of ethnic and social groups moving through the system." The piece ends: "But, despite all the talk about assimilation and [the search for] security, Senator Moynihan, like other Irish-American survivors in politics, wasn't ready to drop completely his Irish-American identity. 'You're not going to put me down as completely assimilated – I'm semi-assimilated,' he said" (D8).

Similarly, George V. Higgins's 1984 Irish American political novel, *A Choice of Enemies*, dramatizes at least semi-assimilation. Despite a cast of characters with Irish name after Irish name and enough corruption to satisfy any commission looking for it, this is not an Irish American political novel as, let's say, *Ward Eight* and *The Last Hurrah* are. The confession of protagonist Bernie Morgan about his own ethnicity intimates as much. Morgan says that he's:

> mostly Scotch and English on my father's side, and about a quarter Irish and God knows what else on my mother's . . . But just about the time I showed up in politics, Tobin here and J. Howard McGrath and Farly, Jim Farly, and Frank Murphy and all of them fine broths of lads in Washington was into politics and elbowing folks aside to make room for all the other Irishmen that wanted to get in. And that was going on here [Boston]. And I look Irish, and I drink like people more or less expect an Irishman to drink, and I found I got along all right with the micks who thought I was one anyway, so, noticing no reason to correct them, I took me place in line and waited for me proper turn. And here I am. (280)

As Daniel Casey and I have written elsewhere: "So in the normal course of events, older issues of politics and religion, for instance, are transmuted and find new manifestations in writing of matters and in ways that could not have been even imaginable or found acceptable in the nineteenth century or earlier twentieth century" (3).

After all, with fewer than 20 serious Irish American political novels written from 1902 until the present, we have hardly seen the end of new possibilities in political fiction or in fiction in which politics figures prominently. Moreover, the current influx of thousands of legal and illegal Irish immigrants into the United States promises additional variations. Doubtless, William Kennedy, probably today's most important Irish American novelist, would subscribe to the view that much remains to be said. The following exchange appears in a Kennedy interview with Peter Quinn:

INTERVIEWER: A final question. We've talked about the "Irish-American experience," literary and otherwise. I don't know if we've come to any conclusion but, in your opinion, what is it that unites us?
KENNEDY: What unites us? It's song, drink, wit, and guilt.
INTERVIEWER: No politics?
KENNEDY: That's included in all four. (81)

Note

This essay originally appeared in *MELUS* 18:1 *Irish-American Literature* (Spring 1993): 47–60 and is reprinted with their permission.

References and further reading

Browne, Joseph. "The Greening of America: Irish American Writers." *Journal of Ethnic Studies* 2 (1975): 71–6.

Carroll, James. *Mortal Friends*. Boston: Little, Brown, 1978.

Casey, Daniel J., and Robert E. Rhodes. "The Next Parish: An Introduction." In *Modern Irish-American Fiction: A Reader*. Eds Daniel J. Casey and Robert E. Rhodes. Syracuse: Syracuse University Press, 1989. 1–21.

Dinneen, Joseph F. *Ward Eight*. New York: Harper, 1936.

Dunne, Finley Peter. "Archey Road." In *Modern Irish-American Fiction: A Reader*. Eds Daniel J. Casey and Robert E. Rhodes. Syracuse: Syracuse University Press, 1989. 23–5.

Fleming, Thomas J. *All Good Men*. Garden City, NY: Doubleday, 1961.

Fleming, Thomas J. *King of the Hill*. New York: New American Library, 1965.

Fleming, Thomas J. *Rulers of the City*. Garden City, NY: Doubleday, 1977.

Higgins, George V. *A Choice of Enemies*. New York: Knopf, 1984.

Horan, James D. *The Right Image*. (1st edn 1967.) New York; Dell, 1968.

Joyce, James. "Gas from a Burner." In *The Portable James Joyce*. Ed. Harry Levin. New York: Viking, 1947. 660–2.

Kennedy, William. *Billy Phelan's Greatest Game*. (1st edn 1978.) New York: Penguin, 1983.

Lynn, Frank. "Decline of the Irish-American in New York Politics." *New York Times* (April 10, 1978): D8.

McGoldrick, Monica. "Irish Families." In *Ethnicity and Family Therapy*. Eds Monica McGoldrick, John K. Pearce, and Joseph Giordano. New York: Guilford, 1982. 310–39.

McIntyre, John T. *The Ragged Edge: A Tale of Ward Life and Politics*. New York: McClure, Phillips, 1902.

O'Connor, Edwin. *The Last Hurrah*. (1st edn 1956.) New York: Bantam, 1957.

O'Connor, Edwin. *All in the Family*. (1st edn 1966.) New York: Bantam, 1967.

Quinn, Peter. "William Kennedy: An Interview." *Recorder* 1 (1985): 65–81.

Shannon, William V. *The American Irish: A Political and Social Portrait*. (1st edn 1963.) New York: Collier, 1974.

Sheed, Wilfrid. *People Will Always Be Kind*. New York: Farrar, Straus and Giroux, 1973.

Sheehan, Edward R. F. *The Governor; Being an Embittered and Bemused Account of the Life and Times of the Brother of the Irish Christ*. (1st edn 1970.) New York: Signet, 1971.

Sylvester, Harry. *Moon Gaffney*. New York: Henry Holt, 1947.

US Department of Commerce. *1989 Statistical Abstract of the United States*. Washington, DC: Government Printing Office, 1989.

Grandmothers and Rebel Lovers: Archetypes in Irish American Women's Poetry

Patricia Monaghan

A canon is forming in Irish American literary studies. Who is to be taught in surveys of Irish America, who included in bibliographies? To whom are dissertations to be devoted, to whose work should journals pay mind? Like all political processes, canonization has its special procedures. Veneration must precede beatification which, in turn, precedes canonization; and the list must shorten at each stage so that the finally elect are indeed the holiest or, in this case, the most distinguished. Selected lists of the beatified who are promoted for elevation are now being published with some regularity. John Duff offers a slate of Eugene O'Neill, F. Scott Fitzgerald, James Farrell, and John O'Hara (22). William Shannon can go with O'Neill and O'Hara, but argues for Finley Peter Dunne and Philip Barry (254). Andrew Greeley plumps for Farrell, O'Hara and Fitzgerald, but insists as well on Edwin O'Connor and J. F. Powers (254).

But even the Chicago machine would take note of a problem here. Where are the women? Where are Carson McCullers, Joyce Carol Oates, Mary McCarthy? Where are Mary Gordon, Helen Vendler, Tess Gallagher? What happened to Flannery O'Connor, Kate Chopin, and Margaret Mitchell? How about Nelly Bly, Maeve Brennan, Margaret Culkin Banning?

As the canon has been forming, criticism of the Irish American literary tradition has invariably focused on male writers. For instance, in the otherwise fine resource *Irish American Fiction* (Casey and Rhodes), only 15 percent – 8 out of 52 – of the authors listed are women. Of the male authors, one – William Alfred – is deemed worthy of inclusion solely on the basis of a single six-page article in the *Atlantic Monthly*, while another, Joe Flaherty, makes it on the grounds of having produced a single novel. Surely there are women too who boast such résumés.

Not only is the percentage skewed, so is the critical attention awarded each author. Only Elizabeth Cullinan merits a whole essay to herself. Most of the remaining women – Ellin MacKay Berlin, Mary Doyle Curran, Mary Deasy, Mary McCarthy, Ruth McKenney, and Betty Smith – are crammed into a single article. And Flannery O'Connor – arguably the most important writer of the bunch? She's merely listed in the bibliography; no mention of her work illuminates the text.

Why this disproportion? Do Irish American women not write? Do they choose novenas over novellas, the confessional booth over the confessional poem, communion over communication? Or are they all so dreadful, so devoid of literary talent, that they are fittingly cloistered from critical mention? Hardly. In fiction we can claim, in the first rank, Kate (O'Flaherty) Chopin, Mary McCarthy, Joyce Carol Oates, and Flannery O'Connor. Close behind are Kay Boyle ("Year Before Last"), Maureen Howard (*Pick Up to End*), Bernice Kelly (*Sweet Beulah Land*), Maureen Daly (*Seventeenth Summer*), Kathleen Coyle (*The Widow's House*), Betty Smith (*A Tree Grows in Brooklyn*), and Elizabeth Gurley Flynn (*The Rebel Girl*). More recently, Irish America has given us Elizabeth Cullinan, Mary Gordon, Alice McDermott, Alice Munro, Maeve Brennan, and Mary Doyle Curran.

Among nonfiction writers, there's Nelly Bly (Elizabeth Cochrane), who exposed the terror of the insane on Riker's Island and went around the world in under 80 days; more recently there's Korean War correspondent Maggie Higgins and Vietnam correspondent Frances Fitzgerald (*Fire in the Lake*). Among playwrights, there's Ruth MacKenney (*My Sister Eileen*) and Megan Duffy Terry (*Viet Rock*). There's also Mary Coyle Chase, who wrote *Harvey* – no surprise to find an Irish American woman writing about invisible creatures. There's biographer Katherine O'Keefe O'Mahony, critic Helen Hennessy Vendler, essayists Anna Quindlen and Mary Maguire Colum, and children's writers Martha Finley, Ann Nolan Clark, and Elizabeth Yates.

How many writers does it take to make a tradition? Is this list not substantial enough, both in length and in eminences, to be called that? But no. By the definition of Irish American literature, these authors can't fit. They don't write about classic Irish American themes; for example, "the solidarity of male companionship and the at least incipient violence accompanying drink and pub life," as Robert E. Rhodes put it in the *Irish Literary Supplement* (22). The problem is women writers don't create characters that reflect the lives of critics, as Shannon (254) claims James Farrell does: "Studs [Lonigan] is one of the major fictional creations of the twentieth century. Few college-educated Irish Catholics reach manhood without making his acquaintance." A large proportion, let us remember, never reach manhood at all.

If women don't write about pub life, they also don't address some of the other themes said to define the Irish American writer. They don't write about long-suffering mothers; perhaps they're too close to becoming long-suffering mothers. They don't write much about guilt; there is, in fact, an almost overbearingly cheery guiltlessness to some of them. They hardly ever write about priests. Thus they have been discounted in studies of the Irish American tradition.

The tradition could be enlarged to include women, but first we must discern what tradition, if any, these women writers do share. But if there is an Irish American women's tradition – and this essay of course argues that there is – it's extraordinarily hard to trace. Many of the mechanisms charted by Joanna Russ in *How to Suppress Women's Writing* are found in action here. There is, as a primary problem, the unavailability of the work. Books by women writers pass out of print all too quickly; it is difficult to find a book by Phyllis McGinley today, or most of Kay Boyle's works. If it's difficult to write a critical article about someone you've never read, it's even harder to follow in the footsteps of the invisible. This Russ calls *lack of models*. "When the memory of one's predecessors is buried," she says, "the assumption persists that there were none and each generation of women believes itself to be faced with the burden of doing everything for the first time . . . Without models, it's hard to work; without a context, difficult to evaluate; without peers, nearly impossible to speak" (93–5).

Not only is it difficult to locate the works of many women of Irish heritage, it's hard to locate the women at all. It is difficult to use standard references to search them out because of the patriarchal tradition of stripping women of their birth names in order to label them with a husband's patronymic; thus may Miss Mayo become

Mrs Hapsburg and lose her ethnic identity. Conversely, women of other heritages may marry Irish, change their names, and thus thwart the researcher. Finally, because the tradition is uncharted, biographical references simply fail to mention the ethnic heritage of many women who should, in fact, be categorized as Irish American writers.

Yet there is a tradition, one ripe for reclaiming. In poetry alone, a galaxy of Irish American women writers flourished in the middle of the nineteenth century. Most prominent were Alice and Phoebe Cary, both widely praised in their lifetimes. Alice, the older, was "The Singer" of John Greenleaf Whittier's famous poem; she was the hostess of New York's most significant literary salon from the 1850s to the 1870s. A feminist, she wrote in female personae, including that of the unwed mother, "not mother, wife, never bride," who commits suicide. Another of her personae was the woman who retained her strength after marriage:

> We've married! Oh pray that our love do not fail!
> I have wings flattened down and hid under my veil:
> They are subtle as light – you can never undo them,
> And swift in their flight – you can never pursue them,
> And spite of all clasping and spite of all bands,
> I can slip like a shadow, a dream, from your hands.
> (Mainiero: I, 309)

Phoebe Cary, less prolific than Alice but considered one of the century's finest parodists, was deservedly renowned for her lampoons of Longfellow. Devoted to her sister, she died only five months after Alice (Mainiero: I, 311).

Like the Carys, Anna Charlotte Lynch Botta was hostess to one of the nineteenth century's most important literary salons. She was a prominent poet; one of her books, which influenced Poe, went through three editions. She was also the author of the *Handbook of Universal Literature*, the classic college text through the end of the century. She is practically unknown today (Mainiero: I, 196).

Some of the nineteenth century's best-known Irish American poets wrote religious verse. One was Katherine Eleanor Conway, whose nearly 20 books concentrated on the question of women's role in the home and the church; she found that "the highest good – for a woman" was "simply, the perfection of her womanhood." Emphasizing "large-hearted simplicity" and "lack of self-consciousness," she advised women to attempt to change nothing in this world but the habits of their husbands and the diapers of their children. When she attempted to take on grander themes, the results were often embarrassing, as when the "Little Dying Son" sees God as he passes away: "His arm is underneath my head! – Oh, it is splendid! – being dead" (Mainiero: I, 394).

The same sort of sentiments inspired Mary Elizabeth McGrath Blake (Mainiero: I, 173), widely published in the latter half of the century in newspapers and magazines. She too devoted her verse to the theme of men's need to serve God, and women's need to serve men. Similarly, Jessie Fremont O'Donnell (Mainiero: III, 192) wrote conventional, hymn-like paeans to God in nature; she specialized in occasional poems on Catholic holidays.

In the twentieth century, the best-known Irish American woman poet was Phyllis McGinley, the astonishingly prolific Pulitzer Prize winner. It's said that she intended to be a serious poet until she discovered the *New Yorker* paid more for light verse than for heavy. Once she had found her voice, her wit filled dozens of books from the 1930s through the 1950s. Her epigrams are memorable gems:

> "How To Tell Portraits from Still-Lifes"
> Ladies whose necks are long and swanny
> Are always signed Modigliani.
> But flowers explosive in a crock?
> Braque.
>
> (69)

> "The Absolute Law of Evelyn Waugh"
> Englishmen of the upper classes
> Are more amusing than the masses.
>
> (72)

And, from her family portraits, "The Adversary":

> A mother's hardest to forgive.
> Life is the fruit she longs to hand you,
> Ripe on a plate. And while you live,
> Relentlessly she understands you.
>
> (44)

Like the others we've considered, McGinley's oeuvre is being quickly lost. She died as recently as 1978, but although she remains a popular children's author, it's increasingly difficult to find her works for adult readers; she is rarely mentioned in critical analyses; she is dismissed by those teaching survey courses. Despite her renown during her lifetime, which certainly more than matches that of William Alfred or Joe Flaherty, she is fast becoming as invisible as the Carys or Anna Botta.

Examining these nineteenth- and early twentieth-century poets, we find two divergent types. On the one hand is the poet who is sentimental and, to a large extent, hypocritical. Such a poet struggles to affirm society's norms while diverging from them personally: herself unmarried, she writes endless tracts in praise of marriage; traveling ceaselessly, she lauds the home. If there are women writing in this tradition still, they are not in the secular mainstream of literature. There we can, however, find the heirs to the tradition's second stream: the woman who tests norms or flouts them, women who forge independent existences and independent poetic identities. The life and works of Alice and Phoebe Cary, Anna Lynch Botta, and Phyllis McGinley correspond to and prefigure those of today.

But we cannot say that they influence today's poets. In fact, contemporary Irish American women poets, however ethnically self-conscious they may be, write without acknowledging these foremothers – very likely without knowledge of them. Thus this essay does not attempt to trace direct connections between the poets of yesterday and those of today. Instead, it relies on analysis of shared archetypes in contemporary work. For, unaware though they may be of their ethnic literary tradition, today's women poets still reach back, through the family, to a common ground. In their heritage, these women poets find similar material. Just as the Irish American man writes of the pub because he knows it so well, his sister poet writes of grandmothers and rebel lovers because she knows those characters so intimately.

We will deal here with the works of only five contemporary Irish American women poets: Tess Gallagher, Kathy Callaway, Mary Swander, Ethna McKiernan, and Renny Golden. But there are others. Some are obviously Irish: Julie O'Callaghan, Nuala Archer, Maura Stanton, Patricia McGinty, Patricia Kirkpatrick, Julia Connor, Susan Donnelly. There are others, however, who claim an Irish ethnicity but whose names are less obviously so: Jody Aliesan, Patricia Barone, Colette Inez, Elisavietta Richie, and Patrice Vicchione all have recently identified themselves to publishers as Irish American poets (Truesdale: p.c.). Therefore, this discussion of shared images in Irish American women poets' works is intended to be not exhaustive, but introductory.

Within the works of our five selected women, two figures appear astonishingly often: the grandmother and the rebel lover. Reflective of the poets' ethnic background, these figures are also parts of their dreaming or creative selves – alter egos of the poets. The poet had a grandmother; she may have known or loved rebels. But, more deeply, the poet is the grandmother; she is the rebel. When she writes about them, she is writing about herself, about her desire to stay within the roles assigned to her and her desire to break free of them. The figures are deeply ambiguous and self-contradictory. While it might seem that the grandmother would represent tradition against the rebel's resistance to it, the opposite is also true: the grandmother is the adventurer who left her native land, while the rebel is a traditional character in Irish history. These multivalent characters offer a rich field for the poet to work.

First let us consider the grandmother. For many contemporary writers, she is the last Irish-born member of the family; even when she is not herself Irish-born, she stands generations closer to Ireland than does the poet, thus forging a link between Ireland and America. The grandmother is intensely familiar – and at the same time, she embodies the strangeness of a land abandoned. Born in Ireland – that land we hear described with such soft wistfulness when we are children – she leaves it. She becomes, thus, a liminal figure: the immigrant, no longer at home in Ireland but never fully American. The fact of immigration remains close to our poetic consciousness, providing a primary image for the search for new ground. The grandmother amply represents the complexity of creation. She is the ancestor, and she is an adventurer; similarly, her granddaughter poets innovate within traditions.

Ethna McKiernan's "Going Back" recounts a visit to the very place from which her grandmother departed for America. She stands looking toward America, her own homeland:

> where you stood,
> One hand raised to shade your eyes
> against the harsh Atlantic
> Grinding shoulders with the rocks below . . .
> I see the girl you were
> walking back alone to your father's house
> Caught between two hungers.
>
> (68)

The poet, re-enacting the grandmother's gestures, finds similarities between them: "my bones were formed / from that same air / that made your bones first stir" (69). Like the grandmother, the poet finds that she "cannot make my roots take hold" in Ireland, and acknowledges that she feels similarly rootless in America. For McKiernan, the grandmother is the part of the psyche that remains an immigrant, forever homeless, forever seeking shelter, forever abandoning that shelter. She is a strong image of the woman poet who enters new territories of language and the spirit, escaping the hunger of women's social repression while seeking to satisfy her own artistic hunger.

Mary Swander, whose book *Succession* concentrates on her Irish heritage, depicts the grandmother as holding the secrets to the family system, the sense of heritage that is both limiting and consoling:

> I simply follow the family pattern
> My Irish grandmothers knit into sweaters
> for their sons.
>
> (49)

To Swander, the grandmother is the primary link in the family chain, the woman who passes on not only life but the rituals of the family, whether that be brushing one's hair at night ("Dutton's Place"), or keeping the house in order ("Winter, 1975"). She – and the family she represents – both holds one back, and holds one up:

> My grandmother's arm wrapped around me,
> holding me, propping me up in the air,
> my shoulder locked into hers, her elbow bent like a hinge.
>
> (29)

So important is the grandmother image to Swander that one entire section of her collection *Driving the Body Back* is devoted to it. In this book the old woman dies – but not without a fight:

> Her dying was so long and hard
> the priests came around
> three different times
> running through all your cotton balls.
>
> (73)

Frail as she is, old as she is, she takes a long time dying. She holds onto life fiercely. Where McKiernan sees in the grandmother a rootlessness which mirrors her own, Swander sees a reflection of strength that inspires her:

> She called my name and I came to her . . . I wanted to stay there
>   and sing to her.
> I saw myself floating away with her . . . wrapped in her skin.
>
> (*Succession*: 36)

For Kathy Callaway, the grandmother offers a vision of lost family wholeness; she is a distant character in the family drama, but one whose life holds hope that meaning will emerge from it. Grandmother, a pioneer who traveled west in search of a better life, is a woman whose existence remains mysterious even to her daughter. When her missing journal is found, the poet describes it to her mother: "stained like an old map, and over the landmass, / your mother's writing leans like Conestogas – / clear, windblown, so hopeful – " (12) She hopes that the grandmother's restoration into the family presence – by the proxy of her diary – will somehow restore not just the family closeness that was lost, but even the voice with which mother and daughter can communicate. "You call me / by my own name now, it's *daughter*, the word / falling through these pages like streaks on a pine-forest floor, / prints disappearing behind the walker" (13). Callaway identifies a hopeful vigor with the grandmother figure; she, in turn, identifying with the grandmother, hopes to stake out new emotional terrain within the family.

The grandmother substitutes for the mother in some of these poems. For "mother" is, to a woman poet, a highly charged relationship, hard to sort out and even harder to write about, while "grandmother" offers an accessible, expressible form of the mother. Mama Mor, Ethna McKiernan calls her, "great mother," an expression of both tenderness and distance. Both connection and freedom from constraint are important in this relationship, the latter (as McGinley has shrewdly pointed out) being notoriously hard to gain from one's mother. And because it is relatively easy to gain distance from one's grandmother, the poet reaches instead to connect. No matter how unconventional the grandmother in fact may have been, she represents the force of heritage to these poets. To McKiernan, the grandmother is the heritage of not-fitting, of being torn between the hunger to stay and the hunger to move on; to Swander, it is the heritage of bonding and bondedness; to Callaway, the heritage of distance and disappearance, of aloofness and dependency. The grandmother is a contradictory image, representing two things that are opposed yet contained within a single being. The poet, reaching out to her heritage, finds both sameness and difference in the grandmother.

There is another, complementary figure who haunts the poems of Irish American women poets; we can call him – for usually it is a man – the rebel. Not necessarily a political rebel, this character sometimes takes that form; sometimes the rebel is merely a wild or lawless person, a "rebel without a cause." Just as the grandmother is a mutated form of the mother, the rebel can be construed as a variant father image, one who can encompass the expression of both anger and sexuality. Both are parts of the poet's Irish heritage and both, as we have mentioned, are contradictory characters. If the grandmother represents the contradictory bonds and supports of heritage – both holding up and holding back – the rebel represents the freedom and pain that come from breaking free of such contradictions. Ironically, for the Irish American, the rebel is also part of her heritage. In breaking out, in breaking free, the rebel is utterly traditional.

In the work of Renny Golden, the rebel makes many appearances. Herself an activist and author of books on America's Sanctuary movement and on the women of San Salvador, Golden consciously allies herself with the rebel:

> Twenty years ago,
> I wanted to know a saint,
> now it's a revolutionary.
> Someone who means the part
> about losing your life to find it.
> (*Unlacing*: 53)

Golden's words, addressed to the rebel, are deeply erotic, for the rebel seems to embody passion. She writes of the rebel for whom "Passion has no coals, only this flaming," who "pluck[s] your life from the fragrant air" (*Struggle*: 21). However passionate, Golden's rebels are ascetic ones, fervently in love with their ideals. The rebel in Golden's work is always a rebel with a cause – a cause that gives self-sacrifice meaning. Such devotion allows the rebel to attain a sense of purpose in which art and politics unite: "you, shining in the new light, have become the song" (*Unlacing*: 53). Love is the source of Golden's attraction to the rebel, for to rebel against injustice is for her a loving gesture that in turn makes the rebel worthy of love.

For Callaway, too, the rebel is connected with passion. To her, the very act of sex entails rebellion. "It's never America, that place where you unfolded your fresh body," (3) she begins, pointing out that the lovers bring all the boundaries of class and culture to bed with them. But however undemocratic the sexual act is, she finds in it an anarchic power that obviates the past and the messages it writes upon our bodies: "My brother, there is no America of the body. / We cross these borders to obliterate the design." Every act of love is an act of rebellion against the structures of a world in which people are divided; sex is thus the ultimate act of the rebel.

The same idea appears in McKiernan, where the rebel appears as the adulterous lover – "too beautiful, too cruel" – who, himself rebelling against his marital promises, puts the poet in a morally ambiguous situation. Like a political rebel who must believe sufficiently in a cause to accept the innocent sufferings it creates, the "other woman" of McKiernan's poem is aware of the pain she causes the lover's wife: "At night he comes to you once more, / and you are not innocent" (61). The wife in the poem is distinguished by the fact that "everything here has roots," while the poet is rootless. The "other woman," in joining her lover in a rebellion against marriage, is shut out of the gentle world of her rival – a world she both desires and despises. McKiernan's rebel, while eroticized, is also a demonized vision of the disruptive power of sexual knowledge.

In the works of Tess Gallagher, undoubtedly the best-known Irish American poet writing today, we find several incarnations of the rebel. In one appearance, he is simply lawless, albeit mysteriously attractive: "the kidnapper" who draws the woman to himself with innocent questions. Suddenly she finds herself beside a road, apparently abandoned by her abductor. When at last he returns, he lovingly lifts her back to life:

> "You must have been cold," he says,
> covering me with his handkerchief,
> "You must have given me up."
> (*Instructions*: 11)

In this dreamy poem, the powerful and dangerous figure of the rebel is intensely seductive; he whispers her name and "says it again, the name of someone he loves" (12). Although frightened, the poet responds; at the end, it is clear she has been waiting for him.

In another poem, set in Belfast, the rebel is more tangible. A political rebel this time, he steps from dreams to show the poet, through a strife-torn city, his personal history:

> You are leading me back to the burned arcade
> where you said I stood with you
> in your childhood last night, your childhood

which includes me now,
as surely as the look of the missing face
between the rows of houses . . .
Now when you find me next in the dream,
this boundary will move with us.
We will both come back.

(*Stars*: 24)

Experiencing the city through the rebel's eyes, the poet becomes part of his dream as much as he is part of hers. In both cases the rebel is outside the poet, a figure both menacing and enticing.

But in Gallagher's most famous poem, "Instructions to the Double," the rebel is clearly part of the poet. No longer someone outside, luring her into rebelliousness, the "double" is an androgynous being, "little mother of silences, little father of half-belief" (*Instructions*: 67). The poet sends the double out into the world to "get into some trouble I'll have to account for." While the poet is a tame being, with "hands trained to an ornate piano in a house on the other side of the country," the double is "Lizzie Borden. Show him your axe, the one they gave you with a silver blade, your name engraved there like a whisper of their own."

And what is the double to do on her "mission"? "Go / to the temple of the poets," and "Say all the last words / and the first: hello, goodbye, yes, / I, no, please, always, never" (68). It is the rebel-double, this "slut, mother, / virgin, whore, daughter, adulteress, lover, / mistress, bitch, wife, cunt," who, unconstrained by social norms, offers the poet a chance to transcend the world of "the country-club poets":

It's a dangerous mission. You
could die out there. You
could live forever.

(68)

This is the apotheosis of the rebel in contemporary Irish American women's writing. Acknowledged as part of the poet herself, the divisive yet dynamic rebel powers the woman into a new relationship with language itself.

These two figures have much in common. The rebel, who takes life, also offers immortality in a cause greater than the self; the grandmother, who helped give us life, eventually must die. The figures are more similar than they seem. The grandmother rebelled against her life in Ireland and left to establish a new family, a new life, in America.

The rebel, conversely, is fully alive only in opposition to society and therefore cannot really move beyond it. Each partakes of the other and, similarly, within the Irish American woman poet, contradictory forces struggle to be heard. In writing, she must both acknowledge tradition and break with it; she must reach back into the family and reach out into the world; she must make order out of passion. From her ethnic heritage, and from her dreams, she draws forth these two figures to help her.

Note

This essay originally appeared in *MELUS* 18:1 *Irish American Literature* (Spring 1993): 83–94 and is reprinted here with their permission.

References and further reading

Callaway, Kathy. *Heart of the Garfish*. Pittsburgh: University of Pittsburgh Press, 1982.

Casey, Daniel J., and Robert Rhodes. *Irish-American Fiction: Essays in Criticism*. New York: AMS, 1979.

Duff, John B. *The Irish in the United States*. Belmont, CA: Wadsworth, 1971.

Gallagher, Tess. *Instructions to the Double*. Port Townsend, WA: Graywolf Press, 1976.

Gallagher, Tess. *Under Stars*. Port Townsend, WA: Graywolf Press, 1978.

Golden, Renny, and Sheila Collins. *Struggle is a Name for Hope*. Minneapolis, Minnesota: West End Press, 1982.

Golden, Renny. "Renny Golden." In *Unlacing: Ten Irish-American Women Poets*. Ed. Patricia Monaghan. Fairbanks, AK: Fireweed Press, 1987.

Greeley, Andrew. *That Most Distressful Nation: The Taming of the American Irish*. Chicago: Quadrangle, 1972.

McGinley, Phyllis. *Times Three*. New York: Viking, 1961.

McKiernan, Ethna. *Caravan*. Minneapolis: Midwest Villages and Voices, 1989.

Mainiero, Lina. *American Women Writers: A Critical Reference Guide*. 4 vols. New York: Frederick Unger, 1979.

Rhodes, Robert. "J. P. Donleavy's Sins and Graces." *Irish Literary Supplement* 6.1 (1987): 7.

Russ, Joanna. *How to Suppress Women's Writing*. Austin: University of Texas Press, 1983.

Shannon, William. *The American Irish*. New York: Macmillan, 1963.

Swander, Mary. *Driving the Body Back*. New York: Knopf, 1986.

Swander, Mary. *Succession*. Athens, GA: University of Georgia Press, 1979.

Chapter 14

Emergent Ethnic Literatures: Native American, Hispanic, Asian American

Cyrus R. K. Patell

> Basketball is like this for Walt Whitman. He watches these Indian boys
> as if they were the last bodies on earth. Every body is brown!
> Walt Whitman shakes because he believes in God.
> Walt Whitman dreams of the Indian boy who will defend him,
> trapping him in the corner, all flailing arms and legs
> and legendary stomach muscles . . .
>
> There is no place like this. Walt Whitman smiles.
> Walt Whitman shakes. This game belongs to him.
>
> (Alexie, "Defending": 15)

These whimsical lines from Sherman Alexie's poem "Defending Walt Whitman" (1996) dramatize the predicament faced not only by Native American writers, but also by Asian Americans, Hispanic Americans, and indeed all US writers who belong to emergent literary traditions. As a Spokane/Coeur d'Alene Indian, Alexie is playing a game in which he is the underdog and Whitman the favorite: Whitman dominates the landscape of US poetry; his powerful shots "strik[e] the rim so hard that it sparks"; the "game belongs to him." The poem imagines "Indian boys" who must defend against Whitman, who must prevent him from scoring by blocking his shots. Yet it also imagines other Indians, those who are Whitman's team-mates: "Some body throws a

351

crazy pass," Alexie writes, "and Walt Whitman catches it with quick hands." These Indians work with Whitman; they defend *him* against those who oppose him. The poem pays homage to Whitman by adopting his free verse idiom and by describing the game from his perspective. At the same time, however, it shows us a Whitman who is out of place, who is awed by the "twentieth-century warriors" surrounding him, whose "beard is ludicrous on the reservation," who "stands / at center court while the Indian boys run from basket to basket," who "cannot tell the difference between / offense and defense." The poem's title is a pun, simultaneously with Whitman and against him. The poem celebrates Whitman, even as it seeks to contain him within the context of "a reservation summer basketball court."

The Chinese American novelist Maxine Hong Kingston achieves a similar effect when she gives the protagonist of her novel *Tripmaster Monkey: His Fake Book* (1989) the name "Wittman Ah Sing." Both tipping her hat to the great poet of American individualism and gently mocking him, Kingston's novel depicts a young poet-playwright who wants to be another Whitman – a Great American Artist – but finds that first he must disengage himself from the subordinate place that American culture has made for him on the basis of his ethnicity. *Tripmaster Monkey*'s narrative registers the pain of being caught between two cultures. Wittman wants to define an identity for himself that can truly be called "Chinese American," but to do so he must prevent the "Chinese" from being marginalized by the "American." In the course of the novel, Wittman discovers that his cultural identity is necessarily hybrid, and he suspects that every American identity is, in fact, so, though mainstream American culture has worked hard to deny that fact.

Alexie and Kingston thus dramatize the problem faced by all US minority cultures including the three whose literatures we are considering here: how to transform themselves from marginalized cultures, often regarded as "foreign" or "un-American," into *emergent* cultures capable of challenging and reshaping the US mainstream. My conception of cultural emergence here draws upon Raymond Williams's analysis of the dynamics of modern culture, an analysis that has served as the foundation for minority discourse theory. Williams characterizes culture as a constant struggle for dominance in which a hegemonic mainstream – what Williams calls "the effective dominant culture" – seeks to defuse the challenges posed by both residual and emergent cultural forms (123). According to Williams, residual culture consists of those practices that are based on the "residue of . . . some previous social and cultural institution or formation," but continue to play a role in the present, while emergent culture serves as the site or set of sites where "new meanings and values, new practices, new relationships and kinds of relationships are continually being created" (122–3). Both residual and emergent cultural forms can only be recognized and indeed conceived in relation to the dominant: each represents a form of negotiation between the margin and the center over the right to control meanings, values, and practices.

Like much early poststructuralist literary criticism, emergent US literatures set themselves the task of identifying and deconstructing modes of binary thinking in which the two halves of an opposition are not created equal. For many minority writers, this process meant understanding the ways in which they and those like them were portrayed as different, incomprehensible, inscrutable, uncivilized – in short, portrayed as "others" who could not be assimilated. Immigrants in the early decades of the twentieth century were described as "hyphenated Americans," and President Woodrow Wilson famously declared that "any man who carries a hyphen about with him carries a dagger that he is ready to plunge into the vitals of this Republic whenever he gets ready" ("For the League of Nations," speech delivered 6 September 1919, Des Moines, IA). This is the impasse of hyphenation, the idea that the American who belongs to a minority group is caught between two incompatible identities, the minority (Asian, Black, Hispanic, Native) and the majority (American). Identity becomes a matter of either/or: either "American" or whatever it is that precedes the hyphen.

The Chinese American writer Frank Chin calls it the problem of the "dual personality." Like Leslie Marmon Silko, Chin traces the source of this bifurcation of subjectivity to the imposition of Christian beliefs onto cultures that are founded upon other religious and mythological traditions. In his manifesto "Come All Ye Asian American Writers of the Real and the Fake," published in the anthology *The Big Aiiieeeee!* (1991), Chin argued that:

> the Chinese American "identity crisis," the Japanese American "dual personality," the yellow/white either/or that distinguishes Christian Chinese American autobiography from the work of the Chinese American writers included in this volume is the product of the Christian missionaries who dominated Chinatown history before the war, and their self-serving imaginative biographies, autobiographies, and novels. (Chin: 14)

Indeed, the burden of the dual personality – and its roots in Christianity's missionary impulses – serves as the point of departure for many of the most prominent works of fiction produced by Asian American, Chicano/a, and Native American writers during the twentieth century: for example, Sui Sin Far's *Mrs Spring Fragrance and Other Stories* (1912), John Okada's *No-No Boy* (1957), José Antonio Villarreal's *Pocho* (1959), Rudolfo Anaya's *Bless Me, Ultima* (1972), N. Scott Momaday's *House Made of Dawn* (1968), Silko's *Ceremony*, and Louise Erdrich's *Tracks* (1988).

The potential for resistance is a crucial component of cultural emergence: according to Williams, a truly emergent culture must be "substantially alternative or oppositional" to the dominant (123), and it is an article of faith among minority discourse theorists that the experience of antagonism toward the dominant culture is an experience that all US minority cultures share. One strategy that can be found across Asian American, Chicano/a, and Native American writing is to use non-European mythological beliefs and stories in order to resist the ideologies of mainstream US culture. Native American authors draw upon what remains of their tribal cultures, in part because tribal ways represent an integral part of their personal identities, but also because their depictions of tribal cultures help to preserve them, not simply in memory but as living cultures.

Emergent ethnic writers often give prominence within their fictions to figures or places that embody the ideas of subversion and resistance. One such figure is the trickster, who appears throughout Native American tribal mythologies in such manifestations as Coyote, Crow, Jay, Hare, Loon, Raven, Spider, Wolverine, and Old Man. Sometimes a heroic, even god-like figure, the trickster can also be a liar and a cheater, a fool and a bungler, but he is almost always connected to the telling of stories. The Native American writer Gerald Vizenor (Chippewa) has argued that the trickster is a natural resource for both Native American tribal narratives and for postmodernism because he is the embodiment of deconstructive strategies – "chance and freedom in a comic sign" (Vizenor, "Trickster Discourse": 285) – and thus disrupts and resists institutionally sanctioned ways of reading. In *Love Medicine* (1984; expanded edition, 1993) and *The Bingo Palace* (1994), Louise Erdrich draws on Chippewa tales of the trickster Nanabozho to create figures of both comedy and subversion in Gerry Nanapush, a member of the radical American Indian Movement, who has a knack for escaping from prison by squeezing into unimaginably small spaces, and his son, Lipsha Morissey, who embarks on a vision-quest for three days and ends up having visions of American fast food. Vizenor draws attention to the parallels between the Native American and Chinese trickster traditions in his novel *Griever: An American Monkey King in China* (1987), whose protagonist, Griever de Hocus, a visiting professor at Zhou Enlai University in Tianjin, is described as a "mixedblood tribal trickster, a close relative to the oldmind monkeys" (34). Perhaps the best-known trickster figure in late twentieth-century American fiction is Kingston's Wittman Ah Sing, who seeks to revolutionize American literature by tapping into the transformative storytelling powers of the legendary Monkey King, Sun Wu Kong, whose adventures are chronicled in Wu-Cheng-en's sixteenth-century Chinese folk novel *Hsi Yu Chi* (translated into English as *The Journey to the West*).

For Chicano/a writers, the most potent deployment of mythical belief has been the collective reimagining of Aztlán, the Chicano/a homeland. In the Nahuatl language of ancient Mexico, "Aztlán" means "the lands to the north," and it is used by Chicanos today to refer to what is now the Southwestern United States. According to the novelist Rudolfo Anaya:

> The ancestors of the Aztecs named their homeland Aztlán and legend placed it north of Mexico. Aztlán was the place of origin, the sipapu, the Eden of those tribes. There they came to a new relationship with their god of war, Huitzilopochtli, and he promised to lead them in their migration out of Aztlán. (235)

That migration southward led to the establishment of the new Aztec nation of Tenochtitlán, which would eventually be conquered by Cortés in 1521. The modern invocation of the myth of Aztlán thus represents the conscious deployment of an ancient myth of origin for the purpose of political and cultural resistance. Chicano/a poets such as Alurista (Alberto Urista), Gloria Anzaldúa, Inés Hernández, Miguel Mendéz, and Lin Romero claim Aztlán as the source of Chicano/a culture in order to emphasize the Native American roots of Chicano/a identity and thus de-emphasize the importance of the Spanish conquistadors, the first invaders and occupiers of America, forerunners in that sense of the US government. In 1972, the radical dramatist Luis Valdez co-edited an activist anthology of Mexican American Literature entitled *Aztlán*; Anaya entitled his second novel *Heart of Aztlán* (1976) and pushed the mythopoetic techniques used in his prize-winning debut *Bless Me, Ultima* (1972) even further: in *Heart of Aztlán*, myth becomes not just a way of interpreting the world but a way of revolutionizing it.

A second strategy shared by writers from these three traditions is to understand hybridity as a crucial fact about identity and to depict the ontology of hybridity as an ontology of violence. Their writings dramatize the shortcomings of a logic that is dominant within US culture, a logic founded upon *ontological individualism*, the belief that the individual has an *a priori* and primary reality and that society is a derived, second-order construct. From Ralph Waldo Emerson to John Rawls, American theorists of individualism have typically sought to shift the ground of cultural and social inquiry from culture and society to the individual, translating moments of social choice into ones of individual choice. This methodological strategy is a literal application of the motto *e pluribus unum* – "from many, one" – which expresses the idea that the American nation is formed through the union of many individuals and peoples. In the hands of thinkers like Emerson and Rawls, the customary sense of this motto is reversed: they move from the many to the one, to the single individual, paring away differences in order to reach a common denominator that will allow them to make claims about all individuals. And one of the most powerful claims that American culture makes about individuals is that cultural hybridity is a contingent, incidental, and ultimately irrelevant aspect of individual identity.

Writers such as Momaday, Silko, Oscar Zeta Acosta, Jessica Hagedorn, and Kingston would disagree: they depict characters who seem to embody within themselves the violence implicit in Williams's conception of culture as struggle. "Decolonization is always a violent phenomenon," wrote the cultural theorist Frantz Fanon, whose work has become one of the cornerstones of contemporary postcolonial theory (Fanon: 35). Being emergent in America means recognizing that the dominant culture has transformed cultural hybridity into a state of violence, and it also means being willing to do violence, when necessary, to the traditions from which the work springs – not only the tradition of canonical American texts but also the literary, mythological, and cultural traditions that have given these writers the opportunity to be "emergent" in the first place. Frank Chin accuses Maxine Hong Kingston of attacking Chinese civilization by rewriting some of its fairy tales and myths. The novelist and critic Paula Gunn Allen (Laguna) accuses Leslie Marmon Silko (Laguna) of violating Native American religious and ethical traditions by transcribing and interpolating into her written texts stories that are meant to be spoken – and spoken only within a clan for specific purposes.

Kingston and Silko, however, take a dynamic view of traditional myth, believing it to be not a static relic of the past but an ongoing process in the present. So Kingston declares, in a personal statement included in a volume of essays on her autobiographical fantasia *The Woman Warrior: Memoirs of a Girlhood Among Ghosts* (1976):

> Sinologists have criticized me for not knowing myths and for distorting them; pirates correct my myths, revising them to make them conform to some traditional Chinese version. They don't understand that myths have to change, be useful or be forgotten. Like the people who carry them across oceans, the myths become American. The myths I write are new, American. (Kingston: 24)

Silko provides a similar answer to critics like Allen, an answer embodied in the character of Betonie, the medicine man in *Ceremony*, who includes newspapers and telephone books among his implements of magic.

For writers like Silko and Kingston, tampering with the myths and unleashing great power often means bringing to bear techniques of literary representation drawn from canonical American literature. Like Wittman Ah Sing, many of the most prominent writers in the three traditions that we are considering here have been educated in American universities and have read widely in canonical American literature and the Western literary tradition; many hold professorships of literature or creative writing in universities today. The Chicano critic Hector Calderón comments that while Chicano/a literature "may inform the dominant culture with an alternative view of the world filtered through myth and oral storytelling or offer an oppositional political perspective, this is done so from within educational institutions. Almost all Chicano/a writers of fiction have earned advanced degrees in the United States" (Calderón: 99). We must realize, writes Calderón, "how institutionally Western [Chicano/a] literature is" (99). According to Rolando Hinojosa, who like Américo Paredes taught at the University of Texas at Austin, "Chicano Literature, which at times passed itself off as a people's literature, . . . is actually a child of us, the academicians who make up one of the last privileged classes in our native land" (Hinojosa: 41). As a result of both their training and their teaching, these authors, like Kingston's Wittman, find themselves deeply influenced by canonical traditions of American, English, and European literature, and the literature they produce is almost necessarily a hybrid of mainstream and ethnic forms.

Historically, the concept of hybridity was a conceptual leap forward for theorists of minority discourse, postcoloniality, and emergent literatures, opening up what Homi Bhabha has called "the Third Space of enunciation." In his study *The Location of Culture* (1994), which was the most influential account of cultural hybridity to appear during the 1990s, Bhabha uses Mikhail Bakhtin's conception of hybridization as "a mixture of *two* social languages within the limits of a single utterance" (Bakhtin: 358) to redescribe a binary relationship in which the two opposed terms are unequal in force: the colonial situation. "Hybridity" shifts the balance of power between colonizer and colonized – at least partially. It allows the empire, as it were, to write back, by demonstrating that the colonizer is always changed by the fact of colonization, existing in a Hegelian master–slave relationship of co-dependence with those who have been colonized. The inequality between the positions of colonizer and colonized is not fully redressed by the mobilization of "hybridity," but it is at least *addressed*. Hybridity opens the door for cultural emergence.

Bhabha begins the introduction to *The Location of Culture* with a section entitled "Border Lives," pointing to "in-between" spaces that "provide the terrain for elaborating new strategies of selfhood . . . that initiate new signs of identity, and innovative sites of collaboration, and contestation" (1). Attuned to the in-between spaces of the US–Mexico border, Chicano/a studies paved the way for a paradigm shift within American studies, away from the frontier and toward the borderland as an organizing trope for the field. In her autobiographical text *Borderlands/La Frontera: The New Mestiza*(1987), which became one of the founding documents of the new border studies, Gloria Anzaldúa describes herself as the product of two different cultures:

> I am a border woman. I grew up between two cultures, the Mexican (with a heavy Indian influence) and the Anglo (as a member of a colonized people in our own territory). I have been straddling that *tejas-*Mexican border, and others, all my life. It's not a comfortable territory to live in, this place of contradictions. Hatred, anger and exploitation are the prominent features of this landscape. (19)

Writing in a hybrid mixture of poetry and prose, English and Spanish, Anzaldúa imagines the borderlands as a space where mainstream systems of classification break down: "To live in the Borderlands means you are neither *hispana india negra españa / ni gabacha, eres mestiza, mulata,* half-breed" (194). *Borderlands/La Frontera* depicts the borderlands as a place of unspeakable violence, but also a place of incredible promise, a place that cannot be tamed by hegemonic culture, a place where new selves and kinds of selves can be born: "To survive the Borderlands / you must live *sin fronteras* / be a crossroads."

For critics of late twentieth-century emergent US literatures, the borderlands would become a powerful trope. What these literatures have in common is the desire to negotiate the borderlands between traditional cultures, to live without frontiers, to become a crossroads where Sherman Alexie can meet Walt Whitman in order to collaborate in the making of what Whitman called "the greatest poem" – the United States itself.

A watershed moment for twentieth-century Native American writing occurred when the novelist and poet N. Scott Momaday (Kiowa) was awarded a mainstream prize – the Pulitzer – for his novel *House Made of Dawn*. The Pulitzer jury's decision took author, publisher, and reading public by surprise: according to Momaday's biographer Matthias Schubnell, "Momaday at first refused to believe the news, and some of the senior editors at Harper and Row could not even remember the novel" (TuSmith: 196 n.4). The novelist James Welch (Blackfeet/Gros Ventre) describes Momaday's winning the Pulitzer as a crucial turning point: "suddenly people started to notice Indian literature, [and] the way kind of opened for Indians; . . . younger people who didn't think they had much of a chance as a writer, suddenly realized, well, an Indian can write" (Coltelli: 197). Momaday's novel coincided with a renewal of political and social activism among American Indians that gained national attention with the publication of Vine Deloria's *Custer Died for Your Sins* (1969), Dee Brown's *Bury My Heart at Wounded Knee* (1970), and the occupation of Alcatraz Island for 19 months from late 1968 to 1971. Identifying Momaday, Deloria, and Welch as the writers who initiated a tradition of written Native American literature that did not exist before, the poet Simon Ortiz (Acoma Pueblo) describes the decade of the 1960s as "inspirational," "creative," and "invigorating," because it was a "worldwide phenomenon of third-world peoples decolonizing themselves and expressing their indigenous spirit, especially in Africa and the Americas" (Coltelli: 110). And, Ortiz argues, this "process of decolonizing includes a process of producing literature" (Coltelli: 110).

For Native American writers, decolonization has meant exploring the dynamics of both racial and cultural hybridity. The mixed-blood war veteran Abel in Momaday's *House Made of Dawn* (1968) experiences his mixed blood as a clash between contradictory frames of reference, a clash that fractures his consciousness, leading him to treat wartime combat as if it were ritual, and ritual as if it were actual combat. Welch's *The Death of Jim Loney* (1979) is a bleak narrative in which the liminal space between white culture and Native culture is portrayed as an existential no-man's land from which Loney cannot escape.

Loney is a hybrid character: he is a half-breed abandoned by his parents – his white father, Ike, and his mother, Eletra Calf-Looking – and he finds that he can feel no connection to either parent or to either of their cultures. Accidentally killing his high school rival Myron Pretty Weasel while the two are hunting, Loney lets the tribal police believe he has committed murder and allows himself to be shot in Mission Canyon, a site believed to be a gateway into the next life. Tayo, the protagonist of Silko's *Ceremony*, is a half-breed, taken in by his aunt "to conceal the shame of her younger sister," who returns to his reservation where he tries to keep himself from killing his nemesis, a Native veteran named Emo, who carries around a bag of teeth taken from Japanese corpses. Similarly, the ironically named John Smith, one of the protagonists of Alexie's *Indian Killer* (1996), is a man who is at home nowhere. Native American by blood but raised by white parents and baptized a Catholic, John Smith is regarded by the teachers at the St Francis school (in which he is one of four nonwhite students) as "a trailblazer, a nice trophy for St. Francis, a successfully integrated Indian boy" (19). John is a cultural hybrid, but he is not "successfully integrated": he is a cultural hybrid who finds his hybridity intolerable. *Indian Killer* is a novel that is full of hybrid figures who exist uneasily at the margins of society. Indeed, the novel suggests that all Native Americans are in some fundamental way homeless, victims of displacement, dispossession, and cultural damage. The young Native activist Marie Polatkin, one of the protagonists of Alexie's novel, believes "that homeless people were treated as Indians had always been treated. Badly. The homeless were like an Indian tribe, nomadic and powerless . . . so a homeless Indian belonged to two tribes, and was the lowest form of life in the city" (146).

At the close of the twentieth century, the Native American novel became darker and more pessimistic. The hopes for change that marked Native culture as a result of the revolutionary fervor of the 1960s seem to have been worn down, overtaken perhaps by the desire for entrepreneurial success that motivates Erdrich's Lyman Lamartine in *Love Medicine* and *The Bingo Palace*. While Erdrich maintains her faith in the healing powers of human love and traditional Native American beliefs, she seems increasingly to be the exception rather than the rule. The shift in Silko's work may perhaps be an indication of the direction in which the Native American novel is headed. The healing of wounds that takes place at the end of *Ceremony* with Tayo's disavowal of violence and the departure of his nemesis, Emo, is replaced in Silko's massive second novel, *Almanac of the Dead* (1991), by a sense that the evil represented by men like Emo is resilient and powerful and not so easily dismissed. In form and subject matter, *Almanac* is as difficult and jarring as any of Vizenor's novels, but it lacks Vizenor's sense of the comic. Described by Silko as a "763-page indictment for five hundred years of theft, murder, pillage, and rape," *Almanac* portrays a nightmarish world of violence, sexual perversion, and corruption at every level of society, a world in which the "witchery" has won out. None of the characters in *Almanac* is capable of love, and few of them seem capable even of hatred. The triumph of individualism has created a hierarchical, mechanistic, misogynist culture, in which the ontological norm might well be the stupor of the drug addicts who abound throughout the novel.

Silko told an interviewer in 1992 that "*Almanac* spawned another novel about a woman who is a serial killer" whose victims are only "policemen and politicians." It was, she said, "way more radical than *Almanac*," but she set it aside because she believed that it was too soon "to serve the narrative again on something so hard." Asked by the interviewer "what happened to the nice, charming Leslie Silko who used to write poems," Silko laughed and described "what happened" as "classic," simply a matter of "development," the result of "reading, learning," and emerging from a "sheltered" life (Perry: 338–9). What Silko sees in her own life is the inevitability of encountering the violence that is inherent in cultural emergence, a violence that is increasingly being given life in the Native American novel, embodied in characters like Vizenor's tricksters, Alexie's Indian Killer, and Silko's drug addicts, sadists, and imagined serial killer. The revolutionary politics that have always been a thread in the Native American novel seemed at the end of the century to be more pressing and aggressive than ever.

Hispanic American literature also flowered during the 1960s, though the Chicano/a and US Puerto Rican writers who came to notice during that decade saw themselves as part of a tradition of literature by Hispanic authors (written most often in Spanish but occasionally also in English) that existed on what is now US soil as far as back as the sixteenth century. The expedition of Juan de Oñate (1598–1608) produced the first New World example of the European tradition of epic poetry, *Historia de la Nueva México* (1610), written by Gaspar Pérez de Villagrá (1555–1620). The poem's 30 cantos, full of allusions to classical epic and Christian doctrine, culminate with the brutal suppression of the Acoma pueblo. In the aftermath of the conquest of Nueva España (which later became Mexico), Spanish-speakers created a vibrant oral culture that was a New World descendant of the medieval Spanish peninsular tradition of ballads and dramas. In the mid-nineteenth century, this Spanish culture, which had displaced the indigenous Native American culture, was itself displaced as a result of the Mexican–American War, which ended in 1848 with the Treaty of Guadalupe Hidalgo. The history of Chicano/a expression begins with the resulting Americanization of a vast area that had once been part of Mexico, and US Puerto Rican poetry continues to contend with the cultural aftershocks of Spain's loss of Puerto Rico to the United States in 1898.

The two dominant strains of twentieth-century Hispanic American poetry thus have much in common: Chicano/a literature and US Puerto Rican literature share a Latin American heritage, a deep connection to Spanish language and culture, the experience of being a minority within US culture, and an abiding interest in racial and ethnic mixing (*mestizaje*). Both poetic traditions make frequent use of "code-switching" between English, Spanish, and other vernacular forms, a kind of linguistic *mestizaje* that serves not only to represent accurately the sociocultural situations of their communities but also to empower bilingual readers. Spanish represents the most visible and viable challenge to the hegemony of the English language in the United States, and the debates over bilingual education have been driven largely by the issue of classroom instruction in Spanish. The use of Spanish by US Hispanic writers, either exclusively or in combination with English, serves as a challenge to the idea that "American literature" should be written in English.

There are, however, significant differences between these two dominant traditions of Hispanic American writing. Chicanos have a far more conflicted attitude toward their Spanish heritage, due in part to the fact that Mexican culture underwent two periods of anti-hispanism, once after independence in 1821 and then again during the Revolution of 1910. Many of the important early Chicano/a writers sought to stress their Indian heritage as the key to Chicano/a identity. In contrast, many Puerto Rican writers rebelled against the process of

Americanization that began in 1898 when Spain ceded Puerto Rico to the United States and continued with the granting of US citizenship to Puerto Ricans in 1917. A hispanist strain of Puerto Rican writing arose that sought to achieve a "pure" poetry of lyricism, metaphor, and strong identification with Spanish culture. In addition, Chicano/a literature is grounded in a continental sense of geography, oriented in northern Mexico, while US Puerto Rican literature is very much part of a Caribbean tradition of island writing. The history of European imperialism transforms this geographic distinction into a racial distinction: Chicano/a culture views itself primarily as a mixture of Native American and Spanish heritages, while Puerto Rican culture stresses its mixture of Spanish and black.

The flowering of Chicano/a literature is often considered to be the result of the Chicano Movement, which arose during the early 1960s in tandem with other movements aimed at gaining civil rights for disenfranchised minority groups. The etymology of the term "Chicano" is still hotly disputed among Chicano/a scholars. The most likely derivation is from "Mexicano," with the "x" pronounced the way it was at the time of the Spanish Conquest, as "sh." But the term "Chicano," which came to prominence during the student movements of the 1960s, has not been universally accepted by those whom it is intended to describe. Various other terms have gained currency in different regions, however: for example, "Hispano" and "Spanish American" have been the preferred terms in southern Colorado and northern New Mexico, while "Mexicano" has been widely accepted in south Texas and in many of the border regions. The first major literary work produced by the movement was *I am Joaquín*, an epic poem written in 1967 by Rodolfo "Corky" Gonzales, who founded the Crusade for Justice in Colorado. In his introduction to the poem, Gonzales describes *Joaquín* as "a call to action" for Chicanos "as a total people, emerging from a glorious history, traveling through social pain and conflicts, confessing our weaknesses while we shout about our strength" (1).

The construction of a heroic tradition was the project of much early Chicano/a writing, and the publication in 1958 of Américo Paredes's groundbreaking study *"With His Pistol in His Hand": A Border Ballad and its Hero* is often cited by the Chicano/a writers of the 1960s as an inspiration, both because it made them aware of an existing literary tradition of proto-Chicano/a writing and because it served as proof that Chicano/a writers could indeed be published in the US. The *corrido* is a narrative ballad, generally anonymously composed, and sung or spoken to musical accompaniment. Related to ballad forms that had been brought by the Spanish to Mexico, the *corrido* flourished in the border region south of Texas where relations between Mexican and Anglo-Americans were particularly troubled. In contrast to earlier ballad forms, which generally dealt with incidents from daily life, the *corrido* emphasizes drama and conflict, particularly the resistance of an individual to forces of oppression along the border. Its protagonist is often the Mexican cowboy, the *vaquero*. True to its name, which is derived from the verb *correr*, "to run," the *corrido* generally offers a swiftly paced story, most often told in stanzas of four eight-syllable lines.

José Antonio Villarreal's *Pocho* (1959), the first novel by a Mexican American author to be published by a mainstream American publishing house, uses the world of the *corridos* as its point of departure. Taking its title from the Mexican epithet for an Americanized Chicano, the novel is a *Kunstlerroman* that tells the story of Richard Rubbio, a Mexican American boy growing up in California whose father, Juan, was a companion of the legendary Pancho Villa and a hero of the Mexican Revolution. The novel charts Richard's gradual assimilation into US culture; in the end, he takes up his father's old vocation – he joins the US armed forces – but it is a gesture that represents the final break with the culture of Mexico that his father still embraces. The first Chicano/a novel to be published by a mainstream US press, Villarreal's *Pocho* holds a foundational place in twentieth-century Chicano/a writing, although by 1970 its assimilationist vision had come to seem problematic and even outdated. The blurb on the back cover of the paperback edition published in 1970 offers this apology: "To many young Mexican-Americans who seek an identity rooted in their own cultural heritage, the pocho represents much of what they, the chicanos, are trying to change."

Two years later, Luis Valdez, the director of the radical Teatro Campesino, would write that the Chicano people "are a colonized race, and the root of their uniqueness as Man lies buried in the dust of conquest. In order to regain our corazon, our soul, we must reach deep into our people, into the tenderest memory of their beginning" (Valdez and Steiner: xiii–xiv). And then he quotes the poet Alurista:

> razgos indigenas
> the scars of history on my face
>   and the veins of my body
> that aches

vomito sangre
y llora libertad
I do not ask for freedom
I AM freedom . . .

The Teatro Campesino had arisen out of the experience of "La Huelga," the strike led by César Chávez's National Farm Workers Association (NFWA) – later the United Farm Workers (UFW) – which began on September 16, 1965, when the *campesinos* of the NFWA voted to join the Filipino grape pickers who were on strike. La Huelga would last for five years and gain national attention with the grape boycott begun in New York in 1968.

Valdez established the bilingual company El Teatro Campesino in 1965 "to teach and organize Chicano farm workers" (Valdez and Steiner: 359). In plays such as *Los Vendidos* (1967), *The Militants* (1969), and *Soldado Raso* (1971), he updated Mexican and Spanish dramatic forms to dramatize issues that were important to the membership of the UFW. Their preferred form was the comic *acto*, a one-act play of less than half an hour that, according to Valdez, dealt "with the strike, the union and the problems of the farm worker" (Valdez and Steiner: 360). Satirizing the opponents of the UFW, the Teatro toured across the country in 1967 "to publicize the strike, performing at universities, in union halls and civic auditoriums, at New York's Village Theater, at the Newport Folk Festival and in the courtyard of the U.S. Senate Building in Washington, D. C.," receiving an Obie award in 1968 "for creating a workers' theater to demonstrate the politics of survival" (Valdez and Steiner: 360–1). Valdez argued that "Chicano theater must be revolutionary in technique as well as content. It must be popular, subject to no other critics except the pueblo itself; but it must also educate the pueblo towards an appreciation of social change, on and off the stage" (Valdez and Steiner: 356). In 1969, the Teatro filmed a version of "Corky" Gonzales's *I am Joaquín*, and in the following year Valdez introduced a second genre, the *mito* (myth), which he described as "a new more mystical dramatic form," designed to "complement and balance" the *acto* (Valdez: 10). "Our rejection of white western European (gabacho) proscenium theatre makes the birth of new Chicano forms necessary," he wrote, "thus, los actos y lost mitos; one through the eyes of man, the other through the eyes of God" (Valdez: 10). With its combination of parable and ritual, the *mito* allowed the Teatro to present longer narratives and to explore the Indian elements of Chicano identity. In 1971, Valdez published

Actos: The Teatro Campesino, a collection of *actos* written between 1965 and 1971. "We will consider our job done," he wrote the next year, "when every one of our people has regained his sense of personal dignity and pride in his history, his culture, and his race" (Valdez and Steiner: 361).

Drawing on the cultural energies let loose by El Teatro Campesino, a group of Chicano academics at the University of California, Berkeley, founded Quinto Sol Publications in 1967 to make works by Chicano authors available. Seeking to foster the growth of an identifiable Chicano literature, Quinto Sol began by publishing a journal called *El Grito*, which the novelist Tomás Rivera described in 1980 as the "one milestone" to date in Chicano literature (Bruce-Novoa, *Chicano Authors*: 160). Two years later it produced the first anthology of Chicano/a creative writing, *El espejo/The Mirror* (1st edition 1969), edited by Octavio Romano-V. and Herminio Rios-C., leading Rivera to remark to the critic Juan Bruce-Novoa that the Chicanos were the first people to have an anthology before they had a literature (Bruce-Novoa, "Canonical and Noncanonical Texts": 202). The writers who became associated with Quinto Sol were self-conscious experimenters, who sought to break down boundaries between fiction and nonfiction, poetry and prose, in order to capture the modern-day Chicano/a experience, while remaining true to the folk traditions that arose in Mexico and the Southwest. Many Chicano/a poets sought to take advantage of their bilingualism, blending Spanish and English in their poetry. The very existence of Quinto Sol gave Chicano/a authors a sense of empowerment.

Instead of waiting – perhaps in vain – for one of their writers to win a prize like the Pulitzer, the publishers established their own prize in 1970, El Premio Quinto Sol, a cash prize designed to establish a canon of Chicano/a novels; the project lasted for three years and its recipients – Tomás Rivera, Rudolfo Anaya, and Rolando Hinojosa – would become the most widely read and studied of Chicano/a novelists.

The first Quinto Sol prize was awarded to Tomás Rivera's novelistic collection of sketches about migrant workers, . . . *y no se lo tragó la tierra* (. . . *and the Earth Did Not Part*, 1971), which epitomized the Quinto Sol sensibility. Unlike *Pocho*, which depicts the displacement of traditional Chicano values by the individualist ideology of Anglo-America, *Tierra* portrays the survival of those values in the face of discrimination and economic hardship. Although, like Villarreal's *Pocho*, *Tierra* seems to focus on one young man's search for self-understanding, Rivera's narrator, like Sherwood Anderson's George

Willard in *Winesburg, Ohio,* floats through the different sketches, some of which are told in the first person, others in the third: the effect is less that of the traditional bildungsroman than of the portrayal of collective experience. What happens to the Chicano bildungsroman as it moves from Villarreal to Rivera is that it becomes a form in which what is at stake is the development not simply of the individual protagonist but also of the community and culture to which he or she belongs. In novels of development like *Tierra* and Sandra Cisneros's *The House on Mango Street* (1983), as well as autobiographies like Ernesto Galarza's *Barrio Boy* (1971), individual identity and communal identity develop simultaneously and are inseparably intertwined.

The winner of the third Quinto Sol prize, Rolando Hinojosa's *Estampas del valle y otras obras (Sketches of the Valley and Other Works,* 1973), shares certain features with Rivera's *Tierra:* it is written in Spanish, makes use of the *estampa* or sketch form popularized by Julio Torri in Mexico, and takes as its setting southern Texas. Unlike Rivera's irony, which is always tinged with melancholy and bitterness, Hinojosa's is tinged with humor, as he describes human behavior that ranges from the heroic to the depraved. Where Rivera limited himself to the experience of migrant farm workers, Hinojosa aims to portray a far more representative version of Chicano/a life, which proves ultimately to be Faulknerian in its sweep.

Sandwiched between Rivera and Hinojosa as winners of the Quinto Sol prize was Rudolfo A. Anaya, whose *Bless Me, Ultima* (1972) is written in English. Like *Pocho, Bless Me, Ultima* focuses on the experiences of a young boy who aspires to be a writer. Set in New Mexico just after World War II, the novel also maps the ways in which a community responds to cultural change both within and without. Antonio Marez is a boy who embodies liminality, torn as he is between the two different subcultures – the plains and the farmland – from which his parents hail. The novel's first person narrative includes italicized passages depicting the dreams of the young Antonio, whose boyhood is profoundly influenced by his friendship with the old *curandera* (folk healer) Ultima, who comes to stay with the family as the novel opens. Through Ultima, Antonio learns about pre-Christian forms of spirituality and knowledge that do not supplant but instead supplement the Christian teachings that he learns in school and at church. What the novel ultimately suggests is that the fusion of spiritual traditions will enable Antonio not only to mediate conflicts within his community but also to help that community maintain its sense of identity and coherence in the face of a consuming Anglo culture.

The Quinto Sol prize project succeeded in establishing the core of a Chicano/a canon, but as the critic Juan Bruce-Novoa has argued, it was a canon constructed around the desire to present a positive image of Chicanos and their culture (Bruce-Novoa, "Canonical and Noncanonical Texts": 200–3). Excluded were the works of writers like John Rechy, whose novels focus on questions of gay rather than Chicano/a identity, or Oscar Zeta Acosta, whose social satire refuses to exempt Chicano/a pieties. Even Tomás Rivera fell victim to the desire to promote communally correct portraits of Chicano/a life: the Quinto Sol editors are thought to have rejected "Pete Fonseca," now considered to be one of his finest stories, because it was held to be unflattering to Chicanos.

Writings by Chicano/a authors have dominated discussions of fiction by Hispanic Americans, in part because of the conscious attempts to found a Chicano/a literary canon described above, and in part because Chicano/a literary scholars have been prominent participants in the development of minority discourse theory. Though centered from the outset on the work of male authors, the Chicano/a canon is already shifting to include writings by Gloria Anzaldúa, Ana Castillo, Sandra Cisneros, and Cherríe Moraga. At the moment, Chicano/a fiction out-strips that produced by writers of Puerto Rican, Cuban American, and Dominican American descent both in sheer volume and in critical attention, but this situation is likely to change in the near future.

In the early years of the twenty-first century, American studies finds itself in flux again as a discipline, as scholars ask what it might mean to use the term *American* in its most exclusive sense, as the signifier of a hemispheric rather than a national culture. Where Chicano/a studies once led the way for a shift away from the frontier and toward the borderlands as an organizing paradigm for American studies, now Caribbean studies seems to offer a model for a comparative American studies that places US culture into a hemispheric context. With its linguistic diversity and its multitude of diasporic cultures, the Caribbean can be seen as a microcosm of the Americas, and the challenges that Caribbean scholars face in studying the lines of affiliation among the different cultures in the region prefigure the challenges facing scholars who seek to replace or at least supplement the old "American literature" with a field that might be called "literatures of the Americas."

These developments in literary and cultural criticism are likely to spur an interest in literature produced by US authors with ties to the Caribbean and thus to shift the balance of power between Chicano/a literature and the literature produced by other Hispanic American traditions. As the twenty-first century begins, Puerto Rican American literature still remains best known for "Nuyorican" poetry, and any incipient canon of Puerto Rican American prose would have to be centered on Piri Thomas's personal narrative *Down These Mean Streets* (1967), which remains a classic of Hispanic American literature, and on the work of two women whose writings dramatize the difficulty of growing up in situations of cultural hybridity: Nicholasa Mohr, the author of the novel *Nilda* (1986) and a dozen short story collections, and Esmeralda Santiago, best known for her memoir of childhood, *When I Was Puerto Rican* (1993), and the author of two novels, *America's Dream* (1997) and *Almost A Woman* (1998). With the commercial success of Oscar Hijuelos's *The Mambo Kings Play Songs of Love* (1989) and the critical accord given to Cristina García, Cuban American fiction seems to be entering a new stage of development. The best-known Dominican American writer is Julia Alvarez, whose novel *In the Time of the Butterflies* (1994) was a finalist for the National Book Critics' Circle Award. The commercial and critical success already achieved by these writers suggests that the twenty-first century will see an expansion of the field of non-Chicano/a Hispanic American literature.

For Asian Americans, the 1960s offered a different legacy. Considered unassimilable aliens until World War II, Asian Americans would in the aftermath of the war become cast in the role of the "model minority," in contradistinction to those minorities – particularly African Americans and Chicanos – who were growing increasingly militant in their calls for social equality. Taking aim at the stereotype of Asian Americans as the model minority, the editors of the groundbreaking collection *Aiiieeeee! An Anthology of Asian American Writers* (1974) lament that "seven generations of suppression under legislative racism and euphemized white racist love have left today's Asian Americans in a state of self-contempt, self-rejection, and disintegration" (Chin et al.: xii). As of 1974, they maintain, fewer than "ten works of fiction and poetry have been published by American-born Chinese, Japanese, and Filipino writers," not because "in six generations of Asian-Americans there was no impulse to literary or artistic self-expression" but because mainstream American publishers were only interested in publishing works written by Asian Americans that were *"actively inoffensive to white sensibilities"* (3–4).

Aiiieeeee! was intended to counter the accepted wisdom that a literature that could be called "Asian American" simply did not exist. "My writer's education owes a big debt to this first *Aiiieeeee!*," writes the Filipino American novelist and poet Jessica Hagedorn:

> The energy and interest sparked by *Aiiieeeee!* in the Seventies was essential to Asian American writers because it gave us visibility and credibility as creators of our own specific literature. We could not be ignored; suddenly, we were no longer silent. Like other writers of color in America, we were beginning to challenge the long-cherished concepts of a xenophobic literary canon dominated by white heterosexual males. Obviously, there was room for more than one voice and one vision in this ever-expanding arena. (xxvii)

In 1990, the editors of *Aiiieeeee!* produced a sequel entitled *The Big Aiiieeeee!*, which dropped the requirement of birth on US soil but restricted itself to Chinese American and Japanese American literature. In narrowing its focus, *The Big Aiiieeeee!* contributed to the perception that "Asian American literature" essentially consists of literature by Chinese and Japanese Americans, with sporadic contributions by writers of Southeast Asian and Asian Indian descent.

By the end of the twentieth century, however, critics working in the field of Asian American literature preferred to include under the rubric of "Asian American literature" texts written by people of Asian descent who were either born in or migrated to North America. Although the term "Asian American" had been invented in order to promote political solidarity among Americans of Asian descent, the idea of a unifying "Asian American" sensibility that depends on being born in North America has come to seem stifling, particularly after the sharp increase in Asian immigration that followed the 1965 Immigration and Nationality Act, which abolished the quotas that favored immigrants from northern European countries. By century's end, the label "Asian American" had been broadened to include native and naturalized Americans of not only Chinese, Japanese, and Filipino but also Bangladeshi, Burmese, Cambodian, Indian, Indonesian, Korean, Laotian, Nepalese, Thai, and Vietnamese descent. This new breadth was not represented, however, in the Asian American literary canon, which continued to be dominated by Chinese American and Japanese American authors, with increasing contributions by writers of Korean, Filipino, and South Asian descent.

The original *Aiiieeeee!* anthology contained fiction and drama but no poetry, and in general Asian American poetry has lagged behind the other genres in achieving prominence on the literary landscape. *The Big Aiiieeeee!*, however, brought attention to a recently recovered tradition of Chinese American poetry, written by immigrants to the San Francisco Bay area during the first two decades of the twentieth century. During this period, poetry had been appearing in two daily newspapers written in Cantonese and published in San Francisco's Chinatown: the *Chung Sai Yat Po*, which was established in 1900 and began issuing a daily literary supplement in 1908, and the *Sai Gat Yat Po*, which was established in 1909. Chinatown had a number of literary societies, which sponsored poetry competitions, and in 1911 the prominent bookseller Tai Quong Company published an anthology of 808 vernacular poems, entitled *Jinshan ge ji* (*Songs of Gold Mountain*, after the popular name given to the United States by Chinese sojourners); a second volume, published in 1915, collected an additional 832 folk rhymes. Together, these poems present a rich account of the experience of early Chinese immigrants in the United States, and many of them express the loneliness, despair, and frustration of discovering that American practices do not always live up to American ideals: "So, liberty is your national principle," writes one of these anonymous poets. "Why do you practice autocracy? / You don't uphold justice, you Americans, / You detain me in prison, guard me closely . . . When can I get out of this prison and free my mind?" (Hom: 85). An additional set of 135 poems, which had been scribbled in Cantonese on the walls of the Angel Island Immigration Station by those detained there, were preserved when two detainees copied them down and brought them to San Francisco.

The only postwar Chinese American poet included in *The Big Aiiieeeee!* was Wing Tek Lum, who was born and raised in Honolulu. His first volume of poetry, *Expounding the Doubtful Points* (1987), was awarded the Before Columbus Foundation's American Book Award. It contains poignant lyrics about family life, describing his difficult relationship with his father ("a gruff old fut") and – in sharp contrast to the contentious mother–son relationships that are found in many works by male Asian American writers – his more tender relationship with his mother, who died of cancer when he was just 16. Other poems treat sociopolitical issues such as the melting pot, pluralism, and Eurocentrism, while still others – such as "To Li Po" – meditate on the practice of poetry. Another American Book Award winner, Mei-Mei Berssenbrugge, also cites Li Po as a part of her "poetic tradition"; as befits a writer who was born in Beijing, China, of Chinese and Dutch parents, and raised in Massachusetts, she includes among her other influences Sappho, Dante, Yeats, Vallejo, Rilke, Stein, Whitman, Dickinson, Pound and Ashbery, as well as Tu Fu and Wang Wei.

Lum and Berssenbrugge, like most Chinese American poets, are interested in finding ways to make use of traditional Chinese poetics and the long history of Chinese poetry within the context of modern poetry written in English. This is particularly true of poets like Arthur Sze, who studied Chinese literature at the University of California, Berkeley, and Carolyn Lau, who invokes Chinese philosophy in poems like "A Footnote to a Dispute among Confucius's Disciples." Paradoxically, such interests put these poets squarely within a central tradition of American Modernist poetry: Conrad Aiken, Amy Lowell, Ezra Pound, William Carlos Williams, and many other "American" poets of the early twentieth century sought inspiration by turning to China.

Other poets, however, view traditional Chinese culture with more ambivalence. In "My Father's Martial Art," Stephen Liu portrays traditional Chinese culture as an anachronism in modern America. The narrator of Marilyn Chin's "We Are Americans Now, We Live in the Tundra" sings "a blues song" to China and bids "farewell" to her "ancestors / Hirsute Taoists, failed scholars" (Lim and Tsutakawa: 17). Li-Young Lee has said that "when I'm writing, I'm trying to stand neck and neck with Whitman and Melville, or, for that matter, the utterances of Christ in the New Testament or the Epistles of Paul. Those are as important to me as and perhaps even more influential than Asian American writers" (Cheung, *Words Matter*: 278). Moreover, women poets like Chin, Diana Chang, Genny Lim, Diane Mark, Nellie Wong, and Merle Woo often fault traditional Chinese culture for its misogyny and discover that finding a poetic voice is often linked to rebellion against patriarchal traditions, personified in the figure of the father and implicit in the communal life of Chinatown.

The typical American Chinatown began as a segregated ghetto for immigrants who were still designated "aliens ineligible to citizenship" under the provisions of the Nationality Act of 1870, so that in the early years of the twentieth century they were largely communities of immigrant bachelors. Planning merely to sojourn in the United States in order to earn money, many early immigrants found it too expensive to bring their wives with them, and in 1870 the ratio of Chinese men to women in the United States was 14 to 1. This gender imbalance was frozen into place by the provisions of the Chinese Exclusion Act of 1882, which prohibited further immigration from China, and by the fact that Chinese men were forbidden by US law to marry white women. For many Chinese American novelists and poets, particularly those who are the children of pre-World War II immigrants, it is often Chinatown that is their primary link to Chinese tradition.

The "Chinatown book" of the mid-twentieth century, a genre that includes novels as well as autobiographies and other nonfictional accounts, helped to foster the idea that Asian Americans were indeed assimilable: for example, the novel *Chinatown Family* (1948), written by the Chinese émigré Lin Yutang, presents an idealized portrait of Chinese American family life that draws on the model of the Horatio Alger success story, suggesting that success can be achieved through a mixture of hard work and well-deserved good fortune. Jade Snow Wong's autobiography, *Fifth Chinese Daughter* (1945), adopted the narrative strategy of "orientalizing" Chinatown, making it seem exotic but safe, and achieved considerable commercial success; the book was reprinted several times in paperback and translated into a variety of languages. Perhaps the most accomplished of the Chinatown novels is Louis Chu's *Eat a Bowl of Tea* (1961), which portrays the last vestiges of bachelor society in New York's Chinatown from the inside, from the point of view of the waiters, barbers, and laundrymen who comprised it.

For later Chinese American writers, however, Chinatown would often become a symbol for less appealing traditional Chinese values such as patriarchy, as well as for US racial oppression. Finding themselves caught between cultures, many Chinese American poets lace their work with history and politics. A powerful example is Alan Lau's "Water that Springs from a Rock," which merges the lyrical and the historiographic as it recounts the massacre of Chinese workers for the Union Pacific Railroad in Rock Springs, Wyoming, in 1885. Genny Lim, Nellie Wong, and Merle Woo write about the ways in which Chinese women have been objectified by white male culture, while poems like Arthur Sze's "Listening to a Broken Radio" and John Yau's "Rumors" question the value of the American Dream. A humorous but apt dramatization of the project of late twentieth-century Chinese American literature can be found in the meal prepared by the narrator of Wing Tek Lum's "T-Bone Steak":

> No, it was not
> Chinese, much less
> American, that pink piece
> sitting in my rice bowl. It was,
> simply, how our family
> ate, and I
> for one am grateful for
> the difference.
>
> (Lum: 91)

Twentieth-century Chinese American literature makes use of a set of recurrent motifs: traditional Chinese culture, the idea of the United States as the "Gold Mountain," working on the railroads, the bachelor culture of Chinatown, the feminization of Chinese culture, and racial discrimination. In contrast, the history of twentieth-century Japanese American literature centers on a single historical moment: World War II and its immediate aftermath.

Japanese American poetry written in English during the twentieth century was produced almost exclusively by *nisei* (second-generation) and *sansei* (third-generation) authors. The *issei*, first-generation immigrants who came to the United States mainland and to Hawai'i between 1885 and 1924, did write poetry that was published in Japanese-language newspapers on the West Coast and in Hawai'i, usually in haiku or in other traditional Japanese poetic forms. One *issei* poet, Bunichi Kagawa, not only published in Japanese-language news-papers but also wrote poems in English, which were collected in the volume *Hidden Flame* (1930). From the 1920s on, *nisei* writers began publishing in the English-language sections of Japanese American newspapers, and for the most part their poetry is strongly influenced by Western literary conventions. Chiye Mori was one of the first poets to explore the political dimension of *nisei* identity: her poem "Japanese American" (1932) likens the *nisei* to "clay pigeons traveling swiftly and aimlessly / On the electric wire of international hate / Helpless targets in the shooting gallery of political discord" (Cheung, *Interethnic*: 129).

A recurring theme in *nisei* writing is the oppressiveness of the *issei*'s attempt to replicate Japanese culture on American soil. Milton Murayama's novel *All I Asking for Is My Body* (1975) depicts life in the sugar cane plantations of Hawai'i in the 1930s as seen through the eyes of a young *nisei* named Kiyoshi Oyama. A similar generational split is dramatized in Okada's *No-No Boy*. In these novels, the *issei* in Murayama's and Okada's novels live in a fantasy world in which Japan can do no wrong and could not possibly have committed such atrocities as "the rape of Nanking." One *issei* character in *No-No Boy* simply refuses to believe that Japan has lost World War II. The cul-tural divide between *issei* and *nisei* is one of the abiding themes in the short stories of Toshio Mori, whose collection *Yokohama, California* was scheduled for publication in 1942 but did not appear until after the end of the war.

The bombing of Pearl Harbor in 1941 and the subsequent intern-ment of 110,000 Japanese and Japanese Americans produced feelings of bewilderment and betrayal among many of the *nisei*, whose rights as United States citizens were ignored by the US government. Some, such as the members of the Japanese American Citizens League (JACL), sought to prove their loyalty as Americans by supporting the US government's wartime policies toward American Japanese, while others remained bitterly disillusioned, particularly after the government sought to recruit *nisei* volunteers into the armed forces in 1942. Those *nisei* internees who answered "no" to two questions about their loyalty and willingness to serve were subject to imprisonment, a policy whose consequences are vividly dramatized in Okada's *No-No Boy*. The English-language magazines that were produced in three of the internment camps – *Trek* (Topaz, Utah), *Tulean Dispatch* (Tule Lake, California), and *The Pen* (Rowher, Arkansas) – reflect the struggle between these perspectives, though critical points of view were blunted by government censorship. The wartime poetry of Toyo Suryemoto uses a façade of natural metaphors to convey the bitterness and despair brought about by internment.

This split perspective about the necessity of internment continues in Japanese American writing after the war. In prose, it is reflected in the gap between the conciliatory rhetoric of Monica Sone's autobiography *Nisei Daughter* (1953) and the bitter ambivalence of Okada's *No-No Boy*. *Issei* poets such as Shumpa Kiuchi and Shusei Matsui wrote poems that harked back to heroic traditions in Asian literature, while many *nisei* authors, writing in the JACL's national paper, *Pacific Citizen*, and in such Japanese American newspapers as *Rafu Shimpo* (Los Angeles) and *Hokubei Mainichi* (San Francisco), devoted themselves to the projects of forgetting the miseries of internment and reintegrating themselves into US culture. Hisaye Yamamoto's celebrated story "Seventeen Syllables" charts the gap that exists between a young and increasingly Americanized *nisei* woman and her mother; the daughter, Rosie, pretends to appreciate the haiku that her mother has just composed, because she is ashamed to reveal just how shaky her command of Japanese really is.

The poet Mitsuye Yamada, born in Japan and therefore an *issei* but raised among *nisei* in the US, cuts across the grain of these generalizations. Her first collection, *Camp Notes* (1976), brings together pieces written during and after her internment at Minidoka and poems written during the 1970s. Written with an ironic detachment and an eye for poignant detail, her poems adopt the anti-racist and anti-patriarchal attitudes that are usually attributed to *sansei* writing about the war. Writing in the aftermath of the civil rights movements of the 1960s and the Vietnam War, *sansei* poets such as Lawson Fusao Inada and Janice Mirikitani sought to make their poetry a vehicle for the reconstruction of Japanese American identity. In the introduction to his second volume of poetry, *Legends From Camp* (1993), Inada wrote, "More and more, artist and audience are becoming one – for the greater cause of community and mutuality . . . I began functioning as a *community* poet – with new people, places, and publications to work with" (Wong: 299). Sharing Inada's sense of political commitment, Mirikitani adds a strain of self-reflective meditation on the limits of what poetry and thought can accomplish. After listening to the experiences of a Vietnam veteran, the speaker of "Jungle Rot and Open Arms" asks:

> so where is my
> *political education*? my
> *rhetorical answers* to everything? my
> *theory into practice*? my
> *intensification of life in art?*

Some *sansei* writers have sought to ground their poetry in a new regionalism: Juliet Kono's collection *Hilo Rains* (1989) explores the ways in which three generations of her family have been shaped by the land of Hawai'i, while Garret Kaoru Hongo writes about Hawai'i and about other communities where Asian Americans live, seeking to draw connections across regional and ethnic boundaries.

Cathy Song is another poet whose work crosses ethnic boundaries. Born in Honolulu to a Chinese mother and a Korean father, Song's poetry is deeply rooted in both the Hawai'ian landscape and her dual Asian heritage. Her first collection, *Picture Bride*, draws inspiration from Korean and Chinese traditions, even as it uses memories and images drawn from family life to explore the ways in which these traditions are restrictive, particularly for women. Myung Mi Kim, a Korean who came to the US at the age of 9, found herself influenced by what is perhaps the best-known Korean American text in academic circles, Theresa Cha's formally experimental *Dictée* (1982), which explores the after-effects of the Japanese colonization of Korea, while taking aim at US national narratives of assimilation. Kim's first collection, *Under Flag* (1991), portrays the fragmentation of Korean American subjectivities, as a result of the loss of language and homeland and the corrosiveness of US racism. Kim has characterized her use of language as "an English that behaves like Korean, an English shaped by a Korean," a kind of third language "beyond what is systematically Korean and English." The question of whether Korean immigrants should produce literature written in Korean or English is debated among Korean American intellectuals. The poet Ch'oe Yun-hong has suggested that Koreans' lack of interest in the problems of Korean Americans has discouraged the production of American poetry written in Korean, and scholars of Korean literature have suggested that Korean American literature should distinguish itself by turning to English and focusing on immigrant life rather than memories of Korea. Ch'oe suggests that the harshness of life for many Korean Americans has fueled a "desire for poetry," but at the end of the twentieth century, Korean American poetry remains an underdeveloped corner in the field of Asian American poetry. Korean American fiction, however, has risen in prominence after the glowing reviews that greeted Chang-Rae Lee's first novel, *Native Speaker* (1995), which may turn out to do for Korean American fiction what Momaday's *House Made of Dawn* did for writing by American Indians.

Another as yet underdeveloped but increasingly vibrant area of Asian American literature is Filipino American writing. Because the majority of Filipinos immigrants have seemed to take pride in their Americanization, Filipinos have been regarded as an "invisible minority," with many Americans unaware of the history of existence of a Philippine–American War in 1899. One of the earliest Filipino American poets to publish in the United States was José García Villa, who lived the bohemian life in Greenwich Village and counted among his friends W. H. Auden, e. e. cummings, and Edith Sitwell. In addition to short stories, Villa wrote poetry that was strongly influenced by the intellectual climate of Modernism. His contemporary Carlos Bulosan is perhaps best known for his autobiography *America Is in the Heart* (1946), but he wrote poems that continued his exploration of what it means to be an outsider in US culture while still believing in the nation's ideals. In the aftermath of the 1960s, Filipino American poets began to explore the contours of US racial discrimination. Serafin Syquia writes paeans to solidarity among US ethnic minorities in poems like "i can relate to tonto" (1972), while Sam Tagatac's "A Chance Meeting between Huts" (1975) focused on an "act / of recognition" between two Asian Americans who learn to see outside of US stereotypes. In "Rapping with one Million Carabaos in the Dark" (1974), Alfred Robles tells his fellow Filipino Americans to "put down your white mind / . . . / & burn up all that white shit / that's keeping your people down" (Tachiki: 114–15). The success of Jessica Hagedorn's novel *Dogeaters* (1990) sparked new interest in Filipino American literature and was followed by the publication in 1996 of two anthologies – *Returning a Borrowed Tongue: An Anthology of Contemporary Filipino Poetry in English* and *Flippin': Filipinos on America* – that contain a richly diverse set of Filipino and Filipino American poets.

Literature by Americans of South Asian descent was also a growing field at the end of the twentieth century, despite the fact that South Asians are still being omitted from mainstream collections such as Shawn Wong's *Asian American Literature: A Brief Introduction and Anthology* (1996). South Asian American fiction has not yet coalesced as a distinct literary field: in its nascent stages, it has been dominated by Bharati Mukherjee, who lived in Canada from 1966 to 1980 before emigrating to the United States, and by two Canadian writers of South Asian descent, Rohinton Mistry and Michael Ondaatje. In his first volume of poetry, *The Loss of India* (1964), Zulfikar Ghose, born in pre-Partition India and Pakistan, explores the dislocation that occurs when a South Asian chooses to write in English and to live in the West. Writing in both English and Kannada, the Indian-born poet and translator A. K. Ramanujan explores the dynamics of the Hindu family, weaving together past and present, India and Chicago, his adopted home. The list of significant South Asian poets working in North America includes two Canadians of Sri Lankan descent – Rienzi Crusz and Ondaatje, the latter best known for his Booker Prize-winning novel *The English Patient* (1992); Agha Shahid Ali, whose 1979 volume *In Memory of Begum Akhtar* invokes a long tradition of Urdu poetry; and Meena Alexander, who was born in India and raised in the Sudan before settling permanently in New York. To the exploration of postcolonial identity that marks all of the South Asian writers mentioned here, Alexander adds a commitment to feminist aesthetics and politics. In an essay entitled "Is There An Asian American Aesthetics?," Alexander maintains that art "is always political, even if it is most abstract, even if it is a simple visual image of a leaf falling from a tree" (26–7).

The idea that art and politics are inextricably connected has become a staple of these three literary traditions, particularly as new voices emerge from the shadows of cultural marginalization. In the near future, it seems likely that some of these voices will be speaking in tongues other than English. Of the writers discussed in this chapter, it is the Hispanic Americans who have most fully explored the creative possibilities of their bilingualism. Some of the central works of Chicano/a literature – for example, Tomás Rivera's . . . *y no se lo tragó la tierra* and Rolando Hinojosa's *Estampas del valle y otras obras* – were written in Spanish, and Hinojosa has continued to move freely between Spanish and English in his fiction. It is therefore already impossible to write an account of emergent US literatures that focuses exclusively on English-language writings. Several of the essayists in King-Kok Cheung's anthology *An Interethnic Companion to Asian American Literature* (1997) feel bound to comment that their accounts are partial and incomplete because they are limited to texts written in English. This linguistic gap in the field of American studies is currently being addressed by scholarly efforts like the "Recovering the U.S. Hispanic Literary Heritage Project" and those of Harvard University's Longfellow Institute, which (according to its mission statement) "has set itself the task to identify, and to bring back as the subject of study, the multitudes of culturally fascinating, historically important, or aesthetically interesting texts that were written in languages other than English," texts that range "from works in indigenous Amerindian languages, Portuguese, Spanish, French, Dutch, German, Yiddish, Russian, Chinese, and Japanese, to Arabic and French texts by African Americans." The first fruits of their labors can be found in the *Multilingual Anthology of American Literature* (2000), edited by Marc Shell and Werner Sollors.

Emergent literatures are all about breaking down the boundaries that exist among languages, cultures, and literary traditions. Perhaps the dramatic monologues written by Ai, the daughter of a Japanese father and a mother who is a mixture of black, Choctaw, and Irish, might serve as an emblem for the shared concerns of Native American, Hispanic American, and Asian American writers. "It's time to cross the border / and cut your throat with two knives," says a character in Ai's *Killing Floor* (20). Whether or not their ethnic background is mixed like Ai's, emergent US writers recognize that they live in a state of cultural hybridity, caught, as Gloria Anzaldúa puts it, "in the cross-fire between camps / . . . / not knowing which side to turn to, run to" (216). In their novels, poems, and plays, hybridity is portrayed more often than not as a state of violence. For these writers, the beauty of literature is its ability to transform violence into art and thus despair into hope.

References and further reading

Acuña, Rodolfo. *Occupied America: A History of Chicanos.* 3rd edn. New York: Harper and Row, 1988.

Ai. *Killing Floor*. Boston: Houghton Mifflin, 1979.

Alexander, Meena. "Is There an Asian American Aesthetics?" *Samar* 1 (1992): 26–7.

Alexie, Sherman. "Defending Walt Whitman." In *The Summer of Black Widows*. Brooklyn, NY: Hanging Loose Press, 1996. 14–15.

Alexie, Sherman. *Indian Killer*. New York: Atlantic Monthly Press, 1996.

Allen, Paula Gunn. *The Sacred Hoop: Recovering the Feminine in American Indian Traditions*. Boston: Beacon Press, 1986.

Allen, Paula Gunn. "Special Problems in Teaching Leslie Marmon Silko's *Ceremony*." *American Indian Quarterly* 14 (1990): 379–86.

Anaya, Rudolfo A. "Aztlán: A Homeland Without Boundaries." In *Aztlán: Essays on the Chicano Homeland*. Eds Rudolfo A. Anaya and Francisco Lomelí. Albuquerque, NM: El Norte Publications, 1989. 230–41.

Anzaldúa, Gloria. *Borderlands/La Frontera: The New Mestiza*. 2nd edn. San Francisco: Aunt Lute, 1999.

Bakhtin, M. M. *The Dialogic Imagination: Four Essays*. Trans. Caryl Emerson and Michael Holquist. Austin: University of Texas Press, 1981.

Bhabha, Homi K. *The Location of Culture*. London: Routledge, 1994.

Bruce-Novoa, Juan, ed. *Chicano Authors: Inquiry by Interview*. Austin: University of Texas Press, 1980.

Bruce-Novoa, Juan. "Canonical and Noncanonical Texts: A Chicano Case Study." In *Redefining American Literary History*. Eds A. LaVonne Brown Ruoff and Jerry W. Ward, Jr. New York: Modern Language Association of America, 1990. 196–209.

Calderón, Hector. "Rereading Rivera's *Y no se lo tragó la tierra*." In *Criticism in the Borderlands: Studies in Chicano Literature, Culture, and Ideology*. Eds Hector Calderón and José David Saldívar. Durham, NC: Duke University Press, 1991. 97–113.

Cheung, King-Kok, ed. *An Interethnic Companion to Asian American Literature*. Cambridge: Cambridge University Press, 1997.

Cheung, King-Kok, ed. *Words Matter: Conversations with Asian American Writers*. Honolulu, HI: University of Hawai'i Press, 2000.

Chin, Frank. "Come All Ye Asian American Writers of the Real and the Fake." In *The Big Aiiieeeee! An Anthology of Chinese American and Japanese American Literature*. Eds Jeffery Paul Chan, Frank Chin, Lawson F. Inada, and Shawn Wong. New York: Meridian, 1991. 1–92.

Chin, Frank, Jeffery Paul Chan, Lawson. F. Inada, and Shawn H. Wong, eds. *Aiiieeeee! An Anthology of Asian American Writers*. 1974. Rpt Meridian, 1997.

Coltelli, Laura. *Winged Words: American Indian Writers Speak*. Lincoln, NE: University of Nebraska Press, 1990.

Daniels, Roger. *Coming to America: A History of Immigration and Ethnicity in American Life*. New York: HarperCollins, 1990.

Fanon, Frantz. *The Wretched of the Earth*. Trans. C. Farrington. New York: Grove, 1963.

Gonzales, Rodolpho. *I am Joaquín/Yo soy Joaquín: An Epic Poem*. 1967. Rpt New York: Bantam, 1972.

Hagedorn, Jessica, ed. *Charlie Chan Is Dead: An Anthology of Contemporary Asian American Fiction*. New York: Penguin, 1993.

Hinojosa, Rolando. *The Rolando Hinojosa Reader: Essays Historical and Critical*. Ed. José Saldívar. Houston, TX: Arte Publico Press, 1994.

Hom, Marlon K. *Songs of Gold Mountain: Cantonese Rhymes from San Francisco Chinatown*. Berkeley and Los Angeles: University of California Press, 1987.

JanMohammed, Abdul, and David Lloyd, eds. *The Nature and Context of Minority Discourse*. New York: Oxford University Press, 1990.

Kim, Elaine. *Asian American Literature: An Introduction to the Writings and their Social Context*. Philadelphia: Temple University Press, 1982.

Kingston, Maxine Hong. "Personal Statement." In *Approaches to Teaching Kingston's "The Woman Warrior."* Ed. Shirley Geok-Lin Lim. New York: Modern Language Association of America, 1991. 23–5.

Lim, Shirley Geok-lin, and Amy Ling, eds. *Reading the Literatures of Asian America*. Philadelphia: Temple University Press, 1992.

Lim, Shirley Geok-Lin, and Mayumi Tsutakawa, eds. *The Forbidden Stitch: An Asian-American Women's Anthology*. Corvallis, OR: Calyx Books, 1989.

Lincoln, Kenneth. *Native American Renaissance*. Berkeley and Los Angeles: University of California Press, 1983.

Longfellow Institute, Harvard University, Mission Statement. www.fas.harvard.edu/~lowinus

Lowe, Lisa. *Immigrant Acts: On Asian American Cultural Politics*. Durham, NC: Duke University Press, 1996.

Lum, Wing Tek. *Expounding the Doubtful Points*. Honolulu, HI: Bamboo Ridge Press, 1987.

Maitino, John R., and David R. Peck, eds. *Teaching American Ethnic Literatures*. Albuquerque: University of New Mexico Press, 1996.

Perry, Donna. "Interview with Leslie Marmon Silko." In *Backtalk: Women Writers Speak Out*. Ed. Donna Perry. New Brunswick, NJ: Rutgers University Press, 1993. 313–40.

Ruoff, A. LaVonne Brown, and Jerry W. Ward, Jr, eds. *Redefining American Literary History*. New York: Modern Language Association of America, 1990.

Saldívar, José David. *Border Matters: Remapping American Cultural Studies*. Berkeley and Los Angeles: University of California Press, 1997.

Saldívar, Ramón. *Chicano Narrative: The Dialectics of Difference*. Madison: University of Wisconsin Press, 1990.

Shell, Marc, and Werner Sollors, eds. *The Multilingual Anthology of American Literature: A Reader of Original Texts with English Translations*. New York: New York University Press, 2000.

Tachiki, Amy, ed. *Roots: An Asian American Reader*. Los Angeles: Continental Graphics, 1971.

Takaki, Ronald. *Strangers from a Different Shore: A History of Asian Americans.* Boston: Little, Brown, 1989.

Takaki, Ronald. *A Different Mirror: A History of Multicultural America.* Boston: Little, Brown, 1993.

TuSmith, Bonnie. *All My Relatives: Community in Contemporary Ethnic American Literatures.* Ann Arbor, MI: University of Michigan Press, 1993.

Valdez, Luis. *Early Works: Actos, Bernabé, and Pensamiento Serpentino.* Houston, TX: Arte Publico Press, 1990.

Valdez, Luis, and Stan Steiner. *Aztlán: An Anthology of Mexican American Literature.* New York: Vintage, 1972.

Villarreal, José Antonio. *Pocho.* 1959. Rpt Anchor Books, 1970.

Vizenor, Gerald. *Griever: An American Monkey King in China.* 1987. Rpt Minneapolis, MN: University of Minnesota Press, 1990.

Vizenor, Gerald. "Trickster Discourse." *American Indian Quarterly* 14 (1990): 277–87.

Williams, Raymond. *Marxism and Literature.* Oxford: Oxford University Press, 1977.

Wong, Shawn, ed. *Asian American Literature: A Brief Introduction and Anthology.* New York: HarperCollins, 1996.

Wu, Cheng-Tsu, ed. *"Chink!": A Documentary History of Anti-Chinese Prejudice in America.* New York: World Publishing, 1972.

Chapter 15

"I'll Be Your Mirror, Reflect What You Are": Postmodern Documentation and the Downtown New York Scene from 1975 to the Present

Marvin J. Taylor

At first glance, the Velvet Underground, whose haunting ballad "I'll Be Your Mirror" provides my title, may not appear to have anything to do with canonicity or with libraries (other than that some library collections may have their recordings in the media center). And yet, the Velvet Underground, and "I'll Be Your Mirror" in particular, suggest a model for conceptualizing the process of canon-building, the accreditation of literary figures and movements, and the role libraries play in both. I realize this is a peculiar statement, but there are several ways in which it is true.

The Velvet Underground, with Lou Reed as its unsurpassed lead singer and songwriter, founded outsider music. This Lower East Side band, linked to Andy Warhol's Factory where it staged multimedia performances, was one of the most important precursors of the Downtown New York scene. Outsider art, outsider literature, and much that we now understand about the politics of being "inside" or "outside" are reflected in the work of the Velvet Underground. I'd like to frame some thoughts about the development of a postwar American canon of writers by looking at how libraries collect cultural materials. I would like to pose the following questions: what role do libraries play in determining what enters the canon? How do libraries determine what aspects of culture will be preserved for posterity? It is to the metaphor of the mirror in "I'll Be Your Mirror, Reflect What You Are" – the title so important to Downtown New York work that the photographer Nan Goldin used it for her 2002 Whitney retrospective – that I turn as a mode of examining the role of libraries. Further, I'd like to use the mirror to explore how the Downtown New York art scene, which grew out of the same cultural ferment that produced the Velvet Underground, complicates our understanding of canon development and of the process/possibility of documentation in library and archival work.

To boldly generalize, the prevailing image of the library among the general public (and perhaps, actually, among librarians) is that libraries are a repository for our cultural heritage – a mirror held up to reality – the reflection being an accurate accumulation of documents from which we can reconstruct history. But are libraries, even when they attempt to collect comprehensively, really a mirror for culture? Can they reflect "what things are?" Do they preserve the documents that can explain how a culture looked? Do the materials in libraries really allow researchers to understand what it was like to live in a period? Or does the act of bringing something into a library alter the original documents so that their historical context is no longer visible? If so, how do libraries affect these materials? In reality, there are probably two competing images of libraries: the connoisseurship model and the documentation model. Much work since the early 1980s in culture studies has shown the implicit political, racial, gender, and sexual dynamics of connoisseurship to be very complicated and problematic as a sustainable model for collecting. It is beyond the scope of my topic to address the differences in these two models here. I would hasten to note that my critique of the documentation model, which I believe is superior to the connoisseurship model, is not meant in any way as an attack on documentation; rather it is intended to provide a more sophisticated understanding of how we can build collections within the documentation model.

As I've tried to collect the Downtown New York scene, these questions have become central to my thinking about how we build comprehensive collections. The Downtown Collection at New York

University's Fales Library is the largest collection of printed and archival materials related to the Downtown New York scene anywhere. Currently the Downtown Collection contains some 7,000 printed items, including monographs, over 300 periodical titles, 'zines, and other print publications. The archives now hold over 1,200 linear feet of material and include the papers of Ron Kolm, a central organizer and promoter of Downtown work; the archive of the Judson Memorial Church, a major center for avant-garde performance, theater, art, and dance dating back to the early 1960s; the archive of *Between C&D*, the influential literary magazine of the East Village during the 1980s, co-edited by Joel Rose and Catherine Texier; the archive of Serpent's Tail/High Risk Books, the important publishing house for Downtown works headed by Ira Silverberg; the papers of David Wojnarowicz, the noted artist, writer, performance artist, and photographer; the papers of Dennis Cooper, the poet, novelist, and editor; and the papers of many other writers and artists. The nature of these materials, their content, format, the vicissitudes of their production, and their relation to the Downtown scene that produced them have caused me to question some of our most commonly held assumptions about libraries and archives. The Downtown Collection, as it has grown and been processed, has raised questions about libraries' modes of collecting, their role as preservers of cultural history, and their ability to be providers of organized knowledge. I'd like to explore how Downtown works of art, which question the structures of society – the available discourses by which we describe things – question the library as a similar available discourse, one that does violence through categorization of materials that are not beholden to the same philosophical, political, cultural outlook as those discourses that inform the libraries' structures.

Beginning in the mid-1970s a distinctively new attitude toward artistic production surfaced in Downtown New York. It was not a new aesthetic, not a new style, and not a unified movement, but rather an attitude toward the possibility of art and the production of art that, while for the most part unformulated, was shared by a wide range of writers, artists, performers, musicians, filmmakers, and video artists who moved to the relatively inexpensive lofts and tenements of SoHo and the Lower East Side. Influenced by the Beats, the New York School, Dada, pop art, hippies, Marxists, and anarchists, Downtown New York artists began to push the limits of traditional categories of art. Artists were also writers, writers were developing performance pieces, performers were incorporating videos into their work, and everyone was in a band. Along with the profound disruption of artistic specialization, Downtown works themselves undermined the traditions of art, music, performance, and writing at the most basic structural levels. Rather than overthrow traditional forms and establish a new movement, Downtown work sought to undermine from within the traditional structures of artistic media and the culture that had grown up around them.

Robert Siegle, the first academic to write on the Downtown scene, finds a central insurgency against the structures of culture in Downtown works. In his book *Suburban Ambush: Downtown Writing and the Fiction of Insurgency*, Siegle writes:

> It is, then, an insurgency, but not one that expects to break free of some kind of specific corrupt institution. It is an insurgency against the silence of institutions, the muteness of the ideology of form, the unspoken violence of normalization. But it does not expect of itself the pure voice of the Other – it knows its own language is divided against itself, its every move a contradiction that marks the position of the speaking subject at the end of the twentieth century. (4)

Siegle describes Downtown writing as quintessentially postmodern in its approach to the "silence of institutions" and to the "position of the speaking subject"; that is, rather than seeing Downtown writing as something that attempts to overthrow institutions or to define a speaking subject that is universal and nonpositional, he sees it as about understanding how the discourse of institutions constructs who we are, and then uses that knowledge to complicate cultural discourse. Or as Siegle says:

> Downtown writing seeks not liberation but liberty, real rather than full sensation, tactical critique rather than strategic game plan. It opens space – mentally, psychologically, semiotically – where simulation, repression, and convention have converged to predetermine our Being. It shakes up reified relations – roles, genders, social structures – so that at least momentarily experiences of various sorts of Other might take place before the great culture machine swallows it up again . . . [D]owntown writing persists in a sort of hit-and-run guerrilla action. (3)

Without assimilating into the traditional art scene, Downtown artists mounted a full-scale assault on the structures of society that had led to grinding poverty, homelessness, the Vietnam War, nuclear power, misogyny, racism, homophobia, and a host of other problems.

Downtown artists were profoundly aware of the failure of Modernist revolutions, but not willing to abandon the possibility of a better world. They began to explore the cracks and fissures where human experience, the actual events of everyday life, undermine the oppressive, prescriptive structures of society. Hoping to kick culture – both in the sense of forcing it to change and, possibly, in the sense of giving up the stifling, prescriptive structures that are so addictive – Downtown art exploded traditional forms of art, exposing them as nothing more than cultural constructs. Verbo-visual writing, appropriation art, performance art, graffiti painting, Xerox art, 'zines, small magazines, self-publishing, outsider galleries, mail art, and a host of other transgressions abounded in Downtown and dramatically changed how we think about the production of artistic work.

It is important to understand that Downtown artists are not held together as a movement; there is not one unified Downtown aesthetic, and no easily definable genres. Downtown works don't fall into the usual subject categories. What Downtown works do share is:

> a desire to use art in refabricating a basis for individuality in the face of our sharpened sense of the structural determination of our lives. That basis will not look like a Victorian self or a modernist narrative. Far from being defeated by contradictions, these postmoderns take from it the cue for an alternative logic. Far from being rendered hopeless by the seemingly inevitable drift of (inter)national politics, they borrow from disinformation the ironic habitation of familiar forms for crosspurposes. Far from being paralyzed by the anxiety of past masters' influence, they appropriate them for commentary on classic motifs (such as mastery, originality, autonomy, representation) and art-world structures (such as publishing houses, galleries, museums, and criticism). Far from feeling compromised by the investment economics of art, they turn the art market into a microcosm of consumer capitalism. (Siegle: 10)

So what does all of this have to do with the library? As I began to process the books, manuscripts, and other materials we were acquiring as a part of the Downtown Collection, I began to experience problems. Downtown works, by their very nature, did not fit into the neatly defined categories the library had established, did not follow the same rigid adherence to authorship, did not even come from acknowledged publishers or suppliers of materials with whom our accounting office was comfortable dealing. I began to see that the same kinds of disruptions Downtown works effected outside the library were occurring as I brought these materials into a major research collection. Now, rather than questioning the larger structures of society, the systems of the library came under scrutiny.

A few examples of the problems we encountered while processing the Downtown Collection point to an overall normalizing function libraries perform when they process materials. One of the most obvious problems is that of classification. David Wojnarowicz was primarily known as an artist and photographer, though he worked in nearly every artistic medium. His papers include over 5,000 negatives, films, punk songs (both lyrics and performances), performance pieces, poems, prose, diaries, letters, found objects, and a host of other materials. Wojnarowicz also had AIDS and his later writing reflects his experience of the disease, intercut with his experiences of child abuse, drug use, and prostitution. An avid illustrator of his own writing – in fact, the illustrations often appear within the manuscripts for his stories – Wojnarowicz created a text, *Memories that Smell Like Gasoline*. This haunting text about his life as a queer man contains descriptions of his battle with AIDS, but is much broader and depicts the life of an extremely sensitive boy caught in the prescriptive nexus of structures such as sexuality, family, law, and gay life, none of which he fits into easily. With its Curious-George-like illustrations, the book is a quintessential outsider piece and inherently "Downtown" in feel. When the Library of Congress catalogued the book, it applied entries for: "1. Wojnarowicz, David. 2. AIDS (Diseases)-Patients-United States-Biography. 3. Artists-United States-Biography. 4. Gay men-United States-Biography. I. Title," and classified the book under RC607.A26W64 1992, placing it among the medical books about AIDS. This act reduces Wojnarowicz's life and work to his illness.

Wojnarowicz was keenly aware of how culture tried to limit him by labeling his work as simply "AIDS art." He was famous for going into bookstores and moving all of his books from the AIDS section to the general literature section: an act of overt activism against the cultural attempts to define him as an AIDS victim and, thus, to pigeonhole his very transgressive work. The overall effect of the classification is to say that Wojnarowicz is not a writer or an artist primarily, but an AIDS patient. If he were thought of as an artist or a writer, he would be classified with art or with literature. There is, however, a danger in classifying Wojnarowicz's work in literature, too. Such a classification could universalize his experience, undermining the specifics of his life, which are all-important to his work. The risk of universalization seems less egregious than the limitations placed on him by defining him as primarily an AIDS patient.

A similar problem arises with Art Spiegelman's *Maus: A Survivor's Tale*. Spiegelman was not the first graphic novelist. The form was one that many Downtown writers explored, making a direct link between comix, television, and the future of fiction. Structurally, *Maus* is a conventional narrative that happens to be told as comix. It depicts the events of the Holocaust as told by a mouse to his son, and in it the Nazis are depicted as cats. The popularity of *Maus* and its importance for the development of the graphic novel cannot be overestimated. It defined the American graphic novel. The Library of Congress, however, decided that it is not really a novel. *Maus* is classified as D810.J4 S643 1986, placing it in the history classification, negating it as art and literature. The system, unable to accommodate the graphic novel, treats it instead as history rather than art or fiction. This act undermines the important breakthrough that makes *Maus* a very special work.

A third instance of this kind of regularization by libraries indicates a larger pattern by which materials with sexual content are discredited. Dennis Cooper's novel *Try* is widely acclaimed as one of the important novels of the 1990s. This postmodern narrative explores the nature of male–male desire at the limits of representation. Focusing on a group of Los Angeles high school boys, the novel depicts the culture of drugs, sex, and violence that lurks behind the well-manicured suburban LA lawns. Minimalist in style, the text has a haunting, sterile tone that describes examples of violence, gay sex, sexual abuse, and heroin addiction. This is not a text about "Gay men – fiction," though the characters are men who have sex with each other. Neither is it a text that should receive the heading "Erotic stories." The novel is not meant to arouse you with its scenes of sexual violence. (If it does, it is in the way that Genet's *Querelle* might arouse. It is not soft-core pornography.) Cooper's novel is completely misrepresented by the heading "Erotic stories." Further, it is degraded. Lacking a more sophisticated terminology for Cooper's achievement, "Erotic stories" serves to turn most readers away from *Try* as a serious novel. Cooper's work uses extreme expressions of sex and sexuality to examine the nature of desire. Library organization, like that of the culture at large, is uncomfortable with these expressions. This uneasiness is reflected in the lack of sufficient terms for sexuality.

While not technically a "Downtown" book, Judith Butler's *Gender Trouble: Feminism and the Subversion of Identity* serves as a touchstone for many younger Downtown writers and artists. A cornerstone for queer theory, this text, too, suffers from similar misinterpretation by the Library of Congress subject headings (LCSH). Classed in

HQ1154.B88 1989 as though it were a sociological text, the book is really a philosophical treatise. The subject headings applied to it attempt to rectify this by giving the book "1. Feminism – Philosophy" as a heading, but then go further and undermine their intent: "2. Sex role. 3. Sex differences (Psychology) 4. Identity (Psychology) 5. Femininity (Psychology)" (Butler: iv). The LCSH are so strongly inflected by the distinction between humanities and social sciences that Butler's book presents a problem. Having no adequate terminology for her work, the subject headings limit the very intent of the book by placing Butler's argument within the context of psychology. While it is true that Butler examines the work of many psychologists who explore gender, her work is not about psychological aspects of feminism, identity, or femininity. It is about the structures of culture that produce the possibility of understanding femininity. This subtle and central idea of the text is undermined by the subject headings that try to fit the book into a discourse, that of psychology, which the book is critiquing.

A different problem arose as we were processing the books and papers of Ron Kolm, one of the mainstays of the Downtown scene. Kolm amassed a huge collection of printed materials about Downtown writing. Nearly half of the material did not have online catalogue records, presumably indicating that other institutions do not hold copies of these outsider publications. The same was true for the over 300 periodical titles. A few of the better-known writers and artists in the collection had online records. As I looked over the materials and spoke with Kolm and other members of the Downtown scene, I became aware of the great importance of many of the writers whose works were not documented in any library. (It reassured me that we were doing the right thing by collecting them.) I feared, however, that these lesser-known writers, many of whom were friends of people like Kathy Acker, Lynne Tillman, Spalding Gray, Gary Indiana, and others, would simply be lost in the online catalogue and forgotten. In consultation with our cataloguing department, we created a special subject heading of "Downtown writers" and placed it on all materials added to the Downtown Collection. In this way, lesser-known authors will have at least one chance of being remembered and found by researchers.

We made similar decisions that did not follow common practice when processing archival materials in Kolm's papers. Kolm was a natural archivist. When I first visited his apartment in Long Island City, he had an entire room of a two-bedroom apartment full of boxes of Downtown materials. (He and his family were living in the other three rooms.) Along with the printed materials, Kolm had some 20 boxes of archival materials, including correspondence, manuscripts, photos, art, posters, ephemera, videos, sound recordings, and thousands of announcements for openings, readings, and performances. Most of the material was easy to process, but the announcements, which were usually roughly sorted into folders with little organization, presented a special problem.

Announcements were particularly important for reconstructing the Downtown scene. Many Downtown works were intensely collaborative. Readings, performance pieces, gallery shows were often joint ventures and provided important meetings of the Downtown community. By looking at the huge number of announcements Ron preserved, I was able to begin to chart links among artists and writers, to locate the spaces where these various groups performed, and to start to understand the culture that developed in SoHo and the East Village. Rather than following a traditional method of organization, the librarian who processed these announcements sorted them by person if it was a one-person show, and by place if there were two or more people involved. Readings, gallery shows, concerts, punk band announcements (including a ping-pong ball announcement for CBGB's) all received special attention. In many instances, Kolm's flyer may be the only artifact that survives from the reading, the performer, and often the venue. (To give you some idea of what I mean, in the mid-1980s, there were over 200 galleries in a 12-square-block area of the Lower East Side. Today there are only two and neither was there during the height of the East Village scene.) Had we followed standard practices, we would have rendered virtually unusable this wellspring of information about the day-to-day activities of the scene.

Precious little Downtown material was published through major publishers. Small publishers and self-published works abounded. Tracking this material is very difficult. There are no vendors who handle Downtown works comprehensively, though Printed Matter, the SoHo artist's bookshop, has a wide selection. Downtown work falls through all the cracks of traditional publishing and thus does not automatically get into libraries. Many librarians are expert at finding this kind of material; my point is merely to say that Downtown writers chose not to send texts to mainstream publishers – largely to maintain their edge. It is also true that most of their work is so transgressive, in terms of style, format, genre, content, or other elements of expression, that most mainstream houses would not consider publishing it. Libraries collude to a large extent with publishers to support what might be thought of as the academic/publishing/library complex. This term is a reformulation of the "military/industrial complex," which was, perhaps, the first widely known example of how discourses of society collude with one another to structure how we think. It was certainly one that was accessible to many Downtown artists and probably helped shape their larger understanding of the ways in which discourse structures our lives. If your work exists outside an established network, chances are it will not be preserved for future generations to view. We may have plenty of cookbooks, romances, and mysteries – all of which I think are important and essential for us to collect and preserve – but precious few chapbooks of experimental poets, flipbooks by naive comix artists, or edgy fiction with graphic sexual content.

Why is it, then, that libraries limit materials through classification, application of subject headings, genres, and author's intent? Why do we not process some materials as fully as others, privileging the correspondence, manuscripts, diaries, and other written documents of an author over other archival materials? Why do we tend to trust publications by established publishers rather than seriously evaluate small-publisher or self-published works? The usual litany of answers includes the following: it costs too much; publishers weed out bad materials; scholars are primarily interested in academic materials or, in archival terms, in biographical and literary materials about a writer or artist's development. All of these answers are laden with value assumptions with which the library is a complicit participant. Such compliance, even if benign, does violence against those materials that question the processes of validation in our culture – and, in fact, all materials, even those more readily acceptable to mainstream culture. We in libraries can be the greatest enemies of the preservation of culture when we believe we are documenting ideas for the future, but do not knowingly select materials that lie outside the academic/publishing/library complex.

By acquiring and cataloguing Downtown materials, I began to see the modern library as just another discourse of culture: one that constructs authors, fixes subject positions (and subjects), defines movements, solidifies genres, validates publishers, justifies periods, and privileges heteronormative relations. In short, the library is the major thread in maintaining the complex weave of discourses that produce culture and constrain the individual, who can never escape from these discourses. Downtown works, however, have opened for me within the library the same kind of space, "mentally, psychologically, semiotically," as Siegle sees they open up in culture at large. These works "shake up" our common assumptions about "roles, genders, social structures – so that at least momentarily experiences of various sorts of Other might take place before the great culture machine swallows it up again." In this case, Downtown works undermine the stability of the discourse of the library, which, with its classification schemes, processing rituals, and economic modes for assessing historical or literary value, stand as the cultural system *par excellence* that reifies, legislates, represses, normalizes, and creates the possibility of what can be known, who can know it, and how it will be preserved.

I realize that my argument is beginning to sound like one made by Michel Foucault, whose work underpins much of postmodern thought and most of the cultural criticism that has swept through academia since the early 1980s. Foucault's work is related closely to the concerns of Downtown artists; much Downtown work was being formulated concurrently with his. Curiously, for someone who critiqued the effects on the individual of most of the major structures of society, from the language of science and linguistics to law and sexuality, Foucault remained largely silent about the library as yet another discourse of society. And yet, as I hope the examples from the Downtown collection show, it is clear that we are involved in violence against and the silencing of cultural materials when we integrate them into our collections.

For Foucault, there is no overarching knowledge that is not linked specifically to the discourses of the time in which that knowledge was first available. In other words, the structure of our understanding of anything is not atemporal; there is no *a priori*, only ever what Foucault, in "The Discourse on Knowledge," calls an "historical a priori" (*Archaeology*: 127). Within any given historical period, then, and under the governing rules that inform the "historical a priori" of that period, there is an "archive" of information that the specific culture produces. For Foucault the "archive" is not the sum total of the experiences of individuals in a given historical period as preserved through the memory of the culture, but only ever a subset of that "historical a priori," the subset of experiences that can be expressed within the constraints of the available discourses of that culture (*Archaeology*: 129). The "archive," thus, is only the record of those experiences "that appear by virtue of a whole set of relations that are peculiar to the discursive level." For Foucault this "archive" of a culture is never mimetic of the culture, but only a product of the possibilities created by the interwoven discourses of a culture. It will come as no surprise that Foucault believes that "the archive of a society, a culture, or a civilization cannot be described exhaustively" (*Archaeology*: 130). At the same time, however, he believes that "its presence is unavoidable. It emerges in fragments, regions, and levels, more fully, no doubt, and with greater sharpness, the greater the time that separates us from it: at most, were it not for the rarity of the documents, the greater the chronological distance would be necessary to analyze it" (*Archaeology*: 130).

I do not agree with Foucault. I believe he is right that the "archive" cannot be described completely. (Not all experiences are written down – memory is a cherished and fragile medium. Moreover, language itself never can express all the things the body knows – the ineffable, animal truths we each understand at some level prior to and beyond the verbal.) This does not eliminate the possibility of attempting to preserve more materials to make a better reconstruction of the "archive" possible. Through my engagement with the current Downtown scene, I have a special opportunity to preserve more of the "archive" of that scene than a library would normally preserve. In her useful article, "Theorizing Deviant Historiography," Jennifer Terry notes that:

> Gilles Deleuze, in reading Foucault, talks about the new archivist who sees effects neither in a vertical hierarchy of propositions stacked on top of one another, nor in clean horizontal relationships between phrases that seem to respond to one another. Instead the new archivist "will remain mobile, skimming along in a kind of diagonal line that allows him [sic] to read what could not be apprehended before." (56–7)

Following Deleuze's reasoning, I believe it is possible for libraries to collect consciously. If the librarians and archivists who have responsibility for preserving the documents of our culture approach the process of documentation knowing that possibly we can never fully document a culture, then we make very different decisions about what we collect and how we preserve it. If Foucault is right, then we need to preserve as large a body of documents and artifacts as we can so that with the passage of time the documents of our culture, that have become rare themselves, will be available for study.

Foucault presents a curious problem for me. At the end of the passage quoted above, he begins to sound as though the "archive" is something that exists and that can be known at some indeterminate point in the future; if not in its "totality," at least the "fragments" and "levels" of understanding begin to accumulate to make up something that begins to approach an understanding of the "archive." I suggest that Foucault should have looked to the libraries, for it is within their walls that much of the "archive" – but, importantly, not all – will be determined. It is by what we as libraries collect that a large portion of the "archive" will be made knowable. But we cannot just continue to collect in the ways we always have and preserve materials that can document the archive of our "historical a priori." If we had continued to collect in the usual manner for the Fales Library, the Downtown scene would only be known through those few writers and artists who broke through into the mainstream of publishing – those canonized through overlapping criteria established by the media, critics, and other people with cultural power. Much Downtown material has already disappeared; much more would have vanished if we had not begun to collect it when we did – it would only have taken a fire at Ron Kolm's and a huge portion of the Downtown scene would have been lost forever.

I'd like to propose an alternative to Foucault's rather bleak prognosis for documenting the "archive." I'd like specifically to think about his idea that the "archive" "emerges in fragments, regions, and levels," for it is here that we have something to use as a means by which to more thoroughly document the "archive." Oddly enough, we return to the mirror; more specifically, to Jacques Lacan's conception of the mirror stage. In his essay, "The Mirror Stage as Formative of the Function of the I as Revealed in Psychoanalytic Experience," Lacan explains the moment of recognition of the subject (a baby): when standing before the mirror he or she first understands that the reflection in the mirror is his or her self. Or, as Lacan puts it: "The mirror stage is a drama whose internal thrust is precipitated from insufficiency to anticipation – and which manufactures for the subject, caught up in the line of special identification, the succession of phantasies that extends from a fragmented body-image to a form of its totality" (4). What is important for us here is that the child's actual vision in the mirror is not one that is complete; it is not a totality – for obvious reasons: the child does not have sufficient motor control to stand steadily in front of the mirror at the age when the mirror stage occurs. Rather, the mirror stage exemplifies the moment when, based on the anticipation that something actually exists out there, a "succession of phantasies that extends from a fragmented-body image" in the mirror leads the child to project its own identity, his or her own I, or, in the English translations of Freud, his or her ego. The image in the mirror need not be absolutely accurate, sharp, and clear for the child to understand that he or she exists as an active subject.

It is precisely this Lacanian mirror that we can use as a model for documenting cultures. If we collect, as comprehensively as possible, the multiple and varying fragments, shades, levels – the fuzzy images of the areas of culture that our collections encompass – then we are truly collecting something that will have lasting value beyond the highly regimented, approved discourses that culture promotes. Another way to think about this might be to compare how one might conventionally collect the Downtown scene to how I have actually chosen to do it. The conventional approach would have been to develop a list of the very best authors, as noted by the mainstream press, who wrote Downtown, and to put together sets of their first editions. This would give one prescriptive view of the Downtown scene. If I chose to go beyond these authors and look at who Downtown writers felt were important, I could create a collection that could serve both audiences. But to really begin to document the scene, I need to collect much more broadly; to document the interactions of a wide range of artists; to acquire books, papers, realia, ephemera, videos, sound recordings, posters, and varieties of materials that the Downtown scene seemed to have no end of fun producing.

By overlapping these various images of the Downtown scene, some no doubt fantastic, some projected, some politicized, some aesthetic, I have a better chance of documenting the Downtown scene. I have had to posit the identity of the scene. I have had to hold the mirror up to it, but I have not allowed myself to believe that I can reflect what the scene really was like. Rather than mimesis, I am positing the "archive" as a series of overlapping representations that I hope, in their interrelatedness, more accurately reflect the archive than any single one could have done. In this way, I can better attempt to know what the scene was like.

This approach is not without pitfalls. Foucault astutely notes the ways in which disciplines create individualities: "Disciplines constitute a system of control in the production of discourse, fixing its limits through the action of an identity taking the form of a permanent reactivation of the rules" (*Archaeology*: 224). When I posit the Downtown scene as something that exists, even if I posit it as a series of divergent and overlapping reflections of the events and personalities, I engage the larger systems of cultural discourse that reinforce the very possibility of identities and/or rules that govern them. The examples above of how libraries limit David Wojnarowicz's work to

AIDS art and Dennis Cooper's novels to "Erotic stories" represent exactly this kind of control. Libraries limit the transgressive nature of Wojnarowicz's and Cooper's works by creating standard, library-defined identities for them, thus reactivating and reinforcing the traditional cultural rules that govern how these artists should behave rather than describing the works they have created. The library reactivates the rules of culture that define art that engages with the experience of AIDS as somehow less than real art, and reinscribes the notion that serious novels do not use sexuality as the content from which they explore language and the possibility of representation.

What are we to do as librarians attempting to document culture, then, if we cannot escape the possibility of reactivating these larger rules of culture? I have taken my lead from Downtown works themselves. Understanding the processes by which the discourses of culture structure our lives, Downtown work engages in the processes of culture, but always with a knowledge of the operations of those processes. Similarly, as a librarian working in one of the major institutions that regulates culture, I need to act like one of the outsider artists. Whenever there is a chance to critique the processes of the library, to perform a "hit-and-run guerrilla action," I do. In the end, Downtown work suggests a different stance toward how we view our role in relation to the structures of culture. In addition to holding the mirror up to culture to reflect the various and conflicting images that may allow me to preserve a part of the "archive" of the Downtown scene, I have to always be aware that I am not only looking into the mirror, but also – and most importantly – holding it up.

Coda: A Few Field Notes from a Postmodern Curator

After all of this theory, here are a few practical thoughts I hope we all keep in mind when we think about the library, the canon, and the accreditation of literary work:

- Don't assume continuity: Oscar Wilde said "Many men can make history, it takes a great man to write it." Where does history live, anyway? In the object or in the narrative? Libraries should collect multiple, overlapping approaches to their areas of documentation.
- Don't assume that the library's standard classification, processing, cataloguing, and other schemas are benign systems of order that

help us organize our thoughts. All systems of knowledge, especially those in libraries, are more exclusive than they are inclusive. They silence some ideas and privilege others.

- Don't assume publishers know what is good. Publishers are a part of the marketplace and the bottom line is selling what the general public wants to buy. There is nothing wrong with this material. In fact, it is essential to an understanding of the culture we live in. But don't believe it's all that is out there. The more that is preserved, the better. Never assume that publishers are just interested in content, however. The ones who are don't make money.
- Don't assume vanity press publication of imaginative work means something is bad. Not all self-published work is bad. Much of the best Downtown work was produced by small houses or paid for by authors themselves. Because of the experimentation with content, form, genre, or a variety of other elements, mainstream houses wouldn't touch their work. Buy more books produced by the artists themselves. And read them.
- Don't make the distinction between high and low art. In terms of the archive, they're equal. Besides, the notion of high art is really historically located and not a very old idea at that.
- Don't assume content is inappropriate. It is not for us to decide if a work is inappropriate. John in Dennis Cooper's *Closer* describes his art as a "Dorian Gray kind of thing" (5). *The Picture of Dorian Gray* was found to be immoral when it was first published. Dennis Cooper's work, too, has been under attack. Worse, the library has decided it's not literature, but rather "Erotic stories." Which mode of censorship is worse?
- Don't privilege the idea of the author. Authorship is almost always collaborative. The cult of the author has a history, but serious collecting based on author lists is actually a relatively recent phenomenon. It encourages vanilla collections spread across every library, vanilla literary studies, and, worse than all, vanilla literary taste.
- Don't read just traditional books. Culture is made up of a variety of other materials that are an integral part of understanding our world. Collect the materials that make sense for your purposes. Then push beyond them. In the Downtown Collection we have books, pamphlets, magazines, 'zines, letters, manuscripts, Xeroxes, comix, posters, announcements, labels, buttons, pencils, photos, videos, sound records, tapes, artworks, ping-pong balls, artifacts, and safety pins.

References and further reading

Anderson, Laurie. *Big Science: Songs from "United States I–IV"*. New York: Warner Brothers Records, 1982.

Benderson, Bruce. *User*. New York: Dutton, 1994.

Butler, Judith. *Gender Trouble: Feminism and the Subversion of Gender*. New York: Routledge, 1990.

Chartier, Roger. *The Order of Books: Readers, Authors, and Libraries in Europe Between the Fourteenth and Eighteenth Centuries*. Trans. Lydia G. Cochrane. Stanford, CA: Stanford University Press, 1994. 25–59.

Cooper, Dennis. *Closer*. New York: Grove Press, 1989.

Cooper, Dennis. *Try*. New York: Grove Press, 1994.

Deleuze, Gilles. *Foucault*. Trans. and ed. Seán Hand, foreword Paul Bové. Minneapolis: University of Minneapolis Press, 1988. Quoted in Jennifer Terry, "Theorizing Deviant Historiography," *differences* 3.2 (1991): 56–7.

Foucault, Michel. "Un 'fantasque du bibliotheque'" (1964). In *Language, Counter-Memory, Practice*. Trans. Donald F. Bouchard and Sherry Simon. Ithaca, NY: Cornell University Press, 1977.

Foucault, Michel. "Archaeology of Knowledge". In *The Archaeology of Knowledge and The Discourse on Language*. New York: Pantheon, 1972, 3–214.

Foucault, Michel. "The Discourse on Knowledge." In *The Archaeology of Knowledge and The Discourse on Language*. New York: Pantheon, 1972. 215–37.

Foucault, Michel. *The Archaeology of Knowledge and The Discourse on Language*. New York: Pantheon, 1972.

Goldin, Nan. *Ballad of Sexual Dependency*. New York: Aperture Foundation, 1986.

Jagose, Annamarie. *Queer Theory: An Introduction*. New York: New York University Press, 1996.

Lacan, Jacques. *Écrits: A Selection*. Trans. Alan Sheridan. New York: W. W. Norton, 1977.

Siegle, Robert. *Suburban Ambush: Downtown Writing and the Fiction of Insurgency*. Baltimore, MD: Johns Hopkins University Press, 1989.

Speigelman, Art. *Maus: A Survivor's Tale*. New York: Pantheon, 1986.

Terry, Jennifer. "Theorizing Deviant Historiography." *differences* 3.2 (1991): 55–74.

Velvet Underground, The. *The Best of the Velvet Underground*. New York: PolyGram Records, 1989.

Wojnarowicz. David. *Close to the Knives*. New York: Vintage Books, 1991.

Wojnarowicz. David. *Memories That Smell Like Gasoline*. San Francisco: Art Space Books, 1992.

Index